A POSTMODERN REVELATION:
SIGNS OF ASTROLOGY AND THE APOCALYPSE

In this new interpretation of the Book of Revelation, Jacques M. Chevalier examines the relationship between astromythology and Western interpretation. While scholars have noted the influence of ancient astromythology in Revelation before, Chevalier shows how John's heavenly imagery is the key to a polemical dialogue between modes of storytelling in Western history: astrology and eschatology, and naturalism and logocentrism. The book also explains how the 'genealogical' concerns of modern academia about the origins of natural and cultural history have supplanted the future-oriented visions of sidereal divination and Christian prophecy.

The first three chapters and epilogue situate Chevalier's biblical analysis in the context of broader interpretations of astrology and the apocalypse developed by Jung, D.H. Lawrence, Lévi-Strauss, Derrida, Foucault, Cassirer, Adorno, Frye, Barthes, and Morin. They also provide the reader with a solid background in the history of astrological belief systems and exegetic readings of Revelation extending from antiquity to the late twentieth century. The remaining chapters are devoted to two questions. First, how does the imagery in Revelation relate to expressions of astromythology? Second, how do twentieth-century readings of Revelation reflect a 'genealogical' perspective on notions of signs, textuality, and destiny?

A Postmodern Revelation is itself an 'apocalypse,' a revelation to scholars interested in sign theory, eschatology, and the history of astrology. The book does far more than interpret the specific biblical text of John's Revelation: it plays with polemics and parallels in the history of Western thought, tracing the history of signs and their meaning from antiquity to a postmodern era that heralds the end of all myths of the End.

JACQUES M. CHEVALIER is Professor and Chair of the Department of Sociology and Anthropology, Carleton University. His previous books include *Semiotics, Romanticism and the Scriptures*.

Death on a Pale Horse, Joseph Haynes (England, 1760–1829), etching after J. Hamilton Mortimer, Stanford Museum (Leventritt Fund), 1972.172.

JACQUES M. CHEVALIER

A Postmodern Revelation: Signs of Astrology and the Apocalypse

UNIVERSITY OF TORONTO PRESS
Toronto Buffalo London

ISBN 0-8020-4172-8 (cloth)
ISBN 0-8020-7976-8 (paper)

Printed on acid-free paper

Canadian Cataloguing in Publication Data

Chevalier, Jacques M., 1949–
  A postmodern revelation : signs of astrology and the apocalypse

Includes bibliographical references and index.
ISBN 0-8020-4172-8 (bound)   ISBN 0-8020-7976-8 (pbk.)

1. Bible. N.T. Revelation – Criticism, interpretation, etc.
2. Bible and astrology.   I. Title.

BS2825.2.C45 1997   228'.068   C96-932268-2

University of Toronto Press acknowledges the financial assistance to its publishing program of the Canada Council and the Ontario Arts Council.

This book has been published with the help of a grant from the Humanities and Social Sciences Federation of Canada, using funds provided by the Social Sciences and Humanities Research Council of Canada.

A Zélie et Thierry, Pour vos rêves et visions ...

Contents

Plates

Abbreviations

1 Chron.	1 Chronicles	Mal.	Malachi
2 Chron.	2 Chronicles	Matt.	Matthew
Col.	Colossians	Mic.	Micah
1 Cor.	1 Corinthians	Nah.	Nahum
2 Cor.	2 Corinthians	Neh.	Nehemiah
Dan.	Daniel	Num.	Numbers
Deut.	Deuteronomy	Obad.	Obadiah
Eccles.	Ecclesiastes	1 Pet.	1 Peter
Eph.	Ephesians	2 Pet.	2 Peter
Exod.	Exodus	Prov.	Proverbs
Ezek.	Ezekiel	Ps.	Psalms
Gal.	Galatians	Rev.	Revelation
Gen.	Genesis	Rom.	Romans
Hab.	Habakkuk	1 Sam.	1 Samuel
Hag.	Haggai	2 Sam.	2 Samuel
Heb.	Hebrews	Song	Song of Songs
Hos.	Hosea	1 Thess.	1 Thessalonians
Isa.	Isaiah	2 Thess.	2 Thessalonians
Jer.	Jeremiah	1 Tim.	1 Timothy
Jon.	Jonah	2 Tim.	2 Timothy
Josh.	Joshua	Wis.	Book of Wisdom
Judg.	Judges	Zech.	Zechariah
Lam.	Lamentations	Zeph.	Zephaniah
Lev.	Leviticus		

A POSTMODERN REVELATION

1

Ends and Flickers of Doubt

This book explores the confrontation between and downfall of two modes of storytelling in Western history: astrology and eschatology – hence, divination and prophecy, or the cult of stars and the visions of Revelation. While both modes of discourse on time have profoundly marked Western history, they are now excluded from dominant concerns of the modern and postmodern world, having been reduced to pale reflections of the hegemonic signs they used to be. My intention is to bring both grand narratives back to life, if only through a postmodern dialogue with history. The journey begins with an overview of the *longue durée* history of astrology spanning antiquity and the modern and postmodern era, in an endeavour to understand the gradual demise of sidereal divination in the West. We shall see that Christian notions of spirituality and prophetic revelation played an important role in downgrading the spheres of heaven, reducing star-gods to the level of mere signs and subaltern spirits dwelling in the visible heavens, below the immaterial Lord ruling from above. Here, John's Revelation is read in that light, as *a contrapuntal scheme launched against astrological time*. In its own prophetic way, the New Testament Apocalypse is Christianity's response to cults that dare to assimilate the divine (immaterial, atemporal) to the visible and the tangible – to celestial bodies and the signs of heavenly desire governing the cosmos and the wheels of time. In the Book of Revelation, Christian prophecy superimposes itself on the language of 'pagan' divination, disassembling and recomposing it in such ways as to satisfy the higher rule of Logos. Like an old city, Revelation consists of several layers, and 'down at the bottom is a pagan substratum' (Lawrence 1974: 60; see also 194f.). In the ancient heavens lies the foundational material both used and ruined by John's apocalyptic edifice.

Two basic questions are asked throughout this book. First, what relationship do John's detailed imageries entertain with ancient expressions of astromythology? Second, what do twentieth-century scholars have to say about the New Testament Apocalypse, and how do their readings of Revelation betray a modern perspective on ancient teleological scripts (astrological and eschatological)? Both questions are answered against the background of two broader stories: the history of Western astrology (chapter 2) and the evolution of readings of Revelation spanning late antiquity and the twentieth century (chapter 3).

Qualifications regarding the apparent death of astrology in Western culture are in order. At the end of this chapter, I argue that astrology has lost its religious status and has been debunked, banished from higher forms of modern learning. But divination still plays an active role in the mass production of countless little prophecies adjusted to the hopes and fears of 'ordinary people' – to expressions of industrial and postindustrial popular culture. While the apocalyptic language now appeals primarily to conservative segments of the population concerned about crises of the West, astrology continues to address the daily preoccupations of millions of individualized souls searching for meaning in a world that ignores all larger Ends.

Telos, Logos, Genos

Divination versus Prophecy

Present-day horoscopy is a rejoinder to the West's repudiation of its own astrological past (Eliade 1976: 59). Albeit a weak plea, it is the diviner's answer to Western schemes directed against the worldly, forward-looking languages of antiquity. Unlike cultural developments of the twentieth century, the mythical and the astrological traditions of the pre-Christian world converged on a tragic, future-oriented sense of time pervading the entire universe, affecting humans and their gods alike. Ancient Greece developed a mythology that was deeply concerned with the tragic and the erratic in life, epic stories of gods, demigods, messengers, and heroes who experienced unexpected joys and sufferings comparable with the blessings and misfortunes of the people they protected, though on a larger scale. Humans and their legendary gods were subject to hordes of untimely events. Narrative beginnings and endings were constantly divined but were not predictable in the sense of following the strict laws of Fate. Stoic philosophers of the Graeco-Roman period saw stability and constancy in a universe ruled by laws of celestial 'mathematics' (synonymous with astrology), yet the logic of the heavenly spheres did not preclude divinatory explorations and propitiatory manipulations of the future, towards fateful developments of the Stoics' own choice. Nor did Stoicism preclude the idea of great floods and prophetic visions of chaos befalling the universe. Although Seneca and Lucan believed in the timeful logic of all things that come in due season, in accordance with the dictates of Fate, they also recognized the inevitability of world-scale catastrophes (*ekpyrosis*) that play havoc with the universe and result in long astronomical cycles and regenerations of the cosmos (*palingenesis*) (Ulansey 1989: 75f.).

Judaeo-Christianity also expressed faith in a grand narrative *telos* that offered promises and warnings of the future. Unlike 'pagan' expressions of teleology, however, the language of prophecy proclaimed the end of time and the world as we know it. Opposed to horoscopy and astromythology, apocalyptic seers reported visions of the imminent End and the hereafter – hence, the Day of Judgment, when martyrs would be redeemed, and the earth destroyed and purged of all evil.

This brings us to ancient embattlements of myths of the End, or the struggle of Judaeo-Christian prophecy against astralism and sidereal divination. Anti-astrological schemes have a long history, dating back to the battle between 'pagan' divination and Judaeo-Christian prophecy, and culminating in the demise of visionary thought in the age of reason and science. This book deals with the latter struggle as it evolved through time, with an emphasis on the fate of astralism (defined as the worship of stars) and our worldly sense of *telos* – our capacity to project ourselves into future times that do not escape the worldliness and cyclical motions of Being. My contention is that the first sentencing of astromythology is written all over the prophecies of Revelation, a script dedicated to visions of the Endtime. In John's visions, astral signs are reduced to subordinate spirits and mere metaphors, sign-manifestations of an otherworldly Spirit heralding the Day of Judgment. The New Testament Apocalypse downgrades the astral pantheon that once presided over the bodily motions of time and desire, turning star-gods into time markers, metaphors, messages, and 'the hosts of heaven' (messengers, soldiers, saints, angels, etc.) subserving an immaterial Sign Maker dwelling in eternity. Astralism is disassembled into fragments of itself, retributive manifestations and poetic metaphors harnessed to the Lord dwelling beyond the visible spheres.

John's use of prophetic rhetoric is a polemical response to pagan divination. The apocalyptic answer to astralism is developed chiefly through a host of deceitful parallels: using imageries made 'in the likeness of the appearances' of the unspeakable star-gods, harnessing their powers to the higher rule of the Lord. The implication of this argument is *not* that an astrological code governs the language of Revelation, or that what John *really* meant had to do with astrological secrets and mysteries that enrich his message and beg to be decoded and deciphered (as in Exel 1986; Maunder 1923; Gleadow 1968; Fleming 1981; Jurist 1982; Moore 1981: 29; Malina 1995). Unlike other exegeses, my reading of the Apocalypse focuses on what the text insists on not saying, or what the prophet never actually says because it is too incompatible with (and yet so close to) his vision of the future. The reading we are about to undertake speaks therefore to the issue of 'influence' in its original sense: *a force producing events that can be prevented, or what the text could have said had not the prophet made every effort to contradict prevailing signs, preventing competing words and imageries from outruling his Verb.*

The influence of astrology on the Scriptures points to plausible connections between texts and their immediate context. 'We must remember that even the Biblical writers were children of their time, and could therefore hardly avoid expressing their thoughts in terms of the recognized philosophy of their age' (Hastings 1921: 54). But more than being a reconstruction of Revelation in its original *context*, my reading points to a text forming part of a broader *contest*. I am alluding to a dispute between competing world-views, a rivalry written into Revelation from the start, a sign battle conveyed with all the discretion needed to impose silence where lapses of memory are required. Paganism is not an everyday symbolic garment worn by Christianity to convey a radically new and much broader doctrine, as Rahner suggests (1963: 99, 109, 113, 131, 155). Nor is it a secret corpus hiding under the cloak of Revelation. Astralism is neither outside nor inside John's Apocalypse. More to the point, 'heathenism' pervades Revelation by actively standing on its *opposite side*. Notwithstanding his 'symbolic garment' imagery, Rahner (1963: 146) makes the same point when he sums up Christianity's settlement with paganism in the following terms: 'the Church opposes, the Church dethrones, the Church consecrates and in the end the Church brings home.' Religious symbolism is so malleable that it can both expatriate and repatriate contending imageries, all at one stroke.

My reading of Revelation 1–12 attempts to shed new light on the polemics of eschatology and astrology as expressed through the Apocalypse – hence, the sufferings and agony of the star cult in Christian prophetic thought. As we shall see, worldly finalities of cyclical time (*telos 1*) are denounced, silenced, and subsumed by visions of otherworldly ends geared to the End (*telos 2*); prophecy triumphs over divination, logocentrism over Sabaism. But my rendering of the Apocalypse speaks also to three other polemical schemes and apparent deaths inflicted upon ancient expressions of teleology: the anagogical, the sublunar-astrological (*telos* 3), and the genealogical.

Logos and Analogos

The first death is of the spiritual, atemporal kind. It involves a search for the eternal lessons and principles embodied in signs of Logos, the Scriptures, and the heavens. Anagogical schemes and plots applied to Revelation have taken various forms, ranging from the Augustinian hermeneutics prevalent in the early Middle Ages to the twentieth-century emphasis upon timeless symbolic principles, whether viewed from a formal–structural standpoint (as in Farrer), a theological perspective (as in Lohmeyer), or a Jungian approach. In these writings the contribution Revelation makes to our knowledge of future events weighs little compared with what eschatology says about Christian principles or universal operations of symbolling and the unconscious. When interpreted anagogically, the Apocalypse has what is essentially an allegorical appeal, with every detail being deciphered so as to mean 'something and something moral at that' (Lawrence 1974: 206f.).

The early teachings of anagogy are closely associated with the accession of Christianity to power in Rome. As the Church achieved hegemony, threats of an immediate End were removed from the heavenly writ and confined to the distant future. Church Fathers recognized the worldliness of their own institutions, yet the rise and consolidation of Christendom in the West meant that great steps had been taken towards the reign of Christ on earth, or the realm of the Spirit made flesh. Given the triumph of God's people, theologians were not about to predict an imminent End. The world had been transformed as predicted, all in the light of the Lord. A period of quasi-eternal communion with the Almighty could be enjoyed without fear of an impending Day of Judgment, in anticipation of the Second Advent of Christ and his eternal reign on earth. Given the secular strength of Church institutions, the old apocalyptic tradition lost its appeal. The interpretive practice shifted from signs of *telos* to lessons of *analogos*. Visions of eschatology based on teleology (the notion that events have final causes) gave way to anagogy, an understanding of text and history that sees them as analogical manifestations of the eternal Spirit. Teleological world-views, astrological and eschatological alike, were superseded. The teachings of Saint Augustine made wishful predictions of future events either sinful and satanic, as in the case of sidereal divination, or allegorical and mystical, as in the case of Revelation.

The Dark Ages thus moved farther away from a time-bound conception of the cosmos, introducing a great schism between the timeless infinity of the heavens and the lower vagaries of human and natural history. In early Christian theology, while the upper world is ruled by a timeless Spirit, far below lies the realm of earthly time, a mundane reality made finite in three fundamental ways: through the toings and froings of cyclical time, the intervention of free will, and the final day of reckoning. The passing of time on earth is subject to the appointed motions of stars and planets, which involve regularity, but also constant shifts between days, seasons, and years. Human temporality is not, for all that, entirely predictable: events are fashioned by interventions of human will and divine retribution. History is all the more finite as humanity's days are numbered and will be brought to a final conclusion on the Day of Judgment, an ultimate 'apocalypse' that belongs to the distant future.

Sublunar Astrology

Although expelled from religion and the realm of the Spirit, temporality continued to govern all worldly affairs. But what about the Church? Was it not also a subject of history, an institution vulnerable to the trials and tribulations of time? In hindsight, the Church could hardly escape its earthly condition – hence, troubled times of its own and related battles and polemics regarding future outcomes. Minds of the Middle Ages critical of Church corruption produced grand-scale presages and forebodings of future transformations of history and the universe. From the twelfth century onwards, astrological and prophetic belief systems dating back to antiquity were once again given free rein in a world ruled by hopes and fears of another global change.

After a few centuries of anagogical spiritualism, eschatology found its way back into medieval religion and politics. While still rejecting astral religion, the West witnessed a reinstatement of astrology defined as a practical, forward-looking science, a form of learning occupying a legitimate position within a vertical plotting of knowledges presided over by theology and prophetic spirituality. A secularized, 'sublunary' version of scientific astrology was reintroduced and made compatible with Church doctrine. Aristotelian philosophy allowed the science of stars to be applied to visible phenomena, without undermining spiritual knowledge attained through revelation. Correlatively, learned interpretations of the Apocalypse wandered away from the anagogical lessons of Augustinian theology, reverting to a teleological sense (*telos 3*) of history. Biblical scholars renewed their concern with future events, adopting a prophetic perspective supported by the astrological discourse sanctioned in Aristotelian metaphysics. In other words, medieval exegesis conveniently *separated astrology from astralism*, using the former as a scientific instrument to bolster the revival of Christianity's apocalyptic imagination.

Genos

While astral divination and divine revelation were deeply committed to probing signs of future destiny, the distinction between the two thought systems was so critical to early Christian theology that few Church Fathers could admit that astralism had any 'influence' on the visionary writings of John. Accordingly, early exegetic readings of the Apocalypse made no concessions to astromythology. Revelation had to be read teleologically, as a text that spoke to Endtime events (without explicit reference to the laws of sidereal motion), or anagogically, as symbolic expressions of eternal morals and teachings of the Christian faith. Later on, the teachings of biblical anagogy gave way to a revival of astrology subsumed under the principles of Christian theology and apocalyptic prophecy. As long as they were clearly dissociated from the idolatrous views of astralism, explicit sidereal imageries offered the language needed to announce the upheavals and transformations of medieval Church history.

The End envisaged by prophets of the Middle Ages did come about, but mostly in the form of an end to older scenarios of the End. Notwithstanding their impact on medieval culture, astrology and eschatology could hardly survive the great transformations of postmedieval Europe. Despite many periods of social upheaval, the Renaissance and the Enlightenment brought a new sense of finality to the West, including a commitment to achieving ends of universal scope, those of Reason inspired by the ancients and harmonized with Christian principles of timeless spirituality, free will, and the transience of human history. With this relatively optimistic rewriting of classical culture and history, notions of dramatic endings and a tragic End looming large in medieval minds were eroded beyond recognition.

Evocations of John's Revelation continued to proliferate throughout the eighteenth and nineteenth centuries, if only via poets and painters of the 'apocalyptic sublime' inspired by the writings of Blake (Paley 1986). But the growth of secularism, humanism, science, and the individual constituted new trends that sooner or later would undermine darker visions of the apocalyptic imagination. The consolidation of such trends during the modern era resulted in resolutely hopeful conceptions of human evolution, towards the liberation of humans from the servitudes of nature and society, or the sufferings of poverty and social exploitation. The ideals of positivism, liberalism, nationalism, and socialism conveyed visions of history that spoke the language of utopia and heaven on earth, or prophecy with no sense of tragedy. Fears of death and the sufferings of history were disposed of unobtrusively, never to play an essential role in the forward march of modernity.

Utopian narratives – watered-down versions of an older teleological imagination – were not meant to last either. With modernity the 'whole great adventure of the human soul' is 'cut off from the cosmos, cut off from Hades, cut off from the magnificence of the Star-mover. Petty little personal salvation, petty morality instead of cosmic splendour, we have lost the sun and the planets, and the Lord with the seven stars of the Bear in his right hand' (Lawrence 1974: 44f.). Time as we know it now has no End. In the words of Baudrillard, 'we are already more or less disconnected from our history and thus also from its destination. That means, then, that time can slow as it nears its end and that the year 2000, in a certain way, will not take place' (quoted in Dellamora 1995: 8).

Habermas (1987: 13) too suggests that our awareness of time is slowing down and losing energy. Ends have been multiplied *ad infinitum*, adjusted to the wants and anecdotes of billions of individuals and thousands of 'peoples' (nations, states, ethnic groups, etc.) seeking the good life on earth, far removed from the pangs of death and tragic developments of secular history. To make matters worse, dreams and hopes of the late twentieth century have exploded into signs of heteroglossic infinity. Promises of a new earth have given way to postmodern nihilism, and a proliferation of particularistic movements, individual finalities, and islands of history that make a mockery of all previous conceptions of a global *telos*.

Visions of the collective future that were once written all over the skies and projected onto the cosmos have become the lot of right-wing politicians such as Ronald Reagan and fundamentalists such as Hal Lindsey (whose book *The Last Great Planet Earth* sold 29 million copies between 1970 and 1990). Meanwhile, centres of high learning have lost interest in signs of Revelation. 'Where interpreting apocalyptic texts like Revelation once occupied the best minds of an era – St. Augustine, John Milton, Isaac Newton and Jonathan Edwards, among others – today it flourishes on a popular level distant from academic life' (Steinfels, quoted in Carpenter 1995: 108).

Teleology has given way to genealogy. Intellectual developments of the

Renaissance, the Enlightenment, and modernity put an end to the syncretism of worldly (astrological) and otherworldly (prophetic) foreknowledge characteristic of medieval thought. As a result, Western minds are no longer driven to probe the future with knowledge and scripts inherited from the past, harnessing the hitherto to the hereafter; going back to the future, as it were. No longer convinced by visions of *telos*, postmedieval intellectuals have chosen to march into the future via a scientific exploration of the *origins and first principles* of natural and human phenomena; going onwards to the past, so to speak. Paradoxically, what Habermas says of Benjamin's consciousness of time applies to the whole of modernity, an age that twists its surface future orientation 'so far back around the axis of the now-time that it gets transposed into a yet more radical orientation toward the past. The anticipation of what is new in the future is realized only through remembering ("Eingedenken") a past that has been suppressed' (1987: 12).

With modernity, the sky became the subject-matter of astronomers concerned with past and present observations of the heavenly bodies, not with their influence on human affairs and related insights into future finalities. Likewise, the Scriptures became objects of scientific exegesis – searching for all the past intentions and conventions that presided over the original text. Although speaking to eternal truths, John's vision of an imminent future became a revelation of the past, a set of prophecies to be understood scientifically, against the background of early Christian history. Most scholarly interpretations of Revelation written in the modern era will therefore pay some attention to connections between ancient astromythologies and the prophetic imageries of John. This is *not* done with a view to enhancing literal visions of the End with astrological predictions, as in the Middle Ages. Rather, modern exegetes are inclined to argue that astromythology and other circumstances of John's visionary experiences must have exerted some meaningful influence on the writing of Revelation.

Modern students of the Scriptures will all subscribe to the notion that *advances* in biblical scholarship presuppose a scientific *regression* to the history of conventions and meanings, a well-documented *retour aux sources*. And yet serious difficulties lie in the concept of inherent forms and origins. In the genealogical perspective, the subject-matter of a text is treated in the same way as a subject or a material object, two constructs that share a common denominator: they point to a web of fixed attributes and origins that can be assigned to any person, text, or thing, constituting each as a separate 'id-entity' or group of 'individuals,' a class by itself. As in kinship analysis, each and every genealogy requires fixed points in time and can exist only by virtue of the distance that lies between webs of relations and lines of descent. While the genealogical approach transcends the unscientific limitations of former teleological traditions, it tends to leave a fundamental question unanswered: how do 'individuals' relate to one another, forming expanded systems of interaction (intertextual, intersubjective, intercausal) that are in constant motion and that constitute each 'individuality,' assigning it a place within a broader story, giving shape and meaning to the particular text, subject, or object?

Modern exegeses of Revelation are at pains to answer this question. The special status accorded to the genealogical method means that little attention is paid to evolving debates and polemical interchanges developed between 'partly similar' texts and conflicting interpretive traditions. Differences in the successive writings *and readings* of Revelation are explored, and connections between the Christian Apocalypse and astromythological imageries of Chaldean and Graeco-Roman origins are discussed. Yet great emphasis is placed on the originality of a primitive text that constitutes a *new origin*, the beginning of an authentically Christian apocalypse motivated by divine influence. While informed by Jewish and non-Jewish sources, the text is said to depart radically from prior and contemporary variations on similar themes, making it worthy of an extensive genealogical investigation. Scholars will of course admit to 'pagan' parallels lurking behind the surface text, yet the inspiration of Revelation remains essentially non-pagan, transcending all outside motivations. Exegetic faith in acts of prophetic creativity – bringing the word into being from nothing (save inspiration from the Verb) – is to be preserved against external contamination, foreign influences in excess of what an authentic *creation* can tolerate.

By contrast, the exegetic reconstruction of Revelation must remain absolutely faithful to the primitive script, to the circumstances of its production and its inherent meanings and root forms. These two hermeneutic tactics, which consist in asserting maximum distance between Revelation and divination, and minimizing the distance between the Christian Apocalypse and its scholarly reconstruction, converge on the higher truth and enduring relevance of the Apocalypse. Paradoxically, all of this is achieved through a genealogical reading of a teleological text. Exegetes cannot go back to the *genos* of biblical mythology without escaping the narration of origins, a myth involving 'the "double meaning" of "springing from": a shudder at being uprooted and a sigh of relief at escaping' (Habermas 1987: 164). Genealogy combines nostalgia with a resolution to escape teleologies of the past.

Exegetes will insist on showing maximum loyalty to a primitive text that offers a fresh beginning, a script so original as to prove itself thoroughly disloyal to all kindred compositions and its own literary ancestry. Given these premises, little attention is paid to the symbolic schemings and machinations plotted by early Christianity against astralism. Likewise, the relationship between ancient teleological scripts and later genealogical interpretations is never understood for what it is: just another battle of schemes evolving across the centuries, a *longue durée* argument over visions of time.

To sum up, the myth of *genos* constitutes the most recent charge against prophecy and divination. It involves an eminently modern attitude whereby signs and text are a pretext to revisit the historical circumstances, original meanings, formative conventions, and root principles of the written word. In modern scholarship, signs of heaven have lost all prophetic value. To paraphrase Freud (1976: 783), they have in common with dream symbolism the fact that they give us, not foreknowledge of human destiny, but rather knowledge of the past coupled with symptomatic reflections of what we wish our future to be.

In my reading of Revelation 1–12, I respond not only to John's prophetic response to astral divination, but also to later exegetic responses to John, by which I mean the scholarly exegeses that speak to the origins, the spirit, and the logic of the New Testament Apocalypse. In doing this I take issue with all discussions of astralism in Revelation that pay no attention to the intertextual schemings of language: that is, John himself, who never names the gods he struggles to silence, and also exegetes, who spiritualize John's Verb to the point of never grasping its historical embattlement with the language of divination. However, of all the responses to Revelation that call for a critical commentary, the genealogical ones are to be given priority, for they dominate biblical scholarship of the twentieth century. All 'genealogically minded' scholars fall prey to a common temptation: to isolate the original text from broader interchanges, ignoring its polemical exchanges with previous and contemporary 'influences' (astralism), and with later interpretive polemics as well. Questions of external influences and interpretive debates are addressed, but never as essential ingredients of an interlocutory apocalypse. Just as an 'original' Revelation ends up transcending its non-Christian influences, so too its scholarly interpretation ends up surpassing rival exegeses. Truth triumphs on both levels, theological and scientific, driven into foreclosing the endless battles and shifts of words through time.

The *Signum Triceps*

My reading of prophecy's response to astrology is set against the background of a broader polemical triad: the claims and counter-claims of teleology, anagogy, and genealogy. Each interpretive mode has evolved differently throughout the centuries, becoming hegemonic in certain periods of history and serving secondary functions at other times. Notwithstanding these critical shifts in history, all three modes have always coexisted. Allegorical symbolism was an essential ingredient of John's prophetic rhetoric and has become a central issue in modern studies of the root forms of language. Genealogical concerns about past chronology and lines of descent (euhemerism) were part and parcel of early Christian prophetic texts, and of allegorical pronouncements of the medieval Church as well. Finally, foreknowledge of the future had its own role to play in Augustinian theology and continues to be a central preoccupation in modern expressions of popular culture.

The complex interplay of the three interpretive modes outlined above goes as far back as antiquity. As Seznec (1953: 4) points out, the ancients developed different theories to make sense of their own mythology: 'The myths are a more or less distorted account of historical facts, in which the characters are mere men who have been raised to the rank of the immortals; or they express the union or conflict of the elementary powers which constitute the universe, the gods being cosmic symbols; or they are merely the expression in fable of moral and philosophical ideas, in which case the gods are allegories.' The author goes on to say that it was thanks to these interpretations, which integrate mythology 'with world history, natural science, and morals, that the gods were to survive through the Middle Ages, preserved alike from oblivion and from the attacks of their enemies.' To these imageries of the hitherto and the forever, Hellenism and Christianity added signs of the hereafter, visions of the future conveyed through augury and heavenly mythology.

The dialogue among anagogy, genealogy, and teleology – signs of the forever, the hitherto, and the hereafter – is vividly illustrated by a baroque painting attributed to Titian (*c.* 1490–1576). This intriguing Renaissance painting throws light on the basic operations of narrative time, a key factor in the workings of symbolling viewed as a complex *signum triceps*. The painting shows a six-faced monster comprising three male heads placed immediately above three animal heads. The composition brings together the full-face heads of a middle-aged man and a lion, the leftward profiles of an old man and a wolf, and the rightward profiles of a young man and a dog. The symbolism represents the principle of Prudence as portrayed in philosophical allegories of the Middle Ages, a multifaceted virtue combining *Memoria*, *Intelligencia*, and *Praevidentia*. The triple-human-head imagery points to a synthesis of the three ages of life, and related memories of the past, insights into the present, and visions of the future.

The triple-animal facies is apparently older. It dates back to Macrobius's fifth-century description of the three-headed statue of Serapis: 'The lion, violent and sudden, expresses the present; the wolf, which drags away its victims, is the image of the past, robbing us of memories; the dog, fawning on its master, suggests to us the future, which ceaselessly beguiled us with hope' (*Saturnalia*, quoted in Seznec 1953: 120). The iconography points to the lower and darker side of knowledge of the past, the present, and the future. It suggests a sombre aspect to all manifestations of human wisdom; signs of *logos*, *genos*, and *telos* are not without inherent negativity. When transposed to the terrain of language, the lion subjects the present to the rule of the Powerful viewed as the Eternal; the wolf cheats us out of memories that must be silenced and forgotten; and the dog converts visions of hope into fears and apprehensions of the future. Over and beyond the positive gains of Intelligence, Memory, and Prescience, Macrobius's imagery evokes the arbitrary impositions of an eternal present that unavoidably combine with lapses of memory and fears of the future to produce all the losses and tensions inherent in the sign process.

When applied to the history of exegeses of Revelation, the *signum triceps* concept has the advantage of being thoroughly dialogical, with the implication that it can transcend the limitations of competing renderings of the New Testament Apocalypse. By transcendence, however, is not meant supersedure. My reading of Revelation still owes much of its inspiration to previous biblical scholarship. Paradoxically, the debt to genealogical, anagogical, and teleological perspectives that dialogism incurs can never be fully cancelled.

To the genealogical tradition I owe my concern with reconstructing the older schemes of Christian prophecy directed against 'pagan' astrology, using the modern canons of historical scholarship and scientific exegesis. Were it not for the linguistic expertise (which I lack), encyclopedic contributions, and formidable insights of comparative religious history and modern biblical scholarship, I would never have ventured to tackle Revelation's interlocution with ancient astralism, let alone the Western evolution of astrology and the history of readings of Revelation. As for the anagogical method, I owe it this book's unavoidable curiosity about the 'universal mind' – looking into the nature of language, operations of the sign process, and principles of human symbolling. Wittingly or not, the *signum triceps* ends up making a contribution to anagogical reasoning: it too formulates a theory of the unconscious logic (narrative, dialogical) guiding all expressions of allegorical thought.

But of all contributions to this book's conversation with divination and Revelation, it is to the tradition farthest removed from Western scholarship, teleology in its worldly astrological form (*telos* 1), that I owe the most. As in the astrological *Weltanschauung*, it is my contention that all acts of signification point to the logic-of-desire-in-motion, a process where signs are eminently physical and sensuous, just like the visible star-gods that used to inhabit the wondrous skies of antiquity. Like the bodies of heaven, signs of language are inherently

- logical and 'mathematical,' subject to geometric arrangements of similarities and differences that constitute the orderly and variable constellations of language;
- normative and moral – hence, bent on elevating certain signs and destinies above others, in the manner of astrology's rank-ordering of the spheres ruling in heaven;
- repressive and transgressive, applying force against competing signs that are kept alive through measures of co-optation, displacement, and resistance;
- harnessed to the e-motive powers of time, to memories and repressions of the past that come together with expectations and apprehensions of the future to mark the anxieties of narrative time.

Scheme analysis (Chevalier 1990; Chevalier and Buckles 1995: 278–84) is an attempt to bring all five aspects of the symbolic process into a dialogical theory of signification. The theory presupposes that we delve into the logic of similarities, oppositions, and mediations that govern the text(s) at hand. Formal analyses of 'signs of the intellect' are none the less limited. Structuralism neglects one of the most fundamental properties of the sign system defined as a code: the fact that some signs are given greater attention than others. For instance, the lamb-versus-scorpion imagery of Revelation 9 and 12 is heavily biased towards a zoological code servicing the battle of spirits, good and evil. The astrological indices of the lamb and the scorpion motifs are given less attention and are prevented from entering the surface text; they have a negative impact on the composition only by way of displacement. Some meanings are bracketed, while others are brought to the fore. The interplay between the overt and the covert – among the explicit, the implicit, and the illicit – is part and parcel of the process of symbolling. Beyond the plotting of sign relations forming logical schemes, dialogism must seek to unravel the devious 'schemings' of language as well.

My reading of the Scriptures serves to illustrate a basic thesis: the code and the motions of desire are one and the same thing. By means of a dialogical method that goes beyond the strict logic of similarities and differences, each scene is disassembled as follows. To begin with, readers are invited to probe the surface narrative for the dominant signs chosen in preference to all other meanings potentially invested in the same imagery. To use the same biblical example, the scorpion-tailed demons of Revelation 9 are assigned zoological 'appearances' that preclude a literal reading of an astrological code into John's use of the scorpion motif. The animal code is visibly preferred over the astral. By implication, signs forced out of the literal text form the underside of the narrative, an underground plot comprising all the unspeakable fears and latent anxieties subsumed in the visible text. John's commitment to the higher morality of Yahwism requires that the Sabian code be reduced to silence; treating Scorpio as a member of the zodiacal pantheon is simply incompatible with the logocentric distinction between immaterial spirits and the bodies made visible on earth (animals, humans) or in heaven (stars).

But a repressive ban cannot be placed on illicit indirections of the text without the narrative signifying 'the unspeakable,' if only in a roundabout way – hence, by means of distortion. Like all displacements, John's zoological 'misrepresentation' of the astrological idiom borders on transgression: a close reading of Revelation 9 shows how astral religion looms large in deeper layers of the text. Slips of the Sabian code are unavoidable. This is to say, signs of the ruling order contain transgressive measures of their own. Licit expressions of language are in the habit of subsuming illicit meanings under the dominant code, which is but a way of reinforcing the powers-that-be in the realm of speech. Efforts to reduce Sabaism to absolute silence are not enough; the law of Yahwism stands to gain more by actually turning stellar imagery to its own advantage, as John does in his vision of the End of Time. Transgression is a powerful instrument of the Law.

The passing of narrative time is another central feature of the secret pronouncements of astrology deployed in John's vision of the End. The zodiacal evocations of the scorpion-and-lamb imagery can serve to illustrate this point. As we shall see later, demons in the train of equinoctial Scorpio entice readers of Revelation to place their hopes in the almighty Ram well before the actual appearance of the Lamb slain at Easter, the season that marks the beginning of a new era and the end of cyclical time.

Scenes of a moving script are often impatient. Words destined for the surface of a future scene are prefigured, albeit with discretion. Scorpion-tailed spirits of the Fifth Trumpet form the pre-text of the marriage supper of the paschal lamb celebrated at the end of Revelation. Their appearance gives the reader yet another pretext for investing hope in memories of the triumph of Aries at springtime. The scorpion and the lamb are both reminiscent of a heathenish past and shadows of the hereafter, ancient signs of divination lurking behind John's vision of the end of narrative time.

The interpretive strategy outlined above will yield valuable insights, provided that several methodological requirements are met. Briefly, the first measure of any plausible rendering of the schemings of language is one of interpretive scope. To what extent does the reading account for all the semiotic elements observable at the surface of a given composition and related connections? To this criterion should be added a solid measure of ethnohistorical research into independent sources of linguistic, cultural, and ethnoscientific information that can be brought to bear on the imagery at hand. The act of reading is inevitably subject to some requirements of interpretive coherence and consistency as well: if one code is said to correlate with another (for example, astrology with zoological figures in Revelation), then the logic of each classification must be duly reconstructed and the correspondences explicated. The criterion of cultural extensibility – that is, the extent to which semantic patterns from the symbolic material at hand can be extended to a broader cultural environment – should also be considered. A semiotic deconstruction of the biblical scorpion motif becomes all the more interesting and plausible when situated against the background of cultural and political implications of Christianity's battle with astromythology. Finally, the interpretive practice lends itself to the act of *predicting*, a fundamental property of reading and of narrative language. Attentive interpreters have in common with competent readers the ability to anticipate scenes of the past and the future through an in-depth, symptomatic comprehension of the narrative present: the better one's grasp of the immediate configuration, the greater one's sensitivity to potential and probable, short-term and long-term shifts in compositional associations.

The question of relevance should also be addressed: Why the interpretive exercise in the first place? Is it merely for the sake of knowledge? Or is it undertaken in order to critique and alter well-established modes of interpretation and regimes of truth? Could the interpretive activity offer new modes of reading that act as alternatives to habits of literary and cultural expression? More shall be said about this issue at the end of this book. For the moment, we note that the interpretive exercise is more than an accurate rendering of culture as the subject-matter of semiotics, more than a 'truthful' substitution of one discourse for another.

Finally, the implication of an interpretive methodology that stresses the rule of logomachy – signs, words, and schemes in dispute – is two-sided. On the one hand, texts that compete with one another are bound to display striking parallels that must be reconstructed though rigorous analysis, with a scholarly attitude towards the history of language, meanings, and forms. Without these informed analyses of variations on similar themes, in our case the prophetic and the astrological, schematic interconnections between kindred compositions will add up to no more than an exercise in ventriloquism. Comparative analyses undertaken without rigour point to an interpreter's text written and developed by proxy (though possibly interesting on its own). Unscholarly approaches to the history of texts in battle can also be an invitation to the essentialistic lessons of *psychomachy* – hence, spiritual commentaries on perennial conflicts of the soul, *à la* Prudentius (348 – *c.* 410). On the other hand, parallels established between competing scripts can never be so striking as to annul the critical distance that one text must maintain *vis-à-vis* its counter-text. If too faithful to each other, two texts may be suspected of rehashing the same compositional stuff. Likewise, a masterful reading of a text or intertext should never be so faithful to its subject-matter as to add nothing to it. An interpretation worth writing and reading presupposes an exercise of mastery that points to a perspective of its own.

Beyond Post-Structuralism

The outline of sign theory presented above approaches the complex connection between signs as a fivefold 'bar': that is, (a) a relational and fractional measure (homological, oppositional) dividing one meaningful sign from and binding it to another; (b) a place of judgment governed by a profession of faith and morality; (c) a place of confinement – a repressive mechanism bent on thwarting all forces of harmonic mediation; (d) a place of debauchery where the Law appears as an in-fraction of itself; and (e) a musical line of attentions shifting through the narrative score. The schemings of time, morality, repression, and transgression in the code of language converge on the order-of-desire-in-motion (Chevalier 1990: 36).

But how do these various facets of symbolling tally with other accounts of Revelation, astrology, and semiotics? While the first aspect (a) of the act of signification lends itself to a Lévi-Straussian analysis of the encodings of Revelation (Calloud, Delorme, and Duplantier 1977; Prigent 1980), the second dimension (b) stresses the moral value system or Great Code (Frye 1981) embodied in a particular language, a focus that tends to be prevalent in modern biblical scholarship. When showing cognizance of the repressive functions of symbolling (c), however, normative analyses of Revelation usually result in critical studies of 'dominant ideologies' and 'moral regimes' seen from a feminist (Fiorenza 1991; see Carpenter 1995) or a Jungian (Jung 1954) perspective. We shall see that Foucault's *History of Sexuality* applies a similar approach to the discussion of the 'astrological regime of sex' in ancient Greece. Given his critical evaluation of psychoanalysis, Foucault none the less substitutes the 'moral regime' concept for older notions of 'repression.' His reluctance to explore the dynamics of repression and transgression (d) in ancient texts happens to be shared by all exegetic readers of Revelation. Although they are not exercises in biblical scholarship, we shall see that Jung's *Answer to Job* and Derrida's commentary on discourses of the apocalypse are notable exceptions to the latter rule. Albeit for different reasons, both theorists emphasize the indirections and deviations of the sign process in myths of the End.

As for the last dimension of symbolling (e), it is partly dealt with in 'surface form' analyses of the cyclical, recapitulative, or spiralling patterns of Revelation (see chapter 3). Notwithstanding these contributions to the study of John's narrative hermeneutics, a much deeper understanding of textual measures of pre- and post-figuration is still wanting, using a Ricoeurian approach to the 'emplotment' and 'distentions' of time built into the New Testament Apocalypse (Ricoeur 1984).

Before we proceed to closer readings of Revelation's conversation with divination, more should be said about theoretical perspectives on astrology and the functions of language. Consider first the structural notion of the code. Our journey into the history of astrological and apocalyptic mythology presupposes knowledge of the complexities of variable codes, whether they be sidereal, calendrical, botanical, or zoological, to name just a few possible systems of classification. An exercise of this sort aims at unravelling not only the multiple correspondences that exist between these systems, but also transformations that may be observed from one culture to another, and their practical implications as well (agricultural, medical) (Lévi-Strauss 1962: 58; 1975: 216–41). This approach to symbolism is most helpful in that it pays more than lip-service to the 'sensible' ordering of signs in language.

The insights of structural semiotics should not be underestimated. Having said this, there are other components of the astrological 'code' that are equally important and that beg to be studied with tools other than analytic models of the unconscious. As suggested above, there is more to the intellect than a synchronic logic viewed from afar and with grammatical aloofness. According to Lévi-Strauss (1958: 415f.; 1975: 39, 80f.), the social sciences should emulate astronomy in the sense of paying attention to phenomena that are at a great distance from the observer, or the 'outer space' that points to the inner unconscious. Also they should investigate the distances that lie between constellations of signs – hence, the logical and transformational differences constructed within and between codes and cultures. Structural anthropology is thus the astronomy of the social sciences.

Although intellectually appealing, this perspective on astronomy and semiotics is shortsighted. While it addresses the logical features of symbolling and the interpretive practice, it neglects two critical issues, leaving them outside the bounds of science. First, albeit committed to an investigation of the unconscious, Lévi-Straussian intellectualism ignores the struggles of semiosis, oblivious, as it is, to the plotting of signs in dispute. Theories of 'la pensée sauvage' bypass the contentious issues and discursive 'schemings' that preside over all acts of language, whether they are religious imageries or pronouncements of the social and natural sciences. Even astronomy has a darker plot and a secret plan that keeps the discipline alive: the older astrological world-view acts as a remote horizon from which astronomers had to and still have to distance themselves in order to create and practise their science. If anthropology is to concentrate on things that are far removed from sight, then the signs of astrology hiding in the 'great beyond' of astronomical phenomena should be acknowledged and duly explored.

Second, anthropology is caught in the world it observes and must therefore speak to the contested sites of cultural history. This is to say, anthropologists can hardly understand the 'distances' that lie between astrology, astronomy, and religion with the same kind of intellectual detachment that astronomers will show towards 'outer space.' Deeper insights into the issues that concern us require rather a hypermetropic sense of 'vision': looking at all acts of tropology and sign interpretation (teleological, anagogical, genealogical) from afar *but never with aloofness* or indifference *vis-à-vis* the emotions and struggles of semiosis. As argued throughout this book, observers of the sign process can gain insight into the schemes and schemings of language on condition that they delve into the expectations and fears embedded in the plot – *active anxieties concealed from our imme-*

diate sight. Secret concerns of the text are an integral part of our subject-matter and are at the root of science itself. Structuralism and astronomy are not immune to the darker motivations and motions of human discourse. Actually they share a similar impulse, one that haunts the Book of Revelation and Western metaphysics as well: a drive to comprehend the universe logocentrically, appealing to the Spirit, the Logic, and the Order that transcend motions of the body, apprehensions of the subject, and the infinite events of human history. This book seeks to illustrate the anxieties of logocentrism as expressed through the anti-astrological struggles of Revelation. It attempts to make sense of symbolling, illustrating the 'moving thoughts' and e-motive powers of signs of the apocalypse.

As do Adorno, Barthes, and Morin (see below), Foucault goes beyond the formal canons of structuralism. He eschews a purely cognitive understanding of the logic of astrology, cognizant of the role that the astral discourse once played in the construction and regulation of sexuality and the human subject. Broadly speaking, Foucault is careful to avoid the pitfalls of both structuralism and psychoanalysis. In his *History of Sexuality*, the author stresses not so much the logical or repressive functions of discourse as the history of sexual aesthetics. The latter is viewed as a complex field of ethical practices and normative 'codes' that undergo important transformations through time (Foucault 1984: 18, 36f.). The ancient discourse on seasons and stars is a case in point in that it forms an integral part of the genealogy of the modern 'subject of desire' and the Western sense of 'moral selfhood' (10–12, 35).

In his second volume, Foucault explains how astrology contributed to the development of a particular 'art of living' or ascetic 'souci de soi' applied to erotic pleasures. As in early Christian teachings, the discourse on sexuality prevailing among philosophers at the beginning of our era tended to downgrade passions of the body, placing them well below joys of the ethereal soul, never to be pursued as a full-fledged spiritual activity or an art for its own sake. However, sexual activity was never treated as the source of sin and the Fall, as a carnal 'condition' to be either renounced or endured because necessary and unavoidable. The 'labour of love' was not turned into an expression of conjugal duty or self-sacrifice. Nor did philosophers promote hermeneutic confessions of the self, a struggle against sexual pathology, or a strict compliance with invariable norms of purity dictated by external authorities. Sex was rather a vital force that produced pleasures worthy of the human condition, provided, of course, that unbridled passions be avoided at all times. Carnal desires had to be mastered and channelled, enjoyed with caution, countenance, measure, and good taste –

hence, know-how in the art of living. The exercise of self-mastery also entailed the preservation of a code of honour involving unequal statuses assigned to adult men, their younger male lovers, and their wives. When properly applied, these techniques of living and loving served as a stepping-stone to loftier experiences of truth and beauty of the soul (Foucault 1984: 58–60, 66–7, 81, 98, 112, 155, 237, 262, 277).

But how did wisdom of the stars help to achieve these ends? The answer lies in what might be called an astrological regime of food and sex. According to Foucault (1984: 102f., 105, 126–40), good health required a constant exercise of self-mastery based on principles of moderation, adaptation to variations in cyclical time, and a balanced combination of the ingredients of life. A healthy management of bodily needs presupposed that culinary and sexual pleasures be adjusted to variable times of the year (fixed by the equinoxes and the solstices), all of which were classified as cold, hot, humid, or dry. For instance, cold brought by the wintry fall of the Pleiades had to be compensated for by things dry and warm – hence, dry foodstuffs and more frequent sex (especially important for older men whose bodies tend to be colder). In other words, the satisfaction of sexual needs had to be pursued with a sense of measure, with an emphasis on calculations of seasons, temperatures, and levels of moisture. The 'good life' understood morally *and* hedonistically revolved around issues of proper admixture, correct frequency, and judicious timing.

Foucault's analysis goes beyond cognitivism to reconstruct the history of sexual pleasures and regulations. He does this without positing a biological libido universally repressed by moral consciousness. His genealogy also does away with contrast generalizations pitting the overmastering desires of pagan cultures against the strict morals of Judaeo-Christian thought (Foucault 1984: 74, 275). In his rejection of the Freudian repression thesis, however, Foucault tends to go too far, at the expense of his understanding of discursive regimes and the history of Western sexuality. Although briefly expounded, his view of the role of astrology can serve to illustrate some of the weaknesses of his genealogy. A central thesis developed in the chapters that follow is that, in lieu of simply fading from Christian discourse, astrology was recuperated through a conversion of star-gods into markers of time, inferior spirits, metaphors, and signs of the Lord. One implication of this tactical conversion process lies in the apocalyptic recuperation of the sexual and gendered symbolism pervading ancient visions of astromythology. While not a central issue in this book, nor an explicit objective in Revelation, the erotic effects of astral symbolism deployed in John's vision of the End – for instance, a divine woman possessed by the male sun – should not be underestimated (see Chevalier 1990, 1995). The New Testament Apocalypse does not speak openly and systematically to issues of sexual ethics, yet the text is replete with thickly textured imageries, anagogical lessons, and convoluted morals of Eros subserving the higher ends of Logos.

The powers of speech are not reducible to conscious regulations of discursive regimes, the historical variations of which can be understood through comparative analysis alone. Given the intertextual schemings of *la parole*, sign theorists should take care to distinguish between ethical codes of conduct and the broader processes of signification, the former being merely one facet of the latter. By focusing almost entirely on discursive practices, Foucault's analyses miss out on the more complex operations of moral speech, some of which thrive on the mighty works of logomachy and dialogical repression. Foucault's outline of the differences that lie between ancient Greek and Christian sexual ethics could have been strengthened had the author turned these dissimilarities into real disputes and struggles over signs of Eros.

As is true of disputes over the rulings of Eros, ancient formulations of Logos are subject to the entanglements of competing imageries. The Stoic morals of astralism are clearly ruled out by John's Verb, yet the emotive powers (erotic, wrathful) of sidereal and calendrical codes are surreptitiously reintroduced into his teachings by way of metaphor. One idiom triumphs and grows by conquering alien words. Christian asceticism has much to gain from this metaphorical appropriation of 'pagan' aesthetics: it can promote ethics of renunciation while promising the heavenly blessings and rewards of Sabian morality. The calendrical imagery used by John to convey hymeneal hopes of the Church can serve to illustrate this point. Although not couched in a language of moral injunctions, the Eastertime wedding feast of the sun-robed woman and the morning star (the Lamb, son of the Ram), and *routine Sun-day commemorations thereof*, speak eloquently to the calendrical timing of pleasures of the flesh conquered by the spirit. The entire world is destined to be renewed through a sublime marriage celebrated at the proper moment in time: the first spring day of heaven on earth. In lieu of *fading out*, astrological signs of Eros *fade into* the lofty visions of Logos.

Discursive regimes do not exist independently of one another, nor can they be grasped in isolation from the prediscursive operations and historical embattlements of semiosis. Had these factors been taken into consideration (without falling back on reified notions of the sex-driven unconscious resisting the impositions of morality), Foucault could have avoided reintroducing an all-too-familiar thesis otherwise rejected in his own work: the notion that Christianity treats sexuality as inherently evil and sinful, a source of pathology to be confessed and eradicated by means of invariable laws and a pervasive/invasive moral–juridical code. My reading of Revelation's response to astralism shows another side of the Christian code: its ability to impose a particular law that speaks down to alternative morals while also harnessing the powers vested in pagan denials of a timeless, immaterial Logos.

Foucault (1984: 155) recognizes the role of calendrically organized rituals in Christianity's effort to impose a highly regulated economy of sexual activity. But nowhere does he reflect on the 'pagan' (heliotropic) genealogy of such rituals – hence, the interplay of code and counter-code. Even where Christianity has risen to power, the sidereal imagination has never ceased to play a critical role. Albeit denounced and downgraded, the language of time and space governed by signs in heaven continues to operate from both inside and outside the teachings of Church theology. Siderealism remains internally active in the sense of offering a rich source of apparently innocent allegories and ritual metaphors that Christianity can profusely draw from. This symbolic material becomes particularly crucial when assigning concrete expressions to the means and consequences of virtuous conduct and sinful behaviour (e.g., life in or out of an 'otherworldly' heaven). But astrology also has the capacity to act 'from without,' in contradiction (if only partial) of Church doctrine. This can be observed in modern horoscopy, a heterodox activity that provides mass-media culture with a zodiacal and planetary regime of erotic attractions and daily activities charted in heaven. That is, the dominant regime never exists alone, so to speak. Rather, it is constantly faced with forces of resistance *that both reinforce and challenge* the ruling order and the powers of language that be.

Although not conceived as an exercise in biblical scholarship, Jung's *Answer to Job* seems to be the only analysis that approaches the astrological aspects of Revelation from a dialogical perspective, with a sensitivity to the tensions that pit logocentrism against astralism and that are lavishly played out in John's visions of the End of Time. Jung's answer, however, is not without major limitations. Suffice it to say that, while Foucault's analysis overemphasizes the historical boundaries of conscious ethical codes, Jung's tends to extract unconscious archetypes from their linguistic and historical contexts, spreading them around the world. In the postscript to this book, I discuss Jung's contribution to our reading of Revelation in greater detail. For the moment, we turn to a discussion of Frye's and Derrida's approach to signs of the apocalypse.

Frye's reading of Revelation falls somewhere between Jungian phenomenology and structuralism's pursuit of a non-referential Code. In Frye's works, the apocalypse embodies a tremendous emancipation of the imaginative mind, a radical departure from the descriptive, formal, and archetypal phases of literary symbolism which tend to be constrained by the mimesis of nature. The New Testament Apocalypse marks the passage from the archetypal to the anagogical mode of signification, a transition whereby

nature becomes, not the container, but the thing contained, and the archetypal universal symbols, the city, the garden, the quest, the marriage, are no longer the desirable forms that man constructs inside nature, but are themselves the forms of nature. Nature is now inside the mind of an infinite man who builds his cities out of the Milky Way. This is not reality, but it is the conceivable or imaginative limit of desire, which is infinite, eternal, and hence apocalyptic. By an apocalypse I mean primarily the imaginative conception of the whole of nature as the content of an infinite and eternal living body which, if not human, is closer to being human than to being inanimate. (Frye 1957: 119)

John's apocalypse is the antitype of all representational modes of symbolling in that it reveals nothing but its own forms. In lieu of uncovering or describing a reality that lies outside the text, it unravels powers of the human imagination, a faculty as infinite in its range as religion itself (Frye 1957: 125). The distance that Revelation takes *vis-à-vis* the objective world implies a movement away from all systems of correspondence established between culture and nature, including the doctrine of the microcosm which portrays the human being as a miniature replica of the whole of reality. Given this rejection of naturalism, John's prophetic visions preclude a reversion to magical thought based on rituals of divination, older codes where the patterns of human destiny are mapped onto natural phenomena such as the motions of stars and planets evolving in the visible heavens. On this issue of astrology, Frye adds that he does not

find any consistent astrological symbolism in the Bible, but there are many allusions to divination in it, many of them practiced in Israel, such as the mysterious 'Urim and Thummim' on the high priest's costume in Exodus 28: 30 and elsewhere ... There are also such patterns of correspondence as the emphasis on sevens and twelves in the Book of Revelation. Perhaps they are prominent there because by the time this book was written, seven was the number of days in the week and of the planets, and twelve the number of months in the year and of signs of the Zodiac.

Hence these numbers would suggest, more than others, a world where time and space have become the same thing. *But correspondence does not seem to be the central thing that the Bible is saying about the relation between man and nature.* (Frye 1981: 75; emphasis added)

These comments lead Frye to discover in Revelation 'the total meaning of the Scriptures,' symbolizing, as it does, the end of the order of nature. The book heralds 'the destruction of the way of seeing that order that keeps man confined to the world of time and history as we know them. This destruction is what the Scripture is intended to achieve' (136; see also 1962: 45, 144). Frye is conscious that the creative pole of Revelation is overshadowed by feelings of paranoia and also memories of the Fall and humanity's exile from the good world and life of plenty enjoyed in Eden. In the Book of Revelation, however, lie promises of a new heaven and earth. More than any other sacred text, Revelation holds the key of human creativity and the powers of renewal and re-creation. By 'salvaging something with a human meaning out of the alienation of nature,' the Bible can assist humanity in its journey towards the redemption of history (137–8).

While echoing the structural and post-structural critique of referentiality and the metaphysics of representation, Frye's views also speak to issues of narrative desire, a theme neglected in Lévi-Straussian and Foucaultian discussions of the Code. His treatment of how nature and astrology relate to the apocalypse and how signs relate to each other is none the less problematical. Briefly, the notion that Revelation offers a loosely structured, highly creative language that transcends the limitations and strictures of nature poses various difficulties. For one thing, nature will not let itself be pitted against culture so easily: natural phenomena can hardly be grasped without constructions of the imaginative mind, be they astrological, zoological, or botanical. Nor should the 'codifications of nature' be viewed so strictly as to be incompatible with visions of poetic revelation. Codes are highly malleable and variable, subject, as they are, to all sorts of contradictory and mediatory effects that make a mockery of all dualism opposing logic and the human imagination. Finally, the lack of fit between natural and 'supranatural' codes in Revelation is more apparent than real. To be sure, correspondences are not always easily discerned. After all, the works of repression and distortion inherent in the sign process are such that 'texts in battle' cannot be expected to spell out all the rules and codes embedded in the tactical imageries they deploy. Connections between codification of the natural and the spiritual are none the less operative.

Astrology in Revelation is a case in point. As Frye suggests, the prophet is bent on destroying the sidereal codification of nature and time. The point missed by Frye, however, is that John cannot kill the Sabian beast without signifying two things, if only in a roundabout way: the actual corpus that is being dismantled, and the bits and pieces that can be rescued towards an astrological language servicing the order of Logos. In the spoils of this anti-astrological war lie new minions of the Verb heralded as 'the universal creative word which is all words' (Frye 1957: 125). The twelve stones imagery of Revelation 21 is a telling illustration of this co-optation strategy achieved through devious bricolage. As Frye (1962: 253; emphasis added) puts it, 'John's vision of the New Jerusalem also sees it as constructed of twelve precious stones, but they no longer represent the Zodiac *because they are the Zodiac. In the Apocalypse the stars are the stones of fire, and the sun is the Messiah who is the cornerstone of the city.*' Nature works and dies in harness, never in earnest.

Like Frye, Derrida considers the apocalypse to be at the heart of all literary experience. He too makes an argument for the radical non-referentiality of language ('there is nothing outside the text'), but without emphasizing the redemptive forces of desire that will transfigure reality through writing. While Frye contemplates a Revelation without apocalyptic tragedy, Derrida dwells on an 'endtime-without-judgment' (Boyarin 1995: 43) – an apocalypse that brings no final revelation. Derridean deconstructionism delves into 'the element of death within the play of signification (in the broadest sense) that potentially can obliterate the real (Thanatos–apocalypse)' (Robson 1995: 73). What is stressed here are not the infinite forms and redemptive core of symbolic activity, but rather the formlessness and endless decentring of the sign process. With Derrida, Frye's Blakean vision of a human mind dwelling in the Milky Way gives way to

a figure who owes more to Becket than to Blake: the nuclear space of hesitation, Derrida suggests, 'occurs within a "who knows?" without subject or knowledge,' or, even more grimly and with a greater emphasis on finitude, apocalypse would be the 'auto-destruction of the *autos* itself' – Frye's infinite man blowing himself to bits. This contemporary theoretical configuration of the exploding word may be rooted historically in a post-Hiroshima world, but the roots run deeper than that: it is consistent with the double-edged symbolism of biblical apocalyptic revelations, including the smashed tablets of Sinai, the deferred Kingdom of Israel in exile, or Christ as the crucified Logos. The revealed Word, it seems, is always the shattered Word. (Robson 1995: 72)

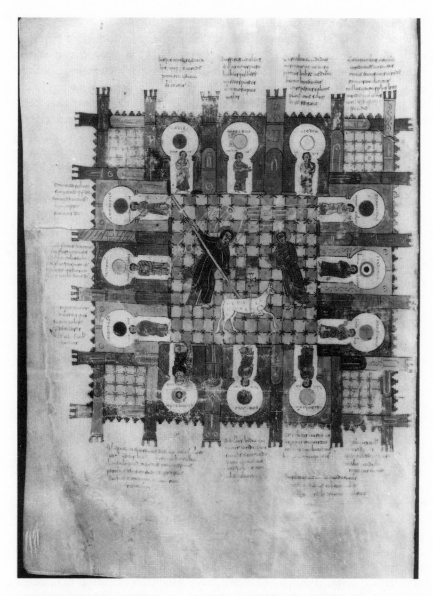

The Heavenly Jerusalem (Apoc. 21: 1–27), showing the Apostles in the gates with their respective precious stones above their heads. Commentary on the Apocalypse by Beatus de Liebana. Spain (Leon), *c.* 950 ce. M.644, f.222v. The Pierpont Morgan Library, New York, Art Resource, New York

Robson's allusion to Hiroshima is evocative of the nuclear bomb and the Second World War, but also Auschwitz and the 'final solution' of Fascism, all of which herald the end of grand narratives of the West – the end of 'the Athenian "beautiful death," the exchange of the finite for the infinite, of the *eschaton* for the *télos*: the Die in order not to die' (Lyotard 1988: 100). With the forward march of the apocalyptic storm or 'angel of history' that Benjamin (1976: 257–8) calls Progress, names of the dead no longer lend themselves to the writings of monumental history.

Imageries of the apocalypse are central to the postmodern deconstruction of literature and the explosion of categories of history and the 'real.' According to Derrida (1984a), our era is characterized by the growth of the literary imagination and the 'textual socius' that comes with it, a specularized society driven by the psychagogic rhetoric of nuclear-war dissuasion and deterrence. Literature and apocalyptic signs and fears of the nuclear age have in common that they both thrive on speculative, fabulously textual events that have no referential reality. Both activities also rely on objective infrastructural conditions that are inherently self-destructive: a world system built around war efforts and the nuclear industry, and a stockpiling of original corpuses and archives arbitrarily assigned to authorial subjects.

All of these conditions are self-destructive. The nuclear-age socius grows in the shadow of a totally devastating Event, an absolute Endtime war that bears a unique name, the first and the last of its kind, a cataclysm that belongs to a class of its own. This rhetorical event is so absurd that it threatens to bring about a remainderless destruction that will annihilate all archives, and the human habitat as well. Nuclear rhetoric points to an End that leaves no trace whatsoever, eschewing and effacing all motions of survival and related works of sublime representation. Given its all-consuming character, the nuclear apocalypse threatens to foreclose the monumental history of typological naming, symbolic mourning, and mnemonic idealization.

Likewise, writing entails the *épochè* of absolute knowledge. Literature is a constant invitation to acts of interpretive deconstruction, interventions that end up decomposing and undermining the archival foundations of writing. Literature and the nuclear epoch are both apocalyptic in the sense of installing humanity in a self-destructive condition of radical fictionality and precarious historicity. But even without deconstruction, writing is subject to a prolonged big-bang effect that keeps scattering elements of signification in countless directions. Whatever the logical and intentional origins and ends of the script may be, the missile-like message of the missive can be counted on never to reach its final destination. Derrida refers to this chaotic dispersal effect as the wandering ways of *la diff-errance*.

The structure of truth itself is inherently apocalyptic in that it always comes as a grand finale, passing a 'last' judgment on all other contending truths that are brought to an End (Derrida 1984b: 24). Truth is essentially eschatological, as it is always the voice of the last human being, the one possessed with a light brighter than all other lights. This may be the voice that proclaims the death of God, the subject, or 'man' (substituted by the 'overman'). Alternatively, the Voice may announce the end of Christian morality, Western metaphysics, philosophy, history, progress, class struggle, patriarchy, or literature (20–3). It could also choose to declare the end of astrology, heralding the triumph of a timeless Verb, as in John's Apocalypse.

My reading of the Book of Revelation has a postmodern apocalyptic tone in that it purports to *uncover* the astrological derailment or delirium of Revelation. I am alluding to the parasitic indirections, intrusions, and deviations of John's logocentric script, all of which converge on the 'galactic under all the milky ways whose constellation' fascinates the Derridean imagination *en passant* (Derrida 1984b: 5). A pagan understanding of the New Testament Apocalypse thus points to the 'phenomena of *Verstimmung*, of change of tone, of mixing of genres, of *destinerrance*, if I can say that, or of *clandestination*, so many signs of more or less bastard apocalyptic filiation' (31). Derrida continues to say that

we know that apocalyptic writings increased the moment State censorship was very strong in the Roman Empire, and precisely to catch the censorship unaware ... we could perhaps think that the apocalyptic discourse can also get round censorship thanks to its genre, and its cryptic ruses. By its very tone, the mixing of voices, genres, and codes, apocalyptic discourse can also, in dislocating [*détraquant*] destinations, dismantle the dominant contract or concordat. It is a challenge to the established receivability [*recevabilité*] of messages and to the policing of destination, in short to the postal notice or the monopoly of posts. (30)

The message of John received from messengers who bear witness to the testimony of Christ who speaks in the name of the Father entails a proliferation of sendings, voices, and tones that are unevenly developed and variably unveiled. The text is all the more apocalyptic since one never knows who speaks or writes, let alone what is actually being said. In the final analysis, if 'the apocalypse reveals, it is first of all the revelation of the apocalypse, the self-presentation of the apocalyptic structure of language ... : that is, of the divisible dispatch for which there is no self-presentation nor assured destination' (Derrida 1984b: 28).

Like Derrida (1984b: 7), I am of the view that the *End of Time* announced in Revelation has already taken place in John's writing, if only through the prophet's dismantling of sidereal measurements of time. Derrida also correctly suggests that the command forbidding John to 'seal the words of the inspiration of this volume' was a double-bind injunction that John 'could only disobey in order to obey' (32). After all, the command to silence astrology had to be sealed as soon as it was obeyed. As already announced, this book reopens the latter seal, with a view to exploring the well-forgotten sources and traces of John's imagery, a disturbing genealogy that offers 'postmodern counterweights to the emphasis on originality, presence, and universality in Christian revelation' (Boyarin 1995: 44).

The contested site where Derrida and I must part company, however, has to do with the question of how many scattered voices a text can effectively mix, and in what actual rank-order, if any. In *Writing and Difference* (1978: 297), Derrida recognizes that the centring effects of language cannot be reduced to idiosyncrasies of a Western metaphysical tradition struggling against the freedom and playfulness of signs. The desire for a centre is rather a vital 'function of play itself.' In Derrida's discussion of the apocalypse, however, the implications of the latter principle are not fully explored. Like most post-structuralist and postmodern theorists, Derrida tends to exaggerate the difference or *différend* that lies between the works of centring and decentring, usually with the aim of privileging the polyphonic, heteroglossic digressions and transgressions of the sign process. While Derrida proposes an inversion of the habitual rank-ordering of centripetal and centrifugal motions of language, his understanding of writing and literature is still based upon a stratified arrangement of the forces at play in language. Paradoxically, the postmodern priority assigned to polytonality over monotonality is yet another confirmation (self-contradictory) of the will to power that plays itself out in battlefields of the Word.

Similar comments apply to the Bakhtinian concept of dialogism. According to Bakhtin, 'high and straightforward' genres such as tragedies, epics, and the Scriptures are so hierarchical, monotonic, and authoritative that they permit no play, no sense of popular or individual freedom, no improvised heroes battling with inconclusive events of the narrative (1981: 35–6, 55). Canonical texts make no concession to varying truths; they preclude a Galilean world of other-languagedness where dialogues and words are written 'with a sideways glance'; and they do not invite compositions of parodic travesty and self-criticism (46, 49, 55, 59–65). By contrast, 'active polyglossia and interillumination of languages' typify heterodox writings ranging from the life-like novel to Cyprian feasts of the Middle Ages, a literature that feeds on the 'speech life of peoples' and a cultural world-in-the-making (17, 30–2, 70, 83).

The problem with these contrast generalizations is that they underestimate the extent to which literary and cultural 'interanimations' and 'arguments between languages' are fundamental to all discursive practices, including the monotonic and authorative. As Bakhtin remarks, 'monoglossia is always in essence relative. After all, one's own language is never a single language: in it there are always survival of the past and a potential for other-languagedness that is more or less sharply perceived by the working literary and language consciousness.' That is to say, 'straightforward genres' are subject to 'the long and twisted path of struggle for the unity of a literary language,' a unity that is never fully gained (1981: 66).

John's apocalypse is replete with signs of dialogical *clandestinations*, not because of a desire to challenge the dominant concordat, as a Derridean or Bakhtinian reading of the text would have it. Rather, the point of Revelation's astrological indirections lies elsewhere: in an attempt to subsume the hegemonic voice of astralism under another Covenant, the Lord's. Carefully oriented transgressions and displacements of the apocalypse are essential to the rank-ordering of signs – raising the timeless Verb above minions of the order of time. Despite their subversive implications, the traps and tricks of Revelation are part and parcel of the well-aimed missives and missiles of Logos. Signs of desire covering the bodies of heavens must be allowed to wander beneath the surface text if they are to deviate from their temporal motions and be enslaved by the Eternal and the Everlasting. Without these erring codes, the West would have lacked the signs needed to speak of the End of Time, the Fall, threats of idolatrous Chaos, sign-mediations of the Verb, the conquering ways of a non-erring Truth, and so on. Machiavellian craftiness and duplicity with the enemy are essential to the ancient 'Head' or 'Sum of Days' (Dan. 7: 9; 1 Enoch 46: 1f., 47: 3) whose apocalyptic rhetoric aims at counting and enslaving all days of the Sabian foe.

What I have just said about the *essential indirections* of the sign process applies to postmodern theories of apocalyptic *diff-errance*. Even when speaking many voices, they too must choose a centre that brings *some* order into the world. An erratic and aleatory big bang that fails to offer a new beginning or fresh vision of the universe should be of little interest to all parties concerned, a matter of universal *indifference*. If this aleatory centre is denied, then what is the purpose of deconstruction? Is it to proclaim the end of all myths of the End, critiquing false prophets who stand accused of denouncing other false prophets (Derrida 1984b: 28)? Is it to foster a post-Renaissance 'world of free and democratized language,' rejecting all sacred words and 'the complex and multi-level hierarchy of discourses, forms, images, styles that used to permeate the entire system of official language and linguistic consciousness' (Bakhtin 1981: 71). When all is said and done, proponents of a postmodern apocalypse should 'make up their minds' and choose among absolute silence, chaotic babbling, or a revelation of their own. As for this book, the preference is clearly for the entitlements of a *Postmodern Revelation*, by which I mean a forward journey aimed at recovering the tragic, sensuous, and desirous *ways of logic* – signs of the primitive *mathematics* and motions of desire (normative, repressive, transgressive) embedded in all words and the powers of speech.

The latter preference implies that we be wary of the Kantian invitation to choose between: (a) a rational philosophy, *savoir-vivre*, or wisdom of life inspired by scientific concepts universally accessible through the labour of pure reason (speculative or practical); and (b) an 'eschatological mystagogy' – a 'derailed' and 'exalted' philosophy that conveys feelings of an enlightened and immediate contact with mysteries of the universe, an intuitive communication with oracular secrets possessed by overlords of knowledge alone.

Derrida's (1984b) reading of Kant's battle against Platonic mystagogy revolves around the issue of mathematics, the key to astrology, and the schemings of Revelation as well. Plato was of the opinion that apocalyptic visions and teophanic interpretations of geometric figures (echoing the Pythagorean mysticism of numbers) should not be revealed to the crowds. This implied an acceptance of the cryptopolitics of knowledge, the opposite of Kant's rational theology. Mystagogues of the modern era will thus cite Plato when resorting to the language of anagogy, poetry, and literature to convey their presentiment of the sun and the goddess Isis hiding under a veil, seeking, as they do, the principles of reason and morality in the sensuous, the visible, and the beautiful. In doing so they assign a false tone of obscure aestheticism to the philosophical pursuit of the moral, the lawful, and the rational.

In other words, and this is a trenchant motif for thought of the law or of the ethical today, Kant calls for placing the law above and beyond, not the person, but personification and the body, above and beyond as it were the sensible voice that speaks in us, the singular voice that speaks to us in private, the voice that could be said in his language to be 'pathological' in opposition to the voice of reason. The law above the body, above *this body found here to be represented by a veiled goddess.* (Derrida 1984b: 19; emphasis added)

The choice is therefore between ethics and aesthetics, the intellect and the affect, the conceptual and the physical, the abstract and the concrete, the orderly and the disorderly, the normative and the transgressive. We have come full circle, back onto home ground. This is the divided terrain that I wish to revisit and contest, with a view to dismantling the all-too-familiar bickerings of Logos and Eros.

This chapter has provided the theoretical background for our journey into the embattlements of 'primitive mathematics' and the apocalyptic imagination, struggles played out in John's visions of the End, and in Western religious history. We shall begin this journey with brief histories of astrology (chapter 2) and exegeses of Revelation spanning the writings of Saint Augustine and scholarly contributions of the twentieth century (chapter 3). Before we undertake these surveys, however, more should be said about the fate of astrology in the nuclear age and present-day manifestations of Kant's 'mathematical mystagogy.'

The Postmodern Middle Ages

Although frequently reported by religious sects and visionaries of right-wing political affiliation, revelations of a forthcoming apocalypse do not form a dominant element of twentieth-century Western culture and the corresponding rhetoric of modernity, let alone the elusive value system of the postmodern world. Christians and theologians still read the Book of Revelation, yet John's imageries are no longer taken literally. When exegetes take these visions of the future seriously, the prophecies are projected onto a distant future that never comes, as in the days of Augustine. By contrast, astrology is a widespread practice that feeds a relatively thriving industry of professionals and semi-professionals catering to the needs of countless individuals prying into what the stars have in store for them.

Astrology is a widespread phenomenon. In the 1970s Eliade (1976: 59) estimated that 1,200 of the 1,750 daily newspapers published in the United States contained horoscopal columns, and that at least 5 million Americans followed horoscopal advice when organizing their daily lives. Horoscopy was then a business with a turnover of hundreds of millions of dollars, a surreal market that kept thousands of practitioners employed. Knowledge of the future was and still is a popular preoccupation in Europe as well. In France half of the daily newspapers offer horoscopal information. A 1980

survey suggested that millions of Frenchmen (12 per cent of those inter-
viewed) took their horoscopes into account when organizing their daily
activities. More than 50 per cent of the adult population consulted
horoscopal columns every now and then. An older study carried out in the
early 1960s showed that at least 30 per cent of adult Frenchmen knew their
zodiacal sign, had a look at their horoscopes once in a while, and thought
that there was some truth to zodiacal personality attributions. In 1967
more than 60 per cent read their horoscopes at least occasionally, and 12
per cent had already consulted a fortune-teller (Morin 1981: 18, 43, 45).

The mass appeal of astrology in the modern age is relatively recent. We
know that from about 1700 until the end of the nineteenth century, astrologers in Europe had lost much of their intellectual respectability. Great
Britain was the only exception; country doctors and annual almanacs published by the Stationers' Company in London preserved the art from
extinction. Predictive almanacs declined in numbers throughout the eighteenth century, save a few publications such as Francis Moore's *Vox Stel-
larum*, which went from 107,000 copies sold in 1768 to 393,750 in 1803.
With the growth of journalism in the 1820s and 1830s, popular astrology
made inroads into the British press, mostly via the writings of Smith in *The
Straggling Astrologer*, Morrison in *The Herald of Astrology*, and Dixon in
The Prophetic Messenger (Howe 1967: 20, 22, 30–4). Astrological journalism was thus born, much to the chagrin of those who wished to preserve an
esoteric science accessible only to the few.

But a full-fledged revival of astrology in Britain did not occur until the
1890s, followed by its diffusion to Continental Europe. The West owes
much of this revival to the growth of Theosophical and esoteric philosophy
at the turn of the century, a new trend that fostered a symbolic and spiritual approach to horoscopy, at the expense of the scientific and utilitarian
attitudes of the Victorian era. In the United States, astrology found fertile
ground in the syncretic combination of Theosophy and spiritualism with
elements of ancient European hermetism and mystical traditions of the
East. In France, a country where nothing on the subject had been published
since Morin de Villefranche's *Astrologia Gallica*, printed in 1661, occultism
of the late nineteenth century produced a mixture of magic, alchemy, and a
Christianized cabbala inspired by the Neoplatonic writings of Renaissance
humanists such as Pico della Mirandola. The statistical works of Paul
Choisnard published in the early 1900s took a more scientific direction and
were instrumental in subjecting horoscopy to quantitative measures of val-
idation (Howe 1967: 54–6, 73f., 77).

Although hermetic sciences had an impact on German intellectual life prior to the First World War, astrology in Germany flourished in the 1920s and the 1930s; more than 400 books and pamphlets addressed mostly to practitioners were published during these two decades (Howe 1967: 102f.). But the strength of German astrology was more apparent than real. In an attempt to achieve academic sophistication and scientific respectability, astrologers such as O.A.H. Schmitz sought to incorporate basic notions of psychology into horoscopy, using the writings of Jung (*Psychological Types*) to expand the characteriological insights or claims of the discipline. Jung himself felt optimistic about this 'widespread and ever-growing interest in all forms of psychic phenomena, including spiritualism, astrology, Theosophy, parapsychology and so forth ... The world has seen nothing like it since the end of the seventeenth century. We can only compare it with the flowering of Gnostic thought in the first and second centuries after Christ' (quoted in Howe 1967: 7; see also 84, 98f.). While characteriology was turned into a highly repressive discourse during the Third Reich, Hitler's regime was not particularly supportive of the organized astrological profession, closing down the German branch of the Theosophical Society in 1937. A gradual distinction was made between unacceptable fortune-tellers and the politically more 'reliable' practitioners devoted to the Nazi regime, including the well-known Swiss astrologer Karl Ernst Krafft (115–19).

Alan Leo, a leading proponent of Theosophy in England, was the first to launch the mass production of cheap, highly simplified, and easily accessible horoscopes. He gave a populist twist to esoterism and occultism, thereby securing the lasting impact of astrology on mass cultures of the twentieth century (Howe 1967: 62, 64–6). As Morin (1981: 43) points out, secrets of the zodiac were removed from the sphere of the occult, where they had been forced to retreat, to be spread among the masses through the press, magazines, and radio broadcasts, at little cost to the individual consumer. Horoscope by phone, computer, television, and Internet is now available to the common run of people and the educated and wealthy alike. Zodiacal charms, lockets, key rings, and jewellery of all sorts are a constant reminder of how the signs of heaven inform popular cultural views of human destiny. However hegemonic they may be, science and religion cannot prevent the art of divination from answering basic individual queries such as 'Who am I?' and 'What does the immediate future have in store for me?'

And yet astrology is no longer what it used to be. First of all, it is no longer the language of the powerful. In lieu of assisting popes, princes, and kings, sidereal divination appeals to weakly integrated segments of society:

mostly women and the young living in cities, populations that are less indoctrinated with the teachings of science or the Christian faith (Morin 1981: 18). Hollywood stars, managers, businessmen, professionals, and wealthy people may take counsel with astrologers, but they do so usually with discretion, with a complementary dose of astrophysical or psychological rationalization, and with some disdain *vis-à-vis* popular, unscientific manipulations of the art. When swayed by more sophisticated formulations of astrology, clients of middle- and upper-class backgrounds will resort to astrology as a back-up rationality, reducing the risks and uncertainties inherent in their own business, profession, or trade. But rarely will they use horoscopal counselling as a substitute for all the techniques and know-how that guide their normal occupational activities (91–3). Some twentieth-century politicians and rulers may also seek guidance in the predictions of astrology, as during the Third Reich (Howe 1967), yet they tend to be exceptions.

As for academics and scientists, they will predictably keep their distance from all forms of divination. Historians and sociologists such as Cramer (1954), Adorno (1994), Barthes (1957), Eliade (1976), Tester (1987), and Morin (1981) will treat astrology as a subject worthy of sociological and historical investigation, yet few will push their enthusiasm so far as to profess to be adepts or practitioners of the art. Fortune-telling is interesting only for social-scientific purposes, dissecting the corpus in search of signs of the times.

Astrology speaks without authority. Religious and scientific objections to the claims of astrology still have the force of law on their side. For all their ideological differences, Christianity, liberalism, humanism, rationalism, positivism, and Marxism have in common a clear aversion to 'primitive astronomy' and related beliefs in the influence of stars and planets on human affairs, claims to knowledge justified neither by reason or evidence nor by any religious canon. An American manifesto published in 1975 by *The Humanist* and signed by eminent intellectuals and Nobel Prize winners condemned the spread of astrology in no uncertain terms: predictions of the future based on astral calculations and propagated by the media are a denial of human freedom, an expression of obscurantism in its worst form, and a show of ignorance *vis-à-vis* basic facts of astronomy. In France the vocal *Union rationaliste* is equally critical of the pretentious claims and irrationality of contemporary astrology. More recently the work of Gauquelin (1985) has been the object of thorough scientific criticism directed by Pecker (1995) at the Collège de France.

By and large, however, public denunciations of astrology are few. This

should not come as a surprise when we consider the institutional and doctrinal weaknesses of astrology. The practice is diffuse, constituting neither
a church nor a science, deprived of any well-organized centre or profes-
sional bodies that can be targeted when the pseudo-science is challenged
and criticized. Acting outside the realms of power, the practice avoids
sparking-off public debates and repressive measures against the profession.
Fortune-telling based on the zodiac is all the more difficult to attack as the
practice tends to be multifarious. Predictions are subject to the intervention
of free will and lend themselves to intricate variations in the actual arithmetic and interpretive modes applied to birth charts and horoscopal
themes, thus providing 'convenient excuses' for errors, as in ancient times
(Pingree 1993: 83; Thomas 1971: 335–7). The methods used by the practitioners range from single measurements to multivariable geometry (zodiacal and planetary 'aspects'), from simple glossaries of zodiacal attributes to
complex blendings of astrology with astronomy, psychoanalysis, Jungian
phenomenology, and Talmudic theology (Barbault 1961; Choisnard 1908;
Mailly Nesle 1981; Dobin 1983).

Unlike their ancient counterparts, the modern 'mathematicians of fate'
exercise limited influence over religion and politics. As Morin (1981)
argues, astrology as it is now practised is primarily a popular-cultural reply
to the inequities and gaps created by the crises of Christianity, positive science, and humanist culture. Established religious responses to broader
questions regarding the human condition have lost much of their appeal in
urban societies of the industrial and post-industrial era. Nor do the ideals
of humanism and high learning in the arts and philosophy provide satisfac-
tory answers to existential questions of workers and the new middle
classes. In any case these ideals were and are still accessible only to a minority of 'cultivated minds.'

Horoscopy intervenes where religion and 'high culture' have failed. It
also compensates for Christianity's neglect of the positive connections that
link human beings to nature and the visible cosmos. Stellar divination permits a reversion to mythical pre-Enlightenment world-views that offer the
language needed to socialize nature and naturalize society (Habermas 1987:
116). In the words of Eliade, astrology grants the self a cosmic status otherwise denied by society and philosophy:

You are no longer merely the anonymous individual described by Heidegger and
Sartre, a stranger thrown into an absurd and meaningless world, condemned to be
free, as Sartre used to say, with a freedom confined to your situation and conditioned by your historical moment. Rather, the horoscope reveals to you a new dig-

nity; it shows how intimately you are related to the entire universe. It is true that your life is determined by the movement of the stars, but at least this determination has an incomparable grandeur ... it means that the universe moves according to a preestablished plan; that human life and history itself follow a pattern and advance progressively toward a goal. This ultimate goal is secret or beyond human understanding; but at least it gives meaning to a cosmos regarded by most scientists as the result of blind hazard, and it gives sense to the human existence declared by Sartre to be *de trop*. (1976: 61)

Christianity's silence *vis-à-vis* the bonds of nature and culture undermine the achievements of science and industry as well, activities of an alienated lifeworld that harness nature and human labour to the exigencies of capital and technology. Science addresses our queries about nature, yet its insights into the world are designed to assist in the subjugation and mastery of nature and the body. In hindsight, science weakens its own case by catering to the literate only (holders of cultural capital duly accredited), by reducing all of nature to pure objects, and by ignoring the role of the subject in nature. Scientific knowledge is all the more partial as it tends not to conceive of the universe as a whole. Astronomy is no exception to the rule. Unlike astrology, astronomy treats the cosmos as an infinite space–time continuum that can be known only partially. As Freud (1973: 34) once remarked, 'no reader of an account of astronomy will feel disappointed and contemptuous of the science if he is shown the frontiers at which our knowledge of the universe melts into haziness.' Our scientifically apprehended cosmos is governed by laws that are so complex as to include multiple centres and theories of the universe governed by principles of indeterminacy and statistical probability, a far cry from the relatively simple rules of correspondence and systemic closure prevailing in horoscopy (Morin 1981: 135).

The gains of astrology achieved through the mass media speak to the crisis of Western culture and rationality, themes explored by critical sociologists such as Adorno, Marcuse, Habermas, and Horkheimer. As Adorno remarks, the rational organization and efficient division of modern sciences have produced a great divide between knowledge of the subject (psychology) and of the universe (astronomy), a gap that astrology attempts to fill. 'What Spengler called the modern caveman, dwells in the cavity, as it were, between organized sciences which do not cover the universality of existence' (Adorno 1994: 118). Chronicles of the stars take up a challenge not conceivable within the limits of science: seeking insights into the most intimate (one's psyche) and the most global (everyone's cosmos) simultaneously, linking the two via the moment and celestial circumstances of each and every human birth. Astrology thus brings together two modes of knowledge cast out from Western science and culture. It offers an accessible 'science of the subject,' pulling the subject out of the narrow confines of psychology and the residual glory hole of confusion and illogicality where subjectivity tends to dwell. I am alluding to the rag-bag where positivism throws everything that fails to behave like a pure object, including critical manifestations of language such as symbolling, metaphor, expressions of desire, and apprehensions of the future.

Horoscopy bypasses science and Christian doctrine as it creates a neo-naturalistic or neo-Romantic approach to the cosmos. It uses astral geometry and psychological analogy to sound correspondences between humans and a number of celestial bodies constituting a finite universe. Through a blend of psychological anagogy and heavenly *mathematica*, constellations and planets are made to influence and partake in the principles that govern human behaviour on earth. Astral bodies are anthropomorphized and humans 'cosmologized' all at once, each signifying the other through laws of cosmic sympathy and 'symbolic configurations' echoing universal forces of the unconscious (Morin 1981: 78–9).

But while responding to the crisis of Western culture and rationality, astrology has also adapted itself to modern times to such an extent that it has inherited many of its inherent problems. As a result horoscopal belief systems are a timid reversion to the integrated world-views of antiquity and the Middle Ages. In lieu of constituting the highest form of learning, astral divination is now systematically ignored or scorned by scientists and theologians alike. As a pseudo-science, it is disconnected from all major achievements of modern positivism, thereby receiving little recognition from established institutions. As a pseudo-religion, it pays inadequate attention to questions of spirituality. The worship of God gives way to the cult of star-things ruled by mechanical laws elevated to the rank of quasi-metaphysical powers, fulfilling Comte's hopes for a quasi-religious commitment to positivism (Adorno 1994: 116). Although inspired by ancient wisdom, few astrologers of today will treat zodiacal constellations and planets as divinities in their own right. Despite their claims to holistic knowledge and millenarian predictions of the New Age, adepts of the art have left spiritual matters out of their agenda. Actually astrologers are now less concerned about the whole creation and events on a collective scale than they are by a world of isolated subjects – an atomized universe of clients and individuals pursuing billions of secular ends.

Astrology in the Age of Aquarius is a monument to modern and postmodern individualism. Stellar configurations play an important role in the art, but they tend to be vaguely abstract and quasi-fictive entities far removed from earthly reality. Few adepts would be able to actually recognize zodiacal constellations in the visible sky, let alone their shifting connection to months of the year. More than the cosmos, it is the individual that matters first and foremost. And so must it be if the ancient art is to fulfil a new function: the quest for identity and the process of individuation in mass-media, urban-market, and state-dominated societies of the twentieth century.

By focusing on the individual and the heavenly circumstances of his or her moment of birth, mass-media horoscopy fabricates a relatively simple yet detailed charting of the client, of his or her personality attributes and daily destiny. Astrology offers the software required to produce not only an encompassing typology accessible to all, but also a combinatory logic of aspects and themes that will generate minute differences operating at the level of the individual and his or her day-to-day activities. Zodiacal reductionism is thus combined with measurements of individuality to produce or reinforce our glorification of the ego and its unique *persona*. Ancient *mathematics* (now computerized and televised) comes to the rescue of individual polyphony, the cult of the sacrosanct subject: totemism *à l'occidentale*.

Astro-psychology plays an integrative function in a complex, highly divided society. It speaks the all-too familiar language of the 'natural subject,' naturalizing differences that can be observed between unique personal 'identities.' Class conflicts, political struggles, ethnic and gender differences, patterns of cultural uniformity imposed on individuals – all disappear under a thick cloak of horoscopal individuation and zodiacal class-psychologism. Class differences are none the less reintroduced into the art. All adepts and clients of astrology seek answers to questions of identity and fate, yet only the wealthy can afford the services of expert counsellors who provide them with fuller descriptions of their finer psyches and sophisticated personalities. Compared with working-class horoscopy, an upper-class ego portrayed *in extenso* (preferably elevated above the common people through some New Age therapy) is worth a small 'fortune.'

Astrology should be credited for having survived the Age of Reason and modernity, playing, as it does, on the needs and wants of the subject yearning for individuality and personal success in the commonplace matters of work, health, and love. As a science of the subject, astrology harks back to ancient issues of narrative destiny and heavenly *desire* (from Lat. *sideralis*, 'concerning the star') – hence, the *desiderata* of humans concerned about their fortune and lot in life. While science ignores the subject, and while sign theories address questions of origins (historical, intentional) and root forms (logical, conventional) only, astrology persists in paying attention to signs of the future and the motions of desire. The wishful investments of 'primitive astronomy' continue to appeal to the 'uncultivated minds' of our times, in total disregard of Augustinian theology, Aristotelian philosophy, and the Age of Reason. Horoscopy is a denegation of thought systems that insist on confining stars to measures and markers of calendrical time, divesting them of their ability to signify motions of the mind and passions of the soul (see Ricoeur 1984: 14–15).

The popularity of astral divination stems from its ability to produce the wishful signs of a narrative composition, harnessing signs of the heavens to memories of the past and hopes and fears of the future – to longings and apprehensions of the soul. Through the vagueness and ambiguities of horoscopal rhetoric, relevant incidents can be given meaning within a plot that keeps moving, linking conjunctural events to the origins of a weighty story and to signs of developments that have yet to come. Like a camera generating motion pictures, astrology projects onto the sky stories that beg to be told as they unfold. Astrology offers a sense of narrative richness and trajectory to life in a world otherwise absurd. It compensates for a social environment where activities are highly fragmented and routinized, where the individual lives in the solitude of anonymous urban sprawls, and where the workers and the unemployed are reduced to component parts and out-casts of some absentee owner's money-making machine.

More than a calendrical system, astrology has always been a logic of yearnings in motion, an activation of wishful dispositions synchronized with orderly movements and 'music of the spheres' (Feldman 1978: 73). The actual contents of this idiom of desire made in heaven, however, has changed considerably since the end of the Middle Ages. By and large, horoscopal divination is now dedicated to the pursuit of individuality and personal identity, as opposed to the larger finalities of national history, the fate of the Church, the cosmos, and all the powers that be.

To the cult of the self-seeking ego, horoscopy adds the intersubjective quest for everyone's *alter ego*, his or her Significant Other. Once mapped out in digest form, a person's chartered identity can be exchanged with others with a view to communicating knowledge of the psyche and disposi-tions towards interpersonal activity. When converted into an intersubjec-tive algebra, zodiacal symbolism becomes a means to deliberate issues of romantic love and their potential outcome. Horoscopy offers evaluations of the alchemy of zodiacal combinations, or the chemistry of sign affinities and fateful incompatibilities. It does this by applying 'sign psychology' to the creation and narration of the sacrosanct couple, the 'wishful relationship' of the private domain (personal, emotional, physical). To combat the solitude and monotony of urban industrial life, astrology delivers the attractions and entertainments of Hollywood romance.

But when compared with more ancient dramatizations of hopes and signs of the future, mass-media horoscopy becomes a feeble expression of the logic of desire. Despite its sensitivity to 'motions of the soul,' astrology has adapted its prophetic inspiration to modern circumstances, turning itself into a watered-down version of its former self. In lieu of prophecies of great things to come, including the messianic millennium and the renewal of the earth, astrological pronouncements have been reduced to a proliferation of modest businesses of *petites espérances*, marginal enterprises catering to billions of small hopes of great concern to their individual owners and their immediate prospects at best. Astrologers will on occasion predict a great future for the science of astrology and related wisdoms (deep ecology, pacifism, Zen Buddhism, etc.) in the New Age of Aquarius. Some will venture to announce events on a national scale, typically at the beginning of each year. But predictions of this sort speak mostly to interests of the profession and competition between individual practitioners vying for public success.

Older views of a dramatic *eschaton* looming ahead will no longer capture the astrological imagination. As argued by Barthes (1957: 167) and Adorno (1994: 102), horoscopes euphorize reality to such a point that they never dare speak of the End and the tragic in life. The possibility that there may be 'horrifying horoscopes, horoscopes *unrivaled* in history, *which freeze the soul*' and which evoke 'the raging of the Apocalypse,' as Rozanov used to say (1977: 283), is rarely entertained. Present-day astrology bathes, rather, in a rosy atmosphere of optimism bordering on ethereal naïvety and great banality. Death is systematically ignored, illness is always passing, old age is full of the blessings of wisdom and maturity, and solitude is about to be surmounted by a great love. Conflicts are misunderstandings soon to be resolved (with a show of goodwill), and no one is unfortunate enough to have mortal foes or to live in utter poverty. Against the deprivations of urban misery, astrology elevates common people above their social rank, treating *Homo horoscopus* in the image of what he or she yearns to be (Morin 1981: 55; Adorno 1994: 61–3). Through 'social catasterism,' horoscopal rhetoric makes everyone into a star. All in all, social problems are without historical and social depth, and the absurdities and sufferings of life are no food for positive horoscopal thought. Horoscopy speaks to a reality without catastrophe, a 'fun world' where 'everything sounds respectable, sedate and sensible.' Signs of heaven converge on Huxley's negative utopia, a Brave New World confirming the principle that 'everybody is happy nowadays' (Adorno 1994: 41, 75).

Ancient preoccupations with timings of the End (the end of one's life, the death of a king, Judgment Day) have been extirpated from today's reassuring astrology. Stoic teachings of wisdom *vis-à-vis* one's inescapable Fate, tragic or glorious, are no longer in fashion either. As in the Middle Ages, the Judaeo-Christian and liberal exercise of free will now informs astral motions that impel but do not compel. Notwithstanding signs of things to come, humans are encouraged to intervene in the unfolding of their own lives. Self-determination, however, is defined along lines that tally with the shortsightedness of the modern and postmodern 'individual.' More often than not, horoscopal advice promotes prudentiality, voluntarism, and opportunism. While difficult circumstances call for a show of caution, flexibility, and self-control, a seize-the-chance morality is conveyed through horoscopal counselling. Provided that predictions are met with actions and efforts that illustrate the ethics of cautious voluntarism, life may be counted on to reward those who behave deservingly. Quick results can be attained by the virtuous who seize a passing opportunity or choose the right solution to an immediate problem. As Barthes (1957: 167f.) notes, astrology compels the heavens to yield before the higher rule of meritocracy: heaven helps those who help themselves, and does so almost immediately and miraculously.

The stars meddle in human affairs in such ways as to express the desires and wishful actions of individuals struggling with problems of inequality, isolation, and alienation. The interventions of astrology, however, are no threat to the powers that be. They have a limited sphere of influence: the individual and his or her immediate well-being. Horoscopy never addresses squarely the sufferings of life, the impositions of nature, or the rigidities and inequities of social forces, all of which are treated as realities beyond common people's reach. While possibilism reigns over private matters, fatalism rules supreme in the natural and public domains. The laws of astrology are the only broader determinations that need careful consideration and strategic action. Without them, *Homo horoscopus* would have no knowledge of self and of things to come – hence, no means to comprehend and influence his or her own destiny. Warnings of the future allow humans to intervene beforehand; forewarned is forearmed.

With horoscopy, however, the basic constraints of life in society are left untouched and unchallenged. In an essay entitled 'The Stars Down to Earth: The *Los Angeles Times* Astrology Column,' Adorno (1994) unpacks the role that modern mass-media astrology plays in reinforcing the dominant regime. In his reading of American horoscopal columns of the early 1950s, Adorno shows how astrology oscillates between prescriptions of work and pleasure, fate and freedom, dependence and ruggedness of character, irrationality and science. The author argues that opposite poles of these familiar dualisms are handled unevenly, with second terms being put to the service of social-control requirements that reinforce totalitarianism and irrationality in its worst form.

A society dominated by science, capital, and bureaucracy thrives on pathological divisions between work and leisure, tensions that pit the *ego* against the *id* and that astrology attempts to resolve in vain. To be more specific, horoscopy sees to it that complementary functions of social organization will be mapped onto separate portions of the day or the year. While hours of daylight are devoted to the reality principle 'at work,' hours of the evening (or weekends and summer holidays) are given over to enjoyments of the pleasure principle. The simultaneous satisfaction of needs of the *ego* and the *id* is denied and broken down into either–or and first–next issues. Bipolar activities are managed through routinized biphasic patterns, where each thing must be done at the right time, one after the other.

The historical modalities of this *ego/id* dualism are covered under a thick cloak of astrological universalism. The 'chores' and 'drudgeries' of life in an industrial society are quite natural and acceptable, provided of course that they will be rewarded in due time, via the 'equally natural' pleasures of daily life. Instead of being a constant feature of human activity, pleasure is converted into a reward for work successfully accomplished, and work into an atonement for all those harmless pleasures consumed at proper times. The latter include the 'normal' activities shared with kith and kin and the simple satisfactions of a standardized and unproblematic family life relegated to leisure time (Adorno 1994: 67–9, 72–4, 99).

The rational *ego* prevails over the indulging *id*. 'The semi-tolerant integration of pleasure into a rigid pattern of life is achieved by the ever-recurring promise that pleasure trips, sprees, parties and similar events will lead to practical advantages,' approved activities seized by rational self-interest and the pursuit of individual status. Likewise, instinctual gratifications are construed as duties to be performed, including sex, which becomes a basic requirement of health. Sexual activity is transformed into a socially approved activity inspired by an antiseptic 'fun morality.' By this Adorno means a constant preoccupation with bodily hygiene, an exaltation of the cleanliness and fitness of the body rendered harmless, odourless, and inoffensive (Adorno 1994: 75–6, 84).

Astrology pretends to address the 'deepest and fondest' aspirations of the unconscious. According to Adorno, however, horoscopy is no more than a dream-factory catering to Hollywoodian 'characters' gone feeble and unheroic, an imaginary industry designed to produce weak egos fed with 'ready-made and predigested expressions of an unconscious rendered normal and socially acceptable' (1994: 49–50).

The fate-or-freedom dilemma is tackled with equal ambivalence and a predictable commitment to conventionality. By the fact of associating individual fate with motions of the celestial spheres, the social conditions of people's lives are hypostasized, separated, as they are, from their exercise of free will and projected onto the stars so as to receive a *raison d'être* otherwise lacking. Feelings of impotence are attenuated and assuaged by means of 'cautious' prophecies, with practical advice as to how people can influence their own fate, allowing for some sharing in the powers of the Almighty Father. Horoscopal advice is none the less indirect and compensatory at best. It never challenges routine activities and habits of sociability constructed by the dominant regime. Rather it conveys 'an implicit metaphysics of adjustment behind the concretistic advice of adjustment in everyday life' (Adorno 1994: 45). The stars just happen to be 'in complete agreement with the established ways of life and with the habits and institutions circumscribed by our age' (59). Signs of heaven are read as recurrent invitations to 'be reasonable,' promoting social conformity and weakness of the ego. Clients of divination are encouraged to yield before pseudo-rational regimes and thought systems that are profoundly irrational, dogmatic, and authoritarian (64, 114, 121). All in all, astrology fosters an uncritical acceptance of the more important features of one's 'fate' and promotes dependence on pseudo-scientific experts and an irrational power system endowed with metaphysical dignity.

Astrological morality makes overt concessions to the freedom and ruggedness of the individual but does so within limits. On the one hand, the organizational demands made by society require that individual pursuits comply with rules of competition. People can act in conformity with their personal needs and aspirations provided that they make plans, allocate their resources, and use their personal assets and 'natural monopolies' to achieve superiority over others. On the other hand, astrology conveys a biphasic morality that goes beyond simple lessons of rugged individualism. After all, clients of astrology must be counselled as to when they should avoid excessive originality and other symptoms of an overinflated ego. They must show a sense of innovation but never act hastily or irrevocably, never stray from their social niche, and never miss a chance to show 'strength' and 'wisdom' through flexibility and adjustment. In the end, compliance of the law-abiding subject *vis-à-vis* the dominant regime remains a priority, which means that conformity to rules of social hierarchy and a 'positive attitude' towards dependency needs must be protected and valued at all times. Ruggedness is taken less seriously than rules of conformity and sub-servience towards the higher-ups disguised as anonymous, benevolent friends (Adorno 1994: 78, 81, 83, 88, 98, 103, 113–15).

Last but not least, astrology speaks to a basic contradiction of the nuclear age, an era where the ruling order perpetuates itself via industries that breed the seed of total destruction. In response to the floating anxieties and feelings of doom associated with this regime, stellar divination con-verts signs of the apocalypse into banal fears and threats of daily life (e.g., car accidents). Horoscopy is all the more reassuring as it professes relent-less optimism, with immediate relief and remedies at hand and compulsive promises that in the end 'everything will be fine' (Adorno 1994: 55). The end-result is a pseudo-rational discourse that makes 'the senseless appear as though it had some hidden and grandiose sense while at the same time cor-roborating that this sense can neither be sought in the realm of the human nor can be properly grasped by humans' (116).

In retrospect, twentieth-century astrology is a late-modern and post-modern revival of ancient and medieval expressions of naturalism, a syncretic paganism after its time. Horoscopy combines computer mathe-matics and electronic media with a neo-archaic amalgam of Babylonian divination, Greek *mathematica*, and Empedoclean four-element cosmol-ogy (Morin 1981: 55). The outcome of this dialogue across time is a virtual reality where myths and facts constantly meet, a New Age spectacle of real events interwoven with diluted Hollywoodian fantasy. To the extent that it mirrors the attributions of the modern subject (individuality, free will) and also the routine problems and short-term preoccupations of the labouring classes, as Barthes claims, astral divination serves to exorcise the real world by actually naming it; astrology is not an 'ouverture au rêve, elle est pur miroir, pure institution de la réalité' (Barthes 1957: 166). Yet astrology may also be seen as reifying and mystifying a petty view of the world, an outlook on life that elevates the fears and hopes of 'shortsighted individuals' to quintessential problems created and deliberated in the heav-ens. The industry of sidereal divination 'prend place parmi toutes les entreprises de semi-aliénation (ou de semi-libération) qui se donnent à tâche d'objectiver le réel, sans pourtant le démystifier' (168). By ignoring larger finalities and the imminence of tragic ends, signs and chronicles of mass-media astrology herald the end of all historical perspective – hence, the trivialization of all wondrous visions of an older prophetic imagination.

The modern and postmodern media industry has brought ancient and medieval paganism out from the sphere of the occult, the Dark Chamber where the Enlightenment confined all irrational thoughts that dare contravene the rule of Reason, Science, and Christianity. Paradoxically, archaic practices have re-emerged, not from a remote past, but from the entrails and depths of late modernity (Morin 1981: 14, 79, 101–3). Through its adaptation to the ideals and rhetoric of liberal individualism, 'primitive astronomy' has come to reinforce the ruling order. But its popularity is also attributable to the exclusionary practices and endemic crises of Church, Capital, State, Science, and Culture – systems of domination that pit the damned against the elect, nature against culture, the poor against the wealthy, the powerless against the powerful, the ignorant against the cultivated. Albeit in digest form, signs of the stars allow all minds and souls to stand as equals before the wondrous heavens, forging plans of their own narrative future and a place in the sun.

But astrology is no more than a postmodern, tongue-in-cheek challenge against all the powers that be, a timid protest that never warrants a full-fledged repression. Neo-archaism is no threat to hegemonic institutions of the West, however conflict- and crisis-ridden they may be. Horoscopal paganism is a 'virtual rebellion' at best, a marginal belief system adopted with discretion and appropriate scepticism, expressed only occasionally and with constant flickers of doubt and well-behaved mimicries of the unconscious (Adorno 1994: 39, 50). Failing a firm commitment to either reason or faith, astrology is incapable of turning into a rigorous science (non-geocentric, non-anthropocentric), let alone a true religion or a compelling morality (37). As a *croyance clignotante* (Morin 1981: 19, 147), neo-paganism is an exercise in double-dealing, an expression of faith in the cosmos undermined by a constant detachment from larger struggles and visions of history. Adepts of postmodern archaism are experts at playing double games, mixing, as they do, faith and doubt, science and fantasy, logic and wishful thinking.

Current readings of the heavenly signs do not simply reflect or deflect – represent or misrepresent – the real conditions of twentieth-century society. Rather, astrology speaks to other speeches. Better said, *it acts meaningfully on other meaningful practices*, those of modern subjects, their disconnection from visions of the future and their alienation from a natural world spoiled by Christianity, Science, and Capital. As argued above, horoscopy exercises an influence from the heart and the margins of present-day history, in ways that both contradict and reinforce the ruling powers of speech. The pervasive yet inconsequential impact it has on our daily lives is in keeping with an older concept of 'influence': the flowing of an ethereal fluid or power from the stars, thought to affect the characters and actions of people, usually in ways that are manipulable and alterable. As with all narratives, horoscopal stories conjure up things that should have happened but never did (events averted though foreseen), or things that did happen but should have failed to occur (events willed by humans though contrary to Fate). Just as astrology constantly speaks to what should and yet might not be (or should not and yet might be), so too it exercises power without ever using force. It exists without being essential, surviving, as it does, without any sense of its own necessity.

Astrology is so unsure of its own fate that the powers of orthodoxy will rarely apply force to its repression and destruction. So it seems. Actually the official powers' silence *vis-à-vis* the twentieth-century, mass-media revival of divination is more feigned than real. As in the Book of Revelation, astrology cannot be ignored, silenced, or forgotten without leaving some trace of the efforts needed to do away with the trivial, the false, and the objectionable.

Casting astrological meanings out of the language of time and desire and into secret chambers of obscure etymologies and colloquialisms is one such effort, a means of actively forgetting what must not be committed to memory. Thanks to the labour of oblivion, we can now safely speak of our 'desires' (Lat. *sidus, sideris*, 'constellation'), our 'desiderata' or things worthy of our 'consideration' without having to invoke the stars. We can discuss questions of 'influence' and never think of fluids emanating from the heavens. We can attach an asterisk to a word and pay no attention to its astral origins. As with months and days of the week, we can speak of 'disasters,' particular diseases ('venereal'), and some personality attributes ('jovial,' 'lunatic') and continue to ignore their planetary significations. We can have Sunday, Christmas, and Easter celebrations and never worship the sun, its solstitial rebirth or equinoctial resurrection. We can talk about Hollywood 'stars,' thank our own 'lucky stars,' and be in 'seventh heaven' without knowing much about catasterism. We can complain about not reaching our 'destination' or about the warm weather of the 'dog days' without evoking older notions of 'destiny' or motions of the Dog Star.

In lieu of simply silencing words and signs that pose a threat to the powers of speech, conventional language will analogize and etymologize the literal meanings it cannot tolerate. The same rule applies to ancient dismissals of astrology. As we are about the see, the logocentric pronouncements of Revelation thrive on the demotion of heavenly signs of the future to mere metaphors and figures of speech.

2

Music of the Spheres

The Assumptions and Riddles of Primitive Astronomy

Ancient astrology rests on the assumption that motions of the heavenly bodies are divine in the sense of being all-encompassing, and also permanent and immutable features of the cosmos. At the same time, these motions are variable, observable, and measurable, and they produce interactive influences that can be acted upon, if only minimally.

In the astrological perspective, attributes of eternity and infinity are predicated upon the lawful universe as opposed to any intangible deity or divine will governing the world from beyond the visible spheres. In the words of Manilius (*Astronomica* 1: 518ff.):

Everything born to a mortal existence is subject to change, nor does the earth notice that, despoiled by the passing years, it bears an appearance which varies through the ages. The firmament, however, conserving all its parts, remains intact, neither increased with length of time nor diminished by old age; it is neither the least bit warped by its motion nor wearied by its speed: it will remain the same for ever, since the same has it always been. No different heaven did our fathers see, no different heaven will our posterity behold. *It is God*, and changes not in time. That the Sun never deviates to the cross-lying Bears and never changes direction, setting course for the orient and bringing forth a dawn born of unwanted lands; that the Moon does not exceed her appointed orbs of light, but preserves the regularity of her waxing and waning; that the stars poised in heaven fall not upon Earth but take fixed periods of time to accomplish their orbits: all this is not the result of chance, but the plan of a God most high.

In this quoted text, it is not entirely clear as to whether an invisible Creator should be distinguished from the visible creation. In the fourth book of *Astronomica*, however, Manilius (4: 883ff.) goes on to say that 'nature holds no mysteries for us; we have surveyed it in its entirety and are masters of the conquered sky; we perceive our creator, *of whom we are part,* and rise to the stars, whose children we are. Can one doubt that a divinity dwells within our breasts and that our soul return to the heaven whence they came?' Ancient astrology thus constitutes a form of pantheism or naturalism centred on the godlike attributes of spheres dwelling in the living sky.

'Movements observed in the sky regulate constant cycles of days, months, seasons, and years – hence, lunar and solar phases, the rising and setting of fixed stars, the march of the planets, and so on. Celestial revolutions preside over invariable periods of time that succeed each other to infinity, thus pointing to the eternal recurrence of things. 'The stars unceasingly pursue their never-ending course; arrived at the limit of their path, they resume without pause the race already run, and the cycles of years, in accordance with which their movements take place, are prolonged to infinity in the past, and continue to infinity in the future' (Cumont 1960: 58). Given these eternal transients, ancient astrology treats the universe as wholly divine.

The cosmos follows fixed laws, but the universe is not static for all that. While the laws of our star-governed universe are unchanging, they regulate orderly variations occurring through space and time. This brings us to another central aspect of astrology: its emphasis on measurable motions and observable transformations of the universe. The calendrical calculations of ancient astrology presuppose the application of measurements to planetary positions, zodiacal signs, and heavenly configurations, a mathematical charting system of Greek origins (Tester 1987: 3, 10–14). The close connection between arithmetic and astral measurements of time is such that, in the Latin world of the first century C.E., the word *mathematici* replaced the word *Chaldaei,* a term commonly applied to practitioners of astrology (Cramer 1954: 244). As Pingree (1990: 290) notes, 'this methodology, of relying on observation as a criterion for establishing general principles, is a strictly scientific one, and was a fruitful forerunner of the observational technique characteristic of true science.'

Through observations and calculations of the periodic motions of heavenly bodies, humans can commune with the divine and accede to the secrets of time, past and future. Just as motions of the divine are calculable, so too the measurable is inherently divine. This is to say, science, divination, and religion form one coherent body of knowledge: scientific measurements of divine motions and conjunctions of heaven lend themselves to predictions of the future – hence, the fate of astral gods and humans alike. By implication, Necessity dominates the universe: 'Fate rules the world, all things stand fixed by the immutable laws, and the long ages are assigned a predestined course of events. At birth our death is sealed, and our end is consequent upon our beginning' (Manilius 4: 17ff.).

Astrology combines the cult of an organized nature with the pursuit of scientific learning. It constitutes a scientific religion, a 'learned theology' verging on 'pure science' (Cumont 1960: xv; Neugebauer 1957: 171). Sidereal divination thrives on numerical measurements, but numbers are not mere figures. 'Just as in ancient times and, above all, in Egypt, the *name* had a magic power, and ceremonial words formed an irresistible incantation, so here the number possesses an active force, the number is a symbol, and its properties are sacred attributes. Astrology is only a branch of mathematics, which the heavens have revealed to mankind by their periodic movements' (Cumont 1960: 18). Knowledge of the gods of heaven is synonymous with an understanding of the laws of mathematics and their application to rituals of divination.

Unlike logocentric, Platonic and Neoplatonic concepts of a timeless and intangible Spirit governing the material universe, astral divinities are embodiments of time evolving in heaven. In lieu of acting as supernatural divinities transcending physical reality, star-gods are part of the measurable order of time, moving with predictable regularity, through everlasting cycles of days, weeks, seasons, and years. The Jewish Yahweh is immortal in the sense of never dying, not even for a while. By contrast, Semitic star-gods are subject to everlasting cycles of life, death, and life after death: 'each time they seemed to sink, they were born again to a new life, always unconquerable' (Cumont 1960: 58). Star-gods possess the secret of life after death, never *life without death*. Accordingly, permanent laws of motion do not preclude the idea of recurrent universal catastrophes ranging from outbreaks of chaos in heaven to great floods affecting the whole universe; the epic writings of Seneca and Lucan, two Stoics of the first century, amply demonstrate the latter point (Cramer 1954: 120ff.).

The marriage of religion and 'primitive astronomical observations' implies that star-gods are fully immersed in the order of time and matter, such that they display attributes and behaviour known to mortal creatures, including passion and strife. As Manilius (2: 603ff.) remarks, 'since many are the signs in which men are born for discord, peace is banished throughout the world, and the bond of loyalty is rare and is granted to few; *and just as is heaven, so too is earth at war with itself*, and the nations of mankind are subject to a destiny of strife.' While far more organized and predictable than the anthropomorphic gods of classical Greek mythology, star-gods of Semitic religions were never perceived as plainly eternal and immutable. 'The resplendent stars, which eternally pursue their silent course above us, are divinities endowed with personality and animated feelings' (Cumont 1960: 79). The sky is thought to display order, regularity, and predictability, but not to the point of eradicating a luxuriant mythology of combats, alliances, and amours plaguing the lives of gods. With astromythology, events written all over the sky are simultaneously governed by the human-like passions of pagan gods and the inflexible laws of cosmic geometry reconstructed through science (Bouché-Leclercq 1879: 218; Cumont 1960: 11). Astralism thus ties the laws of heavenly geometry to the aspirations and emotions of humans dwelling on earth.

Another key aspect of ancient astrology is its aspiration to cosmic integration, a claim eventually passed on to Christianity and the Catholic Church; the word *catholic* (Lat. *catholicus*, Gr. *kath'holou*, 'universal, general') is of astrological origin, denoting activities applying to the whole of humanity and the earth (Cumont 1960: 63). As with the Syrian Baalim, the powers of star-gods are not limited to determinate spaces or times, like some Greek divinities committed to particular cities and related expressions of patriotic loyalties. When viewed collectively, sidereal divinities are Lords of the universe. Star-gods are constantly interacting in such ways that they can never be worshipped in isolation from one another. Individual characteristics and effects of the seven planets and the twelve constellations of the zodiac will vary, yet order exists throughout the universe by virtue of their holistic organization and constant motions performed in synchrony. Since they co-preside over motions of the cosmos, stars and constellations are 'scarcely worshipped save *en bloc*' (66).

The overall circuitry of sidereal divinities is all-encompassing in the sense of being part of the cosmos and dominating the universe from above. Through cosmic radiations, planets and constellations influence one another, and human beings as well. As a result, astrology puts faith in the web of sympathy and correspondences that exists between earthly reality and heavenly phenomena *viewed configuratively*. While star-gods have specific qualities that will affect humans positively or negatively, variable *relations between stars and constellations* will have a profound impact on human lives, social events, and natural history. It is therefore the relative positions, reciprocal relations, or configurational 'aspects' (from Lat. *aspicere*, 'to look at') of the heavenly spheres that determine human fates. Correspondences exist also between astral typologies and other classificatory systems involving units of time (a planet for each day of the week, constellations announcing determinate seasons), climactic events (the summertime heat brought by the Dog Star), and geography (nations, countries). Stars and planets are equally connected to colours, metals, plants, genders, and parts of the human body (the zodiac mapped on to the body; see Manilius 2). As Manilius points out, humans can understand the universe inasmuch as they themselves are made in the likeness of the cosmos.

The 'influence' (an ethereal fluid or power stemming from the stars and affecting the characters and actions of people) exerted by star-gods depends upon not only their inherent qualities, but also their mutual interactions, or the measurable and predictable positions that stars occupy *vis-à-vis* other luminaries in heaven. This variable geometry of stellar aspects consists of concurrent and antagonistic 'influences' preprogrammed for all eternity – hence, mathematical relations that are essential to an understanding of all events occurring under the sun and the moon. The geometry lends itself to a foreknowledge of the future based upon pre-established plans that can be understood through proper divinatory techniques. As in present-day horoscopy, the decisive moment that sets everything in motion is the moment of birth (or the time of conception; see Bouché-Leclercq 1879: 205ff., 238ff., 249).

Ancient astrology entailed a fatalistic view of life and the world. Concepts of predestination, however, were not rigidly defined, that is, without important qualifications and tolerable contradictions. A 'cathartic' approach assuming a reversible influence of astral bodies on personal lives and mundane activities (travel, marriage, business decisions) – hence, some degree of freedom and control over one's destiny – found favour with many practitioners of the art. Subjects amenable to practical interventions of astrology ranged from medicine to geopolitics (divining the fate of armies, cities, foreign nations). Medical astrology was particularly important as it implied the idea that planets and constellations exerted sympathetic influences over different sections of the body (Aries = head, etc.) and also over plants, animals, and minerals that could be used to heal corresponding parts of the human anatomy. Antiochus of Athens, an astrologer of the second century of our era, thought the zodiac to govern not only seasons and ages of life, but also elements, winds, temperaments, humours, colours, temperature, moisture, and texture (Seznec 1953: 47).

Astrology was always an applied discipline, even when faith in absolute predestination prevailed. Efforts to outsmart or change Fate dictated from above was expressed in different ways, thereby turning destiny into a pragmatic 'directional' notion (Pingree 1968: 118; 1993: 85). Prayers, rituals, remedies, and medicine of all sorts were created and promoted to persuade the astral gods to alter their plans or counter their influences (Cramer 1954: 188; Bouché-Leclercq 1879: 14, 205ff.; Ness 1990). Measures were constantly taken to forestall calamities and counter the plans of Fate, even among the most adamant supporters of the Chaldean doctrine. Although imbued with Stoic rhetoric, the history of Roman politics bristles with stories of rulers attempting the impossible: getting rid of opponents 'destined' to accede to the throne. As Cramer (1954: 134) remarks, 'few rulers of the first century would have been convinced enough fatalists – or philosophers – to accept the wistful truism that "no one ever succeeds in killing his successor."' Despite their fear of the inevitable, Roman rulers were hardly passive subjects of the 'necessities' of History.

Those who upheld strict fatalistic views had critical choices to make. To give just one example, a man fully convinced by an astrologer that he would kill the father he loved decided to ask the Roman Senate the permission to commit suicide without prejudicing his right to a proper burial. 'Through [the fear] of parricide it has come to pass that I can kill myself, through Fate that I am not allowed to die: Not the astrologer (*mathematicus*) alone has predicted the deeds of these hands specifically as to period and time, but I myself am also convinced that I shall commit parricide' (quoted in Cramer 1954: 156). While the father argued against the predictive pretensions of astrology, the son assumed that the *mathematicus* had spoken the truth. The young man's position highlights a key contradiction in the astrological world-view: were he to commit suicide, the man would have proven Fate and the astrologer to be dead wrong, but were he to go on living, Fate would inevitably turn him into a parricide. Members of the Senate faced an equally difficult dilemma: they were obliged to prevent the crime from being committed, but if they granted the man permission to kill himself, his death would automatically disprove his claims.

More than an anecdote, the story points to a basic riddle underlying all expressions of astrology. As Bouché-Leclercq (1879: 14) remarks, the future must be immutable in order for astrological divination to be possible, but the whole knowledge system must be conditional if it is to be useful. Foreknowledge without freedom of action serves no purpose. Absolute freedom is also of doubtful value as it disempowers human beings, undermining their capacities for science and prescience. Fate and Freedom are thus two sides of the same coin. One principle depends on the opposite principle, and each, pushed to its limit, destroys the other.

Notwithstanding the prolific writings of astrologically minded philosophers struggling with this issue, ancient thought has never been able to resolve fully the Freedom/Fate paradox. Actually the enigma was a constituent element of the thought system itself, to be passed on to Christian polemics regarding the issue of predestination and later debates concerning theories of causal determination and scientific prediction. Astral fatalism has always been a pragmatic stand. Western formulations of astrology have never been so rigidly mechanistic as to preclude considerable freedom (if not outright confusion) in methods of sidereal computation, and fallible predictions and explanations to account for predictive errors.[1] Nor has astrological determinism precluded deviations from the laws of the universe and the wilful intervention of powerful agencies (human or divine) exercising control over the heavens. In Babylonian theology, the planets (from Gr. *planan*, 'to wander') were endowed with motions of their own, wandering and acting as 'Interpreters' expressing the intentions of the gods (Cumont 1960: 19, 65). They played an active role in manifesting the gods' responses to precise events and human actions. Comets and falling stars were also important in this regard. As Ness (1990) remarks, any heavenly event that was out of the ordinary could be interpreted as an omen, a warning from the gods. From stars whose paths and revolutions never varied or 'erred,'

the Chaldeans had naturally been led to the idea of a Necessity, superior to the gods themselves, since it commanded their movements; and this Necessity, which ruled the gods, was bound, *a fortiori*, to hold sway over mankind. The conception of a fatality linked with the regular movements of the heavens originated at Babylon, but this universal determinism was not there carried to its ultimate logical consequences ... certain disturbances in the heavens, irregular occurrences such as appearances of comets or showers of falling stars, sufficed to maintain the belief in the exceptional operation of a divine will interfering arbitrarily in the order of nature. Priests foretold the future according to the stars, but by purifications, sacrifices, and incantations they professed to drive away evils, and to secure more certainly the promised blessings. This was a necessary concession to popular beliefs which the very maintenance of the cult demanded. (Cumont 1960: 17–18; see also Cramer 1954: 117)

Omen astrology in Babylon was based on observations of heavenly occurrences (comets, eclipses, etc.) announcing events that would usually affect the state or the royal family. It presupposed faith in the star-gods' willingness and capacity to intervene in human affairs. This form of divination preceded the invention of the zodiac (around the fourth or fifth century B.C.E.), and therefore horoscopy – hence, mathematical calculations of the individual future, a more advanced *mathematica* that spread during the

Hellenistic period. With the invention of 'mathematics,' astral omens none the less continued to form an integral part of primitive astronomy, a science enabling humans to understand and communicate better with their gods (Ness 1990).

Although concerned with the lawful workings of the universe, astrology also grappled with conjunctural exchanges and transactions that could bind humans to their gods in heaven. Notions of configurational interactions and cosmic sympathy between all elements and life forms of the universe meant that acts of reciprocity between humans and divinities could be contemplated and actually practised (Bouché-Leclercq 1879: 7). The greatest and smallest happenings may have been 'shaped to accord with the progress of kindly or unkindly star,' as Seneca (see Cramer 1954: 117) used to put it, yet earthlings could influence or alter the plans of sidereal gods through prayers, propitiatory rites, and offerings designed to win their favour or appease their wrath.

There were those who thought it useless to engage in such rituals and upheld a strict Stoic view of life based on the all-powerfulness of Fate. Yet they too derived rules of ethical behaviour from their creed. They elevated to the rank of duty and virtue a human being's cheerful resignation to Necessity. Criminals claiming that Fate was responsible for the unlawful acts they had committed could not expect judges to forgo their sense of moral justice. After all, Fate had already ordained that judges condemn the guilty party. On a more general level, Stoics pinned their faith on acts of piety and religious morality – renouncing pleasures of the flesh in order that the sacred fire of their spirit ascend to the ether, thereby attaining true knowledge (otherwise fallible) and communing with the heavens. Foolish people who 'chose' to rebel against Fate did not ascend to heaven, and experienced pain and grief on earth. In short, notions of Destiny were compatible with all sorts of cultic activities, injunctions of moral behaviour, and discussions of human erring as well (Cumont 1960: 83, 86–9).

The History and Politics of Star-Gods

Greek Mythology and Platonism

Astrology was first developed in Mesopotamia through a history of astronomical observations leading up to an elaborate zodiacal system produced about the middle of the fifth century B.C.E. Astralism was later adopted and expanded as both a religion and a science in Greece and Egypt. From the middle of the third century B.C.E. onwards, it spread from Hellenic civilization to the Roman world. At first, exposure to belief systems brought by astrologers originating from the East affected mostly the Italian masses, not the noblemen and educated minds of Rome, let alone the Greek anti-Stoic thinkers and Sceptics of the second century B.C.E. By the last century of the Republic (51–48 B.C.E.), however, Latin and Greek intellectuals and politicians had given in to a Stoic philosophy rejuvenated by the Chaldean *Weltanschauung*.

The basic idea of astrology – that one's future is determined by astral configurations appearing at the time of one's birth – had been adamantly rejected by followers of Plato, and by Cynics, Epicureans, and Peripatetics as well. By contrast, the influential Stoics (with some exceptions) found themselves very much at home in the Chaldean fatalistic world-view and withstood all the objections of such learned philosophers as Epicurus, Carneades, Alexander of Aphrodisias, and Sextus Empiricus, to name just a few. The Stoic submission to Necessity and the laws of Reason and Causality governing nature and the universe found a perfect ally in the science and prescience of Eastern astrologers. Who could deny that planets and constellations followed invariable laws of motion that faithfully coincided with seasonal changes, weather phenomena, and other observable happenings on earth? On what grounds could anyone refuse to extend these irrefutable laws to all events of nature and human history?

But before we further discuss the marriage between Stoicism and astrology, more should be said about the differences between astralism and the non-sidereal views of early Greek philosophy, prior to the spread of Hellenism under and after Alexander the Great (356–323 B.C.E.). From the seventh century B.C.E. onwards, Greek intellectuals viewed the gods no longer as 'physical agents, but moral – or, if you like, immoral – beings. Resembling men in their passions, they are their superiors in power alone; the close resemblance of their feelings to those of their devotees leads them to mingle intimately in the earthly life of the latter; inspired by a like patriotism ... they are the protagonists in all the causes which are espoused by their worshippers' (Cumont 1960: 23). The founding principles of Greek art, culture, and philosophy since the days of Homer were deeply anthropomorphic, patriotic, and aesthetic – hence, scarcely compatible with the cult of cosmic bodies dwelling in the distant heavens, ethereal spheres displaying neither tasteful forms nor the familiar feelings of the human *persona*. As Aristophanes (c. 450–c. 385 B.C.E.) remarked, human-like divinities such as Hermes had little in common with barbarian idols such as Sun and Moon.

Once introduced into Greek culture, oriental astralism presented many advantages over Greek mythology and philosophy. For one thing, its scientific approach to understanding the universe, and predicting the future of humans and gods seemed far less arbitrary and subjective than Greek methods of divination and speculations regarding issues of logic and life after death (Cumont 1960: 13, 95; Bouché-Leclercq 1879: 247f.; Cramer 1954: 3). Unlike diviners and philosophers, astrologers derived their knowledge from observations and revelations of the skies. Sidereal gods could ostensibly claim to govern the whole universe, and they displayed behaviour that looked far more rational than the conduct of humans and the Olympian heroes and demigods portrayed in their likeness; with their orgies and cruelties, the inhabitants of Mount Olympus were anything but models of virtue detached from the passions and hardships comprising the common lot.

Heavenly gods differed radically from Greek deities who lived among humans and were subject to the same passions and tragedies as creatures of the earth. In lieu of the Olympian superhumans, astrology

conceived everlasting beings, unwearied and invincible, who ceaselessly ran their changeless course throughout an endless series of ages; in place of gods bound to a city or to a country and, so to speak, *adscripti glebae*, differing with the diversity of peoples, it reverenced universal – or, as they were already called, 'catholic' – powers, whose activity, regulated by revolutions of the celestial spheres, extended over all the earth and embraced the whole human race. An almost anarchical society of Immortals, whose feeble and capricious will raised doubts as to their power, was replaced by the idea of a harmonious ensemble of sidereal gods, who, irresistibly guided by the Sun, the heart of the world, the source of all movement and all intelligence, imposed everywhere the inevitable laws of omnipotent Destiny, – last but not least in place of the old methods of divination, now fallen into discredit, of deceitful portents and ambiguous oracles, astrology promised to substitute a scientific method, founded on an experience of almost infinite duration. (Cumont 1960: 76)

The harmony of a cosmos regulated by natural elements (water, fire, earth, air) and the orderly luminaries of heaven contrasted strongly with the whimsical powers of older spirits and fabled heroes of pagan mythology. The insights of Chaldea's 'learned theology,' a pantheism that prioritized the heavenly bodies conceived anthropomorphically and animistically, were to have a profound and lasting influence on the whole of Western history.

The impact of astralism on Greek culture dates back to at least the sixth century B.C.E., resulting from contacts with hemerology, astrometeorology, and other rudimentary expressions of Mesopotamian astrology

(Cramer 1954: 18). Greeks slowly familiarized themselves with Chaldean science and practice during the next two centuries. The first known horoscopes were produced during this period – more precisely, in the late fifth century, in the days of an elderly Socrates and a very young Plato. Cramer (1954: 9) estimates that, by the middle of the fourth century B.C.E., a number of Greek scholars had acquired knowledge of pre-zodiacal and horoscopal astrology. Hellenic science also existed at this time, but it was and continued to be mostly an activity of the laity, not a priestly pursuit, as among the Chaldean *mathematici*.

Greek philosophers thus started assigning special attributes and powers to the luminaries, substituting astral divinities for the old gods and heroes dwelling on Mount Olympus. Given his mystical attitude towards the harmony and numerical relations that governed motions of the stars, the sixth-century Pythagoras had already concluded that musical spheres were divine, 'moved by the ethereal soul which informs the universe and is akin to man's own soul' (Cumont 1960: 23). Life on earth stems from glittering particles of dust that originate from the ether and that pass through water and air before breathing life into creatures on earth. Likewise, Socrates treated planets as divinities in their own right, spirits harnessed to the supreme essence of Being. These thoughts eventually led Plato to lodge accusations of atheism against Anaxagoras, who claimed that there was no more to the sun and the moon than a great mass of incandescent particles and another earth, respectively.

In Plato's *Timaeus*, an intelligent soul dwells in the celestial equator and the ecliptic and inhabits the human head, a microcosm made in the image of the spherical heavens surrounding the earth – a perfect circular shape that Philo saw befitting the stars, the soul, and the mind. An eternal and absolutely perfect Being reigns supreme over the universe and animates visible star-gods with his own life, manifesting himself through sidereal divinities far more powerful than idols of pagan religion (see also Plato's *Laws*, section 10: 899b). Planet gods are worthy of cultic devotion, and astrology comes close to being a 'sacred science.' In lieu of speaking of the planets *of* the gods, Greek philosophers were thus led to portray planets *as* gods, deities assisted by living creatures assigned to the four elements constituting the world (fire, air, water, earth; see Bouché-Leclercq 1879: 226; Flint 1991: 92). As for the gods of the older Greek mythology, they were relocated between earthlings and spirits of the sky.

In the pseudo-Platonic *Epinomis* (section 984a), the stars are explicitly called gods. The author advocates a synthesis between Syrian and Egyptian star-gods and the cult of Apollo honoured at Delphi. The reconciliation should none the less maintain a predominantly Greek character. That is, the onus is on Greek scholars to elevate the cult of stars to a higher level, perfecting it like all other barbarian contributions to human civilization. This Hellenic rewriting of Chaldean naturalism can be achieved by casting star-gods and airy spirits of the sky as intermediaries between the Supreme Being and the earth. In this perspective astronomy becomes synonymous with spiritual wisdom, a theological contemplation of the universe. Although a rival of Plato, Aristotle holds similar views. He too 'defends the dogma of the divinity of the stars: in them, as in the First Cause itself, he sees eternal substances, principles of movement, and therefore divine; and this doctrine, which thus forms an integral part of his metaphysic, was to disseminate itself throughout the ages and throughout the world, wherever the authority of the Master was recognized' (Cumont 1960: 24). The stars have personalities and constitute the efficient causes of the orderly motions of the cosmos.

In deifying astral bodies, Greek philosophers subsumed naturalistic cults and belief systems sustained by popular creed (Cumont 1960: 23). They none the less gave a new twist – the orderly aspects of a rational cosmos – to the luxuriant mythology of Greece's countless heroes, demigods, and divinities. The end-result is a syncretic superimposition of astral naturalism and rationalism on Greek mythology. In doing this,

philosophers may have been influenced by the desire of recommending to the veneration of their disciples beings more pure than those whom mythology represented as the sorry heroes of ridiculous or indecent legends, and to whom fable attributed all sorts of mischievous and shameful deeds. The polemics of the early rationalists had discredited these absurd or odious myths, and the deification of the stars, while saving polytheism, which was practically indestructible, suppressed anthropomorphism, which Xenophanes had already attacked so resolutely. The new sidereal theology has all the appearance of a *compromise between popular beliefs and pure monotheism*. (24: emphasis added)

Cumont adds that astralism found fertile soil in Hellenic concepts of a superior Reason and divine essence governing the universe, concepts well illustrated by the immutable motions and everlasting harmony of the heavenly bodies. Likewise, Bouché-Leclercq (1879: 247f.) considers that Greek philosophical preoccupations with issues of divine omnipotence prepared the ground for a pantheistic conception of the cosmos, a universal organism regulated by the orderly revolutions of stars and planets moving in the lofty heavens.

The Conversion of Rome (250–44 B.C.E.)

While Egypt was pivotal to the development of astrology, ancient Greece played an important role in refining the principles and practice of star-worship. Both civilizations in turn had a profound impact on Roman cultural history. In Greece, stars had already been granted special attention by philosophers such as Plato, yet Mesopotamian notions of cosmic fatalism and stellar divination did not become compatible with Hellenism until the fourth century B.C.E. Hellenic literature and philosophical debates regarding questions of Fate and Freedom started spreading in the Roman world in the third century B.C.E., together with a number of Eastern cults that were to invade the whole of Italy.

Foreign cults which included oracular astralism and sidereal mysticism were first adopted by the lower strata of Roman society. Towards the last century of the Republic, however, they also found favour with the intellectuals and noblemen of Rome. The first contact with Eastern astrological scholarship had already occurred via the teachings of Berossus, a priest of Bel who left Mesopotamia and took up residence on the Greek island of Cos, off the coast of Asia Minor, about 280 B.C.E. Other third-century Chaldean astrologers who contributed to the diffusion of star-worship include Kidenas, and Sudines, an expert liver-diviner who lived in Pergamum, capital of Attalus I, one of the cities addressed by John in his letters to the seven churches of Asia Minor. These Hellenized Chaldeans 'devoted themselves to the task of rendering accessible to the Greeks the treasures of knowledge which were contained in the cuneiform documents amassed in the libraries of their native land' (Cumont 1960: 37).

The growing popularity of astralism in the Graeco-Latin world and the eventual triumph of the *sphaera graecanica* over stellar nomenclatures of Babylonian and Egyptian origins owe a lot to Eudoxus of Cnidos (c. 390–340 B.C.E.), an outstanding Greek astronomer and mathematician of Plato's time whose lost *Phaenomena* was later put into verses by the Greek astronomical poet Aratus of Soli (c. 270 B.C.E.), a younger contemporary of Berossus's. Although initially a follower of Aristotle, Aratus was eventually converted to Stoicism and fatalistic astrology. He in turn influenced the writings of Manilius (first century C.E.), a Latin poet so widely read as to be known by the apostle Paul and a number of Church Fathers, including Jerome and Augustine (Cramer 1954: 26f.).

On the political level, the spread of star-worship can be traced back to the conquests of Alexander the Great and the expansion of Greek culture which the king of Macedon promoted and which was to radiate from Alexandria, Pergamum, and Antioch. The republican nationalism of ancient Greece was eventually replaced by the imperial rule of Roman monarchy, an absolutism that stood much to gain from a global religion preaching submission to the laws of an unchangeable cosmos. Unlike modern astrology, ancient astralism was a religion ideally suited to negating the particularisms of individual subjects, cities, and nations. As Cumont (1960: 32) notes: 'in proportion as the idea of "humanity" spread, men were the more ready to reserve their homage for those celestial powers which extended their blessings to all mankind, and princes who proclaimed themselves the rulers of the world could not be protected save by cosmopolitan gods.' Unlike noblemen of the republican era, the first Roman emperors, such as Augustus (27 B.C.E.–14 C.E.) and Tiberius (14–37 C.E.), had a vested interest in promoting an astral religion that expressed the common denominator of many different cults, thus 'giving to the united Empire the formula of the theology of the future' (49).

Under the Achaemenids of Persia and the Pharaohs of Egypt, astralism professed close connections between kings and star-gods, elevating sovereign rulers above the rest of humanity. This is the kind of religion that Caesarism needed to consolidate its own hegemonic power throughout the Empire. Roman emperors soon became kindred spirits of the sun-god, equally invincible and eternal. But while monarchs would eventually portray themselves as minds capable of grasping the secrets of astronomy (Manilius 1:41) and rulers on an equal footing with the powers of heavens, the practice of astrology was by no means restricted to kings, noblemen, and scholars. Just as Roman rulers appropriated the Chaldean doctrines to reinforce their claims to imperial monarchy, so too opponents of the regime could find ways of harnessing the star-gods to their own cause. Astralism lent itself to expressions of popular discontent, if not outright rebellion against the powers that be. The Sicilian slave wars of the second century B.C.E. are a case in point. They were led by 'men whose claim to leadership was largely if not exclusively based on their reputation as prophets,' a fact that illustrates 'the hold which divinely inspired seers and astrologers had obtained on the lower classes composed of impoverished freemen and slaves. In Rome and Italy in all likelihood similar prophets also flourished among these strata at this time ...' (Cramer 1954: 59f.).

Astralism in ancient Greece and Rome was not merely the site of political struggles between the powerful and the powerless. It was also a deeply philosophical and theological issue. In the second century B.C.E., a debate raged between Stoic allies of astrological fatalism and their opponents, comprising humanists and sceptics who advocated notions of free will.

Compared with Plato, Aristotle, and their disciples, Stoic masters, who were mostly Orientals (Zeno was born in Cyprus), granted fuller attention to sidereal divinities governing the universe. They saw great beauty in the orderly workings and 'adornments' of the cosmos (whence the term 'cosmetic'). 'Since stoic pantheism represented Reason, which governs all things, as residing in ethereal Fire, the stars in which the supreme Fire manifested itself with the greatest force and brilliance, would necessarily be invested with the loftiest divine qualities' (Cumont 1960: 32). As in Chaldean doctrines, Zeno's pantheism considered stars to be direct manifestations of the primordial principle of ethereal Fire animating human reason, souls, and all the forces interacting within the cosmos. Similar views were expressed in the writings of Hipparchus, a Greek astronomer of the second century B.C.E., and in later formulations of Roman sidereal mysticism as well. Unlike the Jewish belief system that placed the invisible Creator above his visible Creation (2 Enoch 48), Stoicism viewed the material world spiritually, and the spiritual world materially: through principles of cosmic sympathy, humans, star-gods, and the world were all essentially made of the same stuff and governed by the same universal laws, those of Time and Fate.

Stoicism introduced philosophical discourse into astrological theology, but it also adapted its own doctrine to the astrological mode of thinking. An orientalized version of Stoicism presented a great advantage: it had faith in the methods of science on its side. Stoic concepts of Necessity found themselves at home with the observable laws of nature revealed by astrologers and the practice of predicting the future based on such laws. While some Greek philosophers expressed objections against astral fatalism, including logical arguments and refutations of astral divination, astrologers typically fell back on refinements of their own 'mathematical methods' to counter these critiques and persuade the Stoics of their times (Bouché-Leclercq 1879: 246, 251).

Posidonius of Apamea (c. 135–c. 50 B.C.E.), a follower of the Stoic Panaetius, was instrumental in synthesizing oriental religion and Greek thought. His teachings made astrology palatable to the most influential scholars. As a result, star-worship became a central ingredient of Western Latin thought throughout the centuries extending from the death of the last great sceptics, such as Cicero and Caesar, up until the fall of Rome. With the new monarchy and the rule of Octavius (d. 87 B.C.E.), Caesar's grand-nephew, sidereal fatalism turned into the official world-view of the upper classes of Rome.

From the days of Posidonius onwards the anti-astrological majority of Roman humanists began to shrink until it became a minority of very small proportions. The sceptics fought their rearguard battle magnificently during the first half of the first century B.C. Fighters against astrology of the calibre of a Lucretius or Cicero (as well as the smilingly sceptical Julius Caesar) made a fine but losing battle against the swelling hosts of educated Roman believers in fatalistic astrology. With the death of these champions of free will, however, an era began which from Augustus to Domitian displayed only a small current of anti-astrological sentiment. Not until the second century A.D. occurred a final and shortlived revival of the earlier scepticism. (Cramer 1954: 63)

Posidonius inspired men such as Seneca and Philo of Alexandria. His influence can also be detected in the *Astronomica* of Manilius, a poetic formulation of astrological fatalism dedicated to the emperor Tiberius. The disciples of Posidonius expressed faith in a rational cosmos 'where no Epicurean–Lucretian atoms "swerved at will," but one in which scientific natural laws reigned supreme and Fate merely signified the immutable application of such laws' (Cramer 1954: 98). Accordingly, they objected to the Epicurean emphasis on pleasures and passions of the body, a libertarian attitude that constituted an obstacle to pious humans elevating their eyes and minds to the starry spheres. Virtuous souls were expected to raise themselves to a higher plane and fly back to their place of origin, the ethereal heavens (Cumont 1960: 83, 102).

The notion that souls could be transported to heaven and revert to a state of ethereal fire points to an important theme in Roman ideology: catasterism, whereby a deceased soul or mythical figure (including animals) is transported to heaven in the form of a comet, a star, or a constellation. Although comets had always been interpreted as signs of ill omen, the northern appearance of a bright star observed during the games dedicated to Caesar's memory was used by Octavius Octavianus to elevate Julius Caesar (d. 44 B.C.E.) to the rank of a star-god. As a result, some northern stars became known as 'Caesar's throne' (Cramer 1954: 118). Astrology thus received the imperial seal and became an integral part of Roman political discourse and Latin culture for many centuries. Through court poets and politicians, astral titles and the honours of catasterism were bestowed upon later rulers (Augustus, Claudius, Vespasian, Titus, etc.), live emperors, and their relatives. Numerous epitaphs, however, show that religious hopes of a stellar life after death were granted to outstanding humans and lowly souls as well. As Manilius (1: 759ff.) suggested, 'perhaps the souls of heroes, outstanding men deemed worthy of heaven, freed from the body and released from the globe of Earth, pass hither and, dwelling in a heaven that is their own, live the infinite years of paradise and enjoy celestial bliss.' The common view in imperial Rome was that the rank-ordering of stars in heaven reflected the hierarchy of mortals on earth. 'The greater one's status on earth, the brighter a star did the soul become in the heavens' (Cramer 1954: 78). The Christian Church in turn inherited this faith in sidereal resurrection: Pope Gregory I (590–604 C.E.) firmly believed that followers of God turned into star-spirits after death.

Catasterism was a double-sided principle. On the one hand, it required that fabled heroes, human beings, totemic animals (e.g., lions, bulls), and sacred objects (e.g., altars) be placed far below the lofty gods of heaven. It presupposed an acceptance of Greek euhemerism, a fourth-century (B.C.E.) theory advocating a demotion of the gods of mythology to the rank of superior mortals and characters of real history. On the other hand, catasterism allowed lower beings and divinities to achieve heavenly status and glory. Given a royal pedigree or exemplary conduct, a human soul could accede to astral life after death. The same 'translational' logic applied to pagan demigods and spirits competing with astral deities. After a proper rewriting of traditional mythologies, older godheads could turn into celestial bodies and configurations ruling over the universe. Although not originally committed to star-worship, much of Graeco-Latin mythology was thus co-opted into serving the higher rule of astralism. The Greeks were particularly successful at translating their own Olympian heroes into astral spirits. From the third century B.C.E. onwards, they assigned to their own gods (Hermes, Aphrodite, Ares, Zeus, Chronos) the planetary titles of Chaldean divinities (Nebo, Ishtar, Nergal, Marduk, Ninib). The Babylonian planets were given Greek names that were eventually converted into Latin, and then passed on to the West through the languages of medieval Europe (Cumont 1960: 27; Cramer 1954: 3). Zodiacal constellations were also adapted to Greek mythology (Bouché-Leclercq 1879: 214f.).

Rather than destroying Hellenic tradition, the rise of astralism implied that Greek tales had to be revised and projected onto the skies. 'There Perseus found Andromeda again, and the centaur Chiron, who is none other than the Archer, fraternised with Orion, the gigantic hunter' (Cumont 1960: 66). Aries 'was the famous ram with the Golden Fleece which had carried off Phrixus and Helle over the sea and had let the maiden fall into the waves of the Hellespont. It might also be that which was the subject of the dispute between Atreus and Thyestes, or again it might be the ram which guided the thirsty company of Bacchus to the wells of the oasis of Ammon' (Bouché-Leclercq, quoted in Cumont 1960: 66). Fabled heroes were thus translated to heaven and made to garb themselves in celestial honours.

From Augustus to Domitian (44 B.C.E.–96 C.E.)

In its republican era, Rome showed opposition to astrology only once, via a ban applied throughout Italy in 139 B.C.E., at a time when civil war was breaking out in the country. Prior to the second-century rule of the Gracchus brothers, astrological practices in the Latin West posed no political threat. Empire-wide restrictions on the practice of astrology did not occur until Augustus. Political concern with the spread of astrology in the Latin world thus coincided with the rise of an imperial monarchy in Rome. As intellectuals, aristocrats, and high-ranking army officers started adhering to the principles of sidereal fatalism, Roman emperors began imposing topical restrictions on the practice of 'primitive astronomy.'

With the expansion and consolidation of the Roman Empire and the influx of merchants, soldiers, and slaves from the colonies, religious influences of the Semitic world spread rapidly to the Latin West. Divinities such as the Persian Mithras, the Phrygian Cybele, and the Alexandrian Isis were solidly transplanted into Roman soil. Although highly heterogeneous, these foreign religions had in common a veneration of the heavenly spheres – hence, stellar belief systems and rituals developed in the ancient temples of Persia, Syria, and Egypt. From the early second century B.C.E. onwards, legal measures were taken by the senators and rulers of Rome to curb the expansion of such cults in Italy, but without much success. During the first century of our era, itinerant astrologers casting horoscopes 'found an eager clientele, not only among the curious urban mob gathering for fairs and festivals, but even in the Italian countryside, where at least the newly arrived hosts of slaves from the east not only nostalgically welcomed those oriental soothsayers, but may also have helped to introduce Italian estate managers to the awe-inspiring "infallible" astrological predictions of such travelling astrologers' (Cramer 1954: 47).

While doubted or opposed by the previous aristocracy and shunned by the Roman masses, the 'mathematical' approach to divination caught on with the intellectuals, the upper classes, and the political leaders ruling in Rome during the first century of the principate (Cramer 1954: 236, 253). Sceptics and Epicureans continued their struggle against astrology, yet the philosophical battle of 'freedom fighters' against the spread of Chaldean fatalism had been lost. Scientific astrologers such as the Greek Thrasyllus (d. 36 C.E.) and his son, Tiberius Claudius Balbillus (d. c. 81 C.E.), became the *éminences grises* of court politics. With the exception of Vespasian, most rulers resorted to their services. The house of Thrasyllus enjoyed great fame and close institutional ties with Ephesus, Pergamum, and Thyatira, cities mentioned in John's letters to the churches of Asia Minor (Cramer 1954: 138). By and large, expert astrologers came from Egypt and the Greek East, unlike Latin aristocratic practitioners of the republican era (Nigidius Figulus, Tarutius Firmanus). Their fatalistic world-view inspired two well-known first-century contributions to astrology produced in the Latin West: Manilius's *Astronomica* and Germanicus's version of Aratus's *Phaenomena*.

Divination was a very sensitive issue in Roman politics in that candidates to the imperial throne were constantly seeking or being offered oracular insights into their own future. Whether directly or through their fathers, horoscopal promises of an imperial destiny were successively made to Octavianus, Tiberius, Caius Caligula, Nero, Galba, Otho, Vitellius, Vespasian, Titus, and Domitian (Cramer 1954: 168). Under the guidance of the knowledgeable and influential Thrasyllus, Tiberius himself is known to have practised the art of Chaldean mathematics.

But the art and rhetoric of astrology was a double-edged sword. While it was effectively used to legitimate the rule of the imperial monarchy, it also served the interests of opponents to the regime. As Cramer shows, these two-sided effects of astrological politics account for the fact that sidereal divination was both institutionalized and criminalized throughout imperial Roman history. It was a well-established science subserving the interests of the ruling classes, but also an invitation to criminal activity among the rebellious segments of society and contenders to the throne. Mathematical divination could be used to predict the successful outcome of plots against the throne and to produce self-fulfilling prophecies of triumphant insurrection.

At first, legal restrictions and bans imposed on the practice of astrology reflected a philosophical rejection of the Chaldean mode of divination, a practice otherwise deemed harmless. The imperial edict passed in 139 B.C.E. is a case in point. Later decrees, however, were temporary measures to counter political tensions experienced mostly in Rome and Italy. Up until at least the fourth century C.E., anti-astrology decrees were motivated by the fear that oracular astrology would result in popular insurrectionary activities, the art being used to guarantee success to those struggling against the ruling powers. This was especially true during the sixty years of political turmoil that plagued Rome under Marius and Octavianus (90–30 B.C.E.). The rise of monarchs to power and the infatuation of Latin aristocrats with Chaldean mathematics created yet another fear: that contenders to the throne would seek encouragement through foreknowledge of their own political future and the death date of the emperor, his heir, or his immediate family. Edicts promulgated in 11, 16, and 49 C.E. made such inquiries into future death dates illegal in Rome and sometimes throughout the Empire, constituting *prima facie* evidence of treason. Throughout Rome's imperial history, countless noblemen known or suspected to hold such information, or to possess imperial horoscopes, were exiled from Rome or executed by imperial order, with a view to protecting the ruler against threats to his throne, real or imagined. Only accredited diviners and the emperor's trusted astrologers were granted immunity. They alone were entitled to seek horoscopal insights into what Fate kept in store for the ruler, potential successors, and conspirators as well. They produced predictions that were designed to reassure the emperor against prophecies of short reign, identify and eliminate contenders to the throne, or dispel false hopes of an impending death, all with a view to maintaining political stability at court (Cramer 1954: 144f., 168, 236, 240ff.; Bouché-Leclercq 1879: 253, 256).

In 11 C.E., Augustus was so concerned about rumours of his own imminent death that he opted to make public his personal horoscope. Twenty years prior to this date, the same ruler countered a wave of unrest and oracular agitation that swept through the capital by ordering a general *auto-da-fé* of suspicious writings with divinatory contents. Advised by Thrasyllus, Tiberius ordered a similar *auto-da-fé* with a view to curbing astrological activities among would-be conspirators of Rome; the event took place in 19 C.E. The emperor also adopted highly repressive measures against the spread of Judaism and the Isis religion in Rome. Later rulers of the first century C.E. kept the Augustan edict in force. Two years before his assassination, the ageing Claudius (41–54 C.E.) obtained a senatorial decree banishing non-accredited astrologers from Italy, thus countering the unrest caused by prophecies of the ruler's impending demise. Vitellius (15–69 C.E.) was particularly fearful of astrological incitements to rebellion and persecuted practitioners of the art without mercy. Vespasian (9–79 C.E.) was such a strong believer in Chaldean doctrines that, as they had with Galba, Otho, and Vitellius before him, prophecies encouraged him to struggle for the throne. When in power, he issued another expulsion order against unaccredited astrologers, a measure which never stopped him from consulting his court astrologer Balbillus, the son of Thrasyllus and a former friend of Claudius's (Cramer 1954: 86, 99, 101, 111, 114f., 135, 138).

Astrological prophecies issued by a man apparently named Asklepios convinced Domitian that he would end up being murdered. Although a self-proclaimed *dominus et deus*, Domitian spent much of his life fearing Fate and suspecting his own relatives and court members of conspiring against him and planning his death. As a result, 'during those last years of

Domitian's reign prosecutions for violations of the Augustan law of topical restrictions were numerous and sentences harsh. With Domitian's assassination in 96 all of his edicts [e.g., expulsion edicts of 89–90 and 93–4] expired automatically, when the Senate in solemn session pronounced the dreaded *damnatio memoriae*' (Cramer 1954: 142f., 151, 246). Under Domitian, a great number of philosophers, astrologers, their clients (real or presumed), and noblemen thought to possess imperial horoscopes were exiled or simply executed.

The emperors of Rome attempted to maintain strict control over the use and abuse of astrology, whether it be through edicts, prosecutions for treason (starting in 16 C.E.), or repressive measures ranging from imprisonment to exile and arbitrary executions. Yet these measures were never entirely successful. Ambitious aristocrats continued to consult well-known astrologers such as Anaxilaus of Larissa under Augustus, Pammenes and Ptolemy Seleucus under Nero, and Asclation under Domitian, all of whom took considerable risks when advising the oppositional nobility (Cramer 1954: 82f.).

The Later Principate (96–235 C.E.)

A small group of influential Stoics were initially opposed to the monarchic rule of Julius Caesar and Augustus. With support from Roman nobles, some Stoics also opposed the principate during the first century of our era (Cramer 1954: 146f., 200). While swayed by the arguments of astrological fatalism propounded by the followers of Zeno, Roman emperors countered Stoic opposition by imposing restrictions on the astrological practice, depriving the oppositional nobility of its rational–prophetic powers and harnessing their science to their own despotic rule. Repressive measures taken against astrologers never entailed a wholesale rejection of the Chaldean *Weltanschauung*, but rather an attempt to exercise control over it. With a few notable exceptions (Columella, Pliny the Elder, Philo of Alexandria), first-century thinkers did not doubt the infallibility of astrological divination. All agreed that the moon governed the tides, that the equinoxes caused predictable weather phenomena, that motions of the sun affected all life forms on earth, and that stellar motions had a direct bearing on worldly events.

Throughout the second century C.E., however, Stoicism started losing support from Rome's ruling stratum. The Stoic world-view faced a new wave of philosophical critique stemming from intellectuals opposed to dominant theories of rationalism and fatalism.

In the second century of our era there developed a renaissance of that struggle which had characterized the second century B.C. ... But just as in the earlier conflict Chrysippus and Diogenes of Babylon, Stoic champions of fatalism, had been forced by a rising tide of Scepticism (culminating in Carneades and his New Academy) to compromise to a degree – a compromise best represented by Panaetius – the Stoics of the second century A.D. sought to reconcile their faith in Fate with a gentler belief in a benign Providence. Their foes, Platonists, Epicureans, Peripatetics, and Cynics in particular, would of course never agree with fatalist concepts of any sort. Indeed there could be no compromise between those on the one side who believed in a rationally organised cosmos and those on the other who either believed in an arbitrary divine rule or denied any cosmic order, insisting that, even if it existed, men would never be able to discern it. (Cramer 1954: 178f.)

Criticisms levelled against Stoic fatalism were not new. Like earlier members of the New Academy founded by Carneades, sceptics attempted once again to keep the claims of astrological determination, especially those of horoscopal divination, within reasonable bounds, thus protecting probabilistic conceptions of reality from rigid notions of Fate. The human ability to comprehend the laws governing the universe was also questioned. Those more inclined to adopt the views of empiricists and peripatetics doubted the adequacy of observational knowledge possessed by astrologers, not to mention the logic of diviners busying themselves trying to counter and contradict Fate. As for the Platonists, they insisted on the existence of a supreme essence governing the world from beyond the visible universe – a divine Providence interfering at will in the lives of mortals. Most of these objections to astrology would later provide the Christian Church with weapons to be used against astrological fatalism and pagan divination.

Given these renewed criticisms, Stoics watered down their notion of absolute Necessity and attempted to reconcile Fate with a measure of freedom, human and divine. Ptolemy argued that certain things are governed by chance and that humans' foreknowledge of future events can help them to cope with life or prevent things from actually happening, as opposed to the idea that everything is rigidly determined by stars and Fate (Cramer 1954: 194; Tester 1987: 70). Logic dictated an attitude of caution towards the fatalistic claims of a cosmic Reason embodied in motions of the heavenly spheres.

Paradoxically, advocates of human freedom had an important point in common with proponents of cosmic Fate: a commitment to Logos, whether it be expressed through a recognition of the great sidereal order governing time and the universe *or* through a logical critique of unfounded astrological speculations. Reason triumphs in both cases. But faith in Reason could also be challenged. Philosophical and cultural developments of the second century started calling Logic and Reason into question. Instead of resolving their differences, philosophers engaged in the Fate-versus-Freedom debate came to a deadlock by the end of the first century. Their intellectual dispute regarding the 'reasonable' gave way to a wave of anti-rationalism that took various forms, including solar mysticism, Neoplatonism, and Christian monotheism.

In hindsight, some of the basic tenets of Stoic astralism were conducive to the rise of mysticism in Graeco-Roman thought, heralding its triumph over the age of reason in antiquity. First, the heavenly 'translation' of older mythical divinities and the interconnectedness of humans and star-gods organized vertically, with the sun and the emperor occupying central positions in the cosmos, laid the ground for a hierarchical conception of human transactions with spirits in heaven – a *sine qua non* of monotheistic theology. Second, non-rationalistic expressions of faith were aided by the idea of redemptive catasterism and the diviners' commitment to elevating souls to a better life on earth and in heaven, through a combination of ritual activity and proper ascetic conduct. Third, the astrologers' secret knowledge of remedies against Fate and humans' pursuit of actions capable of thwarting the plans of heaven could open onto ideas of godly Providence – hence, divine care and guidance obtained through corrective behaviour. Fourth, the Stoic concern with order and reason meant that all belief systems could be subjected to the exigencies of logical criticism, including astrology and rationalism itself. Paradoxically, the entire history of Western debates surrounding the Chaldean art is replete with rational critiques of fatalism (a king cannot kill someone fated to be his successor; all humans born at the same time cannot have the same fate; all humans who meet the same fate simultaneously cannot have been born at the same time; etc.) that endorse the fatality of a compelling logical argument – a legacy of Stoicism and astrology! *Rational attacks against Reason* were bound to open onto new philosophies that wandered away from rationalism.

Theories of sidereal fatalism were logically and culturally vulnerable. But astralism could very well survive the death of rationalism, adjusting its principles to faith in the mysteries of the universe. This is especially true of the popular adaptations of astrology. As Cramer (1954: 148) points out, the 'mass of the Mediterranean population had never taken an active part or even an interest in the intellectual disputes. They had been satisfied to accept the astrologers' claims at face value, but without ever abandoning their faith in religious revelations ... and the reliance on prayers and sacrifices to gods and goddesses for a happy and prosperous future.' While the intellectuals of Rome placed great value on astrological learning and the ethics of *amor fati*, Latin citizens were more interested in cultic activities aimed at knowing and controlling the future – hence, the sacrificial offerings, prayers, and ritual services of oriental haruspices, soothsayers, and star-gazers.

At the institutional level, heliolatry inspired by Eastern cults was to play a vital role in the political survival of astralism in the Latin West. Solarism turned astrology from a rational theology into an imperial expression of cultic mysticism. It transformed a religious science into faith in ritual magic, the powers of providence, and supernatural revelations obtained through dreams and omens of all sorts. In the third century C.E., the sun became the overarching principle that set the whole universe in motion, subjugating all former deities and mythologies of the Roman Empire. This revolution based on Chaldean notions of heliolatry and astro-magic was brought about by a number of late-principate thinkers, such as Philostratus, Apuleius of Madaurus, the Chaldean Julianus, and his renowned son (Cramer 1954: 217ff.). Roman solar-worship echoed earlier formulations of astro-solar mysticism, including the teachings of Apollonius of Tyana, a contemporary and rival of Christ and Paul. Apollonius was a theurgian whose life was later to be told by Philostratus, and then anathematized by Eusebius, the Christian patriarch of fourth-century Constantinople. Although critical of horoscopal astrology, Pliny the Elder had also argued that the sun should be elevated above all other stars. This Roman writer of the first century held the sun to be the sovereign divinity that infused life into human souls and reason into the orderly motions and combined activities of nature and the heavens. In the fiery sun resides the *principale naturae regimen ac numen* (Cumont 1960: 72f.).

These sun-centred ideas (and variations thereof) were politically sanctioned towards the end of the Roman principate, with the imperial enthronement of the sun-priest Heliogabalus, (218–22) representative of the sun on earth. In the year 218 the monarch became 'god and master by right of birth (*deus et dominus natus*), who had descended from heaven by grace of the Sun, and by his grace will reascend thither again after death' (Cumont 1960: 54). Like Domitian and Commodus, who had used oriental cults to elevate their own autocratic rule to celestial heights, third-century emperors of Rome such as Heliogabalus and Aurelian (270–275) converted Semitic expressions of heliolatry into a state religion. *Mathematica* gave way to the cult of an eternal ruler embodying the Invincible Sun, supreme regulator of the universe. In their frantic quest for knowledge of the future, second-century rulers of Rome such as Hadrian, Caracalla, and Septimus Severus had already started abandoning the scientific mode of divination, resorting instead to magic and mystery cults to obtain favours, secret knowledge, and revelations directly from the gods. 'Isis and Mithras, Elagabalus and Asklepius proffered religious certainty instead of scientific, human, and, therefore, fallible methods of astrology. This trend was clearly reflected in Latin and Greek literature of the second and third centuries, before it became politically manifest in the reign of Elagabalus, the apostle of solar monotheism in Rome' (Cramer 1954: 216f.). Late Roman art continues to deploy planetary and zodiacal imageries, but with less emphasis on the celestial mathematics of Fate and divination; heavenly representations speak rather to the sun-god as chronocrator, a Time-Lord governing the calendrical motions of time (Tester 1987: 106). Christianity would soon displace this naturalistic brand of monotheism for a loftier conception of a supreme Lord dwelling in the highest heaven, an eternal and immaterial God governing the universe from beyond the visible spheres.

The history of Mithraic solarism and its rivalry with Christianity is particularly important as it points to the pervasive influence of astralism on religions of the early Christian era. Far from being the offshoot of an Iranian myth, as claimed by Cumont, the Mithraic motifs of bull, scorpion, dog, snake, raven, lion, and cup revolved around astral and solar symbolism. According to Ulansey, Mithraic mythology is basically a narrative mapping of the stars. While the lion stands for the summer solstice, the other motifs 'represent the constellations which lay on the celestial equator on or below the ecliptic when the spring equinox was in Taurus' (1989: 55). Stoicizing philosophers of Tarsus were well aware of Hipparchus's late second century B.C.E. discovery of the precession of the equinoxes (vernal and autumn equatorial points moving from Aries and Libra to Taurus and Scorpius) and seem to have elevated their own native god, Perseus, to the rank of an unconquered deity or cosmocrator putting an end to the Age of Taurus, destined, as he was, to govern motions of the celestial pole and the visible sun; in the words of Hippolytus (c. 160–c. 235), Perseus became 'the winged axle that pierces both poles through the center of the earth, and turns the world around' (quoted in Malina 1995: 74). Mithraic rituals thus equated the demise of the former equinoctial sign with the slaying of the bull by the northerly constellation of Perseus located immediately above Taurus (Ulansey 1989: 93, 110).

Mithraism spread throughout the empire, and heliolatry became the religion of imperial Rome, a monotheistic religion struggling to gain ascendancy over the countless polytheisms of Graeco-Roman and Semitic antiquity. While this represented a new trend in Roman history, rulers deployed old means to exercise control over politically less acceptable appropriations of secret mysteries of the sun and the stars. As Cramer (1954: 212; n.d.) shows, legal actions and repressive measures against subversive usages of astrology persisted well into the third century. Septimus Severus (193–211) ordered the executions of friends and court members suspected of having inquired into the emperor's death date by means of divination. In addition to his bitter persecution of Christians, Diocletian (284–305) temporarily outlawed all divinatory practices throughout the Empire. The repression of astrology would not take on an entirely different meaning – an outright and permanent rejection of astralism viewed as paganism – until the advent of another revolution in the Latin world: the conversion of Rome to Christianity. But before we turn to astrology in late antiquity and the Middle Ages, something should be said about the Jewish background to Christianity's perspective on the heavenly bodies.

Jewish Astrology

The first-century writings of Philo of Alexandria are a good illustration, at least on the philosophical plane, of how Hellenistic astralism could be rejected as a religion while also being retained as a valid source of knowledge and mystical experience, providing an understanding of star-signs compatible with the teachings of Yahweh. In keeping with Judaism and Platonism, Philo objected to religions that defined God materially, an observable being living fully within the natural world. Influenced by the teachings of Carneades and the New Academy, he also objected to belief systems that left no room for the intervention of free will, human or divine. He thus rejected the fatalistic astrology that 'had raised the house of Thrasyllus to the pinnacle of prosperity and political influence in the courts of Augustus, Tiberius, Claudius, and most recently Nero' (Cramer 1954: 126). Stoicism and horoscopy à la Thrasyllus and Balbillus were suspect from the start as they undermined the Jewish ethics of human freedom and godly omnipotence. Instead of attributing their blessings, misfortunes, virtues, and crimes to the all-powerful actions of stars, followers of the Lord must take responsibility for their actions and accept all related rewards and punishments received before and after their death.

Philo's objections to Chaldean mathematics, however, were directed essentially against sidereal naturalism and fatalism, not against astrology taken as a whole. Like Columella, Philo recognized that the heavenly spheres were rational beings that could actually influence human and natural events. The moon and the sun do have an effect on the process of conception, and the Big Dipper does influence sexual activity. But the luminaries are by no means the primary movers of human and natural history; rather, stars must keep the Lord's commandments and come 'in their allotted time,' lest they be thrown into Sheol (1 Enoch 18: 15). Their main purpose is to shed light on the world and to regulate the order of time, announcing normal things to come. For God said, 'Let there be lights in the vault of heaven to divide day from night, and let them indicate festivals, days and years. Let them be lights in the vault of heaven to shine on earth' (Gen. 1: 14–15).

In addition to their regulatory functions, stars can be read as representations of sacred temple objects: the twelve loaves of bread and the twelve stones of the priestly breastplate thus point to a zodiacal imagery, and the seven branches of the menorah to the planetary system (Ness 1990; Gleadow 1968: 122–35). Stars may also act as signs indicating God's plans for the future, plans that go beyond the regular alternations of days, weeks, months, seasons, and years. Alternatively, stars can symbolize or embody spirits acting on behalf of God or struggling against his reign on earth and in heaven. Although dwelling in a spiritual world, God 'presented himself by a descending series of divine representations,' a 'creative and ruling radiation of divine nature ... thought of as the world of forms,' with the heavenly bodies acting as their purest expressions – a collective Logos functioning as a cosmic priesthood serving the immaterial Lord (Goodenough 1958: 210). By wearing his breastplate studded with twelve zodiacal stones, the high priest 'becomes one who bears in his mind the original pattern, so that he is in a sense transformed from being a man into the nature of the cosmos, and becomes ... himself a little cosmos' (quoted in Goodenough 1958: 211). The priest thus puts on the heavenly cosmos, wearing a material cloak in the manner of the Creator donning the veil of his wondrous creation. Through cultic activity, humans commune with the universal Logos.

Philo's discussion of the Jewish principle of sevenness applied to motions of the sun, the passing of seasons, and the renewal of earthly fertility suggests another Jewish appropriation of ancient astralism. 'The sun, too, the great lord of day, brings about two equinoxes each year, in spring and autumn. The spring equinox in the constellation of the Ram, and the autumn equinox in that of the Scales, supply very clear evidence of the sacred dignity of the seven, for each of the equinoxes occurs in a seventh month, and during them it is enjoined by law to keep the greatest national

Festivals, since at both of them all fruits of the earth ripen, in the spring the wheat and all else that is sown, and in the autumn the fruit of the vine and most of the other fruit trees' (quoted in Goodenough 1958: 217). As Goodenough (218) points out, Judaism's heptadic principle embodies human hopes of 'astral immortality granted by that beneficence which, while it came from the relentlessly regular heaven, made all the earth fertile and promised renewed life also to man.'

As in Philo's writings, ancient rabbinical hermeneutics made use of astrology to make sense of scriptural imageries, interpreting them against the background of God's cosmic order, knowledge of which was obtained through observation and revelation (Schiaparelli 1905: 10). Thus the twelvefold tribal system of the Old Testament was often read as reflecting divisions of time (hours, months) and heavenly space (zodiac) ordained by Yahweh. While the Mishnah (c. 200 C.E.) states that lunisolar imageries should not be engraved upon sacred objects, many passages of the Jewish Scriptures evoke astronomical considerations and imageries of astral immortality ('going to heaven') borrowed from the pagan world (Dan. 12: 3; 1 Enoch 72–3; 2 Baruch 51: 10; 4 Ezra 7: 88–99; 4 Maccabees 14: 7f., 17: 5). Excerpts from the Ma'aseh Bereshit account of Creation also show the centrality of stars and signs of the zodiac in Jewish views of the universe.

In his discussion of Jewish concessions to astrology, Goodenough adds a fragment of the early apocalyptic imagery, words that highlight some of the astrological underpinnings of Jewish symbolism, not to mention the astral underside of John's vision of the End of Time, discussed at length later in this book. The fragment announces that 'in time to come, the Holy One, blessed be he, will take his seat in Eden and expound. All the righteous will sit before him: all the retinue on high will stand on their feet. *The sun and the zodiac [or constellations] will be at his right hand and the moon and stars on his left*; God will sit and expound a new Torah which he will, one day, give by the Messiah's hand' (1958: 205, emphasis added).

Interest in the luminaries of heaven was expressed not only through rabbinical teachings and philosophical writings such as Philo's, but also through popular belief systems and artistic representations of Jewish theology. While notoriously opposed to polytheistic equations between gods and bodies of the sky, ancient Jews made use of zodiacal imageries to represent Yahweh bringing order into the universe and placing his chosen people under the protection of the heavenly forces.

In his doctoral thesis, entitled 'Astrology and Judaism in Late Antiquity,' Ness (1990) uses evidence from various sites (Harran, Edessa, Palmyra, Heliopolis, and Khirbet Tannur) to show how astrology was practised throughout Hellenized Syria. Planets and stars were worshipped in such ways as to highlight the power and majesty of a chief divinity ruling the universe through laws of heavenly motion. While gods of the Syrian Bronze Age or classical Greece were relatively egalitarian in that they governed the world like the ruling class of a city or state, later pantheons were hierarchically organized, reflecting, as they did, the imperial regimes of Persia, Egypt, and Rome. Like the subaltern rulers of a King or a Caesar, star-gods, zodiac-spirits, and other lower divinities carried out the orders of an all-powerful Lord called Bel, Baal Shamin, or Zeus. In the Jewish and Christian cosmogonies, astrology functioned in basically the same way, providing a reservoir of powerful metaphors and a host of well-organized angels, godlike messengers, and mediators subserving the monotheistic rule of the Almighty in Heaven. Ancient Jews, early Christians, and their fellow Syrians saw astrology as a tangible expression of a Supreme Deity imposing order and his will on the whole universe. Judaism and Christianity differed none the less from 'pagan' religions in one important respect: although seconded by star-spirits, the Lord of Heaven reigned well above the material world and the visible spheres moving across the sky.

Teachings of the Old Testament and the Hebrew Bible make it abundantly clear that Israelites must have no other gods but the immaterial Yahweh (Exod. 20: 3; Deut. 5: 7). Anyone 'who goes and serves other gods and worships them, or the sun or the moon or any of heaven's array' violates the Jewish covenant with God and should be stoned to death (Deut. 17: 1–7). As in Ezekiel 8, worshippers of the sun are bound to arouse the wrath of God, for they confound the observable creation with the invisible Creator, a confusion that is at the root of all idolatry (see also Deut. 4: 19; 2 Kings 21: 3–5; Jer. 8: 2; Zeph. 1: 4–5). By implication, followers of God should not 'take alarm at the heavenly signs,' for these signs can do neither harm nor good; compared with the will and the wrath of God, 'the Dread of the peoples is a nothing' (Jer. 10: 1–3). Unlike God, star-gazers who predict peoples' fate and offer spells and sorcery rituals to ward off impending dangers are powerless to alter anyone's fate (Isa. 47: 12–16). As confirmed in Daniel 2, only God has the power to 'control the procession of times and seasons, to make and unmake kings, to confer wisdom on the wise,' to reveal mysteries, and to divine the future.

This is not to say that astrology is banned from the Scriptures. Heavenly bodies continue to serve as powerful metaphors, as in Genesis 37, where the sun image is applied to patriarchal Jacob, or Psalms 19, where the sun is likened to a bridegroom coming out of his pavilion and racing across the sky. Stars and planets also play an active role in God's management of the cosmos (giving light, marking time, etc.) and as forces, living creatures, and messengers subserving and manifesting the rule of Yahweh. Given these attributes, many passages of both the Old and New Testaments evoke the astrological belief system while never committing themselves to pagan astralism – to the notion that the highest god can be assimilated to a visible sphere or body in heaven, typically the sun (or the moon). Despite their repudiation of astralism, many scenes of the Scriptures could have been understood astrologically by those who had faith in the powers of 'mathematics,' or at least some familiarity with its teachings.

According to the Sibylline Oracles (3: 20–4, 219–27), ancient Jews did not practise sidereal divination. As God once said to Israel, 'Away with your astrology: for Israel there is no planet!' (Shabbath 156a, quoted in Altman 1971). Although often associated with the teaching and promotion of astrology (see Charlesworth 1983, 2: 202, 799, 873, 880f., 897), Abraham set the example by forsaking the Chaldean art after his conversion to monotheism (1 Enoch 7–10). Given the right rank-ordering of god and his works, however, astrology could be reconciled with Judaism. As Ness points out (1990; see also Charlesworth 1983, 2: 893), Jewish thinkers of the second century B.C.E. such as Artapanus and Eupolemus 'took a "scientific practice" which they believed true and tried to make it look Jewish by associating it with Jewish heroes.' Actually 'this is the approach of most of the Jewish astrological writers, just as it was for the Egyptian astrologers.' Those who study the heavenly works and celestial laws of God as Solomon did can continue to do so provided they be wise enough to recognize Yahweh as the supreme 'Artificer,' acknowledging that his angels can 'thwart' all lesser gods (Wisdom 7: 17–22; Eccles. 3: 1–9; Job 38: 33; Testament of Solomon 15; see Charlesworth 1983, 1: 945, 975; 2: 600). Compared with those who worship things of their own creation, however, star-gazers deserve less reproach. 'If, charmed by their beauty, they have taken things for gods, let them know how much the Lord of these excels them, since the very Author of beauty has created them ... Small blame, however, attaches to these men, for perhaps they only go astray in their search for God and their eagerness to find him; living among his works, they strive to comprehend them and fall victim to appearances, seeing so much beauty' (Wis. 13: 3–7).

We know from the Hebrew and Aramaic Dead Sea Scrolls (second century B.C.E. to 70 C.E.) that ancient Jews engaged in the practice of physiognomy, judging the moral character and destiny of individuals on the basis of physical appearances; the practice is linked with astrology in the rabbinical literature (Alexander 1973–87: 367; see Charlesworth 1983, 1: 250, 568).

The Treatise of Shem, a Syriac tract written at the turn of our era, also shows that ancient Jews were conversant in the art of predicting events (crops, climate, health, political developments) from the sign that marked the beginning of the New Year, a practice elsewhere condemned as knowledge taught to men by a fallen angel (1 Enoch 8: 3) and an affront to the Lord who has 'all the signs of the stars and the signs of the moon' in his hand (Jubilees 12: 16–18). As Charlesworth (1983 1: 477) points out, the Treatise of Shem invalidates the argument 'that astrology in Judaism was never more than a Qumranite or sectarian aberration.'

Writings from the Khirbet Qumran reflecting the beliefs of first-century Jews, towards the end of the Second Temple Period, indicate that astrology was also combined with physiognomy and brontologia to explain and predict human and natural phenomena. People born under certain signs were thought to show particular physical and spiritual characteristics, and thunderclaps appearing in conjunction with certain signs were thought to announce particular events (Ness 1990).

Finally, the Testament of Solomon (see Charlesworth 1983, 1: 944f.) and the Letter of Rehoboam testify to the use of astrologically inspired magic and medicine among the earliest Christians and the first-century Jews. In the Letter of Rehoboam text, planets act as subordinate angels that rule over certain plants and hours of the day and that look after the day-to-day management of God's creation. These planetary gods can receive prayers and offerings from humans provided that practitioners of astrology acknowledge God's supremacy from the start: 'Eternal God, resistless in power, the One who regulates all things which pertain to our salvation, grant us favor that I might make a certain planetary god ... subject to me for the accomplishing of my will' (Ness 1990). Just as the emperor exercises his rule against contenders to the throne and with the assistance of provincial governors and lower-ranking authorities, so, too, Yahweh has enemies and deputies playing subaltern roles in the heavens.

Notwithstanding the constant rejection of full-fledged polytheism and astralism, the three documents mentioned above suggest that 'many Jews, hellenized and unhellenized alike, had adapted scientific astrology to their own tastes by the first century C.E.' (Ness 1990). The same comment applies to the Talmudic writings produced in later centuries, a rabbinical literature that treats the stars and the planets as key players within God's ruling order – hence, lesser divinities ranked below their Creator. This sacred literature (e.g., the Babylonian Talmud, tractate Shabbat) shows again some ambivalence vis-à-vis the concept of astral influence and Fate. While some texts suggest that the fate of the chosen people is governed by

Israel's star, other writings claim that stars do not make patriarchs and nations wise or rich, which means that Israel is free from planetary influence and that her fate is ultimately dictated by God.

A less ambivalent example of rabbinical astral magic practised in late antiquity (and reported by Epiphanius in his *Panarion*) is the Book of Secrets, a Hebrew manuscript written in the second half of the fourth century. While rabbis usually discouraged the practice of astral divination, they prompted learned men to explore the principles of magic. Accordingly, the Book of Secrets describes the cosmos from a Jewish perspective, it goes into spells invoking living stars and planets, and it portrays the sun as an angel possessing invaluable secrets. This manuscript shows once more how astrological mysteries and rituals were 'acceptable if placed in a properly Jewish garb' (Ness 1990). As Ness argues, 'the angels carry out God's orders, and to that extent substitute for His direct action. Portraying them visually is a way of showing God at work, maintaining the world He created. In a sense, they are a substitute for portraying the God Whom even Moses might not see.'

In his study of Jewish astronomical symbols of late antiquity, Goodenough (1958: 167–77) discusses a bronze hanging-bracket for lamps found in Galilee, with a ring perforated by twelve holes, and a lamp probably hanging from the hook below the bracket. Mention is made of a stone frieze from the synagogue of Kefr Birim showing signs of Sagittarius, Taurus, Virgo, and Capricorn, and also a second- or third-century amulet from the de Clercq collection showing the sun, the moon, the planets, and the zodiac. Other amulets depict scenes of astral piety centred on the sun and the moon, echoing Jewish charms that hail Helios as a symbol of deity. Goodenough's discussion includes representations of the sun, the stars, the timeless seasons, the cupids, and the death of Adonis appearing on Roman Jewish sarcophagi and in catacomb ceiling art. Although adapted to Jewish monotheism, much of this imagery was shared with 'pagan' religions of the Graeco-Roman world. As in other cults, this astral symbolism was closely tied to beliefs and hopes in the immortality principle built into the eternal motions of heaven. The imagery harked back to the seasonal cycle and the alternation of 'day and night, the yearly journey of the sun to the southern hemisphere, the phases of the moon, the Cosmic Year of the fixed stars, the cycles of the planets and their influence upon terrestrial events, or the spheres of the planets as methods of ascent, or as seven heavens' (192).

Visual representations of astral mediators interceding between earthly mortals and their invisible Creator can be found in ancient synagogue art dating between the third and the sixth century C.E. First-century Jews such as Josephus used to be critical of humans paying too much attention to products of their own creation, treating them as idols worthy of cultic devotion. After the Jerusalem temple was destroyed, however, this attitude changed considerably. 'Synagogues and tombs of the Talmudic period were highly ornamented with human and animal figures. The eagle, absolutely unacceptable on Herod's Temple, is very common over the entrance of synagogues' (Ness 1990). As astrology was a common source of iconographic representation, zodiacal motifs found their way into several synagogues of this Second Temple Period.

The oldest Jewish zodiac mosaic was discovered in a synagogue located in Naraan, near modern Jericho. The panel in question consists of two concentric circles contained in a large square. A female figure is drawn in each of the four corners labelled after the four Jewish months that marked the four seasons. While these signs run counter-clockwise, the Greek zodiacal icons sighted between the two concentric circles run clockwise; zodiacal constellations are not aligned with the proper seasons. A picture of *Sol Invictus* driving a four-horse chariot appears in the centre circle with his usual apparel: a whip, a crown of rays, and a cloak covered with stars.

Three other synagogue zodiacs were discovered: one in Beth Alpha, on the slopes of Mt Gilboa; another in Husifa, on Mt Carmel; and a third in Hammath-Tiberias, on the western shore of the Sea of Galilee. The Beth Alpha panel differs from the Naraan mosaic in terms of some of the motifs used to represent the seasons and signs of the zodiac, both of which run in the same direction. In the Husifa zodiac, signs and seasons are not labelled and do not correlate. The Hammath-Tiberias zodiac is unique in that signs and seasons are correctly aligned and represented with a purely Greek iconography, including nude, uncircumcised figures standing for Libra and Aquarius. The central sun-god figure has his right hand raised in benediction, with a crescent moon beneath the arm. His left hand holds a whip and a globe with two circles crossing – the spherical universe traversed by the celestial equator and the ecliptic. A seven-pointed star appears beneath the same arm. Other possible examples of synagogue zodiacs have been found in Susiya, near Hebron; in En Gedi, in the Judaean desert; and in Yafia, southwest of Nazareth. The Yafia mosaic shows the twelve tribes of Israel represented by twelve animals, an imagery that rabbinical tradition has commonly equated with signs of the zodiac.

Theories that purport to explain this synagogue art are most instructive. One common view is that Judaism did not see in astralism a valid science, let alone a valid religion, and that zodiacal imagery simply stood for the Jewish calendar, without implying a commitment to any astral belief system. Avi-Yonah (1964) thus argued that signs of the zodiac were combined with inscriptions of the twenty-four priestly courses (each serving in the temple two weeks a year) to represent the Jewish calendar, thereby facilitating calculations of festive dates. Given the non-alignment of seasons and signs in several mosaics, this interpretation has not convinced most expert historians. Another theory is that the zodiacal imagery deployed in the synagogue mosaics is without special meaning, not even calendrical. Urbach (1953) suggests that Jews of late antiquity came into such close contact with non-Jewish cults that they gave in to the idea that pagan images could be exchanged, possessed, or used as ornaments, provided they were not actually worshipped. Both theories are problematical in that they assume that zodiacal imageries could be used without carrying astromythical evocations. The art bears no signs of an effort to subsume astralism under Judaism, appropriating Sabian associations while leaving pagan doctrines behind.

Unlike Avi-Yonah and Urbach, Goodenough claims that the zodiac was part of an artistic genre characteristic of a Hellenized world-view which influenced Jewish popular culture but not rabbinical doctrine. Orthodoxy notwithstanding, Jewish artists used astral and planetary iconography to represent the calendar, the seasons, and the whole cosmos falling under Yahweh's rule, a universe driven not by the real sun, but rather by a sunlike charioteer standing at the centre (as in the synagogue mosaics) and above the heavenly vault, and guiding the whole cosmos. The latter imageries served as mere signs and allegories, imperfect representations and manifestations of an immaterial divinity lying beyond the visible sun and the spheres of heaven. This religious composition à la Philo was not given a 'scientific' meaning, severed as it was from the Graeco-Roman 'mathematics' of human destiny (Goodenough 1958: 168, 178, 209, 215). 'The fact that the seasons were not correlated with the correct signs showed that the congregations either did not know, or did not care, about the details of astrology. Those who did practice astrology kept it in a separate mental compartment from their religion' (Ness 1990).

Prigent (1990) and Ness (1990) propose similar explanations but with less hesitation about the compatibility between rabbinical Judaism and the practice of astrology: zodiacal thinking was by no means confined to Jewish heterodoxy. Some rabbinical teachings made room for astrological mathematics as a wise man's way of paying attention to the wondrous works of God (Prigent 1990: 169–71). Despite his many doubts and reservations concerning the role of astromythology in the New Testament Apocalypse, Prigent sees in the zodiacal belt encircling Helios a confession of faith in the *sunlike* Lord of Israel dwelling in heaven and governing the whole universe. Judaic adaptations of alien symbolism are a credit to the vitality and wisdom of early Jewish theology: synagogue art drew some of its iconographic inspiration from astral imageries that were almost neutral or thoroughly detached from their 'pagan' origins (172). Likewise, Ness claims 'the zodiacs symbolize God, His care for His universe, and especially for His people, the Jews.' Stars and planets were not autonomous divinities in their own right, as the Chaldeans, the Greeks, and the Romans used to believe, but they did manifest the powers of God and his ruling order administered by astral and planetary angels and the laws of astrology.

Thus, it was not possible to portray YHWH directly in a synagogue. But it was possible to portray Him indirectly, by portraying His satraps, the planets. In the examples which survive, Sol Invictus in the centre of the zodiac represents the whole planetary system, *pars pro toto*. The seasons may indeed be a reference to the Jewish calendar. At the same time, they may have reminded worshippers that 'I will never curse the ground again because of man ... neither will I ever again destroy the every living creature ... While the earth remains, seedtime and harvest, cold and heat, and summer and winter, shall not cease' (Gen. 2: 21–2). (Ness 1990)

Ness adds that 'Jews used the same horoscopes, spells, and symbols as their neighbors, but they used them in a Judaic way for Judaic purposes.' Provided that Jews continued to express their faith in Yahweh through proper temple activities, God could be counted on to maintain provisions of the Noahic Covenant or solar pact (the everlasting alternation of days, months, and seasons; cf. 1 Enoch 82) against Chaos and the afflictions of another great Flood.

To conclude, all indications are that Judaism did find means of fitting the language of astrology to faith in Yahweh, using it in such ways as to highlight God's powers over heavenly forces and the orderly motions of time. As Lawrence (1974: 62) puts it, ancient Jews 'looked at the world with the eyes of their neighbours. When the prophets had to see visions, they had to see Assyrian or Chaldean visions. They borrowed other gods to see their own invisible God by.' Jewish appropriations of astrology continued throughout the Middle Ages, as illustrated by the twelfth-century writings of Abraham ibn Ezra, a foremost medieval Jewish interpreter of Scripture (Altman 1971). Given the pagan implications of zodiacal symbolism, however, several major scholars of ancient synagogue art (Avi-Yonah 1964; Hachlili 1988) have denied the importance of astrology in Jewish religious history. In doing so, they have left the synagogue imagery poorly explained and artificially disconnected from broader influences of the Graeco-Roman world. Yet their reservations about the weight of astrological thinking in Jewish theology were by no means unjustified. If by astrology we mean astralism – a deification of planets and stars combined with a mathematical understanding of their mutual relations and influences on human affairs – then there is ample evidence to suggest that Hellenized Jews did keep their distance from the Chaldean *Weltanschauung*. In lieu of being treated as full-fledged divinities, heavenly bodies were demoted to the rank of *sign-manifestations*, *metaphors*, and *messengers* of the Lord whose will and wrath can override the lawful motions of heaven. Moreover, the literature reviewed above shows no consistent interest in the configurational mathematics of stellar geometry – hence, astrology as a full-fledged science. Although showing a preoccupation with adapting the astrological imagination to its own doctrinal needs, Judaism pays little attention to the laws of natural science, and even less to the deification of material spheres, forces bent on usurping the powers of the Highest in Heaven.

Astrology and Early Christianity

From the third century B.C.E. onwards, the Graeco-Latin world adapted and expanded Chaldean astralism by means of new astronomical findings and the philosophical developments of Stoic thought. Though less concerned with its mathematical aspects, ordinary people were amply exposed and attracted to star-worship and mythology following the invasion of Semitic, Persian, and Egyptian cults in Italy. The rational–scientific and strictly fatalistic implications of astralism did not appeal to the masses, but they did find favour with Greek thinkers and the ruling classes of Rome. After some critical reactions to the rise of sidereal fatalism and the demise of the Olympian pantheon, the 'learned theology' of Eastern mathematicians became the dominant creed of Greek and Latin noblemen and intellectuals, reaching its apogee during the first century of our era. The emperors of Rome adhered to its principles and patronized the profession, making every effort to control the political usages of astrological divination and harnessing the powers of Chaldean mathematics to their own rule. By the third century C.E., however, the Chaldean *Weltanschauung* was stripped of its rational–scientific assumptions, giving way to the cult of sun and emperor. Solar monotheism and mysticism were turned into state religion.

Greek mythology in the Republican era was anthropomorphic and somewhat anarchic, with an inclination to emphasize the dramatic and epic nature of life expressed in patriotic and legendary forms. By contrast, astralism propounded an orderly view of the cosmos ruled by empyrean forces and their imperial representatives – hence, the luminaries of heaven and the emperors of Rome. As in Greek mythology, the universe contin-ued to be populated by a host of gods. Although concerned with the rank-ordering of fabled heroes and the heavenly spheres, both the Chaldean and early Greek world-views were essentially polytheistic. But astralism could also take on monotheistic appearances, as attested by the rise of heliolatry in late antiquity. Third-century sun-priest emperors upheld astralism's lofty conception of gods and rulers reigning over the visible world, but they gave a new monotheistic twist to the older sidereal creed. Instead of paying attention to the combined activities of numerous stars and planets moving in heaven, solarism elevated the eternal and invincible sun-god above all other divinities, treating it as the source of all life and intelligence. As a result, solar mysticism de-emphasized the 'mathematically' calculable influences of interacting stars and planets and promoted notions of pro-phetic revelation and divine intervention to counter the rationalistic and fatalistic precepts of Graeco-Roman Stoicism.

In this general movement towards a loftier, monotheistic conception of Divine Will, Christianity went a step farther. To the early followers of Christ, God may be portrayed as a solar charioteer, or *Sol Invictus*, as on pre-Constantinian mosaics of the Old St Peter Shrine (Toynbee and Ward Perkins 1956: 71–5; Kirschbaum 1959: 34f.). Notwithstanding this symbol-ism, God is an immutable and immaterial Spirit that transcends all visible bodies, including the awesome spheres of heaven. The Almighty Father and his Son may be portrayed in the image of men or the sun, yet both of them rise well above the material world and the order of time. Unlike side-real naturalism, Judaeo-Christianity had in common with Platonic and Aristotelian idealisms the concept of a divine essence or Being governing the visible world from outside its limits, not from inside. Pagan religions thus erred in their propensity to worship God's creation instead of the Creator himself, as Philo once argued. Like other expressions of idolatry, astrology threatened the Judaeo-Christian conception of an omnipotent God ruling but never ruled by the heavenly spheres.

Combined with Stoic philosophy, the Chaldean faith in the star-gods brought radical transformations into Graeco-Latin culture and prepared the ground for solar mysticism, and then Christian logocentrism which tri-umphed over astral pantheism. Does this mean that Christianity did away with all expressions of heliolatry and star-worship? Not at all. Like most Church Fathers and rulers of medieval Europe, the Christian emperors of late Roman antiquity showed little tolerance towards non-Christian gods and polytheism in general. Still, some Christian rulers saw no problem in equating the Almighty God with the invincible and eternal sun-god Apollo. Although converted to Christianity, Constantine I (306–337) worshipped the Sun and proudly held the title Helios. 'With Constantius Chlorus (A.D. 305) there ascended the throne a solar dynasty which, connecting itself with Claudius II Gothicus, a votary of the worship of Apollo, professed to have *Sol Invictus* as its special protector and ancestor. Even the Christian emperors, Constantine and Constantius, did not altogether forget the pretensions which they could derive from so illustrious a descent, and the last pagan who occupied the throne of the Caesars, Julian the Apostate, has left us a discourse in which ... he justifies the adoration of the King Star, of whom he considered himself the spiritual son and heaven-sent champion' (Cumont 1960: 55). Given their adherence to solarism, emperors of the mid-fourth century (354–75) continued to use and fear the powers of sidereal divination, persecuting aristocrats deemed to have an imperial future and astrologers and their clients suspected of plotting against the throne.

Emperors translated their fears of subversive astrological predictons into ruthless campaigns against seditious diviners and their aristocratic clients. In 357, Constantius II imposed an empire-wide ban on all forms of divination. Prosecutions and punishments continued to be directed mostly against those suspected of treason, that is, divining the emperor's future and the identity of his successor with conspiratorial intent (Cramer n.d.: 2). While Julian 'the Apostate' (361–63) attempted to restore pagan cults in Rome, the Christian struggle against divination received imperial sanction under Jovian (363–4), Valentinian I (364–75), and especially Valens (364–78), resulting in a series of inquisitions, trials, and mass executions of possible successors to the throne, would-be conspirators, and their 'Chaldean' advisers. Later expressions of Christianity's opposition to divination would go far beyond the 'topical restrictions' of earlier politically motivated bans, to include a full and permanent rejection of astrology and related religions on essentially theological grounds. The execution of Priscillian in 385 by the order of Emperor Maximus, and later canonical declarations of the Council of Braga (560–5) condemning attributions of the zodiac to the patriarchs and to parts of the human body (melothesia), heralded an age of intolerance *vis-à-vis* overt expressions of pagan magic and rituals within the Church (Flint 1991: 94).[2]

Driven underground by a barrage of laws, many of which were included in the Theodosian and the Justinian codes, astrology vanished in the Latin west with the collapse of the western empire in the fifth century. In the Greek east, on the other hand, a surprisingly rich, though chiefly compilatory astrological literary activity flourished from the fourth into the sixth century. Of it Roman law took less and less cognizance, leaving the final battle against astrology to the Christian councils in whose canons the fight against all and every astrological theory and practice continued .... The prohibitions preserved in the Justinian Code expressed the final attitude of Roman Law towards astrology. They were to dominate European legal theory and practice in this matter for a thousand years to come. (Cramer 1954: 232)

The Middle Ages brought about the conversion of Rome to Christianity, the decline of the Mithraic cult to the sun, the fall of the Roman Empire in the West, and the rise of Constantinople as the new Rome of the Byzantine East. While Greek formulations of astralism and sidereal divination survived in Byzantine society, the early Middle Ages sounded the knell of astral religion throughout the Western world. Both the State and the Church repeatedly condemned its practice and forced it either to go underground or to find indirect means of expression, means divested from the cult of star-gods and the mathematics of Fate. Astralism *as a religion* never recovered from the blow inflicted by the Christian Church on ancient sidereal cults. Nor could astrological fatalism be used again to diminish the Christian faith in divine providence and a human being's freedom to obey or contravene the laws of God (Flint 1991: 20). Those who attempted to revive the art of astrology – the eighth-century Persian Stephanus Philosophus, to name just one – had to recognize from the start that stars were heavenly spheres manifesting God's will, not full-fledged divinities with powers of their own (Tester 1987: 95). Likewise, followers of Priscillian (fourth century) held that the main business of stars was to make God's will manifest to all those trained in the mysteries of astrological symbolism (Pingree 1993: 80).

Church Fathers and the ancient philosophers who inspired their world-view played an important role in bringing about the downfall of astrology. The third-century Neoplatonic writings of Plotinus were instrumental in discrediting astralism, using all the traditional arguments against *astrologia*. To these arguments Plotinus added a good dose of Aristotelian philosophy: human beings should never be denied what is properly theirs – namely, a soul that stands well above the physical world and is not subject to its heavenly laws. Through Saint Augustine, Plotinus's theory of the human spirit was to exert a considerable influence on mainstream Western philosophy. While initially attracted to the science of divination, Saint Augustine condemned the astral cult: stars cannot act on their own and should never be elevated above the Christian God. In his view, all those who contend that 'the stars determine what we shall do, or what good things we shall possess, or what evils we shall suffer, must be refused a hearing by all' (Augustine 1950: 143).

Augustine's rejection of astrology echoed Saint John Chrysostom's fourth-century sermons against horoscopal readings of Matthew's Bethlehem-star story (Matt. 2: 1–12). Jews and early Christians may have linked Jesus' birth with the fact that 'Jupiter and Saturn over a period of *eight months* were in conjunction three times in Pisces, the Hebrew zodiacal sign and the sign of the last days [and the new vernal equinox]. Later Jewish and Jewish–Christian astrologers could well have noted the significance: Jupiter, the 'star' that denoted kingship, was linked with Saturn, the 'star' that represented Israel (or Palestine). A derived meaning seems clear: In the last days a great king shall be born in Israel' (Charlesworth 1983, 1: 479–80). Augustine acknowledges that Jesus was born under a special star, yet the son of God was not born by the action of a permanent heavenly body. Rather, a special star played havoc with normal calculations of astrology, and did so because Christ was born, bearing witness to his nativity and the end of idolatry.

According to Prudentius, a fourth-century Latin Christian poet, the Magi were to be credited for having identified the irregular star as the Christ Child 'outshining the trains of the ancient stars.' They saw in the star, not a deity, but rather a sign confirming God's promise to Abraham that his offspring 'must one day be equal to the stars.'

The astrologer watching all night on a height in Chaldea felt his blood curdle with alarm when he saw that the Serpent had given place, the Lion taken to flight, the Crab drawn in his feet in a crippled row along his side, that the Bull was roaring in defeat, his horns broken, the constellation of the Goat, with his hair torn, fading away. Here slides off in retreat the boy with the Water Pot, there the Arrows, the Twins wander apart in flight, the false maiden deserts her silent wooers in the vault of heaven, and the other blazing orbs hanging in awful clouds have feared the new Morning Star. (*Apotheosis*, quoted in Flint 1991: 369)

The Christian theologian Origen (*c.* 185–*c.* 254), a contemporary of Plotinus's, was equally critical of astral causality: stars may be signs or living beings, but not causes. He also raised the issue of the precession of the equinoxes (arriving slightly earlier each year) as an objection against the zodiacal calculations of astrologers. Other Church Fathers such as Tertullian (*c.* 160–*c.* 220) and Epiphanius (315–403) opposed astral divination as a pagan practice undermining human freedom and the omnipotence of God, two central tenets of the Christian faith leading up to the final act of Judgment. Tertullian (and later Church Fathers such as Isidore, *c.* 560–636) suggested that astrology may have been allowed up until the time of Christ, but certainly not after: 'the Magi offered incense and myrrh and gold to the infant Lord as it were to mark the passing of this world's glories and rites, which Christ was to remove' (Tester 1987: 112; cf. 125). The same argument was to be taken up by later Christian theologians such as the influential Bede. As Charlesworth (1983, 1: 479) notes, the notion that early Christian Jews did not practise astrology and that the wise men must have been 'pagans' is still found in modern biblical scholarship.

Readers should bear in mind that the enforcement of State bans and Church prohibitions imposed on astrology has never been entirely successful. Early medieval references to kingly interests in astrological predictions and repeated conciliar condemnations of 'haruspices' (defined by Isidore as observers of the days and hours on which to do things) suggest that 'non-Christian astrologers were sought after and active in very many areas of Europe' (Flint 1991: 95; see also 97). In any case, the latter bans and canonical laws were never designed to silence astrology in all possible ways. Church strategy involved, not a simple repudiation of pagan naturalism, but rather a convoluted attempt to convert and subjugate competing cults, forcing them to serve the higher rule of God. As Cassirer (1963: 102) puts it, there are two ways of conquering the astrological world-view: 'the one consists in negating the *content* of this view; the other, in the attempt to clothe the content in a new *form* to give it a new methodological foundation.' The Church did both. As argued below, the language of stars was systematically subsumed under various facets of Church doctrine: these range from Christian lessons of anagogy, prochecy, and demonology (or angelology) to principles of euhemeristic history and 'natural' astrology.

The anagogical reappropriation of ancient astralism was achieved in part through the introduction of subsidiary solarism in Christianity. The combination of solarism and Christian idealism took various forms. As Cumont (1960) notes, theological idealism found its way in Oriental cults through the imagery of *Iupiter summus exsuperantissimus*: a Jupiter 'Most High' living in an ethereal world, sitting on his glorious throne placed above the vault of heaven. In this cosmogony the perceptible sun becomes a mere reflection or manifestation of an otherworldly luminary, an everlasting Light that would replace the sun come the End of time; so thought the Jews and Christians alike (Isa. 60: 19f.; Rev. 22: 22). 'From the luminary which gives us light was detached that universal "Reason," of which the Sun had hitherto been the focus, and the existence of another purely spiritual sun was postulated, which shone and reigned in the world of intelligence ... and to this were transferred the qualities which henceforth appeared incompatible with matter. We can follow this doctrinal evolution in the works of the Neo-Platonists, and discern its termination in the Mithraic speculations of Julian the Apostate. The "intelligent" Sun ... becomes the intermediary between the "intelligible" God ... and the visible universe' (Cumont 1960: 75).

Lunisolar metaphors in early Christian literature reflected Church rivalry with Neoplatonic, Mithraic, and imperial sun cults. Rahner's (1963) discussion of these polemical parallels goes a long way in showing the Christian 'transfiguration' of astralism, a 'definitive and uncompromising sublimation of all things on to the supernatural plane,' or 'sucking the milk out of the Gentiles,' so to speak. Although Helios is dethroned by God who dwells in what Origen calls 'the heaven of our heart,' figurative comparisons between sun and Christ and between moon and Church can still be found in the writings of Origen and Ambrose. In a similar vein, lunar Church interpretations of Saint John's sun-clothed woman standing on the moon (Rev. 12) are advanced by Methodius of Philipi, Augustine, and Anastasius Sinaita. While the Greek goddess Selene (alias Luna and Artemis) is merely a prefiguration of the Church, the moon evoked by John signifies the child-bearing and light-giving Church wedded to Christ, the Sun of Righteousness and true Apollo–Helios (Rahner 1963: 90–6, 102f., 115, 122, 136, 155f., 161–3, 169f.).

Given these metaphors of Hellenistic inspiration, a baptized Christian can be seen as an enlightened sun-child 'no longer under compulsion from the stars,' as Justin and Methodius used to think. By implication, the sorrows and life-giving pangs of the Mother Church can be assimilated to the periodical darkening and dying of the moon, partaking in the downfall of the Crucified sun and the night of our sublunary world. Year after year, however, the lunar Church gives birth to the sun Christ in December and moves on towards the fullest moon of Easter resurrection, a final restoration prefigured in the weekly Sun-Day celebrations and the monthly replenishments of the moon by the action of the sun. To the extent that it revolves around winter-solstitial and vernal-equinoctial events, the nativity and resurrection of Jesus born from the womb of the lunar Church is thus suggestive of 'one great sun mystery,' a symbolically rich cult where, to quote Origen, Helios and Selene 'carry out their stately dance for the salvation of the world' (in Rahner 1963: 111). Closely related connections between baptismal, dominical, and paschal events and the sun, morning star, and light appearing in the east are made explicit in the writings of Lactantius, Severianus of Gabala, Cyril of Jerusalem, Melito of Sardis, Ignatius, Augustine, Prudentius, Firmicus Maternus, Zeno of Verona, Paulinus of Nola, Jerome, and Clement of Alexandria (105, 108, 114f., 120–2, 124f., 132–5, 168–74). In later centuries, churches were designed and built in such ways as to face the rising sun. Solarism was so pervasive in early Christianity that Tertullian had to defend the Church against accusations of heliolatry: some, he says, 'mistake Sol for the Christian God because they have heard that in praying we turn towards the rising sun and because on the day of Sol we give ourselves over to joy' (quoted in Rahner 1963: 106).

Christian prophets and theologians found various ways of subjugating the older promises of solarism, including the blessings of a heavenly ascent. This was done through a bifurcation of the universe into two realms, the visible world and the great Beyond – hence, a division between the earth and sky and the spiritual heavens, or the lower world and the upper realm to which followers of God could ascend after death. Life on earth and life in heaven or hell were thus subject to different laws. In lieu of forming a hierarchically integrated cosmos, the universe comprised distinct realms operating interdependently yet differently: the visible, with its own rulers and rules, and the invisible, either hellish or heavenly, depending on one's behaviour before death.

Interestingly, iconographies of ancient and early medieval Christianity resorted to one of two strategies to represent the immaterial and immutable heavens. In some cases, realistic imageries of saints and spirits located above the sun, moon, stars, and clouds were used to signify the difference between the two realms. Other iconographies involved simplified versions of Hellenistic views of the sky, with God's permanent heaven being portrayed as yet another sphere or disc situated above the earth and the zodiacal or planetary firmament. The hand of God or an angel coming out of a segment of the disc could also be used to suggest an invitation to Christ's or humans' meritorious ascent to heaven (Grabar 1982).

We know that the triumph of Christianity brought about a reinstatement of the powers of human and divine will – hence, some measure of freedom vis-à-vis the determinations of life. While fatalism was a corollary of ancient astrology, a logical consequence that had to be circumvented in many different ways, the freedom to comply with God's commandments and the expectation of being rewarded or castigated for one's conduct on earth were central precepts of Christian theology and morality. Rewards and punishments received beyond the grave were to be assigned on the basis of merited requital. Criteria of worldly status or some ineluctable Fate unfolding without human intervention or divine Providence no longer held. With the support the Church eventually obtained from the rulers of Rome, the Christian struggle against state idolatry and its heavenly manifestations (catasterism, solarism, cosmic fatalism) thus gave way to a struggle for otherworldly redemption: people of all classes and nations were granted the same freedom to earn themselves an afterlife of eternal blessings in the world of above.

Although formulated differently, Christian hopes of a posthumous ascent to heaven were in keeping with older themes of solar resurrection and catasterism. Towards the end of the Roman Empire, blessed souls were no longer transformed into corporeal stars shining and moving in heaven. Instead they joined an immutable God dwelling in a spiritual heaven, beyond the vault whirling above the earth. While astral divinities led by the sun rule over motions of the material universe, the sunlike God lives in a world of eternal Forms unperturbed by events of history, an immaterial realm 'removed from all desires of the wicked lusts' (Firmicus Maternus, c. 354 C.E., quoted in Goodenough 1958: 181). By reducing astralism to mere metaphor, dressing faith in the afterlife in a new astronomical garb, as it were, men of the declining Empire managed to bridge the gap between religion and science. In doing so, however, philosophers of late antiquity showed that they were 'more concerned to make religious appropriation of science than to develop science itself.' To these men, 'the god ceases to be the old Venus or Dragon or Yahweh in this process and, beyond even physical determinism, becomes the immaterial unmoved Mover. Religion saves its faces, moves over into the age of the new science, as it learns to call the new force by the old name' (183).

The cult of astral gods was anathematized by Christianity. But the language and imagery of stars and planets never ceased to capture the Western imagination. The Dark Ages converted much of this language into lessons of allegory and sign-metaphor. In the next chapter, we shall see that the early Middle Ages saw the rise of spiritual exegesis in Church theology. This is a mode of interpretation whereby signs and visions of God are no longer understood teleologically, as foreknowledge of the future transmitted through prophetic revelation, but rather anagogically, as metaphors and allegories conveying principles of Christian faith. Church Fathers manipulated terms and concepts of astrological origin in such ways as to fit these new requirements of anagogical exegesis. In the writings of Victorinus, the Neoplatonic concept of the human soul originating from the ethereal heaven and receiving the influences of the seven planets along its journey to the earth thus became seven heavens with seven spirits forever subserving the invisible Lord. To Saint Ambrose, another Church Father of the fourth century, the heptad symbolized the seven deadly sins, and also the seven gifts or virtues of the Holy Spirit, beliefs that persisted well into the Middle Ages. Jerome (347–420), a theologian familiar with the writings of Aratus, read into John's 666 metaphor a Greek name (*Teitan*) standing for *Diclux*, the false sun in Latin – hence, Antichrist (Matter 1992: 40). In a similar metaphorical mode, Bede (*c.* 672–735) substituted the apostles for signs of the zodiac (with John the Baptist taking the place of Aquarius). Likewise, medieval theologians such as Bonaventure and Blasius Vegas saw in John's twelve-star imagery (Rev. 12) a zodiacal representation of the apostles. Bonaventure added that Revelation 12: 4–9 may have contained allegorical allusions to the battle of Virgo against Draco, using a stellar language to represent the conflict between Church and Antichrist.

It should be emphasized that the Church Fathers drew on much older traditions of moral-allegorical hermeneutics to reinterpret the meanings and implications of astral imageries and the prefigurative implications of Old Testament stories. Allegorical readings of dream material, prophetic signs, and narrative metaphors were by no means absent from inner exegeses of the Hebrew Bible and the Old Testament. Nor were they foreign to the language of Christian parables found in the New Testament. Likewise, Greek and Roman mythologies were full of personifications of abstract principles (Venus as Beauty, Minerva as Wisdom, etc.) and apologues containing lessons of tale-telling morality. Ancient mythologists availed themselves of similar methods when making sense of their narrative material. Figurative interpretations of mythology go as far back as Heraclitus's *Homeric Allegories* and Anaxagoras's spiritual reading of Homer's combats of the gods (*Iliad*, Book 20). Centuries later, Neoplatonists applied this search for the deeper spiritual meanings of sacred texts to a loftier understanding of Greek mythology and foreign religious traditions, convinced, as they were, that mythical characters were but 'magnificent metaphors – signs or steps along man's way to an understanding of the nature of divinity' (Seznec 1953: 86). Saint Augustine and Gregory of Tours warned Christians against the dangers of glorifying the moral lessons of pagan fables, yet allegorical modes of interpretation were adopted by most Church Fathers, including Tertullian, Cyprian, Origen, Saint Ambrose, and also Prudentius, the author of the influential *Psychomachia*, a text where virtues and vices are systematically personified. The sixth-century writings of Gregory the Great (*Moralia*) and Fulgentius (*Mythologiae*) are monuments to the spiritual-allegorical readings of biblical texts and pagan mythology, respectively.

Christianity recuperated the powers of astralism and solarism through metaphorical language and the hopes of a meritorious ascent to heaven. All the same, teleological concerns were by no means abandoned. Through revelation and prophecy, the Church salvaged from the ruins of astrology much of antiquity's pursuit of foreknowledge of human destiny. We have seen how the cult of sun and emperor in late antiquity undermined the 'mathematical' approach to divination, introducing mystical experiences and propitiatory rituals into the ancient arts of futurology. Christian spirituality went even farther in that it detached the prophetic experience from heliolatry, astralism, and other cultic expressions of naturalism. Faithful to their Judaic heritage, Christians elevated the realm of the wilful spirit above the material world and reinstated the ethics of freedom. But Christianity did all of this without relinquishing its claims to prophetic insights into future events.

Early Christians never thought of freedom as an absolute principle, a precept without limitations or inherent contradictions. Humans make their own destiny and God can intervene in the lifeworld. But Christians were certainly not about to forsake the powers of foreknowledge embodied in their own prophetic tradition. Logically, the two ideas – humans shaping their own future and knowing their destiny before it unfolds – are not easily reconciled. Notwithstanding this riddle that plagued theories of fatalism and free will alike, Christians called upon their own prophets to obtain insights into the future. Mystical visions could be obtained either directly from God or through the intermediation of God's signs and messengers sent from heaven, not from mathematical calculations of the combined activities of stars and planets following predictable movements in the sky. Divine revelation inspired by God was thus substituted for scientific divination.

Christianity did not simply suppress sidereal divination and astromythology. More strategically, it subsumed the language of astral naturalism, incorporating it within its own prophetic genre. This subsumption process implied a competitive or polemical relationship between the two predictive modes, each trying to show its superiority over the other and subordinate the rival language to its own cosmology. These polemical schemes are well illustrated by debates surrounding the predicted death date of the emperor Valens (328–378) at the end of antiquity. While legend has it that astrologers and conspirators successfully foretold his death through divination, Christians attributed a more accurate death prediction to Isaac of Constantinople, a prophecy apparently designed to discourage Valens from pursuing his Arian persecution of orthodox Christians. 'What the pagans laboriously obtained through astrological textbooks and astronomical observations, through complicated sacrifices and elaborate rites, was revealed to a loyal Christian by the simple means of divine inspiration alone' (Cramer n.d.). The Christian controversy regarding the Magi's role in announcing the birth of Jesus is another telling example. Although Augustine associated the Magi and their astrological lore with paganism, the ninth century witnessed their rehabilitation in Christianity, using their ancient knowledge and learning to bolster the powers of Christian prophecy (Flint 1991: 370–2).

The rejection of pagan divination did not mean that such knowledge was simply false. More to the point, visions of the future not inspired by God were condemned as sign-manifestations of evil spirits. As in the Old Testament (Deut. 18: 10–2; Num. 22: 4), foreknowledge based on sources other than God is demoted to secrets obtained by demon power, the heathenish counterpart of prophecy. Throughout late antiquity and the Middle Ages, leaders and followers of Christian orthodoxy did not dismiss divination as mere superstition, prophetic falsities inspired by idols that had no existence whatsoever. Rather, it was believed that pagan rituals could call upon and be answered by the idols themselves, spirits that were in reality demons posing as gods and parading their godlike powers in the sublunary heavens, typically inhabiting the middle portion of the air, well below the incorruptible heavens (as in Plato's *Timaeus*, 40–2; see Flint 1991: 102f.). Since demons were thought to act through stars and astrology, it was not uncommon for preachers to 'go about the countryside expelling "the demons Jupiter, Mercury," etc., from haunts where they have lingered' (Seznec 1953: 45). The powers of such demons were taken very seriously. Despite his struggle againt idolatry, Saint Benedict (*c.* 628–90) was fabled to have been tormented by a monstrous Apollo beast enraged for having been dislodged from his Monte Cassino shrine (Seznec 1953: 48).

In some cases satanic creatures of the sky could secure humans' allegiance by providing valid information about future events and causing these events actually to happen. If the event (e.g., a disease or a death) never happened, the demons could be interpreted as having intervened, responsive as they are to humans' cultic offerings and propitiatory actions. If the event came to pass despite ritual measures to prevent it, then the idol star-spirits had some reason to be angry. Actually, these spirits were so evil that they could produce false oracles with a view to misleading and causing misfortune to diviners and their credulous clients. In short, divinatory practices were prohibited, not because they were misplaced and unfounded, but rather because of the real demonic powers that kept these systems going.

Astrological cults were thus indirectly attested and preserved by Christianity. Astral symbolism of Graeco-Latin and Chaldean origin 'did not die out with idolatry: it was adopted by Christianity ... and up to the Middle Ages these symbols of the fallen gods were reproduced *ad infinitum* in sculpture, mosaics, and miniatures' (Cumont 1960: 62).

Although he rejected the notion that stars can cause human beings to act against their own free will, Augustine recognized that some astrological predictions proved to be correct. This was not because of humans' skilful insights into the future. Rather, the omens came true by sheer chance or the intervention of evil spirits promoting idolatry. 'When astrologers give very many wonderful answers, it is to be attributed to the occult inspiration of the spirits not of the best kind, whose care it is to insinuate into the minds of men, and to confirm in them, those false and noxious opinions concerning the fatal influence of the stars' (Augustine 1950: 151). Church Fathers such as Tertullian, Lactantius, and Augustine resorted indeed to the Platonic distinction between good and evil spirits to explain how some oracles, dreams, and prophecies (e.g., the Sibylline books) were inspired by God, while others could be obtained through pagan divination and idolatry (Bouché-Leclercq 1879: 92–103). This position is reminiscent of Paul's attitude *vis-à-vis* sacrificial feasts: 'Does this mean that the food sacrificed to idols has a real value, or that the idol itself is real? Not at all. It simply means that the sacrifices that they offer they sacrifice to demons who are not God' (1 Cor. 10: 19–20). In his *Divinatione daemonium*, Augustine teaches that demons have existed for many centuries and know a lot about past prophecies and future events. They understand supernatural forces and are capable of reading human minds, interpreting signs of things to come, and moving freely across space and time. They can also cause certain things to happen. Unlike true prophets, diviners make it a profession of tapping these spirits for special information, favours, and powers, thereby entering into 'commerce with the Devil.'

Astrology was turned into demonology. As Cassirer (1963: 99) notes: 'the Christian Middle Ages were able neither to dispense with astrology nor to completely overcome it. They adopted the astrological system, just as they tolerated and continued ancient pagan conceptions. The old gods lived on; but they were demoted to demons, to spirits of inferior ranks ... By virtue of this subjugation, astrology could remain undisturbed as a principle of worldly wisdom.' Stars provided the language needed to portray sign-appearances and agents of the will of God, angels, holy men (apostles, saints, patriarchs) translated to heaven, demons rising against God, or wrathful forces sent from above to punish evil human beings on earth. Unlike older star-gods, celestial forces could be mobilized with a view to bringing chaos into the world and the order of time – hence, playing havoc with God's eternal transients and bringing about the End. Unexpected calamities and blessings originating from the not-so-orderly heavens would thus bear witness to the powers of demons, the impact of God's wrath on his creation, or the Lord's Providential intervention in human affairs.

The Christian Church did not simply abandon the astral imagery. On the contrary, it redeployed the older star-gods by giving them a new twist, treating them as sign-manifestations of God or intermediary spirits (saints, angels, demons) dedicated to supporting or challenging his reign on earth and in heaven. When reinforcing the rule of God, stars and planets could be seen as heavenly sign-letters expressing the magnificence of God's creation. They could also be portrayed as souls in fiery bodies ruled by solar Helios and lunar Selene – subaltern spirits offering prayers to the Lord (see Origen, *On First Principles* 1.7; cf. Rahner 1963: 97). In lieu of fading out, paganism disappeared by vanishing into Christian culture and society (Tester 1987: 175).

Euhemerism was another strategy deployed by the Church to counter the religious formulations of ancient astrology. Although originally used as a polemical weapon against the Olympian divinities, the euhemeristic notion that the deeds and powers of star-gods were mythical accounts of real events attributable to great heroes allowed the stellar pantheon to survive the spread of Christianity. This conciliatory rhetoric had already been used by ancient Jewish writers of history such as Artapanus. In his historiographical glorification of Judaism, Artapanus explains Egyptians gods and the corresponding cults by reference to inventions useful to humanity, which is not to say that the superiority of Moses and the supremacy of Yahweh should ever be questioned (see Charlesworth 1983, 2: 893). Likewise, Church Fathers such as Eusebius, Paulus Orosius, Lactantius, and Isidore of Seville treat pagan gods as key actors in the unfolding of large-scale periods of world history; they represent kings, ancestors of civilization, teachers of humanity, and great heroes of the past worthy of veneration. 'The result was to restore dignity and independence to the personages of Fable; as benefactors of humanity they had every right to be held in grateful remembrance ... By gaining a foothold in history, the gods acquired new prestige' (Seznec 1953: 15).

Although Apollo and Mercury may have indulged in the practice of magic, they can still be viewed as good magicians who made vital contributions to the growth of human wisdom. Armed with this theory, medieval

Christianity converted Cepheus into Adam, Cassiopeia into Eve, zodiacal signs into the twelve patriarchs, Leo into Daniel, Cancer into Abraham, Aries into Job and the Christian Lamb. Similar interpretive tactics were picked up by later chroniclers and compilers of universal history. Scholars such as Ado of Vienne and Peter Comester felt they could place the humanized gods of pagan religions on the same footing as biblical characters and patriarchs of the Old Testament. The Renaissance continues this trend towards the translation of pagan mythology into worldly history, treating non-Christian gods as forerunners of civilization. Mercury was the first musician, Bacchus taught us how to make wine, and Atlas was the man who taught astrology to the Greeks. Peter d'Ailly saw the fabled gods of heavens as rulers whose names had been inherited by various parts of the world. In the late-fifteenth-century writings of Annius of Viterbo, Jupiter is still thought to have been an important king; likewise with Saturn, Caelus, Uranus, Apollo, Bacchus, and Osiris (Seznec 1953: 14–17, 21–2, 50f.).

Euhemerism also provided a foundation for the genealogical claims of late-medieval occupational groups (painters, writers, merchants, etc.) desirous to trace back their vocational activities to mythical heroes and planetary demigods governing their profession (Seznec 1953: 70). Similar genealogical rhetoric was used by aristocrats and people concerned with establishing their pedigree or their letters patent of individual or collective nobility. Pride of descent found a convenient mode of expression in 'ethnogenic fables' and quasi-supernatural genealogies that turned pagan gods into begetters of aristocratic families and 'noble races' of the Middle Ages. Merovingian scholars thus asserted that the Franks and the Romans were descendants of the Trojan Francus and the Trojan Aeneas, respectively. While the dukes of Burgundy saw themselves as descendants of Hercules or Gideon, Charles IX established genealogical connections between characters of fabled antiquity and the sixty-three sovereigns of his own line. Claims to genealogical fame found their way into the Vatican as well. Pope Alexander VI 'used the Borgia coat of arms as warrant for having the ceiling of his Vatican apartments decorated with frescoes representing the story of Isis, Osiris, and the monster Apis' (Seznec 1953: 26; cf. 19–22, 32, 35f., 137). Numerous pieces of art point to these claims of mythical ancestry that marked the European Renaissance and that culminated in the seventeenth-century adulation of worldly power celebrated at the Palace of Versailles.

Another factor that explains the Christian recuperation of astrology lies in the practical functions of stellar observations: travelling, agriculture, medicine, and the reckoning of time (Tester 1987: 126–9). Although clearly opposed to divination, Isidore (*De Natura Rerum*), and Bede (*De Temporum Ratione*) after him, emphasized the distinction between astronomy (laws of heavenly revolutions) and astrology (concerned with the powers of such movements). In keeping with the teachings of Augustine, Isidore made the 'natural' or scientific branch of astrology interchangeable with astronomy, a science acceptable to Christianity. Virtuous minds exercising self-discipline and lifting themselves to observations of the lofty heavens contributed to the teachings of asceticism and the development of a Christian science proper. Unlike sidereal augury, the latter science, known as natural astrology, could legitimately explore the effects of lunar influences (emphasized by Pliny), falling stars, and other heavenly motions on the livelihoods of farmers, travellers, and navigators; on health problems via the workings of the human body; on computations of monastic horarium and calendar feasts; and on the development of a liturgical music inspired by the numerical ratios of sounds, motions, and intervals of the celestial spheres (Flint 1991: 98, 130–2, 136–9). These legitimate applications of astrology lasted throughout the Middle Ages and well into the Renaissance: while Pope Julius II (1503–13) used astrological counsel to establish the date of his coronation, Pope Paul III (1543–9) relied on similar advice when fixing the hour of each consistory (Seznec 1953: 57). In the later Middle Ages, stellar representations (e.g., zodiacs adorning the stained glass of Christian churches) continue to convey time-reckoning significations that point to Church liturgy and the Lord's government over yearly time, as opposed to any infiltration of cultic astralism into Christian doctrine.

Through the influential writings and calendrical computations of Bede, the Church imposed the Dionysian calculation of years from the supposed date of the Incarnation. More significantly, the Church superimposed its own calendar on older agricultural and liturgical divisions of the year, ancient patterns inspired by agricultural and climatic cycles and related cults to the sun, the moon, the planets, and the fixed stars. This superimposition is still evident in the planetary nouns denoting the seven days of the week, astral terms borrowed from Hellenistic and oriental mythologies (notwithstanding early Christian attempts to impose a purely Christian terminology; Seznec 1953: 43). It is also evident in the case of Christmas, a Feast of Nativity echoing the rebirth of the sun at the time of the winter solstice. Heliolatry and related divination rituals were so popular throughout the third and fourth centuries that the Church decided to institute the Christian feast of Epiphany with a view to celebrating the Lord's birthday, thereby consciously co-opting the winter-solstitial 'new sun' celebrations into subserving the official creed. This was done in protest against the pagan solar celebrations of 6 January but also the Gnostic denials of the divinity of Jesus born of the Virgin Mary. With the Julian calendar reform, Jesus' birthday was eventually moved from 6 January to 25 December. The Epiphany was none the less preserved and became an event commemorating the baptismal birth of Jesus in Jordan and the manifestation of Christ to the Gentiles, represented by the Magi.

Easter (from *Eostre*, 'goddess of dawn') is an even more telling example as the actual timing of this chief Christian feast still depends on lunisolar calculations of pre-Christian origins: Easter is held on the first Sunday after the first full moon that coincides with, or comes after, the spring sun ascending above the equinox (taken as 21 March). In the ancient tradition of Asia Minor, the death of Christ was thought to have taken place on 14 Nisan, the day of the spring full moon and the Jewish Pasch (cf. Charlesworth 1983, 2: 837). The date was eventually modified by Constantine, following a long second- and third-century debate regarding the importance of celebrating Christ's resurrection on a vernal full-moon Sunday (Rahner 1963: 110f.).

In their own symbolic way, these events reveal a basic strategy in Western religious history: the subsumption of older calendars and cults salvaged and purified under the higher rule of Logos. As Rahner (1963: 150) puts it, Christian festivities 'served both to combat and consecrate the old Graeco-Roman feeling for the sun.' As a result, Western culture has become profoundly diaheliotropic, showing a constant propensity and sustained failure to turn away from the sun – an inherent tendency to denegate its own heliolatric origins.

The transmission of ancient knowledge through Church educational institutions is yet another factor accounting for the indirect preservation of astrological knowledge throughout the Middle Ages. Paradoxically, the education provided by the medieval Church did not preclude knowledge of astrology. Short of any other system of learning, the Church reproduced the late antique system of 'liberal art' education and considered that all forms of knowledge could be put to the service of true faith and add to our understanding of the Holy Writ, an assumption confirmed throughout this book. In the sixth century, the schooling system revolved around the seven liberal arts of Greek origin, with *astrologia* or *astronomia* as one of the 'freeman's arts' (in addition to Grammar, Rhetoric, Dialectic, Arithmetic, Geometry, and Music). Rudiments of astrology were learnt from the writings of Bede, but also from those of Macrobius, Isidore (565–636), and Cassiodorus (490–583). Charlemagne was taught principles of astrology by Alcuin, an influential theologian who made the court at Aachen a centre of great cultural revival. Although critical of astrology as a pagan activity, the Church introduced Christian students 'to the illicit subject of astrology. The idea, at least, of a potentially valid science of astrology was kept alive by the very authorities who condemned it' (Tester 1987: 126). While no substitute for visions revealed by God, some understanding of *astrologia* was thought to shed light on the insights of ancient lore, the nature and errors of idolatry, and the workings of God's creation. Astrology could assist the Church in understanding signs of the Lord's will appearing in heaven, and the powers of subordinate spirits acting on behalf or against the Lord.

To sum up, with Christianity stars are no longer empowered to make destiny, nor do they foretell a future that is inexorable and immutable, impervious to human action and divine Providence. The heavenly spheres are not, for all that, dismissed as mere bodies in the sky. As Flint points out,

tempered belief in the powers of the sun, moon, and stars, and in the influence of demons and angels, and Christian invocation of, and control over, storms and rains and pestilences, came to seem to these others an excellent way of combating the prevalence and popularity of the non-Christian earthly magic purveyed by conjurers and witch doctors and necromancers, love charms and potions, spells and the powers of the dead. And there was, in addition, a great deal in the content of the magic of the heavens that was of itself attractive and could be rendered at least inoffensive and perhaps again helpful to Christians. This was plundered with more eagerness than we have always understood. (1991: 128)

Although anathematized, elements of astrology continue to be transmitted by the Church through its liberal-art education system. Astrology is disassembled and recuperated in such ways as to provide Christianity the language needed to talk about: (a) anagogical representations of constant principles (promises of heavenly resurrection, the sun-likeness of God, etc.); (b) prophetic sign-manifestations of future events willed by the Lord; (c) subordinate spirits and demigods subserving or challenging the reign of God; (d) measurable alternations of time decreed by God and guaranteed by his solar pact with Noah and his faithful descendants; and (e) the practical effects of astral motions on climate, agriculture, human health, and so on. In lieu of being worshipped as full-fledged divinities governing the order of time, the sun, the stars, and the planets are turned into moral symbols, contested signs, visible spirits, and time-regulating bodies moving between mortals on earth and God enthroned above the vault of heaven.

The Christian attitude towards astrology, a cultic idiom anathematized and recuperated all at once, was symptomatic of profound religious and political transformations that were occurring in the Latin West towards the end of antiquity. But the Christian response to siderealism was by no means new. Actually much of the argument I have just made regarding the Christian Roman treatment of signs of 'primitive astronomy' applies to earlier New Testament writings and to the Jewish world-view as well, issues to which we shall later return.

From the Middle Ages to the Renaissance

The influential handbook entitled *Mathesis* is the last important astrological manual to have appeared before the fall of the Roman Empire in the West. It was written by Firmicus Maternus, a Christian and Neoplatonist prose writer during Constantine's reign. Throughout the four or five centuries that followed, few manuals and masters of the art were available to transmit Greek knowledge in the field. Firmicus's text and other manuscripts of late Greek astrology did not emerge from obscurity and start circulating widely again until the twelfth century. This was a time when Western scholars and philosophers had long ceased ranking astral bodies on par with God and craved a better understanding of the Aristotelian, Stoic, and Neoplatonic world-view of early Christendom. The growth of Church education, sciences, philosophy, and scholasticism from the ninth century onwards, coupled with monastic (especially Benedictine) concessions to magical beliefs of the countryside (Flint 1991: 145), prepared the ground for a revival of an *astrologia* adjusted to the requirements of a firmly established Christianity no longer at war with paganism.

Given the scarcity of textbooks in astrology, it was through Latin, Hebrew, and Jewish-Spanish translations of Arab versions of late Greek writings (e.g., those of Firmicus Maternus) that astrology re-entered the liberal-art teachings of the High Middle Ages (Beer 1971; Pingree 1990, 1993: 83). Although eventually translated directly from Greek, the Alexandrian science first reached the West from the Muslim lands of Spain and Sicily, preserved, as it had been, by Arabs whose understanding of the heavens had gone through Persia, and perhaps India. It was thus 'late Greek astrology, from the first four or five centuries of our era, coloured by its passage through Persian and, to a lesser extent, Indian hands, which most filled the minds of medieval astrologers, and only rather less the restrained art of Ptolemy's *Tetrabiblos*' (Tester 1987: 168).

An exchange of tracts between the Emperor Manuel Commenus and a monk by the name of Michael Glycas is revealing of a new trend in Western religious thinking developing around the twelfth century. The emperor was of the opinion that the Christian doctrine could be reconciled with a soft, despiritualized version of astrology. He claimed that astral influences were real and that they point to the lawful operations of God's universe, but without the stars being alive, acting as causes of earthly events, or showing a will of their own. Signs of God's natural works and of his intervention in human affairs – for example, a star and an eclipse marking the birth and death of Jesus, respectively – were thus to be taken seriously. There is no reason for the astrological practice not to receive the recognition that is granted to medicine, two disciplines bound together since Graeco-Roman antiquity. Glycas thought differently. In his view, knowledge of the future can be obtained from God only. It cannot be attained through humans' mastery of an astrological science that transforms heavenly signs into living causes and undermines humans' freedom and accountability before God (Tester 1987: 96f.).

While rehashing the familiar polemics regarding stellar divination in a Christian perspective, the incident points to a softening of Church attitudes *vis-à-vis* the pagan art. A letter written by Berthold of Regensburg in the year 1270 sums ups the Church's attitude to astrology: the stars may have been empowered by God to rule over the visible world (weather phenomena, human sicknesses, etc.) but not over a human being's free will, let alone his or her soul. Although widely accepted and in keeping with basic tenets of Christian doctrine, this opinion was essentially two-sided, allowing a variety of attitudes regarding the actual practice of astrology, ranging from 'more or less full acceptance to a qualified rejection' (Tester 1987: 178). Two issues were particularly controversial: whether heavenly bodies will actually cause physical events to occur (as opposed to merely signifying them), and whether judicial astrology (genethlialogy, interrogations, elections) will permit humans to predict or prevent events caused or signified by the heavenly spheres. Negative answers to the latter question were voiced by John of Salisbury (Bishop of Chartres, d. 1180), Oresme (Bishop of Lisieux, d. 1382), and Peter d'Ailly (Archbishop of Cambrai, d. 1420), to name just a few.

Notwithstanding the variety and frequent ambiguities of responses to these questions, very few questioned the validity and usefulness of astrology or astronomy; these two terms were used interchangeably, as the science of heavenly motions could hardly be separated from its practical applications. Those who thought it to be incompatible with their faith in divine Providence and a human being's free will could still encourage Catholics and theologians to acquire a good understanding of the Alexandrian science, if only to gain a better understanding of the Scriptures and the errors of all fatalistic conceptions of the human condition. This was the recommendation put forward by Thomas Bradwardine, Archbishop of Canterbury, in the first half of the fourteenth century. While Peter d'Ailly conceded that heavenly motions may alter the atmosphere, and human behaviour as well, Oresme granted that stars may incline humans to behave in certain ways and affect their fortunes. Astrology can therefore serve noble ends: 'to know great matters; to learn of the Creator; and, less important, to ascertain certain dispositions of this lower and corruptible nature, whether present or to come' (Tester 1987: 198).

Aristotelian philosophy made a crucial contribution to this medieval squaring of the circle – combining concepts of astral influence, free will, and divine Providence. While early medieval philosophy was predominantly Neoplatonic and Augustinian, a new philosophical trend emerged in the twelfth century with the rediscovery of Aristotle. By the thirteenth century, influential theologians such as Bonaventure and Aquinas had become adepts of the Aristotelian world-view. Unlike the Stoics and the Neoplatonists, who had a highly integrated view of the cosmos, Aristotle argued that laws that govern souls, spirits, and the heavens differ radically from those that apply to the sublunary world. The latter phenomena, which include a human being's physical make-up, are affected by motions of the stars and are subject to astral influences. Given the distinctiveness of sublunary physics, philosophers and theologians could use *astrologia* in a broad range of legitimate scientific pursuits, such as medicine, meteorology, alchemy, and divination, without ever denying the omnipotence of God or the human being's exercise of free will and his accountability to the Lord. Since the human soul and body are intertwined, stars may be said to incline humans to choose certain courses of action but without ever forcing them to obey the laws of Necessity. In short, stars incline and impel; they do not compel. Given the powers of free will that God has granted to humans, and God's miraculous interventions in human history, 'the astrologer only claimed to identify tendencies in his client's disposition; he could not tell whether or not he would succumb to them' (Thomas 1971: 335f.).

In addition to its scientific implications, an Aristotelian approach to astrology was conducive to a reflection on the Christian sense of morality and free will – hence, humans' triumph over the forces of nature and related inclinations of carnal desire. For instance, Arnold of Villanova (d. 1313) was of the opinion that, while the heavenly spheres dispose humans to behave in certain ways, the wise person will make every effort actually to master the stars. This ideal of a human being's spiritual emancipation from our astrologically dominated world is reminiscent of Paul's critique of people's enslavement to false gods and the 'elemental principles of this world' (Gal. 4: 3, 9). It reproduces Tatian's second-century notion that 'we are exalted above the fate, and in place of the planetary daemons, we know but one ruler of the world, and him immovable' (quoted in Rahner 1963: 94). It also echoes the teachings of Bardesanes, a Syrian Christian scholar of the second and third centuries C.E. (154–222) who thought that 'the stars govern only the elemental world, leaving the soul free to choose' (Pingree 1993: 80).

By and large, Thomas Aquinas was also willing to concede to the science of astrology everything that was compatible with Christian theology and the sublunary physics of Aristotelian philosophy. In his *Summa Theologica*, Aquinas suggests that 'very many men follow their passions, which are motions of the sensitive appetite, alongside which passions the heavenly bodies can work; few men are wise enough to resist passions of this kind. And therefore astrologers, as in many things, can make true predictions, and this especially in general; not however in particular, for nothing stops any man from resisting his passions by his free will. Therefore the astrologers themselves say that "the wise man is master of the stars" (*sapiens homo dominatur astris*), inasmuch as he is master of his passions' (quoted in Tester 1987: 181). In the later words of Pierre de Ronsard (1524–1585), 'Les Estoiles adonc seules se firent dames de tous les corps humains, et non pas de nos âmes' (*Hymnes des astres*). The same theme of humans being called upon to triumph over the passions of sublunary physics can be found in the *Divine Comedy* (1308–20), a work whose author had assigned sciences of the Trivium and the Quadrivium to influences of the seven planetary spheres (*Convivio* 2: xiv). Jewish doctrine differed little in this regard: Abraham ibn Ezra and Abraham ben David of Posquières taught that true faith and purity of soul could result in Yahweh's overruling fate dictated by the heavens (Altman 1971).

Christian appropriations of astrology precluded rigid formulations of naturally ordained destinies that would remove guilt and moral responsibility from human behaviour. The medieval Church saw little problem in the natural side of astrology, or the agricultural and medical applications of the art. By contrast, theologians exercised greater control over applications that dealt with human behaviour, and therefore the realm of morality and the soul. As Thomas (1971: 361) notes, they 'saw greater danger in an exact social science that they did in a natural one.' While astrology enhanced the exercise of freedom by offering a choice between inclinations of the body and struggles of the soul, it also furnished potential explanations and justifications for humans' immoral conduct.

In *King Lear* (act I, scene ii), a weighty exchange of words between Edmund and Edgar captures the latter tension between faith in human morality and fate governed by the stars. Mortals have every reason to fear the deleterious effects of eclipses in the sun and the moon on the bonds of kith and kin. However, to use the sardonic words of the bastard son to the Earl of Gloucester,

This is the excellent foppery of the world, that, when we are sick in fortune, – often the surfeit of our own behaviour, – we make guilty of our disasters the sun, the moon, and the stars: as if we were villains by necessity; fools by heavenly compulsion; knaves, thieves, and treachers by spherical predominance; drunkards, liars, and adulterers, by an enforced obedience of planetary influence; and all that we are evil in, by a divine thrusting on: an admirable evasion of whoremaster man, to lay his goatish disposition to the charge of a star! My father compounded with my mother under the dragon's tail; and my nativity was under *Ursa major*; so that it follows, I am, rough and lecherous. 'Sfoot! I should have been that I am, had the maidenliest star in the firmament twinkled on my bastardizing. Edgar —— [*Enter* Edgar] and pat he comes, like the catastrophe of the old comedy: my cue is villanous melancholy, with a sigh like Tom o' Bellam, O, these eclipses do portend these divisions! *Fa, sol, la, mi.*

In reply to Edgar's inquiry about his brother's meditative mood, Edmund says that he is pondering the predicted consequences of an imminent eclipse.

I promise you, the effects he writes of succeed unhappily; as of unnaturalness between the child and the parent; death, dearth, dissolutions of ancient amities; divisions in state; menaces and maledictions against king and nobles; needless diffidences, banishment of friends, dissipations of cohorts, nuptial breaches, and I know not what.

Edg. How long have you been a sectary astronomical?

Although full of riddles and tensions, the reconciliation of astrology with Christian theology and ethics was generally successful. By the early fourteenth century, princes, bishops, and popes had astrological counsellors in their immediate surroundings. Some of these advisers exceeded the licit powers granted to them and were severely punished for it. By order of the Inquisition, an astrologer at the court of Florence (Cecco d'Ascoli) was burnt at the stake in 1327 for his application of astrology to the birth and death of Christ and the coming of Antichrist, as if Necessity could rule the life of the Son of God and the world's future.

Notwithstanding these expressions of heresy, late-medieval astrology was an eminently practical activity, a science that served many functions and that did not offend the Church. Knowledge of heavenly motions was put to the service of cartography, navigation, and agriculture. It was used to mark time, to predict weather, to cast natal charts, and to identify the proper time for undertaking all sorts of activities. It provided the knowledge needed to alchemize metals and also to diagnose, forecast, and treat individual illnesses and large-scale diseases such as the Black Death of the 1340s (thought to have been caused by the heavenly conjunction of three planets).

In different countries of Europe, almanacs were essential instruments of medical practice; astronomical tables had to be produced for medical purposes by university professors up until the late eighteenth century. Astral divination and science were such close companions that even Francis Bacon (1561–1626), the arch-prophet of the modern natural sciences, considered that an inductively verified astrology could play its role in predicting 'meteors, inundations, drought, heats, frosts, earthquakes, fiery eruptions, winds, great rains, the seasons of the year, plagues, epidemics, diseases, plenty, famine, wars, sedition, sects, transmigration of people; and all commotions or great innovations of things natural and civil' (quoted in Tester 1987: 222).

Although an age of great scientific discoveries, the Renaissance did not eradicate all forms of knowledge later to be branded as illogical and unscientific. Actually the Renaissance pursuit of worldly culture made astrology more attractive than ever (Cassirer 1963: 100). At first, rational conceptions of the universe highlighted the primary role of the heavenly spheres in regulating the sublunary motions of time; semi-divine cosmocrators of antique and barbaric origins were instrumental in promoting the higher rule and primordial decrees of the eternal God. Telling examples of this syncretic imagery include zodiacal representations of Renaissance Vatican art, the art work of Agostino's Chigi's Farnesina palace and the cupola of his tomb, and sidereal demigods appearing in the fifteenth-century fresco cycles of the Palazzo della Ragione in Padua and the Palazzo Schifanio in Ferrara (Seznec 1953: 76–82).

But it is mostly the practical and empirical claims of astrology that preserved the art of ancient *mathematica* against a premature death. If anything, the seventeenth century witnessed the apogee of sidereal divination. The latter science was so useful as to offer foreknowledge of the future, but also countless measures to prevent impending misfortunes and related explanations for predictions that never came true; as with God's miracles, humans' wilful interventions could alter the course of individual and collective histories and 'frustrate the portents of Heaven.' Astrology was a form of knowledge that provided explanations for all aspects of life, reflecting, as it did, a theory of macrocosm and microcosm inherited from Neoplatonism, passed on to the Middle Ages via the teachings of Boethius (c. 480–524), and then expanded through the twelfth-century writings of Bernard of Tours and the encyclopedic literature of medieval scholasticism.

Melothesia was a telling illustration of how humans were connected to the heavens and the universe. Representations of zodiacal constellations distributed over parts of the body were commonly engraved on calendars and prayer-books of the late Middle Ages and the Renaissance. This imagery can be found on a page of the *Très Riches Heures* of the Duc de Berry. Astrological thinking yielded microcosm pictures of the planets mapped on to the human body or the seven orifices (ears, eyes, nostrils, mouth) of a person's circular, firmament-like head. Apart from their medical implications, visual representations of melothesia suggested that human beings were inevitably 'tied' to influences of the heavenly spheres. This is true of late-medieval miniatures that show different parts of a human puppet-like body pierced by linear rays stemming from planets and constellations of the zodiac (Seznec 1953: 63–8).

European aspirations to a systematic understanding of manifestations of *natural order and causality* in the universe resulted in the formulation of all sorts of predictable connections, as between city horoscopes and urban fires, seasons and suicide rates, star-governed weather phenomena and the economics of harvest, famine, and rebellion. In their own way, these 'speculative thoughts' were rationalistic prefigurations of later developments in the natural and the social sciences, including history, psychology, and sociology, as acknowledged by Comte (Thomas 1971: 324–37). The astrological *scientia universalis* took it upon itself to develop, among other things, a complete understanding of periods of history and an exhaustive system of human typology, mustering all available erudition 'to build an artificial edifice out of disparate elements ... chosen from the immense reservoir of pagan or Christian antiquity' (Seznec 1953: 287). The knowledge thus constructed was such an influential force in society that it could occasionally generate predictions that came true by virtue of humans' faith in their veracity. As William Fulke argued in 1560, to predict a famine was to encourage farmers to hoard foodstuffs, thereby creating scarcity, price inflation, and the probability of famine.

In the seventeenth century astrology thus continued to be applied in many different ways:

First, it sheweth us the causes of the admirable dissimilitude, not only as concerning regions, but touching the wits of men and their manners, under diverse climates. Secondly, it remonstrateth what is the cause, that so great diversity ariseth. Thirdly, what destinies or events at certain times are like to fall upon countries, being called Judicial Astrology. Fourthly, it foretelleth the variable state of the air, and other elements at every moment. Fifthly, it telleth us the happy or unhappy increase of fruits, be it corn, wine, oil, or whatsoever else the earth bringeth forth: which was experimented by Thales; who, foreknowing a dearth to come, kept in his fruits, and sold them at an high rate. Sixthly, wars, famine, unusual drought, inundations, death of cattle, changes of kingdoms, destructions of princes, and so forth. Seventhly, what times are fit to sow, plant, or to do any other thing appertaining to the art of husbandry. Eighthly, it giveth much light to those who profess physic, take upon them to be pilots, discoverers of countries and kingdoms, or will gain them any knowledge in the art apodemical. Ninthly, from this science are made prognostications and ephemerides, needful for all sorts of men. Last of all, it sheweth us the temperature of all kinds of individuous, all kinds of hourly, daily, weekly, monthly, yearly dispositures, alterations and inclinations. (William Ingpen, *The Secrets of Numbers*, quoted in Thomas 1971: 323)

The applications of astrology listed above involved predictions affecting entire populations. This collective approach to issues of fate was to fade away with modern reformulations of astrology. Present-day horoscopy is more concerned with personality attributions and individual hopes than with national profiles and large-scale prospects of human history. But late-medieval and Renaissance clients and practitioners of the art were also bent on seeking answers to individual concerns. As Thomas (1971: 307, 315–18) shows, astrologers of the seventeenth century dealt with all sorts of personal problems, including issues of health, lost property, the whereabouts of missing persons, business and journey prospects, not to mention a host of delicate family problems such as identifying a child's true father or probing the sentiments or wealth of a potential spouse.

Astrology served yet another crucial function, one that ties in directly with the central topic of this book: visions and warnings of the Apocalypse. In the eyes of medieval astrologers, events observed in the sky could be read as signs of the hereafter unfolding according to laws of the sublunary world. But they could also be interpreted as *teleological signs* heralding the last day – hence, the order of time and the universe coming to a final end, as foretold by Saint John in the New Testament. The sky differed little from Revelation in that it too could be read as a divine book, a many-layered script inspired and ruled by the Verb, providing insights into future history.

One event that heralded the rise of *eschatological astrology*, a discourse that was to mark medieval religious politics from the twelfth century until the Renaissance, is the double eclipse and conjunction of all the planets in Libra announced for the year 1186. Prior to the event, a series of prognostications were made by a number of influential astrologers stationed mostly in the Islamic world of Spain and Sicily.

According to one there were going to be great natural and political disasters, to the benefit of the Franks and the discomfiture of the Saracens, with the generations after the calamity living a much fuller life ... Then there was William's, a clerk of the Constable of Cheater, who reckoned that a great Christian prince was to rise, who should also be 'numbered among the prophets,' because Jupiter signified prophecy; but since England too would suffer from this conjunction, 'since as every astrologer knows, this region is under Saturn, and the Moon is with him ... there is but one remedy, that the king and the nobles should take this counsel, serve God and flee from the devil, so that the Lord may turn aside these threatened punishments.' (Tester 1987: 149)

Cecco d'Ascoli is only one of many medieval theologians and philosophers who saw in astrology a means of divining the future of Christendom, deploying astrological wisdom to cast light on the timing of John's prophecies and related scenes of the Final Judgment. Even Bacon recognized 'the possibility of foretelling when Antichrist would come' (Tester 1987: 180).

This eschatological approach to astrology implied a rather strange amalgamation of prophecy and divination, two perspectives that early Christianity had found difficult to reconcile. In the next chapter we shall see that exegetic readings of Revelation developed by Church Fathers in late antiquity and the early Middle Ages eschewed the teleological or millenarian mode of interpretation, preferring instead an anagogic strategy, an understanding of the Scriptures that looked for allegorical sign-manifestations of the timeless principles of Christian spirituality. However, exegetic approaches to the apocalyptic literature started to shift in the eleventh and twelfth centuries as new monastic movements challenged the established order of State and Church. These movements sought to renew Church institutions from inside and were later followed by pressures to reform the Church outside the confines of Catholicism. Anxieties regarding *the future outcome* of struggles against Church corruption was a critical factor in the revival of astrology and many old forms of divination. Far from being caught up into a past that showed little concern for 'progress,' medieval Europe was literally obsessed with divining the future, using human free will and reason to transcend the forces of nature and related dispositions of visible bodies, towards profound transformations of Church institutions and human history.

The religious and political troubles of Germany experienced around 1524, a year marked by the conjunction of all planets in Pisces, were particularly conducive to the proliferation of apocalyptic prophecies couched in the astrological language. Actually the sixteenth and seventeenth centuries are full of examples of how the art could be applied to polemical predictions of political events and large-scale historical prospects, including the death of a king and the downfall of Rome, Presbyterianism, or the English monarchy. In England, successive governments thus 'displayed keen interest in the activities of contemporary astrologers, and did not hesitate to censor their texts, prohibit their publications, and call them to account for their activities. Tudor printers, booksellers and almanac-makers were frequently in trouble when their forecasts were thought to have over-stepped the mark' (Thomas 1971: 344). Some astrologers of the fifteenth century were executed because of their calculations of the ruling monarch's death date. All rulers of the Tudor dynasty had to face somber astrological predictions advanced by dissident groups who were hopeful that such forecasts would be accurate if only because of their impact on human courses of action. But the rhetoric of astrology was not used by dissident groups alone. For instance, it was generously exploited by both sides in the 'Great Rebellion' of the 1640s, a conflict triggered by parliamentary and middle-class Puritanical opposition to the Stuarts' claims to rule by divine right (Thomas 1971: 299, 325f., 342–8).

While eschatologically minded, medieval and Renaissance Europe persisted in using the anagogical methods of interpretation inherited from Augustinian theology. The medieval Church was clearly opposed to fatalistic conceptions of judicial astrology, yet this did not mean that sidereal imageries could not serve useful purposes, such as applying heavenly metaphors to lessons of the Scriptures. As with early Christian treatments of astromythology, allegorical lessons *à la* Fulgentius could be salvaged from the ruins of judicial astrology. Throughout the Middle Ages anagogy has been a standard interpretive instrument applied to exegeses of ancient myths and sacred texts. In the twelfth century the *Metamorphoses* of Ovid were thus reinterpreted in such ways as to serve the cause of sacred truth. It was also in this period that 'Alexander Neckam related the gods to those virtues which, according to Saint Augustine, had prepared man by degrees for Christian wisdom; that William of Conches, in his commentary on Boethius' *Consolation of Philosophy*, interpreted Eurydice as the innate concupiscence of the human heart and the giants as our bodies, formed of primeval slime, which are in constant rebellion against the soul, Jupiter' (Seznec 1953: 91). Three centuries later, Ficino and the quattrocento Platonists were still making abundant use of anagogy to extract scriptural meanings from mythical texts. It was as if all religious traditions converged on the teachings of Christ, if only by way of allegory and prefiguration. Florentine art of the late fifteenth century produced masterpieces of allegorical representations, among which Botticelli's three Venuses and his Pallas. The sixteenth-century infatuation of scholars with the science of hieroglyphs, cryptograms, and mythical emblems had religious didactic overtones as well (Seznec 1953: 97–105, 112–19).

Allegorical thinking lent itself to an eclectic amalgamation of motifs and imageries borrowed from many different sources, Christian and non-Christian alike. In late-medieval and Renaissance Europe, planetary gods continue to be identified with the Olympians, but with such interpretive freedom that Venus could easily be turned into Eve, Perseus into Saint George, Saturn into God the Father, and Marduk Jupiter into one of the evangelists or a monk holding a chalice. Armed with the anagogical method, Christian mythologists could turn Cupid into the Angel of Annunciation, or Minerva into the Virgin Mary. Mercury could be represented as an ecclesiastical dignitary, a portrayal harking back to the divine Nebo, the Babylonian scribe. Many descriptions and illustrations of the gods thus ended up betraying oriental influences. A case in point is Michael Scot's mid-thirteenth-century astrological treatise composed for Emperor Frederick II. Through moral-allegorical commentaries, the treatise attempts to reconcile Islam and Christianity. It reinterprets elements selectively borrowed from various texts, including an influential medieval manual of astral magic entitled *Picatrix*, a Latin translation of a tenth-century Arab manuscript (*Ghâya*) of oriental and Hellenistic inspiration.

While containing some elements drawn from the classical authors, allegorical treatises on the gods reflected most of all the writings of medieval mythographers and scholiasts, describing and reproducing other descriptions and reproductions of older texts. The end-result was a bookish and baroque compilation of mythological descriptions and glosses betraying a mixed and uneven erudition. Fourteenth-century illustrations of this intellectual eclecticism can be found in the anonymous *Libellus de imaginibus deorum*, John Ridewall's *Fulgentius metaforalis*, and Boccaccio's *Genealogy of the Gods*. In Boccaccio's work, the same myth can be explained in various ways: Perseus's heavenly ascent may have been a true event (euhemerism), a symbol of human ascent to virtue, or a mythical reformulation of Christ's ascent to his Father. Late-medieval minds revelled in a cosmopolitan carnival of deities, committed, as they were, to syncretic mélanges of imageries derived from different intellectual and spiritual traditions. 'Just as the illustrator of the *Libellus* composed his Apollo out of extracts from Servius, Lactantius Placidus, Fulgentius, Martianus, or Isidore, so Zaltieri assembles the *membra disiecta* of the immortals, and combines them as best he can into awkward and baroque shapes' (Seznec 1953: 255).

Christian reappropriations of foreign mythologies served various functions. As in the educational program of the sixteenth-century Jesuits, 'pagan letters' fulfilled a moral-allegorical role and could be used didacticly, making the invisible visible – a true challenge in the Judaeo-Christian tradition. Allegorical reinterpretations of ancient fables meant also that threats of pagan heresy and Church censorship could be countered at a single stroke (Seznec 1953: 156–62, 167–8, 178, 220–3, 269–75).

The practical, eschatological, and allegorical applications of astrological imagery were central ingredients of late-medieval and Renaissance culture. Throughout the sixteenth and seventeenth centuries, astrology continued to be supported by merchants, artists, intellectuals, aristocrats, and members of the clergy as well. While a good proportion of William Lilly's mid-seventeenth-century clients comprised domestic servants and seamen, clergymen and Englishmen of 'social distinction' also had recourse to his services (Thomas 1971: 292, 301, 319–22, 380). Astrology found favour in Rome with all popes of the first half of the sixteenth century (Julius I, Leo X, Clement VII, Paul III), in England with Elizabeth I, and in France with Catherine de Médicis (counselled by Nostradamus) and Louis XIV. With the invention of printing, astrology reached a public wider than ever before and was put to all sorts of day-to-day uses: deciding when to plant a field, build a church, undertake a journey, launch a battle, celebrate a marriage, bleed an animal or a patient, have sex, and so on. Almanacs that included astrological prescriptions of the latter kind, together with weather information (derived from the day of the week that marked the beginning of the year) and larger-scale prognostications (based on readings of comets, planetary conjunctions, and eclipses, such as on the Black Monday of 29 March

1652), were printed by the millions. By the mid-seventeenth century, numerous handbooks describing the practice started to be published in English (Thomas 1971: 294–9, 304).

The Renaissance none the less propelled the West into a new era, releasing European culture from the hegemony of Church institutions. It allowed scholars to probe and master nature in ways that lay the ground for modern culture, science, and industry. Paradoxically, the Renaissance did all of this by gradually abandoning medieval preoccupations with the future and final ends of humanity, reverting instead to the classical values inspired by the ancients. The spread of humanism, aestheticism, and rationalism involved a radical shift of interest, from visions of the future to an investigation of root forms and first principles: the origins and laws that lay the foundations of all things. This progressive search for new beginnings led scientists and scholars to establish clearer distinctions between the physical world and the realm of the spirit, philosophy and religion, natural sciences and metaphysics – astronomy and astrology. To these distinctions can be traced back the downfall of the 'science of astrology,' a development that becomes apparent mostly towards the end of the seventeenth century.

A practical distinction between astrology and astronomy, the two components of Chaldean mathematics, emerged from medieval universities, paving the way to a fuller separation that was to mark the late Renaissance and the whole of modernity. Peter Abelard (1079–1142) and Saint Victor (1097–1141) had already defined astronomy's subject-matter as the laws of stars (positions, motions, cycles), as opposed to astrology, which is *discourse about* the stars. The latter discourse is said to be 'natural' when dealing with heavenly influences on weather, the earth, and the human body, but superstitious when applied to events that fall under human control (Tester 1987: 143f.). While these definitions implied a critique of the anti-Christian usages of 'mathematics,' they reaffirmed the compatibility between astronomy and legitimate forms of astrology. Sidereal divination was acceptable as long as it was applied exclusively to sublunary physics governed by natural forces and passions ranked below a human being's soul and free will.

In order to understand the beginning of human illnesses and predict their evolution, 'physicians' had to acquire education in astrological 'physics,' which required in turn that they understand the circuitry and motions of the heavenly spheres, without prejudice to Christian notions of metaphysics. Students of medicine in late-medieval and Renaissance universities had to be familiar with instruments and concepts of astral and planetary computation that belonged to what was to become the science of astronomy proper. Astrolabes, maps, and almanacs describing the heavens were essential requirements of medicine and astrological prediction, instruments that had to be produced and studied before they could actually be used. 'Within *astrologia*, as within alchemy, really lay two subjects – astrology and chemistry – which were the preparatory ground for the others, the arts of astrology and alchemy' (Tester 1987: 201). By the mid-thirteenth century, a wholly astronomical *sphera* had been produced by John of Sacrobosco, providing a scientific basis for any scholar interested in practising astrology and in further exploring the laws of the heavenly bodies.

While later students of medicine had to study Sacrobosco's influential *Sphera*, they also had to read Ptolemy's *Geography*, the standard geographic work throughout the Middle Ages, and also his *Almagest*, which gave a full account of Greek astronomy and an earth-centred view of the universe. The dissemination of Latin versions of Ptolemy's works in the sixteenth century led to a non-Arabic reappraisal of his geocentric system, a reappraisal that favoured a probabilistic approach to heavenly influences. This 'conjectural' rethinking of Ptolemy was essential to preserving Christian principles of free will and divine Providence against Arab versions of sidereal fatalism.

The development of science eventually resulted in the Copernican and Galilean revolution, a new astronomy that refuted the Ptolemaic system and placed the earth and the planets squarely in the orbit of the sun. Combined with the discovery of new continents, this revolution laid the foundation of an entirely different conception of the universe. Even though converted to heliocentrism, astronomers continued for a while to view the cosmos as a finite system governed by relatively small distances and a fixed number of component stars, assumptions that allowed astrology to maintain its claims to scientific validity even after the Copernican revolution. But the discovery of new planets and stars (as in 1572 and 1604) and the growth of astronomy as a relatively autonomous science was bound to undermine the astrological assumptions of a geocentric cosmos and the fixed circuitry of a limited number of stars and planets. While Galileo observed imperfections on the surfaces of the sun and the moon, Halley and Tycho Brahe showed that comets followed regular paths and evolved far above the moon. These findings undermined the commonplace Aristotelian distinction between the perfect superlunary heavens and the corrupt sublunary world plagued by comet-related disasters.

These and later discoveries of the science of astronomy have been so profound that we can no longer claim to inhabit a compact universe conceived as an interlocking organism. Not only the earth and the sun, but even our

galaxy has ceased to form centres of cosmic activity. We now live in a plu-
rality of worlds of infinite dimensions, a multicentred universe composed
of a multitude of stars dispersed in a boundless space, asterisms separated
by vast and unequal distances that contradict all astrological conceptions of
space (Pecker 1995: 26; Thomas 1971: 349f.). As a result, modern astronomical science undermines the esoteric measurements of zodiacal signs
and lunar houses affecting natural phenomena and human behaviour. It
also puts an end to all medieval (Judaeo-Christian and Islamic) assumptions of a 'living sky' composed of bright stars and planets moving within a
closed celestial-vault system and directly influencing minute events on
earth.

The new astronomy reflected a new attitude towards the material universe, one in which observations of celestial phenomena were of equal
importance compared with anagogical and teleological readings of the sky.
Before the Renaissance, astrology could pervade all aspects of life without
being overly preoccupied with issues of astronomical reckoning. Empirical
descriptions of the sky mattered less than the logical, pragmatic, and moral
implications of the art. While Arab representations of astral divinities incorporated observable distances and configurations of the stars, Western imageries concentrated chiefly on the symbolic aspects of sidereal bodies. They
also borrowed unhesitatingly from various traditions, producing highly
baroque and anachronistic mélanges of motifs derived from different cultural geographies and periods of history. Despite claims to the contrary,
mythographers such as Giraldi and Cartari 'pay no attention to place or
time. They mix together all the gods, regardless of their place of origin, the
most ancient with those of later times' (Seznec 1953: 241; cf. 154, 235, 253f.).

From the second half of the fifteenth century onwards, however, the
West witnesses a change of attitude regarding issues of accuracy, be they
astronomical, physiological, or historical. From one mode of reversion to
origins – remembrance by syncretic degeneration – European culture
started moving into a new mode: a 'deliberate return in order to get back to
the roots again, for a new start' (Lawrence 1974: 194). Dürer's chart of the
heavens (1515), the first ever to be printed, thus shows a reversion to classical figures of heaven, picturing the skies in ways that are more closely
aligned with stellar geometry and the descriptive imageries of ancient texts.
In addition to moving closer to perceptions of the sky, anthropomorphic
and zoomorphic representations of constellations are truer to plastic forms
of the body, as in classical art and mythology. As with other stellar figures,
Hercules is given back his original physique, an athletic body mapped onto
perceptible spheres of heaven. Seznec (1953: 187f., cf. 320) suggests that

Dürer's map is a sign of the times, for 'to recover the forms used by the ancients as well as their learning, their poetic imagination, and their knowledge of the universe – to reconcile, as they did, mythology and geometry – such was to be the dreams of the greatest spirits of the Renaissance.' In his own prophetic way, Dürer renounces an excess of allegorical content and opts instead for a synthesis of plasticity and authenticity, reconciling aesthetics with observations of the bodily spheres. His chart conveys a genealogical concern for intrinsic configurations and original significations, as distinct from the anagogical and teleological lessons of previous formulations of astrology.

Prior to the Renaissance, genealogical methods of interpretation were confined to issues of mythical descent (euhemerism) and boastful claims to knowledge of ancient manuscripts. With the Renaissance, however, genealogical reasoning is extended to questions of root meanings and forms, with the assumption that immanent systems and pristine sources do exist. While heavenly order is not subject to variable models of astronomical phenomena, original texts cannot be disassembled into composite influences. Classical iconographies are true to form and cannot err, let alone encourage an intermingling of foreign sources and disorder of its own kind. Towards the end of the sixteenth century, this search for root meanings produces various genealogical hypotheses, including the view that all languages are derivatives of Hebrew, that all gods are descendants of the Egyptian pantheon, and that all 'pagan' mythologies are corruptions of biblical revelations (Seznec 1953: 250). Although too linear, these speculative reversions to the past and theories of evolution laid the ground for the seventeenth-century studies of comparative religion à la Huet, Bochart, and Vossius. They also coincided with the development of archaeology and the excavation of thousands of ancient coins, reliefs, and statues, findings that provided direct knowledge of antiquity. The taste for archaeology, however, generated new scruples about aesthetic manipulations of mythology, a cautious attitude which is at the root of the modern separation between religious art and the scholarly knowledge of art history.

An era of crisis and reaction then dawns. The gods no longer arouse the same sentiments. Zeal is succeeded by admiration grown reticent and overscrupulous; intoxication with beauty, by a cold archaeological interest, by scholarly curiosity. From being objects of love, the gods are transformed into a subject of study ... Increasingly erudite and diminishingly alive, less and less felt but more and more intellectualized – such, from now on, it seems, is to be the inescapable evolution of mythology. (Seznec 1953: 321)

Together with new knowledge of history and the heavens, the Renaissance added a crucial ingredient in Western views of the cosmos: humanist pride in the intrinsic worth of humans and their centrality in the universe. The Age of Reason affirmed the superiority of logic and the mind over all things material, thereby bringing the older Logos closer than ever to the earth, a fundamental prerequisite of modern thought. At first, this re-evaluation of human beings' place in the world did not entail a rejection of astrological belief systems. On the contrary: the growth of humanism initially encouraged the pursuit of astrology defined as *scientia universalis*, a comprehensive science invading natural philosophy and confirming astral notions of causality in many new ways. But, as Cassirer (1963: 89–122) shows, the longer-term consequences of humanism were not favourable to the survival of sidereal divination. In the words of Seznec,

the bonds which attach man to the universe ... now cease to be thought as a form of imprisonment. Marsilio Ficino still adheres to the notion of 'superior' powers with dominion over 'inferior' beings (the stars sending their influences down toward the earth). Nicholas of Cusa no longer accepts this subordination of earth to sky; he sees only harmony and correlation, not dependence. Paracelsus goes even further; he suggests that the influence may operate in the other direction – from man to the stars, from soul to thing, from the inner world to the outer ... The decisive word has been spoken: mind is superior to matter. (1953: 59)

Pomponazzi of Mantua (1462–1524) and Marsilio Ficino (1433–1499), the latter a self-avowed melancholic child of Saturn, propounded concepts of astrological causality that were in many ways compatible with modern views of nature. Actually their approaches to astrology played an important role in bringing about a worldly approach to reality, detaching observable events and natural occurrences from the interventions of God, his agents, and his demonic enemies. Although still committed to siderealism, 'even Pomponazzi's strange and abstruse work helped pave the methodological way for the new, exact scientific conception of natural occurrences' (Cassirer 1963: 106). In his writings the created world gains more autonomy *vis-à-vis* its Creator – hence, natural science *vis-à-vis* knowledge obtained through revelation. One implication of this is that the secular history of religious leadership and faith, including the rise and fall of the Christian Church, may be subject to natural laws and the motions of heaven. Different gods and thought systems have different times regulated by moving stars. Other Renaissance thinkers such as Nicholas Cusanus and Paracelsus refuse to place the heavens 'above' human beings and the earth, preferring instead to talk of correlations and kindred connections between elements of the world organism. As for Pico della Mirandola, he opts to place the creative powers of humanity and the destiny-making works of great thinkers, statesmen, and artists squarely above the stars. Geniuses are not created by stars, never to free the 'heaven of their mind' from compelling movements of the sky. Rather, they are indebted to Almighty God for being the products of loftier minds, with the implications that miracles of the spirit outweigh the wondrous forces and tyranny of the visible spheres of heaven. In his *De dignitate hominis*, Pico treats constellations as fictitious symbols of the mind that differ from signs of mathematical physics in that they are without demonstrable effects on real events. This is to say that minds exercise far more influence than stars in heaven. Similar thoughts are later expressed by Kepler, who saw his inspiration, not in Mercury or Mars, but rather in the 'influential' works of much closer 'stars': Copernicus and Tycho Brahe (Cassirer 1963: 107–11, 117–22).

Astrology lost ground on the religious front as well. By and large the Reformation broadened the distance between science and theology, physics and metaphysics. As with Luther, who scoffed at astrology (but none the less feared the conjunction of planets in Pisces in 1524), Calvin had serious theological reservations against astrological divination. In his *Advertissement contre l'astrologie* (1549), a response to the fashionable pro-astrological writings of Saint-Gelais, Calvin admits that bodies in heaven will influence the lower bodies (humans, the earth, etc.) and that astrology can be used in medicine, agriculture, and social activities. God should be thanked for his wondrous works deployed in the heavens. The Lord may use signs in heaven to manifest his will to humans, with the implication that astrological predictions may come true. Some predictions, however, will be borne out because fulfilled by the Devil himself with a view to promoting idolatry or heading a mission of divine wrath. As with many secrets and mysteries that are explored through diabolical means, foreknowledge obtained in this fashion is a product of the Devil's University. Having made several concessions to *astrologia*, Calvin downplays the role of all intermediations between God and humans, preferring knowledge obtained by direct revelation over insights achieved through mathematics. The theologian also stresses the rewards and punishments (and final Judgment) that the Lord dispenses in proportion to human deeds, acts of retribution performed through special sign-manifestations (e.g., comets), not through regular motions of the heavenly bodies.

The Counter-Reformation Church also showed increased opposition to astrology, as expressed in the Tridentine decrees and the Papal Bull of 1586 and 1631. Both Catholic clergymen and Protestant ministers had to maintain some distance from the astrological profession as 'they were competing agencies, offering rival methods of divination. The godly man might be able to prophesy by prayer and revelation, just as the astrologer made predictions after studying the movement of the heavenly bodies. But was there room for both?' (Thomas 1971: 363). The usual reply to this question was that only prayers and virtues of the soul could offset natural inclinations of the bodily sphere. When abiding by these rules, Protestant astrologers such as Lambe, Lilly, and Napier were given episcopal licences authorizing them to practise their science.

Puritan Presbyterians, Quakers, and Baptists, however, were particularly adamant that Christianity be purged from all traces of Roman Catholic iconolatry. 'Astrological images and sigils paralleled the charms worn by the Catholic laity, and the notion that a separate sign of the zodiac ruled each part of the body recalled the Popish belief that there was a saint for every disease' (Thomas 1971: 368). Presbyterians were strongly opposed to any belief system that allowed humans to penetrate mysteries of the world by natural means and that contradicted the notion of God's omnipotence. Astrological rhetoric was deployed by radical sects of the Civil War of 1642–52 and was also an integral part of the seventeenth-century Behmenist doctrines of illumination and cosmic sympathy. On the whole, however, the puritanical emphasis on God's all-powerful Providence made rival concepts of astrological fatalism more intolerable than ever: the moral and theological teachings of predestination and the election of grace could hardly be reconciled with secular lessons of eternal destiny and sidereal elections.

Some Catholic theologians became wary of astrology's concern with God's presence in the visible world and the art's latent concessions to pantheism and materialism. A revival of Stoic, Platonic, and Neoplatonic philosophy in Italy led theologians such as Pico della Mirandola to de-emphasize the physical world, moving human beings closer to God and promoting imageries of the Beyond via the mystical world-view of hermetism and the cabbala. Unlike Pomponazzi of Mantua, who saw in astrology the science of natural laws ordained by the Creator, Pico ended up having no need of Aristotelian physics. While other Renaissance Platonists such as Marsilio Ficino thought astrology to be compatible with Christianity, Pico launched in 1394 a twelve-volume attack against *astrologia*, using all traditional arguments to denounce its judicial applications. Pico was initially condemned by the Inquisition, but his writings were to become influential in later campaigns instigated against the use and abuse of sidereal divination. All this occurred at a time when astrologers exerted enormous influence in Italian courts, constantly producing birth charts, annual prognostications (for a region, a country, or the whole world), and election-charts for important activities and events. Later centuries witnessed a shift away from offshoots of Islamic astrology, back to Hellenistic texts, resulting in 'the fullest flowering of astrology in western Europe, frequently in conjunction with Neoplatonism and Hermeticism' (Pingree 1993: 83).

Alchemy and astrology persisted in laying claims to scientific validity well into the Renaissance, and the influence of astrology on medicine lasted until the nineteenth century (Tester 1987: 186). Notwithstanding their contribution to modern astronomy, Copernicus, Galileo, Kepler, and Tycho Brahe (a devout Protestant) were adepts of the art of sidereal divination. Few well-known scientists, however, were to practise astrology after the seventeenth century. The French rationalists and encyclopedists ignored astrology altogether, and scientists like Newton and Leibniz became 'mathematicians' in the full modern sense of the word. After 1700 new scholarly and university contributions to astrology (in a Christian perspective) were no longer produced, save perhaps the writings of the Dominican Tomasso Campanella (1568–1639) (Tester 1987: 213). Given their lack of interest in the subject, eighteenth-century philosophers and scholars left satirists the task of critiquing and ridiculing the claims of *astrologia*. Government and Church persecution of astrologers gave way to relative freedom in the exercise of a severely discredited science that had lost much of its impact on political events and religious life as well (Thomas 1971: 304, 344f., 352–6).

By the early eighteenth century, most scientists, philosophers, and theologians had lost interest in astrological futurology. Thus died Western astrology, at least in its scholarly form. The ancient science of divination could hardly continue its activities without the support and recognition of science and university education. In the modern age, the distinction between astrology and astronomy – horoscopes and the science of the heavenly bodies – is understood by all and considerable distance is kept between the two forms of knowledge and the corresponding professions. But while left stranded by the evolution of culture and science, astrology never disappeared from Western culture. Through the use of almanacs and mass-media literature, practitioners of the art have kept astrology alive in most Western countries, if only as a concession to the individual quest for identity and promises of the immediate future.

Shifts in Western attitudes towards astrology parallel in many ways the history of interpretations of Revelation, a prophetic text originally embattled with astralism and signs of heavenly divination. In the next chapter, I address the issue of variations in readings of the New Testament Apocalypse, with an emphasis on major shifts in exegetic perspectives applied to John's vision of the End.

3

A History of Revelations

Although there is only one New Testament Apocalypse, there are many interpretations of the book, alternative readings which exegetes are bound to address when delving into the original text. 'Explaining' John's writing thus entails doing several things: scrutinizing the reference text, exploring its response to its immediate context, showing how it speaks to particular audiences and other texts (Jewish, pagan), situating one's reading *vis-à-vis* other exegetic contributions, and then addressing the relevance of it all from the standpoint of modern readers. Far from being a simple hermeneutic reconstruction of one text through the writing of another – a straightforward encounter between author and scholar – the interpretive act is merely one moment in a moving battle of conflicting viewpoints traversed with multiple interests and changing perspectives. In the words of Fiorenza (1991: 2), 'authorial aims, points of view, narrative strategies, persuasive means and closure, as well as audience perceptions and constructions, are rhetorical practices that have determined not only the production of Revelation but also its subsequent interpretations.'

This book is an exercise in scheme analysis – entering the scholarly conversations with Revelation from a particular perspective. The approach is essentially twofold. On the one hand, scheme analysis presupposes an intertextual and dialogical understanding of Revelation, situating the script in its interaction with other ancient texts and their overall context. This task is pursued in later chapters, with an emphasis on polemical exchanges and rhetorical disputes between ancient astromythology and Christian logocentrism. On the other hand, scheme analysis requires that we address other ways of making sense of Revelation and formulate our response to other strategic answers to John's reply to astrology. This brings us to the history of commentaries on Revelation. Reviews of the exegetic literature

on the New Testament Apocalypse are many, and the typologies somewhat variable, usually quite detailed, and list-like. In reality, however,
hermeneutics applied to Revelation revolve around three fundamental paradigms: the anagogical, the teleological, and the genealogical.

The anagogical paradigm treats the original text as a work of wisdom
reflecting timeless propositions of the Christian spirit, kernels of truths
wrapped in symbolic imagery. Through allegories and metaphors, the text
speaks to an eternal present understood theologically. While Revelation is
visibly concerned with things that have yet to come, events of the hereafter
belong to a distant future, they highlight principles that transcend history,
and they point to the End of Time – a guiding principle of anagogical
thought. By and large, spiritually oriented exegeses of Revelation are not
conducive to literal predictions of large-scale world transformations (the
millennium, the Day of Judgment), nor do they foster subversive analyses
of human history. Rather, they lend themselves to Church accommodations with the secular order.

The teleological paradigm is different in that it accepts John's presentation of his book as a work of prophecy and visions of things to come. It
applies the Seer's imagery to a reading of later history, events recorded
after the writing of Revelation. Students of the Scriptures adopting this
approach take God's planning of history most seriously: 'For he has
weighed the age in the balance, and with measure has measured the times,
and by number has numbered the seasons: neither will he move nor stir
things, till the measure appointed be fulfilled' (4 Esdras 4: 36f.). Predictions
of the future (the interpreter's past) serve to promote particular analyses of
Church and world history, usually in ways that are critical of secular powers (imperial Rome, the corrupt Church of Rome, etc.). While teleological
exegeses are often geared to visions of an imminent millennium or End
affecting the Church gone evil, some interpretations advocate a long-term
eschatological perspective. In the latter case, the Book of Revelation speaks
to the distant future only, not to a crisis-ridden world about to come apart,
let alone to events recorded well before the interpreter's time.

Unlike the two other paradigms, the genealogical mode of interpretation
is a product of the Renaissance, modern humanism, and the growth of scientific scholarship. As we shall see, the genealogical approach to textual
material emphasizes issues of context, sources, root meanings, and original
forms. Questions of origins are certainly not absent from ancient and
medieval hermeneutics dealing with mythology and the Scriptures, but
they tend to be confined to the dating and recording of prophecies and
events, and the tracing of lines of descent, whether it be from a tribal-

patriarchal or a euhemeristic perspective. Modern genealogical hermeneutics extends this older notion of descent to issues of meaning and signification. Cognizant of the weaknesses of teleology and anagogy, the genealogical perspective on signs stresses neither future time nor the timeless principles of scriptural writings. Rather it upholds a disciplined, well-documented reversion to the 'original text' and a value-neutral examination of its sources, authorial intents, literary patterns, and inherent logic, not to mention the context of its initial production. 'Genealogists' are distrustful of the primacy that earlier exegetes, modern preachers, and sectarian commentators assign to John's predictions of history and to his words of eternal wisdom. Committed as they are to biblical scholarship, they take it upon themselves to reconstruct ancient webs of significations. Anagogical and teleological readings of the Scriptures emphasize the validity of Revelation from the interpreter's standpoint, usually at the expense of the author and his first-century readership. By contrast, the genealogical strategy assigns meanings to the author's time, thereby undermining later applications of John's apocalyptic teachings. 'The rights of the text must be respected, and the chasm between the world of the text and that of the present-day interpreter must be maintained' (Fiorenza 1991: 1).

Before we proceed to a detailed review of these approaches to Revelation, readers are asked to bear in mind that not all readings of Revelation fall neatly into three homogeneous paradigms. Our typology does not preclude middle-of-the-road exegeses, partial or precursory formulations of a given paradigm, or dominant modes subsuming subsidiary hermeneutic strategies. Nor does the typology exclude important variations occurring within each mode. Teleological interpreters have quarrelled over critical questions such as Antichrist's historical identity (the Roman pontiff, Luther, Napoleon?) and also the exact timetable of the millennium and the Endtime events. Likewise, genealogists have debated the historical conditions (dating, current crisis if any, etc.), religious influences (pagan or mostly Old Testament sources?), authorial intents (did John want to announce an imminent End?), and literary patterns of Revelation (liturgical, cyclical, recapitulative?). Finally, interpretive differences observed both within and between these paradigms are not merely the result of logical comparisons carried out with scholarly intent. More important, these hermeneutic differences constitute a complex field of interpretive schemes and polemical manipulations developed and changing over many centuries. They involve divergent readings and crucial disputes over visions of the past and the future; forces of good and evil; the relationship among Christianity, Judaism, and pagan religion; the role of the papacy in Church history; the relative weight of divine inspiration *vis-à-vis* authorial intent; the primacy of compositional logic over literary imagination; and so on. The following literature review points not so much to unevenly successful readings of Revelation as to a multitude of perspectival Revelations, competing readings and counter-readings loaded with polemical implications and adaptations to history.

Despite their differences, anagogical, teleological, and genealogical accounts of the Scriptures share an important assumption. They have in common this peculiar notion that the historical flow of conversations with Revelation can and should be finally arrested or transcended. Interactive discussions and shifting interpretations of the Apocalypse give way to the primacy of timeless truths, final endings of the future, or an 'original narrative' reconstructed in its eternal present – an act of literary 'creation' superseding its own sources and unaffected by later embattlements of competing exegeses. In all cases, little attention is given to polemical writings and readings of Revelations evolving through time. As we shall see, the propensity on the part of Revelation to *deliberate or debate* its own context and countertext (astromythology) is never *fully* addressed, nor are interpretations of John's book ever presented for what they really are: arguments launched against other readings of the Apocalypse.

Anagogical Exegeses

Revelation was written, and then centuries went by without its vision of the End being fulfilled. Faith in prophecies of the imminent reign of Christ on earth could not last forever. As time passed by, history failed to deliver the literal promises made to John in Patmos. Meanwhile, chiliasm – the material, worldly understanding of the coming kingdom – became a threat to Christianity's reconciliation with Roman rule. During the second century C.E., Christian communities proliferated through the Roman Empire and reorganized themselves, developing their own Church institutions conceived as instruments of salvation. On the political front, this growing Church developed more stable connections and accommodation with Rome. As a result, Christianity had to downplay its vision of Christ rising again to manifest the full kingdom of God on earth. In their struggle against the Montanist expression of millenarianism, some Church Fathers went so far as to claim that Revelation had been originally written by the heretic Cerinthus, the enemy of John the Beloved. With Constantine's conversion to Christianity in 312 C.E., Church institutions were incorporated within late Roman imperial culture. The 'Church grew into more solid institutional forms and developed more complicated (if essentially safer) relationships to the temporal power of the empire' (Matter 1992: 39). Apocalyptic millenarianism became more disruptive than ever. With the conversion of the Empire, Rome and her emperor could no longer be equated with Antichrist.

A new exegetic trend thus emerged, towards a spiritual understanding of John's visions, an anagogical approach opposed to chiliastic renderings of the Apocalypse. The anagogical hermeneutic strategy consists in seeking those moral and theological principles that govern the Scriptures, using historical events as illustrations of spiritual forces and struggles of good and evil that preside over human history, to be fully resolved at the End of Time – an End that humans cannot possibly predict. 'But as for that day or hour, nobody knows it, neither the angels of heaven, nor the Son; no one but the Father' (Mark 13: 32). The dualism between the present aeon and the aeon to come is maintained, such that the Church remains concerned with signs of the End of Time, an eschatology that feeds into Christian promises of an eternal afterlife and threats of damnation directed against the sinful and enemies of the Church (Sweet 1990: 1). John's prophetic imageries, however, should not be literally applied to humans' understanding of the precise course of history. In the anagogical perspective, the interpreter's task is to extract, distill, or unravel timeless essences, theological laws, or atemporal truths from both Church history and apocalyptic mythology. Events and images of Revelation are 'mere container or cloak' (Fiorenza 1985: 23) that hold, cover, or convey the spiritual knowledge revealed to John. Given the enduring validity of John's Verb, all periods of history will illustrate theological principles that stand above time, spiritual rules that may be understood through insights into the allegories and mysteries of the Scriptures.

Rudiments of the anagogical method can be found in the teachings of Origen of Alexandria (*On First Principles*, early third century c.e.), the first exegete of the Christian Church. In keeping with the growing influence of Greek thought in Christian theology, Origen accepts the idea of a future millennium but rejects literal millenarianism on the grounds that a difference is to be made between the literal Judaistic imagery of Revelation and the Christian soul and spirit of the text, a distinction also found in the writings of Jerome and still used in twentieth-century discussions of the Apocalypse. While Revelation is inspired by the Holy Spirit, its deeper spiritual meaning is couched in an allegorical or typological language that requires constant figurative explanation. To give one example of this method, the seven heads of the dragon have no specific historical content; according to Origen, they merely represent seven deadly sins.

Victorinus of Pettau played an important role in the development of a spiritual reading of John's Apocalypse. On the one hand, the bishop of the period of the Great Persecution (shortly after 300 C.E.) thought that the trials of his time corresponded to woes of the sixth seal in Revelation. He was firmly committed to prophecies of Nero's return from the dead and to visions of the End and the imminent reign of Christ on earth. On the other hand, Victorinus offered spiritual commentaries on Revelation and is the first known exegete to have applied the recapitulation approach, treating John's vision as a prophetic account of things to come but in the form of complex repetitions and alternative accounts of the same message. In this perspective the plagues of the bowls are parallel with those of the trumpets, not sequels to the latter trials. This simple rule was to become a strong argument against linear historical readings of Revelation and an important principle of medieval apocalyptic thought.[1]

It was left to Jerome (340?–420) to revise the teachings of Victorinus in such ways that better reflect a Church no longer at war with the Empire. The Latin Church Father shifted from a literal to an allegorical mode, rejecting earthly-kingdom prophecies and the 'fable of one thousand years.' He reaffirmed the principle of recapitulation, with the implication that 'the Apocalypse presents a series of typological events *recurring* in sacred history from the time of the patriarchs, through the unknown future on earth, to the *parousia*' (Matter 1992: 39). Likewise, Methodius of Olympus, a Christian martyr of the early fourth century, argued that Revelation is not concerned with real historical events, not even the birth or deeds of Christ, but rather eternal truths expressed symbolically. In his *Symposium*, the male child of Revelation 12 alludes, not to the real Christ, but rather to the spiritual Christ engendered in each faithful Christian; the woman with the child is the Church; the ten horns of the dragon of Revelation 12 are demonic inversions of the ten commandments; the fallen stars are false prophets who claim knowledge of manifestations of heaven; and so on. This line of reasoning is later picked up by Andreas, a sixth-century archbishop living in Asia Minor, who adds an important eschatological reservation: Revelation speaks also to mysteries of an ultimate future, to be unfolded at the End, when good shall triumph over evil. As did Tyconius and Augustine, Andreas believes that the millennial kingdom started with Christ, yet he holds that the number 1,000 merely signifies multitude and completeness, not a literal millennium. Babylon is a metaphor for all worldly powers, the temple stands for the Christian Church, and the number 666 is a mystery that will be understood in due time, when Antichrist arises (from the tribe of Dan) to persecute followers of the Lord (see Prigent 1959: 12f.).

The rise of anagogical accounts of apocalyptic literature did not eradicate all claims to prophetic visions of a new earth. North African Christians of the fourth century opposed to accommodations with Rome formed a Donatist front of 'enthusiasts' who considered theirs the only true Church. The community kept its distance from the Roman Empire and felt persecuted by a corrupt Church hierarchy. Like the author of Revelation, they vested all their hopes in the festive joys of God's imminent kingdom on earth (Fredriksen 1992: 24).

Tyconius was a lay product of Donatism. Although his written commentary on Revelation is no longer available, his anagogical interpretation of North African millenarianism was to have a major influence on Western medieval exegesis via the works of Augustine. The Donatist theologian advocated a historical understanding of apocalyptic prophecies, interpreting them in the light of the Donatist battle against the State Church and worldly embodiments of the Beast. Despite his commitment to millenarianism, however, Tyconius denied that the precise timing of the End[2] and the identity of the redeemed could be known. This agnostic attitude towards the timing of God's interventions in history was derived from a larger hermeneutic agenda developed in his *Liber regularum*. In this book, Tyconius identifies seven basic rules of biblical composition that govern scriptural meanings and that reflect the mysteries of biblical knowledge:

1/ *De Domino et corpore eius*:
When the Bible speaks of the Lord, it may mean his body, the Church.

2/ *De Domini corpore bipertito*:
The Church-body is bipartite, with beauty and ugliness, goodness and evil constantly coexisting.

3/ *De promissis et lege*:
Law and promise are realized throughout history and arouse faith in the predestined.

4/ *De specie et genere*:
Scriptural references to events (*specie*) may serve to express general truths (*genere*).

5/ De temporibus:
Numbers are so malleable that future events prophesied in the Scriptures cannot be dated.

6/ De recapitulatione:
Scriptural references to sequential events may be mere repetitions or recapitulations of the same narrative.

7/ De diabolo et euis corpore:
Passages that speak of Satan may intend his body – hence, his followers.

The laws of God and conflicts between good and evil reiterate themselves through the individual salvation process and through general principles of world history (rules 3, 4, and 6). God intervenes in human times, yet he does so in such mysterious ways that good and evil cannot be assigned to particular people (rule 2), nor can prophets predict precise events (rule 5). Grand battles between the 'body-of-followers' of God (e.g., Donatists) and Satan (e.g., Rome, sinners within the Church) cannot be interpreted as signs of the imminent *parousia* and the End (rules 1 and 7). Whether victorious or persecuted, the Church is in no position to proclaim the arrival of *parousia*. Through synecdoche (substituting the whole for the part, or vice versa), numbers and periods of time can be manipulated and assigned various meanings, which means that the millennium may have started with Christ, but no one knows when this era of Church history will end. 'Scriptural numbers do not and cannot quantify; rather, they symbolize and indicate spiritual truths' (Fredriksen 1992: 28). Tyconius's account of the Scriptures

emphasized the historical [reiterative, non-linear] realization of prophecy while denying the sort of social and temporal transparency to the text which would allow for a millenarian interpretation. A radical agnosticism controls his estimate of both current events and traditional prophecies: neither persecution nor relative peace indicates God's ultimate timetable; and no exterior fact (like persecution), conforming to a church's view of itself as holy (hence persecuted), can actually confirm that view. The time of the End is unknowable in principle; and until it comes, the Church must remain a *corpus permixtum*, containing both sinner and saint. (Fredriksen 1992: 29)

Concerned with the credibility of Church tradition, Augustine (354–430 C.E.) also warned Christians against using wars and portents to claim foreknowledge of apocalyptic events – prophecies eventually mocked and disproved by an End that never came. Remindful of what the Lord said to the apostles, that 'it is not for you to know times or dates that the Father has decided by his own authority ...' (Acts 1: 7; cf. Matt. 24: 36), the Church Father recommended in his *City of God* that Christians refrain from indulging in calculations of future history. God's interventions in the present or future are inscrutable. Visions of the inevitable Day of Judgment notwithstanding, 'history's time frame is known only to God, and if the hour of the End is unknowable in principle, it cannot serve to impose a plot on time – none, rather, that those living *in* time can discern' (Fredriksen 1992: 34). The Lord knows what the future has in store for humans, yet the capacity to act freely and to engage in sinful or virtuous behaviour is an integral part of God's plan and his foreknowledge of the powers granted to humans. God's will is 'to give power to wills.' While by no means incompatible with principles of moral freedom, the prescience of God, once denied by Cicero, precludes human beings' foreknowledge of their own fate (Augustine 1950: 152–9).

Given this profession of historical agnosticism, the first resurrection announced in Revelation 20: 1–6 speaks, not to collective events of the future, but rather to the redemption of the individual soul achieved through baptism and life in the Church. Visions of the millennium reflect the spiritual reign of the Church, sustained through contemporary battles and miracles of the saints (Lerner 1992: 52). Augustine thus *moves the millennium back into current Church history*: in the Church lies the Kingdom of Christ. During this period the devil is bound and his power bridled, yet the faithful must cope with the coexistence of good and evil within the individual, the Church and the world. Against millenarianists, he insists that the seventh millennial Sabbath age should not be taken literally and should be understood simply as a 'total' period or 'all generations,' which means an indeterminate portion of time. Visions of Judgment Day and the Second Coming of Christ continue to be central tenets of Christian theology, but they apply to the *spiritual* redemption of bodies in heaven, a salvation that will occur not with material delights, not on earth, and certainly not before the End of Time.

Tyconius and Augustine brought about a profound revolution in biblical exegesis. In many ways, the spiritual attitude they adopted towards the apocalyptic literature was designed to offset the subversive claims of heterodox millenarianism. Their contributions are thus to be understood historically, against the background of religious developments of the fourth and fifth centuries, a period of history marked by the consolidation of

Church institutions, but also the Donatist schism, the Arian heresy, and the Vandal invasions of the Western Empire – troublesome events that fostered millenarian counter-readings of John's Apocalypse.

The interpretive themes and methods developed by Victorinus, Jerome, Tyconius, and Augustine found their way in medieval exegesis principally through the sixth-century writings of Primasius,[3] bishop in the North African province of Numidia. Primasius's interpretations were in turn transmitted to exegetes of the Carolingian age, mostly through the commentaries of the Venerable Bede (c. 730) and Ambrose Autpert (c. 760). From the eighth century onwards, readings of the Apocalypse became closely linked to commentaries on the Songs of Songs, an association reflecting 'the tradition of allegorical exegesis in the ecclesiological mode' (Matter 1992: 46). In this tradition it is assumed that concrete imageries express universal truths, and that mysteries of the Scriptures speak essentially to the survival of the Church on earth, a central concern throughout the early Middle Ages in Latin Christianity.

Before we move on to teleological accounts of John's Apocalypse, mention should be made of the Mariological application of Tyconius's fourth *de specie et genere* rule. According to this rule, the sun-robed woman of Revelation 12 can be seen as the mother of Jesus, who in turn represents (qua *specie*) the Church (*genere*), an identification later to be rejected by biblical scholars of the Reformation. Early proponents of this thesis include Ambrose Autpert and the sixth-century Cassiodorus and Oecumenius. As Prigent (1959: 25f.) notes, interpretations based on Tyconius's fourth rule lent themselves to the introduction of historical events and characters in Revelation. In their search for concrete manifestations of the universal truths of Revelation, anagogically oriented exegetes did allow history to be read into the Apocalypse, if only by way of metaphor. The text, however, did not refer to history; rather, history illustrated the text.

Teleological Exegeses: Eschatology and Church History

Although early Christian history kept holding back the End, millenarian readings of Revelation lasted up until the fourth century. Many Christians 'continued to view imminent apocalypticism as normative' (McGinn 1992: 11). As long as Rome was bent on persecuting Christians, the New Testament Apocalypse (especially Rev. 20) provided a source of comfort and hope in the impending triumph of God's kingdom ruling the earth for a thousand years. This was true of the followers of Montanus, a Phrygian bishop and enthusiast of the second century who prophesied the earthly realization of the heavenly Jerusalem. An eschatological view of Revelation was also proposed by Justin Martyr (*Dialogus cum Tryphone, c.* 150). He was the first post-apostolic writer to comment on John's Apocalypse, a book which he thought predicted a literal millennial kingdom for the earthly Jerusalem, followed by the final days of resurrection, judgment, and the new earth. Among other patristic authorities who held chiliastic views, Jerome mentions Tertullian, Victorinus, Lactantius, and Irenaeus (140–200 C.E.). With Irenaeus (*Adversus Haereses*), the Roman Empire personifies the Beast hostile to God. The exegete, however, refrains from naming any particular emperor and adopts in some cases a purely symbolic approach to John's imagery. The beast numbered 666 is a case in point. According to Irenaeus, by repeating the digit 6, the text 'recapitulates' the wickedness and apostasy of 6,000 years of human history. As for the four Living Creatures placed around the throne of God, they symbolize Christ's attributes of kingship, humanity, priesthood, and the prophetic office.

Hippolytus, bishop of Portus Romanus in the early third century, professed the same views as his master, Irenaeus, yet he did not think that the millennium would come before the year 500. In his rendering of Revelation, the great harlot and Babylon imagery stands for Rome and is pitted against the sun-robed woman of Revelation 12, who represents the Church. Antichrist comes out of the tribe of Dan and is personified by Antiochus Epiphanes, king of Syria.

From the fourth century onwards, the anagogical readings of Revelation developed by Victorinus, Jerome, Tyconius, and Augustine supplanted the future-oriented views of early Christian Church Fathers and the 'heresies' of later millenarian movements such as Donatism. Teleological renderings of Revelation, however, were bound to flourish again: millenarian hopes for a period of peace on earth before the End had not been completely crushed by timeless-symbolic theology. In his eighth-century reading of Revelation (*Explanatio Apocalypsis*), Bede thus made extensive use of linear historical reasoning. He divided world history into seven ages (*periochas*) which he described in a sevenfold text evoking the gradual development of the Church moving towards sacred time. While Bede pictured these *periochas* with broad allegorical strokes, later exegetes of the twelfth and subsequent centuries used his framework to reintroduce concrete historical events and expectations into their understanding of John's Apocalypse. Although not meant to sanction what he considered to be millenarian heresies, Bede's notion that the death of Antichrist would be followed by a brief Sabbath of earthly silence (Rev. 8: 1), a thesis initially developed by

Jerome, gave further ammunition to later versions of millenarianism (Lerner 1992: 54).

Other adepts of the historic-prophetic approach include Berengaudus (*Expositio super septem visiones*), a ninth-century commentator who saw in the first six seals of Revelation the first part of human history, a lengthy era extending from Adam to the fall of Jerusalem. The first six trumpets led up to contemporary Church struggles, and the horns of the beast stood for barbarian tribes overthrowing the Roman Empire. Mention should also be made of Rupert of Deutz (*Commentum in Apocalypsim*), a German theologian of the twelfth century who explored the parallels between Revelation, the history of Israel, and the first four centuries of Christianity.

In the anagogical perspective advocated by Tyconius and Augustine, the thousand-year reign of Christ and the binding of Satan were thought to have started with the appearance or resurrection of Christ. Antichristian powers were still at work in human history and were to be unleashed in their full strength at the end of the symbolic millennium, not at the end of a literal thousand years. When a real period of 1,000 years (after Christ) came to its end, however, Christianity witnessed general unrest and great eschatological anxiety about the loosing of Satan and the outburst of a great conflict, the last. These fears that spread in the tenth and eleventh centuries (especially in France) were eventually dispelled, if only because of the passing of time. Prophetic-historical views of history did not disappear for all that. As Beckwith notes, the critical period passed by, and neither Antichrist nor the Lord manifested himself, yet

the expectations which had been so actively aroused were not at once allayed; great interest in the coming of the Last Days continued, eschatological thought was busy. The Lord's appearance was believed to be not far off, and this foreboding was soon intensified by the condition of the Church itself, which now entered on a period of unconcern and self-content. Relieved as it was from fear of the sufferings believed to be predicted for the time now past, secure in its imperial domination, it beheld in its present state the fulfillment of the promises of millennial glory. Naturally deterioration and worldliness followed as the result in both official administration and individual moral life. Devout observers saw in these forces at work in the Church the presence of Antichrist and his agents. Such a predominance of evil could not continue, – in its very presence lay the presage of the End as near. (1967: 327)

Against Augustine's personal and spiritual understanding of reform and salvation, new religious movements of the eleventh and twelfth centuries sought to renew Church institutions. Their avowed objective was to 'liberate the clergy from lay control and to bring both clergy and laity under papal control in order to achieve their aim of making Latin Christendom truly "the body of Christ" on earth, purified from the corruption they perceived around them' (Daniel 1992: 77). Like Donatists of an earlier age, new religious orders objected vigorously to the worldliness of a Church hierarchy aligned with dominant political regimes.

Richard of Saint Victor (*In Apocalypsim Ioannis libri septem*) and the author of the 'Ordinary Gloss' compiled around 1120 drew heavily on Bede's Sabbath thesis and sevenfold understanding of Church history but without drawing millenarian conclusions from it. Influenced by Richard's work, however, the Dominican Hugh of Saint Cher (*c.* 1236) put the short worldly Sabbath promise to the service of triumphant evangelization and missionary activity, emphasizing a life of preaching and poverty. But it was the Calabrian abbot Joachim of Fiore (*c.* 1132–1202) who took up the task of drawing full millenarian implications from earlier exegeses of the New Testament Apocalypse, highlighting the crucial rule of monasticism in God's plan of human evolution. His understanding of history was to have a lasting influence on later readings of Revelation, transforming John's prophetic text into a weapon used by the Franciscans, the Dominicans, and the Reformed Churches in their struggle against papacy, the Catholic hierarchy, and the worldly Church. Although Joachim never gave his writings an anti-papal character, 'with the followers of Joachim and with all who set themselves against the corruption of the Church and the hierarchy it became an axiom that the Pope was the Beast, the Antichrist, and that papal Rome, or the Roman Church, was the woman sitting on the scarlet-colored beast. Their destruction was foreseen as near, many reckoned the year or the decade' (Beckwith 1967: 329).

In Joachim's exegesis (*Expositio in Apocalypsim*), John's visions are translated into a systematic account of Church chronology, a progressive purification of historical Christianity. World history is divided into three ages, the first one (the Father's, the Old Testament) spanning from Creation to the birth of Christ. The second age (the Son's, the New Testament) is to end in the year 1260 and is ruled by the institutional Church, a Holy Roman Empire marred by the imperfections and corruption of secular history. Note that the first coming of Christ is merely one turning-point of history; in teleological readings of Revelation, the interpreter's own time tends to be more crucial to an understanding of the Apocalypse than the remote past or the timeless present. When brought together, the first and second ages are to last six consecutive millennia. They will be followed by a seventh millennium forming the third age – the Holy Spirit's. In this age of final rest and contemplative spirituality lies the promise of a future Sabbath, an *ordo spiritualis* or perfect monastic Church governing the earth. The Sabbath will prevail between the death of Antichrist and the final consummation of all things, to occur in the eighth age – the End. Instead of arriving suddenly through an act of God, the coming order of monks constitutes the end-goal of a lengthy process that begins with Adam. In keeping with orthodox Bedean and Augustinian theology, however, the Sabbath will last a short while only, less than a year. The closer History approaches the End, the shorter the 'days' are; 'since the Lord had accomplished much more during the world's sixth age (lasting from the Incarnation to Antichrist) than he had in the previous five together, it followed that his work would be even more compressed during the Sabbath' (Lerner 1992: 52).

Alexander Minorita, a north German Franciscan monk (*c.* 1235), was the first medieval commentator to give the millennium a literal signification. According to his calculations (in *Expositio in Apocalypsim*), the millennium had already started with the triumph of the Church under Constantine, with the implication that the Last Judgment would come around the year 1326. Alexander refrained from assigning a precise date to the future Sabbath, yet he further developed Joachim's chronological and ecclesiological approach to Revelation and got rid of the principle of recapitulation advocated in previous centuries. The Parisian theologian Nicolas of Lyra (*Postilla super totam Bibliam, c.* 1270–1340) also read into Revelation predictions of the entire course of Church history divided into seven ages. He too abandoned the principle of recapitulation, extended the events of the seals into the reign of Domitian, discovered predictions of Arian heresies and the spread of Muhammadanism in later scenes of Revelation, and announced that Satan was about to bring the millennium to a close.

Towards the end of the thirteenth century, the southern French Franciscan Peter Olivi (*Lectura super Apocalypsim*) lifted all restrictions on the enduring earthly Sabbath thesis. Critical of Church corruption and fearful of persecution, the mendicant monk used Revelation to predict a lengthy period of rest and earthly glory granted to opponents and victims of Antichrist. The Holy Spirit could be counted on to exercise his reign through monastic orders for a period of 700 to 900 hundred years (ending around the year 2000). Unlike other mendicant commentators of Revelation such as Bonaventure (1221–1274), Olivi was convinced that the Church had become 'infected from head to toe and turned, as it were, into a new Babylon' (Burr 1992: 96).

Our commentators are unanimous on the sixth period: It is that of Antichrist. The only dissenter on this score is Olivi, who differs from the others in portraying the sixth period not only as the time of Antichrist but also an age of renewal initiated by Saint Francis. Olivi sees this period as closely connected with the seventh and with the eternal bliss that comes after judgment. A new age of peace and contemplation begins in the sixth period, is perfected in the seventh so far as is possible in this life, and attains complete fulfillment in eternity. Thus the sixth and seventh periods correspond to the inauguration and fulfillment of Joachim of Fiore's age of the Holy Spirit. (94)

Olivi was convinced that leaders of the renewed Church would be persecuted by heads of the carnal Church, thereby implicating Catholic Church authorities, and even the Pope, in such persecutions. The notion that Roman rule would eventually be destroyed by a pagan army and that 'a minion of Antichrist or perhaps Antichrist himself will don the papal tiara' (Burr 1992: 96) was bound to provoke Church anger, resulting in what Olivi had already foreseen – Church repression.

Millenarian readings of Apocalypse were professed by the anonymous author of the Colombinus Prophecy (c. 1300), Ubertino of Casale (c. 1305), a disciple of Olivi, and Arnold of Villanova (c. 1290), a Catalan physician turned evangelist.[4] As expected, the Church became intolerant of expressions of evangelical zealotry, the growth of the Olivi cult in Languedoc, and spiritual glorifications of mendicant orders pitted against the 'carnal church.' Despite a period of intellectual liberality that prevailed during the pontificates of Boniface VIII (1235?–1303) and Clement V (1305–14), orthodox Church pressures against commerce with 'diviners and dreamers' led John XXII to 'take the firmest measures against potential schismatics and subversive prophets' (Lerner 1992: 65). Ubertino was forced to leave the Franciscan order; in 1317, Olivi's commentary was put on trial, condemned, and banished from Church teachings; and the Olivi cult was repressed through inquisitorial campaigns. On a broader European scale, John's Apocalypse became a powerful instrument in the hands of the thirteenth- and fourteenth-century reformers, including followers of Wycliffe in England, Waldo in France, and Huss in Bohemia, all fighting against the Scarlet Woman of Rome.

Exegetic debates about the millennium and the End of Time were part and parcel of medieval European realpolitik. The political signification of the Apocalypse was such that 'when Innocent III [1161–1216] summoned the Church in the West to undertake a new Crusade, he declared officially that the Saracens were, according to the Apocalypse, the true Antichrist, and Mohammed the false Prophet; and that the end of their power was at hand, since its duration was limited to 666 years, which should elapse from the appearance of Antichrist in Mohammed' (Charles 1913: 24). Gregory IX's quarrel with the German emperor Frederick II (1194–1250) also involved eschatological rhetoric: while the pope condemned the emperor as an embodiment of the Beast evoked in Revelation 13, Frederick II claimed that 'the Pope himself is the great dragon who has seduced all the world, the Antichrist whose forerunner he has declared me to be' (quoted in Charles 1913: 24).

Reform-minded exegetes, however, were far more vulnerable to repression than kings and emperors. Influenced by Olivi and Arnold of Villanova, John of Rupescissa was one of those late-medieval scholars who used the Apocalypse to trot out the spiritual-versus-carnal-churches thesis and spent many years in prison for it. In his *Liber secretorum eventuum* (*c.* 1349), he reads Revelation as prophesying the coming of Antichrist in 1366, followed by his downfall in 1369, and then a Sabbath that would last for a full, literal millennium. His prophetic writings became very popular throughout Europe. The revival of millenarian eschatology *à la* Rupescissa led to a renewed interest in the early Christian writings of Lactantius. More important, it inspired the millennial movement of the late fourteenth century, led by the German Franciscan Frederick of Brunswick. It also coincided with a proliferation of prophets challenging Augustine's mystical view of the millennium, 'proposing different extended lengths of time for an imminent earthly Sabbath other than an exact thousand years ... Faith in a wondrous earthly future was growing just when Western Europeans were poised to storm the globe and survey the heavens' (Lerner 1992: 70f.). On the latter point, it should be remarked that the discovery and colonization of new territory were conducive to projecting the 'pastoralism of conventional Promised Land imagery' to American lands viewed as the New English Canaan: 'for the Puritan settlers, historical space was textualized because the experience of the New World had been typologically prefigured in the Bible. When the Puritans fled persecution, they repeated Exodus' (Robson 1995: 61).

With the Reformation, spiritual exegeses of Revelation are still advocated,[5] yet interpretive efforts to establish parallels between Church history and John's Apocalypse become the norm. In his preface to his 1534 translation of Purvey's *Commentary on the Apocalypse*, Luther presses John's visions (from chapter 4 onwards) into the service of a Protestant view of Church history. In his review of this period, Prigent (1959: 57–71) goes through a long list of commentators who adopted the prophetic-historic approach to Revelation, all with a view to establishing a direct equation between Satan and Roman papistry, announcing its imminent defeat and judgment at the hand of God. Scholars who saw in Revelation a lengthy history of religious persecutions leading up to the Antichristian reign of papistry include Meyer (*c.* 1534–54), A. Osiander (*c.* 1580), J. Fox (1596), J. Durham (1660), D. Paraeus (1622), J. Cluverus (1647), J. Gerhard (1645), H. Kromayer (1662), Calov (1676), and Pierre Jurieu (1686). By and large, these commentators view their own age as crisis-ridden years filled with expectations of the forthcoming End.

As already mentioned, the earliest exegeses of Revelation were of an eschatological nature, concentrating on visions of current crises of the world and an earthly millennium soon to follow. With early Christianity, readings of the New Testament Apocalypse are primarily concerned with events of the immediate future viewed cosmologically. Care is taken *not to establish* systematic connections between apocalyptic imagery and explicit events or characters of the historical past or present. By contrast, heterodox exegeses of the late Middle Ages tend to press Revelation into the service of a global Church history, using the Scriptures to plot out worldly events of a distant past (i.e., John's distant future) leading up to the interpreter's age, the millennium, and the Day of Judgment. Eschatological and Church-history interpretations of Revelation thus place different emphases on how much knowledge of history is needed to make sense of what John has to say about God's presence in the world and about things to come, including the end of history.

While Church-history expositions of Revelation served the cause of both Catholic and non-Catholic reformers struggling against the worldliness of Church power, eschatological interpretations of the book were revived by propapal Jesuit scholars of the sixteenth century. Opposed to Protestant versions of an Apocalypse predicting the downfall of the Church of Rome, Jesuits such as Ribeira (*Commentarius in Apocalypsim*, 1591), Blasius Vegas (*Commentarii exegeteci in apocalypsim Ioannis apostoli*, 1606), and Alcasar (*Vestigatio sensus Apocalypsis*, 1614) advocated a future-oriented approach to Revelation, treating the text (or at least everything from the sixth seal to the end of the book) as a series of visions of the end of the world, a last age to be fulfilled literally, strictly according to prophecy. Their commentary on Revelation thus echoed the teachings of Irenaeus, Hippolytus, and Victorinus, and those of Bonaventure as well. A century later, however, the French theologian Bossuet (*L'Apocalypse avec une explication*, 1688) chose rather to turn the Church-history method against the Reformation: Bossuet saw in the Turkish invasion of Europe and the teachings of Luther the realization of John's vision of Gog and Magog (Rev. 20: 8). Meanwhile, as millenarianism was eventually condemned by Protestant Churches via the Confessions of the Lutheran and Reformed Churches, some non-Catholic scholars (Napier 1593, Conradi 1560) abandoned the continuous world-historical method and fell back on the recapitulation method to discredit Roman Church history. As the Protestant ban on chiliasm was without authority in England, scholars such as Mede (1627) applied a combination of recapitulation and chiliastic principles to the Book of Revelation. Disciples of Mede, including Sir Isaac Newton and Whiston, predicted that the millennium would arrive soon, in the year 1715, and then 1734 according to Whiston. Through the writings of Bengel (*Erklärte Offenbarung Johannis oder vielmehr Jesu Christi*, 1740), prophecies of the End achieved great popularity in eighteenth-century Germany.

Scholarly debates between eschatological and Church-history renderings of Revelation lasted until the nineteenth century. Commentators who adopted the Church-history perspective fell into two categories: those (de la Chétardie 1701, Louis Elies du Pin 1714, Reeves 1802, etc.) who attempted to show correspondences between Revelation and early Christian history (usually up to the reign of Constantine), and those (Swedenborg 1766, Holzhauser 1784, etc.) who went beyond the late antiquity to include events of the Middle Ages and later centuries. The latter include Auberlen (*Der Prophet Daniel u. die Offenbarung Johannis*, 1854) and his followers who saw in John's Apocalypse predictions of the principal epochs of Church history and its spiritual progress in its struggle against the forces of evil. Hengstenberg (*Die Offenbarung Johannis erläutert*, 1849–51) and a few others adopted the same approach, but with a strong anti-papal bias. As for the eschatological method, its major proponents were Kliefoth, Lange, Zahn, Stern, Kremenz, and Waller; mention should also be made of a few eschatologists (e.g., Joubert 1762, Bridou 1818) who read into John's writings prophetic visions of the final conversion of Jews to Christianity (see Prigent 1959: 91–105).

To conclude, the notion that Revelation is a blueprint for Church history, with many of its prophecies directed against Catholic papacy and the millennium being reckoned from either Christ or Constantine, was an integral part of early reform movements within the Catholic Church and later Protestant exegeses. Roman interpreters returned the favour by portraying all heretics, including Luther and other Reformation leaders, as embodiments of the Beast and Antichrist. Or they reverted to future-oriented expositions of Revelation, thereby undermining Protestant applications of apocalyptic imagery to Church history. The popularity of teleological accounts of Apocalypse adapted to each interpreter's time, his view of previous history, and hopes for a better future lasted well into the nineteenth century. In these accounts,

> place is found in the visions for the subsequent course of the Roman empire, for the invasions of the Goths and other barbarian tribes, for the Turks and their conquest of Christian lands, for the Crusades, the wars of the Reformation, the French revolution, and also for great historic figures, e.g. Constantine, Luther, Gustavus Adolphus, Napoleon, and so on with endless variety, as the phases of history changed and the fancy of scholars dictated. With some the recapitulation theory is adopted, each of the two series, the trumpets and the bowls, repeating and making clearer the series of the seals; but generally the three series are viewed as unfolding a continuous history. (Beckwith 1967: 330f.)

Teleological exegesis postulates that world history proceeds inevitably towards its own End, a denouement planned from the beginning of Creation and revealed to John in the first century C.E. Church history moves towards the interpreter's critical age, reaching the eve of a profound transformation involving a global dualism between good and evil. Apocalyptic thought thus presupposes a radical contrast between 'two aeons or ages, the present evil age and the good, messianic era to come. But we should not exaggerate this sort of dualism into one of a metaphysical Gnostic or Manichaean sort' (McGinn 1992: 8). After all, God manifests himself throughout human history, through the deeds of his faithful followers and the mediation of the millennial age, a messianic kingdom that prepares humanity for the blessings of an everlasting life in the New Jerusalem.

Genealogical Exegeses

Back to the Beginnings

Teleological accounts of Revelation can go in two different directions. The interpretation may speak to issues of continuous history, embracing long-term movements and turning-points in the history of the Church (*kirchengeschichtlich*) or the world (*weltgeschichtlich*). Or it can adopt an eschatological stance (*endgeschichtlich*), placing the events foretold by John entirely in the Last Days. In all cases, the original text is deemed to convey prophetic visions of things that have yet to come, not with eternal truths sought through anagogical reasoning.

Teleology and anagogy are radically different approaches. Yet they have an important point in common that sets them apart from modern biblical exegesis: their propensity to transcend the narrative present, seeking meaning well beyond the text and its original context. Signification resides outside John's time, in future events or in expressions of a timeless spirit. Interpretive meanings are formulated in ways that can *transcend* the primitive text and circumstances of its production.

Insofar as exegetes have understood Rev. as a descriptive or predictive account of factual events of the past and the future, or of timeless theological statements and principles, they have tended to reduce the imaginative language of Rev. to a one-to-one meaning. They thus have historicized the sequence of images and visions, objectified symbolic-allegoric expressions, and reduced mythopoeic vision to abstract theological or philosophical problems. (Fiorenza 1985: 23)

By contrast, modern exegeses of Revelation are concerned with origins, committed, as they are, to a genealogical perspective on the Scriptures. As Fiorenza points out (1985: 15), 'it is universally acknowledged that Rev. has to be understood in its historical-cultural and religious context.' Thus 'contemporary scholars no longer dream of finding predictions for history or for the future within Rev.' (35). Unlike teleological and anagogical expositions, genealogical accounts seek explanations in terms of how the text actually 'began' – beginnings defined as the sources and origins of a text. Given their commitment to a scientific recovery of 'first meanings,' scholarly readings of the Scriptures purport to be disinterested, apolitical, and value-free. While Revelation can be treated as a window to its own time, its interpretation must remain detached from all contemporary politics, including battles over religious doctrine.

As with other perspectives on Revelation, the genealogical approach is conducive to various modes of interpretations. For one thing the 'source' of a text can be defined extrinsically. The original text is then understood against the background of contemporary circumstances (*zeitgeschichtlich*), social and political, and current religious, cultural, and literary influences. The book is understood 'from the standpoint of its first-century historical setting' (Mounce 1977: 41). But the sources can also be intrinsic, internal to the text itself, by which I mean immanent properties that belong to no other text and that are thought to constitute the source of its fixed meaning. Words have original significations and intentions (including hopes of the future), the narrative has an inherent structure, and the text exhibits thematic patterns that produce narrative order and the lessons of a particular theology or literary genre. In all cases, scholarship requires that the text be

looked from the point of view of the text itself, its author, or the circumstances of the original readers – the times (cultural, political) at which Revelation was written or immediately before. In the words of W.G. Kümmel,

to be sure, today we are one in principle to the correct method of exposition of the
Apocalypse, at least where such exposition proceeds from scientific presupposi-
tions: The Apocalypse can only be understood in accordance with the intentions of
the author and with our historical distance from his time, if we first of all ask about
the traditional meaning of the images and conceptions *(traditionsgeschichtliche
Methode)*, then seek to determine which expectations the author proclaims in
respect to the imminent end *(endgeschichtliche Methode)*, and finally observe to
what extent, by means of reference to the history of the immediate past or present,
the time of the end is regarded as already realized in the present *(zeitgeschichtliche
Methode)*. (quoted in Court 1979: 19)

We now proceed to a more detailed discussion of these various applications
of the genealogical method to Revelation, starting with the contemporary-
historical approach.

Contemporary-Historical Analyses

According to Charles (1913: 4f.) and Beckwith (1967: 335), exegetic scholarship in the modern age thrives on the contemporary-historical mode of
analysis. In this perspective explanations are arrived at by reference to
events contemporary with the author and the original text, events that must
have been well known to the writer and reader 'who did not think of docu-
menting what were to him obvious identifications' (Court 1979: 13). The
central task of the interpreter is thus to explore the interaction between text
and context, unravelling historical connections that used to be implicit and
that exegetes must now reconstruct through rigorous documentation.

Rudiments of contemporary-historical readings of Revelation can be
found in the sixth-century writings of Oecumenius (Prigent 1959: 28) and
the twelfth-century teachings of Richard of Saint Victor. More fully developed versions of this approach, however, date back to commentaries of six-
teenth- and seventeenth-century scholars who objected to the interpretive
speculations and anti-papal rhetoric of prophetic-historical exegesis. From
the Reformation onwards, many scholars, especially the Jesuits concerned
with Roman Church credibility, combined their anagogical or teleological
readings of Revelation with an interest in archaeology and early Christian
history – hence, knowing the facts and conditions of the writer's own time.

Encouraged by intellectual developments of the Renaissance and the rise of humanism, philological contributions to apocalyptic exegesis were also attempted by a number of scholars of the sixteenth and seventeenth centuries, all of whom delved into the original meanings and linguistic aspects of Revelation (see Prigent 1959: 83).

While he emphasized the eschatological underpinnings of Revelation, the Jesuit Ribeira (1591) was one of the first to argue that the first five seals of John's visions spoke to events occurring during the period extending from the preaching of the Apostles to the persecution of early Christians under the emperor Trajan. John's visions were thus concerned with issues of immediate history and the final End, not with the unfolding of subsequent Church history. Similarly, Bibliander (*Diligens atque erudita enarratio libriapocalypsis Johannis*, 1547) insisted on the importance of first-century persecutions of Christians for an understanding of Revelation. Alcasar (1614) claimed that Revelation 5–19 reflected early Christian Church conflicts with Judaism and the heathenism of the Roman world, a line of reasoning later picked up by Eichhorn (*Commentarius in apocalypsim Johannis*, 1791). In his exposition of the premillennial part of the book, Alcasar explored possible connections between the text and events that fell within the age of the prophet and early Christianity, without reference to events recorded after the reign of Constantine.[6] For Ribeira, and to a lesser extent Alcasar, the text no longer foretells events intervening between John's time and the Last Days. Theirs is a postmedieval invitation to a science of history, a scholarly inquiry into the early Christian setting of John's visions of the End.

In the eighteenth and nineteenth centuries, two formulations of the contemporary-historical approach were developed. On the one hand, several scholars (Abauzit, Harduin, Wetstein, Harenberg, Herder, Züllig) contended that John's prophecies were essentially directed against Judaism and Jerusalem: details of the visions thus spoke of the historical Jerusalem – for example, the seven hills in the neighbourhood of the holy city. On the other hand, other contemporary scholars (Corrodi, Herrenshneider, Semler, Bleek, Ewald, de Wete, Lücke, Volkmar) interpreted Revelation 20 chiliastically (rightly so, according to Charles 1913: 48) but thought it more accurate to read into the bulk of Revelation signs of antagonistic relations between Christians and the Roman Empire. Antichrist was thus to be identified with *Nero redivivus*, who stood for heathenry and the Roman Babylon, an archenemy still alive and soon to return to persecute members of the true Church. As Feuillet (1961: 46) notes, most exegetes of the twentieth century reach similar conclusions concerning the importance of early

Christianity's conflict with Rome in the Book of Revelation, especially chapters 12 to 21. But the question of how Judaism and Christianity meet and depart from each other in Revelation has not disappeared altogether from modern biblical exegesis. On the contrary, the influence of Old Testament imagery and literary forms remains a central issue in genealogical debates over John's Apocalypse.

With Ernest Renan's *L'Antéchrist* (1871), a new shift in the contemporary-historical perspective occurs: numerous motifs of Revelation are shown to be grounded in economic or ecological events of John's time. For instance, the scenes of Revelation 6: 6 and 8: 8 are best understood in reference to the famine prices of 68 C.E. and the fall of a water-polluting meteorite, respectively. Another product of this archaeological approach is Sir William Ramsay's study of Asia Minor archaeology and history in *The Letters to the Seven Churches of Asia Minor and their place in the plan of the Apocalypse* (1904). In Ramsay's work, 'the Apocalypse reads the history and the fate in the natural features, the relations of earth and sea, winds and mountains, which affected the cities' (quoted in Court 1979: 12). In a similar vein, there is Hemer's (1986) more recent excursion into the cultural-archaeological setting of the letters to the seven churches of Asia Minor.

As the social and political setting of Revelation will be taken up in the next chapter, no review of twentieth-century debates over the historical circumstances of John's Apocalypse will be attempted here. Suffice it to mention a particular brand of contemporary-historical exegesis, one that maintains a teleological interest in questions of linear Church chronology. In his *L'Apocalypse et les cultes de Domitien et de Cybèle* (1935), Touilleux reacts against Allo's use of the recapitulation principle and takes a preterist stance (*zeitgeschichtlich*), arguing that John's prophecies had already been fulfilled when the book was originally written. John thus adopted a 'fundamentalist fiction' strategy characteristic of Jewish apocalypses, one whereby he reports his visions as if they had occurred about 68 C.E., nearly thirty years before his time. Having written these prophecies *ex post facto*, events recorded at later dates (between 68 and 95 C.E.) served to enhance the credibility of John's apocalyptic prophecies and his vision of greater things to come.

Similar 'prophetic predating' arguments were taken up by Gelin (1938) and Giet. In *L'Apocalypse et l'histoire* (1957), Giet emphasizes parallels between scenes of Revelation and Josephus's account of the three phases in the Jewish War with Rome – hence, events occurring during the reign of Vespasian. While Hopkins and Feuillet (see Fiorenza 1985: 38ff.) are not concerned with the correspondence between Revelation and concrete events of early Christian history, they too consider John's visions to be founded on a theology of linear history. After the *genus litterarium* of Jewish apocalypses, events of both mythical and real history (e.g., Christ's) are organized into discrete periods and segments of time such that an understanding of both the present and the eschatological future can be derived from past salvation history. Faith in the Redeemer, his prophetic messenger, and his promises of a glorious future is thus strengthened through past realizations of God's plan.

Literary-Historical and Source Analyses

As Charles once remarked (1913: 58ff.), modern exegesis generally accepts the view that Revelation as we know it betrays the influence of other writings and sources. Not only should the text be situated in its proper historical context, but it should also be understood *in relation to other ancient texts*. The implication of this simple comment is that the influence of other texts, and also later revisions of John's original Apocalypse, may be of such critical importance that the unity and authenticity of Revelation can be either seriously questioned or firmly established, depending on the results of close analyses of the relevant sources.

Although philological commentaries on Revelation date back to the Renaissance, studies that seek to question or confirm the unity of John's text are a development of nineteenth-century scholarship. The issue of textual unity had already been raised by Grotius (*Adnotationes in NT*, 1644), who argued that parts of the text were produced in Patmos under Claudius, while others had been put in writing in Ephesus. Revelation thus brought together several visions experienced in different places and at different times, mixing conflicting elements written down before and after the destruction of Jerusalem.[7]

More recently, literary history has produced a great number of hypotheses concerning the composite nature of the New Testament Apocalypse, most of which speak to the delicate issue of how much incoherence (lack of temporal linearity) and how much Jewish material could have formed an integral part of the original Revelation. Briefly, these hypotheses fall into three categories (after Charles). The first position is known as the *redaction hypothesis*. It states that one or several editors can be shown to have edited the original Johannine text. This is the position presented in the final writings of Völter (*Das Problem der Apokalypse*, 1893), a German exegete who saw in Revelation the influence of several Judaistic sources but also a

Christian text written by John and revised ten years later by the heretic Cerinthus. While adopting a similar mode of analysis, Vischer (*Die Offenbarung Johannis*, 1886) and his followers (Iselin, Rovers, Holtzmann, Kohler, Von Soden) concluded that the text had so many Jewish parallels that it had to be a Judaistic composition later edited by a Christian who also added the letters to the seven churches. According to Weyland (*Omwerkings-en Compilatie-Hypothesen toegepast op de Apokalypse van Johannes*, 1888), the book was rather the final product of an able Christian editor who brought together the original Johannine Apocalypse and two Jewish sources. Charles (1920) is another major proponent of the redaction hypothesis. He recognizes that the author of Revelation made use of various sources, especially of Jewish tradition, and that while John wrote in Greek, he thought in Hebrew. He adds that John's text must have been later revised by a rather unintelligent disciple. Deviations from Classical Attic Greek are consistent features of John's style, yet the language and rhythm deployed in Revelation also points to numerous repetitions, interpolations, glosses, and corruptions introduced through later editorial activity. These distortions of the primitive text must be identified with a view to reconstructing the linear order originally intended by the author.

By contrast, the *source hypothesis* emphasizes the loosely integrated sources at play in Revelation, to the point of doubting the original unity or logic of the New Testament Apocalypse. According to Spitta (*Offenbarung des Johannis*, 1889), the original text merely compiled a number of superficially edited sources: during the reign of Trajan, a Christian editor put together a primitive Christian Apocalypse (written soon after 60 C.E.) and two Jewish sources (written under Caligula and Pompey, respectively). Briggs (*The Messiah of the Apostles*, 1895) went to the extreme of discovering six independent sources, the combination of which had gone through four different editions. Later contributors to this source-critical literature include Wellhausen (*Analyse der Offenbarung Johannes*, 1907–9) and Stahl (1923). Using the repetition criterion, M.E. Boismard (1949) reached the conclusion that the prophetic parts of Revelation (Rev. 4–22) reflect three different texts written by the same author but at different times (the letters, a text written under Nero, and another after 70 C.E.)

A middle-of-the road strategy consists in admitting that an original, single-authored text must have existed, but not without distortions and incongruities. The *fragment hypothesis* advocated by Weizsäcker (*Die Offenbarung Johannis*, 1904), Sabatier (*Les origines littéraires et la composition de l'Apocalypse de St. Jean*, 1887), Bousset (*Die Offenbarung Johannis*, 1906), and others thus holds that fragments of pagan or Jewish material (e.g., the sealing of the twelve tribes of Israel in Rev. 7) were loosely incorporated into the text. This was done more or less successfully, and without an adequate understanding of their original meaning.

It should be emphasized that, while they challenge the internal unity of the Johannine Apocalypse, literary historians never abandon the notion that 'original source-texts' (*Grundschrift*) exist in the first place. It just happens that Revelation as we know it is not coherent enough to classify as a 'primitive text.' There is so much confusion, idiosyncracy, and diversity of sources at play in this book that it cannot be considered to have the 'oneness' – logic, coherence, unity – of an 'original' text.

By and large, twentieth-century exegetes of Revelation have retained the literary-critical interest in questions of textual dating and authorship. Source-critical manipulations of the book, however, are no longer in fashion. With a few exceptions (Ford 1975), scholars have now abandoned the twofold assumption that (a) Revelation is essentially a composite text full of inconsistencies and essentially foreign elements; and (b) that the task of the exegete is to decompose the mixture of the Jewish and Christian material at hand so as to identify its component parts – parts that represent primitive texts combined into a derivative product. Most scholars now view Revelation as a single-authored, authentically Christian Apocalypse (Fiorenza 1985: 36).

Comparative Religious Studies

The development of comparative religious studies over the last two centuries has had a major impact on readings of the Scriptures. The search for parallels between Revelation and contemporary or earlier religious traditions (*traditionsgeschichtlich*, *religionsgeschichtlich*) was anticipated by Cornelius (*Commentarius in acta apostolorum*, 1627), the first exegete to discuss similitudes between Revelation 12 and Greek mythology (Prigent 1959: 82). But it is only well into the modern era that scholars have recognized the extent to which the symbolic material of Revelation is not entirely original, reflecting, as it does, not only Old Testament sources, but also contributions from traditions beyond Judaism.

The list of scholars who have contributed to this literature is beyond the scope of this chapter; some of them will be discussed throughout the analyses developed in this book. Suffice it to mention here the main schools of thought and a few key advocates of the comparative method (see Feuillet 1961: 92). One criterion that can be used to classify comparative-religion analyses is the cultural-influence area emphasized by the exegete. For instance, A. Dieterich (*Abraxas*, 1891) found John's inspiration (especially in Rev. 12) in the Greek Zeus–Leo–Python mythology, whereas Jeremias (*Babylonisches in Neuen Testament*, 1905) and Lohmeyer (1926) stressed Babylonian-based Mandean parallels. W. Bousset (1906) chose yet another direction: his reading of Revelation points to striking similarities in the Iranian and Egyptian Horus–Isis–Set mythology. As for the influential Gunkel (*Schöpfung und Chaos*, 1895), he favoured the Babylonian Marduk–Damkina–Tiamat mythology, as did Bousset, Pfleiderer, Holtzmann, and Moffat. In Gunkel's view, traditions other than the Judaeo-Christian are at the origin of much of John's apocalyptic symbology. Although the prophet gave his foreign material a new Christian turn, he could not interpret it with absolute freedom, nor did he have a full grasp of all the imageries thus borrowed. Unlike the latter exegetes, H. Lietzmann (*Der Weltheiland*, 1909) rejected any particular cultural influence and instead emphasized the widespread Near Eastern distribution of the heavenly Saviour figure.

Another criterion that can be used to situate Revelation in relation to other ancient texts or belief systems is the dominant theme that pervades the visions and language of John. In the works of F. Boll (1914), ancient astromythology plays the latter role: Revelation is merely a literary elaboration of astrological religions of Babylonian origin and further developed in the Graeco-Roman world. A similar thesis first appeared in Dupuis's *Origine de tous les cultes*, published in 1795. According to Dupuis, the seven churches addressed by John harked back to the seven spheres or planets moving in the sky, and the conflict between the Beast and the sun-robed woman of Revelation 12 reflected the Virgo–Draco antagonism in heaven. This line of reasoning was later revived by Jäger and Hommel (*Reformation*, 1909), with an emphasis on the zodiacal correlates of John's celestial imagery, and then by Boll. Students of Revelation influenced by Boll include Loisy (1923) and N. Morosow (*Die Offenbarung Johannis eine astronomish-historische Untersuchung*, 1912). Sir William Ramsay and Lepsius saw in John's imagery signs of the seven planets, constellations marking the four seasons, the twelve stellar gates of the firmament, and the twenty-four constellations of the northern and southern hemispheres. In light of the evidence marshalled by these scholars, Charles (1913: 54: emphasis added) was led to conclude that 'behind several of the figures and conceptions in the Apocalypse lay astronomical ideas he [the student] will be the first to acknowledge, but he will at the same time be convinced that to the Seer the astronomical origin of these conceptions was in most cases *wholly unknown*.' While he thought Ramsay had unduly committed himself to the astronomical method (in spite of his own warnings against it),

Charles (1920, 1: clxxxvi) was also led to contradict his own method and read conscious astrological references into Revelation. For instance, in his short review of the interpretations of Revelation, he notes that the 'order of the twelve precious stones ... points to our author's knowledge of the heathen conception of the City of Gods and of contemporary astronomy, and his deliberate deviation from them.' To this notion of deliberate misappropriation of astrological sources we shall return at length throughout our reading of John's Apocalypse.

While the majority of twentieth-century biblical scholars deem it useful to understand Revelation against the background of non-Christian traditions, there is also a widespread tendency to exercise exegetic caution *vis-à-vis* the multitude of 'foreign keys' to the Apocalypse discovered through comparative analysis. Parallels that are only partial can lead to false conclusions regarding the actual meaning of John's imagery. Moreover, the fact that Revelation may display themes or patterns found in other traditions does not necessarily indicate a relationship of real literary dependence. To avoid losing sight of the truly Christian and profoundly original character of Revelation, many exegetes will now accept a literary-dependence argument if and only if two basic conditions are met: the parallel between the two traditions must be extensive and systematic (covering all details of a given scene, chapter, or theme), and their nearness must be temporal and geographic as well. If the second condition is not met, then it cannot be assumed that one tradition has influenced the other. Given these methodological requirements, New Testament scholars will often argue that a comparative understanding of Revelation need not go beyond Judaism and Old Testament sources. In the words of Fekkes (1994: 59), 'there is no denying that Revelation is a complex of various traditions and even multiple genres, and this should warn any who would attempt to build an interpretation on the basis of one tradition only. Yet the sheer magnitude, variety and consistency of John's use of the OT certainly constitutes this area as a fundamental starting place for the exegete.'

Fiorenza (1985: 17f.) recommends that, when making sense of Revelation, exegetes go beyond Jewish traditions. In her words, 'contemporary scholarship tends to elucidate especially the Jewish apocalyptic and OT matrix of the images and patterns in Rev., but does not sufficiently acknowledge that the cultural-religious milieu of Rev. and its communities is also Greco-Roman and Asian culture.' She adds that, 'instead of trying to isolate different traditions and backgrounds, scholars might consider that the author, consciously or not, drew on and fused together traditions, motives, and patterns at home in very different cultures and mythologies.'

While scholars may choose to follow Fiorenza's recommendation, there is yet another way of downplaying traditions other than the Judaeo-Christian at play in John's Apocalypse: the text can be interpreted as being unique, constituting its own origin, transcending all previous sources and 'influences' that were fed into its composition. Exegetes will quarrel over the relative weight of 'pagan' sources in Revelation, yet most would accept Fiorenza's conclusion that whatever raw material and literary patterns John may have borrowed, the prophet did succeed in reworking his sources 'into a new and unique literary composition' adjusted to the historical circumstances of his time (Fiorenza 1985: 22; cf. 134, 163). The insights of the Seer are such that he can be said to have worked his Jewish and non-Jewish source material into 'an independent literary form and a personal theological conception,' thereby showing an 'independent use of available material' (Fiorenza 1985: 36). Kraft (1974) is also of the opinion that the author of Revelation was such an artist that he was able to integrate different traditions and achieve 'a unitary composition and optimal configuration of artistic form and theological content' (see Fiorenza 1985: 17; cf. 163). Beasley-Murray seems to object to the notion that the text has no counterpart in ancient literature, a notion that encourages 'undisciplined *freedom* in the elucidation of the book.' But he goes on to suggest that freedom did prevail in the writing of the book: that is, John '*freely* makes use of existing material' and gives old meanings a new purpose (1974: 12, 18; emphasis added).

We are thus faced with the somewhat paradoxical notion of foreign sources that are effectively used but never entail literary dependence. Beasley-Murray's discussion of John's Antichrist figure may serve to illustrate this point. The figure betrays varied influences, the most important of which is the Babylonian story of Tiamat. John combined the latter story with emperor-worship imagery and the myth of evil Nero returning from the dead. Having said this, Beasley-Murray goes on to say that

it is doubtful, however, whether we are justified in viewing any of these factors as *originating* the figure of the Antichrist ... Contrary to the supporters of the history-of-religions school, however, it is more likely that the watery Tiamat gave rise to the Antichrist than the Babylonian hero-god Marduk created the concept of the Christ and his kingdom. Back of the Antichrist stands the Devil, who for John as for Job never rises beyond being an instrument of God; and back of Christ stands the almighty God who promises redemption to his people. The cartoon of Tiamat and her host provides a means of expressing convictions whose *sources lie in very different origins.* (42f; emphasis added)

John must have been acquainted with the Babylonian dragon myth. But since his concept of salvation is essentially Christian, our reading of Revelation must begin with Christ, not Tiamat (40f.).

According to Feuillet, we should admire the author of Revelation for his mastery of the sources deployed in his visions and his ability to 'make his own everything he borrows' (1961: 66f.; my translation). The final product is not a mosaic of citations or a mere accumulation of disparate prophetic oracles, but rather a 'grandiose création littéraire.' Charles (1920, 1: clxxxvi) recognizes that the Apocalypse reproduces and reinterprets traditional forms of figures, symbols, or doctrines, yet it is important that we distinguish new meanings from original significations and that we recognize that 'in nearly every case our author has transformed or glorified the borrowed material.' Some imageries foreign to the essence and spirit of Revelation may be inapplicable to the author's purpose, or even unintelligible to him, but 'it is probable that these defects and inconsistencies would have been removed by our author if he had had the opportunity of revising his book.'

We shall return to this rather bizarre yet well-established notion that a text can make extensive use of existing traditions while also being fully independent of its source material, a truly 'original creation' – a unique literary act that brings the composition into existence from nothing save sheer inspiration.

Literary Genre and Form Analyses

In recent decades formal and literary genre analysis has generated a whole new range of interpretative claims and contributions to biblical scholarship. The basic assumption pervading these studies is that the text must be viewed as a patterned whole, not a mere sum of imageries begging to be dissected word by word, verse by verse, chapter by chapter (Ellul 1975; Sweet 1990: 13f.). By and large, the exegetes advocating this approach focus on *either* the dominant thematic features of Revelation in comparison with other literary genres, *or* the form–content configurations of the text – its compositional structure and overall architecture.

Interpretive findings achieved through the *literary-genre* approach have sought to fit Revelation into an overall tradition, model, or type characterized by certain compositional-thematic patterns. These recurrent themes and compositional conventions may be typical of the epistolary apostolicism of Revelation (Fiorenza 1985: 23), or they may reflect the logic of the Jewish calendar of feasts (Farrer 1949). Alternatively, John's text may be read against the background of the Yotser liturgy; Near Eastern 'myth and ritual' patterns (Hooke 1935, in Sweet 1990: 41); or the hymnic language, Eucharistic liturgy, and cultic settings of early Christianity (Shepherd 1960; Feuillet 1961: 61f., 71f.; Prigent 1964: 12, 77f.; 1981: 379). The festal and cultic aspects of Revelation could in turn point to the stages and scenes of the imperial games celebrated in Ephesus (Stauffer 1965). Revelation could also contain the component forms of Greek tragedy, with its 'dramatis personae, stage props, chorus, a plot, and a tragic-comic ending' (Fiorenza 1985: 166; see also Palmer 1903 and Bowman 1955). 'Other patterns are taken over from Jewish apocalyptic (judgment/salvation, cosmic week, messianic reign), from Near Eastern (divine warrior pattern or the assembly of the gods), from Hellenistic mythological (divine child, sacred marriage, divine polis) or early Christian tradition patterns (e.g., Synoptic Apocalypse or the apostolic letter form)' (Fiorenza 1985: 17).

In recent decades, biblical scholars have debated whether Revelation should be charted as a product of the prophetic or the apocalyptic genres (see Hellholm 1983). The criteria used to capture the apocalyptic genre and possibly lacking in the prophecies of Revelation include pseudonymity, secrecy, historical periodization, journeys in heaven, and a list of things revealed (Fiorenza 1985: 168; McGinn 1992: 12). Most scholars are now critical of the distinction (Caird 1966: viii). Unconvinced that the two types are essentially different, some simply prefer to 'place Rev. within the wider context of Greco-Roman revelatory literature which would allow us to understand it not just in relation to Jewish apocalyptic literature but also to Gnostic "apocalypses"' (Fiorenza 1985: 18).

Less concerned with the actual contents and recurrent themes of Revelation, other exegetes have stressed the formal-structural patterns of the Book of Revelation. This formalistic literature ranges from Calloud's and Fiorenza's (1985: 174ff.) structural exegeses to surface analyses of the overall plan of Revelation (see Lambrecht 1980: 77–104; Prigent 1980). Regarding the latter plan, Fiorenza rightly observes that one

can almost find as many different outlines of the composition as there are scholars studying the book. It is debated whether the apocalyptic part Rev. 4–22 is independent of the letters, or whether the letters are an integral part of the architectonic structure of the book. Other issues of debate are whether the book is totally composed in seven cycles that recapitulate each other or whether only the explicitly numbered visions are intended as seven cycles. It is also discussed whether Rev. consists of two rather even sections (1–11 and 12–22) or whether its architectonic pattern is the concentric ABCDC'B'A' pattern. Another issue is whether the narrative is cyclic, linear or moves in a conic spiral. (1985: 21f.)

While some scholars (e.g., Charles 1920) have attempted to reconstruct the linear order of symbols and scenes deployed in Revelation, others (e.g., Allo 1933; Bornkamm 1937) have emphasized the recapitulative–cyclical organization of John's apocalyptic material, showing how the same message or situation is repeated through a variety of consecutive visions and images. An interesting combination of these two opposite principles lies in the conic-spiral model, a framework where the narrative moves in concentric cycles but also 'from the present to the eschatological future' – hence, 'with the end-oriented movement of the whole book' (Fiorenza 1985: 5, 171ff.). Much of this surface-structure analysis hinges on the compositional role exegetes attribute to the 'almost-oppressive numerical symbolism' (McGinn 1992: 14) of John's visions, or 'sacred numbers and figures, which have an affinity to the astral myths of late antiquity' (Fiorenza 1985: 167). The number seven applied to the letters, the seals, the trumpets, and the bowls of Revelation is usually singled out as central to John's overall plan. Whether the whole book, however, is reducible to the heptadic rule (Farrer 1949; Gager 1975; see also Collins 1976: 12ff.) is still open to debate. Other formal features of Revelation's presentational logic include anticipatory visions, hymnic interludes, inclusions (a new sequence contained at the end of the last), and intercalations (two contiguous episodes interrupted by a third), all of which serve to interweave numerical series and thematic units into a highly integrated text (McGinn 1992: 14; Fiorenza 1985: 171ff.).

Teleology Subsumed

As Fiorenza (1985: 15) remarks: 'although most exegetes have replaced the classical approaches to the interpretation of Rev. with the historical-critical approach, they still maintain a combination of the preterist or futurist interpretation, or insist that Rev. reveals the course of salvation history or timeless historical principles.' As argued below, genealogical interpretations of the Scriptures have not simply supplanted older anagogical and teleological readings of John's book. More significantly, they have subordinated prior methodologies to their own readings of the Apocalypse.

Eschatological preoccupations with future time have not disappeared from genealogical excursions into the past. Although most biblical scholars now advocate a return to the original text, its inherent features, or the times and circumstances of its writing, many still insist that we should not ignore the truly prophetic character of Revelation. For instance, H. Morris (1983: 14) argues for a literalistic, futuristic, premillennial interpretation of John's visions. Beckwith (1967: 336) considers that the book is not only a writing that is truly apocalyptic in its genre, but also a vision that speaks the genuine apocalyptic truth. Revelation is what it claims to be: 'the message of a prophet sent by God and guided by the Spirit.' Given their dedication and devotion to the word of God, biblical scholars will maintain cultic reverence towards their object of analysis and the truth value of Revelation. While committed to the pursuit of academic exegesis, most scholars will invite readers to overcome the historical distance and idiosyncrasies of Revelation and to invest faith in the transcendental implications of Revelation and its relevance to our understanding of the End. Mounce (1977: 44) thus suggests that 'the predictions of John, while expressed in terms reflecting his own culture, will find their final and complete fulfillment in the last days of history.' To use the words of Charles, 'even according to the Contemporary-Historical Method, there remains a certain prophetic or eschatological element in the book, which arises out of and yet is inexplicable from the events of the present. The writer was no mere mechanical apocalyptist. He claimed to be *and wrote as a prophet*, though he was hampered in some measure by a body of apocalyptic tradition, which possessed in his eyes an undoubted sanctity, but which required to be interpreted afresh' (1913: 5; emphasis added).

A scholar's confession of faith in the prophetic truth of the Apocalypse may not be incompatible with his or her methodical exposition of biblical material; there are of course exceptions to this rule (du Plessis 1936; Sickenberger 1942; Zahn 1924; see also Feuillet 1961: 12ff., 100). Given their commitment to modern scholarship, exegetes now seem to agree that the Scriptures cannot be seriously used to predict *precise events* that were recorded after its writing, let alone historical moments that have yet to come. Compared with questions of prophecy, however, issues of denominational doctrine and related polemics (e.g., Mariological readings of the sun-robed woman of Revelation 12, the Jewish inspiration of Revelation) will have far more impact on the actual exposition of meanings of the Scriptures. More important, a great divide has separated biblical scholarship from sectarian and popular interest in the graphic predictions of Revelation. Faith in the literal prophecies of John's Apocalypse has never disappeared from the public, usually sectarian or political appropriations of the Scriptures. Despite the rise of humanism and the growth of science in Western culture, millenarian sects have used Revelation to promote their own views and prognostication of Church and world history. Literal millenarian readings of the book have been adopted by Taborites (radical Hussites) of fifteenth-century Bohemia; Anabaptists of the sixteenth century, French Labadists of the seventeenth century; and also Darbyites, Mormons, Adventists, and Jehovah's Witnesses of the nineteenth and twentieth centuries, to name just a few. Nowadays, while scholarly studies of Revelation are few, popular interpretations adopting a fundamentalist perspective are legion.

John's prophecies have made their way in politics as well. Not too many years ago Ronald Reagan was quoted saying that 'Ezekiel tells us that Gog, the nation that will lead all the other powers of darkness against Israel, will come out of the North. Biblical scholars have been saying for generations that Gog must be Russia. What other powerful nation is to the north of Israel? None. But it didn't seem to make sense before the Russian revolution, when Russia was a Christian country. Now it does, now that Russia has become communistic and atheistic, now that Russia has set itself against God' (quoted in Halsell 1986). Apocalyptic imagery was an integral part of the neo-conservative rhetoric of the 1980s. The Moral Majority and the New Christian Right movement thus made generous use of Lindsey's *The Late Great Planet Earth* to legitimate nuclear armament as the only way to defeat communism and the Soviet Union at the final battle of Armageddon. Fiorenza (1991: 8) also cites Walvoord's popular *Armageddon, Oil and the Middle East Crisis: What the Bible Says about the Future of the Middle East and the End of Western Civilization* as another example of how political fundamentalism can co-opt Revelation into serving contemporary right-wing politics (against Saddam Hussein as Antichrist incarnate).

As with the separation of astrology and astronomy, expositions of Revelation have bifurcated into two interpretive modes: the popular teleological and the scholarly genealogical. Modern exegetes will make concessions to eschatology as long as it is not understood realistically; prophecies of the End can be taken seriously but not literally. But there is another way, perhaps more significant, in which teleology can be subordinated to scientific scholarship: through a secular reassessment of the end-goals of human history. In the modern era, hopes in the new aeon and the renewed earth have given way to faith in the discoveries and revelations of science. Despite their faith in John's Verb, both Prigent's (1959: 77) and Charles's reviews of exegetic commentaries on Revelation, writings that span more than 2,000 years, are committed to this evolutionary view of exegetic history, an optimistic outlook on commentaries progressively and inevitably moving towards the end-goals of scholarly knowledge inspired by the 'spirit of science.'

It is remarkable that a century [eighteenth] that gave birth to the most boundless subjectivism should have also called the historic sense into active existence. Hope at last dawns on the long journey we have taken down the centuries. From this time forward we can reckon, on the whole, on a steady advance towards the solution of the problem. Progress may have occasionally to be made by roundabout ways, wrong paths may for a time be pursued, side issues be mistaken for the problems-in-chief, and criticism thereby be obliged to retrace its steps after apparently spending its energies in vain. But, notwithstanding, possession in part of the promised land has been won, and its entire conquest is only a question of time. (Charles 1913: 44)

Left-wing intellectuals have also found ways of using the Apocalypse to further their own struggle towards a better world. John's Apocalypse is often given a conservative, fundamentalist twist, but it can also serve to strengthen progressive 'visions of a just world' and classless society, as in liberation theology. According to Fiorenza (1985: 25; see also 1991), exegetes now tend to view Revelation more and more as a Christian composition *sui generis* as opposed to a slightly adapted Jewish writing, a shift in perspective 'due to many different developments in NT exegesis and theology. It is especially fostered by a renewed methodological interest in the literary character of NT writings, on the one hand, and the challenging theological questions of liberation theology, on the other hand.'

Finally, modern exegetes have incorporated teleological reasoning within their own analyses by imputing ends and endings, not to history, but rather to all the signs, imageries, and literary forms deployed in John's composition. Instead of being understood literally and historically, the 'final causes' of Revelation are now viewed individually and compositionally: the *end-goals of the text* lie in expressions of original authorial intentions, reflections on contemporary history, or the execution of an overall narrative plan (linear, cyclical, numerical, epistolary, etc.). The prophet made use of symbolic material with the aim of communicating thoughts and visions to his readers. His revelations followed precise developmental arrangements (from the hitherto of Rev. 1 to the hereafter of Rev. 22) and spoke to political and religious circumstances of his time, to which he added memories of the immediate past and hopes of the future as well. Having abandoned all notions of predictable finalities of history, scholars now seek the meaningful end-goals of author, text, and plot.

Exegetes who make it a central point to probe John's thoughts and hopes as conveyed in Revelation will deal with history but only from an authorial perspective. The question is no longer how events depicted in the text tie in with real Church or world history, but rather what were the *prophet's perceptions of past and future times*. Prophecies of the End thus express John's claims and expectations regarding things already realized and things yet to come. A central question to be asked here is whether the *author wanted* to convey the idea that the final time had already begun with the death and resurrection of Christ, or was he also concerned with imperfections of the Christian community and hopes in future atonement, victory, and salvation (as Holtz and Fiorenza argue; see Fiorenza 1985: 43ff.)? Also, was John writing about God's overall plan of long-term Endtime events, or was it first and foremost the immediate coming of the Lord that concerned him (Fiorenza 1985: 46–8)? Although they will answer these questions in various ways, scholars concerned with these issues share one basic assumption: the meaning of Revelation lies in the author's view of history.

Anagogy Subsumed

Genealogical questions about the original circumstances, sources, intentions, and plans of Revelation do not preclude teleological preoccupations with the aims and end-goals of the Apocalypse. Nor do they prevent exegetes from developing timeless-symbolic interpretations in an anagogical fashion, searching for the moral and spiritual implications of John's allegorical language (see Prigent 1959: 95–7). The commentaries of Claudel (1952), Farrer (1949), and Ellul (1977) are openly committed to the latter approach. Charles (1920, 1: cvii) adopts the same language when he says of Revelation that it is 'permanent truth' transmitted in a symbolic 'vehicle and vesture.' 'If it is the expression of a great moral and spiritual truth, it will of a surety be fulfilled at sundry times and in divers manners and in varying degrees of completeness in the history of the world.' The author adds that

the Seer seeks to get behind the surface and penetrate to the essence of events, the spiritual motives and purposes that underlay and gave them their real significance. Hence apocalyptic takes within its purview not only the present and the last things, but all things past, present, and to come. Apocalyptic and not Greek philosophy was the first to grasp the great idea that all history, alike human, cosmological, and spiritual, is a unity – a unity following naturally as a corollary of the unity of God. And yet serious N.T. scholars of the present day have stated that apocalyptic has only to deal with the last things! (1: clxxxiii, clxxxvi)

Other traces of the Augustinian quest for universals can be found in Lohmeyer's notion of an atemporal Johannine salvation concept that dissolves past and future in the eternity of God and Christ (Fiorenza 1985: 44). Lohmeyer (1926) ends up being so distrustful of historical explanations that he considers even the letters to the churches to be pure fiction. Minear's (1968) discussion of a comprehensive, transhistorical model lurking behind John's accounts of specific times and places reflects a similar exegetic strategy. Anagogical reasoning also informs Schlier's claim that the Roman Empire is the 'one cruel and drunken-city of all times,' with the implication that 'in the different historical events of various times the same thing respectively takes place' (see Fiorenza 1985: 43, 184f.). Specific events illustrate constant truths traversing all times, thereby confirming the enduring validity of the New Testament Apocalypse and its relevance for all periods of history, including the interpreter's own time.

Fiorenza's discussion of essentialism and 'above-timeness' in expositions of Revelation points to the persistence of anagogical teachings in modern biblical scholarship. In her view, studies of Revelation have tended to advocate a dualism between the Jewish character of John's outside imagery and the essentially Christian nature of Revelation's inner contents. The idea of Christian kernels of truth wrapped in a Jewish literary shell, an old theme dating back to Origen, 'has ever since marred the discussion of apocalyptic literature.' It has been used to dehistoricize John's symbolism through abstract principles, archetypal forms, and ontological concepts (1985: 23; cf. 2f., 25, 37, 186f.).

Although usually emphasizing questions of origins and the formal, literary, and contextual ramifications of Revelation, modern scholars have sought basic principles that make John's vision still relevant to its modern readership. This has been done from a particular denominational perspective or from the standpoint of feminism or liberation theology, using Revelation as a resource language against malestream ideology and colonialist oppression (Fiorenza 1985: 25; 1991: 5–14). It should be mentioned that students of Revelation who end up reproaching John for advocating a theology of vengeance, 'a veritable orgy of hatred, wrath, vindictiveness, and blind destructive fury that revels in fantastic images of terror' (Jung 1954: 121ff.), also interpret Revelation in the light of moral universals, but with a negative assessment of John's contribution to Christian ethics. Just as Luther doubted the Christian character of Revelation, so D.H. Lawrence (1980) regarded the book as the Judas of the New Testament. By contrast, others stress the positive aspects of Christian love and redemption and hopes for justice deployed in the New Testament Apocalypse (Beasley-Murray 1974: 27; Sweet 1979: 13, 51; Fiorenza 1985: 198f.).

But of all subsidiary expressions of anagogical thinking in biblical scholarship, the most important lies not so much in professions of faith in universal principles as in the widespread assumption of an 'eternal present.' By insisting that we return to the original circumstances, first meanings, and intentions of the text and its inherent logic, genealogists have arrested the flow of time. They have extracted from the text its entanglements and embattlements with previous texts (mythical, ritual, scriptural). Sources are recognized and discussed at length, yet the exercise is usually of a *comparative* nature. The aim of source analysis is to look at the similarities and differences between comparable texts, not the rhetorical disputes and polemical exchanges traversing the composition at hand. Moreover, exegetes often reach the conclusion that the author of Revelation has managed to supersede and transcend his own Jewish and non-Jewish sources, freeing himself from his origins and 'creating' an entirely 'original' text. The writing is turned into a composition *sui generis*, with its own Christian meanings and forms: John's handling of his sources ends up being 'always original and independent' (Swete 1951: cliv).

Genealogists have a fragmented view of history. They can also be criticized for not having done justice to Revelation's interaction with future times. Problems of the future are limited to narrative preoccupations with either the End or current developments of the Church under Roman rule (e.g., Christian accommodation with Rome, Judaism, or pagan cults in Asia Minor). The notion that Revelation is a text 'under way' or in constant motion – a text that transforms itself into new readings of the End and polemical reinterpretations of John's own embattlement with previous visions of history and the cosmos – is never considered. By defining the act of interpretation as an exercise in literary-historical *reconstruction*, exegetes downplay the role of discursive positioning in biblical scholarship. In doing so, they tend to overlook their own historically conditioned replies and responses to answers of the past and problems of their own times. When concerned with 'first meanings' only, scientific hermeneutics presuppose 'a discursive suppression of present-day socioecclesial locations and theological interests' (Fiorenza 1991: 1).

A text is not merely a response to its immediate historical context or subtext (Fiorenza 1985: 183, 192). In reality, all interpreters are engaged in hermeneutic disputes that move and evolve with the passing of time. From the moment that exegetes attempt to make sense of Revelation, they *log onto and connect into a moving 'dialogue.'* In the words of Fiorenza, 'in the act of interpretation one does not just understand and comprehend texts and symbols (hermeneutics), but one also produces new meanings by interacting with them.' This argument applies to all exegeses of Revelation, but also to John's interaction with his own context. Although Revelation may 'reflect' the first-century circumstances of its writing, it is important that these circumstances not be reduced to social and cultural factors 'revealing themselves' through John's visionary material and acting from outside, so to speak. As argued below, there is more to Revelation than a specific environment informing a particular script and providing the appropriate symbolism to attain the end-goals of the author and the text at hand. In lieu of being treated as external context, the latter conditions should be viewed as part of an *overall contest built into the text, a polemical exchange pervading the language of the New Testament Apocalypse.*

Text, Symbols, and Context

Much has been written about the social and political conditions under which Revelation was initially produced. In recent decades, a majority of scholars have reached the following conclusions regarding the circumstances surrounding the New Testament Apocalypse.

1 In keeping with some ancient sources, most biblical historians agree that the Book of Revelation was written at the end of the first century (*c.* 95 C.E.), during the reign of Domitian.

2 While Revelation contains memories of the trials experienced during the Neronic era, there is no conclusive evidence of severe religious persecution suffered by Christians in Asia Minor under Domitian. Revelation appears to have been written at a time when there were few martyrs and when Christians enjoyed comparative affluence and peace.

3 The imperial cult, however, was strongly promoted under Domitian, the self-proclaimed *Dominus et Deus*. With the assistance of the high priests of Asia Minor and in union with local cults, emperor worship was firmly established throughout the provincial cities addressed in Revelation 2–3.

Ephesus was the seat of the proconsul and competed with Pergamum for primacy. Like Smyrna it was a center of the emperor cult, had a great theater, and was famous for its gladiatorial games. Pergamum was the official center of the imperial cult. Already in 29 B.C.E. the city had received permission to build a temple to the 'divine Augustus and the goddess Roma,' which is probably referred to in Rev. 3:13 by the expression 'the throne of Satan.' In Thyatira the emperor was worshipped as Apollo incarnate and as the son of Zeus. In 26 C.E. Sardis competed with ten other cities for the right of building a temple in honor of the emperor but lost out to Smyrna. Laodicea was the wealthiest city of Phrygia and had especially prospered under the Flavians. (Fiorenza 1985: 193)

Christians who refused to submit to Roman religion were not persecuted systematically, yet provincials who were accused of being Christians by informers and were unwilling to recant and renounce their faith could be executed if found guilty (Sweet 1990: 29).

4 All indications are that the 'Apocalypse's call for divine judgment on the world is more rooted in a conflict of world views than in reaction to particular events of the day' (McGinn 1992: 13). A close reading of Revelation suggests that John objected strongly to Rome's dominion over all aspects of life, including rituals and religious beliefs woven into local trade and political activity. The prophet denounced false Christians who accepted the latter regime, compromising their faith through libertarian practices. He condemned the 'lukewarm' who adopted a low-profile Jewish lifestyle, avoiding overt witness-bearing and indulging in pagan cults. John showed no sympathy towards self-interested Christians who refused to withdraw from regular city-life events such as fertility cults, trade-guild ceremonies, and pagan temple feasts involving the eating of animals sacrificed to idols (Sweet 1990: 33). His Revelation seemed to have been a reaction against the complacency of worldly Christians who prospered under Domitian, forgot the hardships of the Neronic era, and no longer vested hopes in Christ's imminent return.

Revelation was John's response to Christian and Jewish accommodations with Rome. The prophet was reacting to pressure to adapt to civil religion in Asia Minor, pressure that came from Roman and provincial officials who denounced Jewish–Christian aloofness as 'atheism and hatred of the human race; public religion, as opposed to private belief, was part of the fabric of human life and abstention brought danger to society; earthquake, famine, plague – any natural disaster was interpreted as the wrath of the gods, and could be blamed on the "atheists"' (Sweet 1990: 31). Rome increasingly viewed Jewish customs and religion with suspicion, objecting to the antisocial character of ritual activity performed outside of Roman religion. Pressure to conform must have been exerted by some Christians as well, especially those from a Greek background who objected to Jewish–Christian intransigence and wished to participate in city life (31). Likewise some Jewish communities must have wished to maintain stable relations with imperial Rome, including certain privileges such as exemption from military service and the right to practise their own religion. These communities stood to lose a lot from being closely associated with 'antisocial' Jews and Christians. While the privileges and well-established traditions of Judaism attracted adherents from among the Christian ranks, Jews had to take their distance from sects, heretics, and other subversive elements that could have provoked Rome to anger. In any case members of the synagogue must have had little tolerance for active Christians who not only antagonized Rome but also applauded the fall of Jerusalem in 70 C.E. and claimed to form the true Israel, an elect people led by the self-proclaimed 'holder of the key of David.'

5 John's critique of Christian complacency entailed a rejection of Nicolaitan Gnosticism, a theology used to justify religious concessions to Roman laws in religious matters. In the Gnostic perspective, what mattered above all was individual salvation expressed through knowledge of spiritual mysteries, involvement in sacramental rites, and contempt for the material world. Instead of constituting a reward for one's sacrificial conduct, redemption had already been achieved through Christ's death and resurrection. Salvation was thus a matter of spiritual experience, without the experience being affected by real-life situations or physical behaviour of any kind (ritual fornication, eating idol food). In practice, this meant that Christians could participate in pagan activities knowing well that idols had no real existence. The claims made by God and the Roman emperor belonged to radically different orders, and involvement in the physical, worldly realm could hardly affect one's spiritual communion with God. 'Jesus Christ's claim to kingship and power is not of a political nature but pertains to the spiritual-religious life of the church, since Christians are taken out of this world and by virtue of their baptism already share in the kingly power of their Lord. No one, not even Satan, can harm the elect for they have insight into the very depth and mystery of the demonic and divine' (Fiorenza 1985: 196). Revelation condemned Christians who adopted this overly enthusiastic view of salvation, treating spiritual redemption as something already achieved and completely divorced from everyday life and ritual activity. Unlike Paul, who thought that evil originated mostly from cosmic forces, John warned Christians against bending to the power of Rome lest they provoke God's wrath and never achieve final redemption, never to 'exercise their kingship and priesthood *in the eschatological future*' (Fiorenza 1985: 125; emphasis added).

But if these are the real circumstances that motivated John's vision of the imminent End, why does the prophet use symbols of cosmic proportions to reflect on religious politics in Asia Minor? If he is adamant about Christians not giving in to the *unholy league of state idolatry, Judaism, and pagan cults* in Asia Minor, why does he show so much discretion and convolution in his portrayal of these evil influences usurping the attributes of God? Why use a generously esoteric language to *reveal* God's message to the world and disclose things otherwise hidden to his readers? As H. Morris puts it, Revelation

was written to show those things which were coming to pass, not to obscure them in a maze of symbolism and dark sayings. Great blessings was promised to all who would read (or even hear) the *words* of the book of this prophecy (Revelation 1: 3), but how could anyone be blessed by words he could not even understand? It seems anomalous that so many different exegetes of a book that was written as an unveiling of the future would publish such an unending variety of differing interpretations as to leave most seekers after such knowledge altogether confused. Such was certainly not the purpose of its original writer John, nor of Jesus Christ who sent it by John, nor of God who gave it to Christ. (1983: 20)

As should be expected, answers to these questions vary considerably, but they all revolve around the critical issues of language, symbol, and metaphor. To some biblical scholars, what John had to say was readily intelligible to his original audience. The actual meanings and political evocations attached to his words made perfect sense and were immediately accessible to first-century Christians. Later readers and interpreters, however, are not privy to these tacit connections built into the primitive text, and it is precisely the task of the exegete to recover these linkages through literary-historical analysis. As Sweet (1990: 21) remarks, 'it was not the author's concern to say which emperor was reigning – he was not writing for posterity but for his contemporaries, and they did not need to be told.' In his discussion of the sea-dragon imagery (harking back to the Babylonian Tiamat mythology), Beasley-Murray (1974: 17) takes a similar stand. He considers that earliest readers of Revelation must have recognized John's symbols as loan words taken from the Book of Daniel and applied to the oppressors of John's day. 'What to the uninitiated modern reader appears grotesque imagery, spoke with power to John's fellow Christians. The same applies to other symbols drawn from the stream of tradition, perhaps above all to those linked with the typology of the second exodus, and those relating to the city of God, wherein the images of Old Testament prophecy and of contemporary non-Christian religious beliefs flow together to produce a picture of unparalleled beauty and power.'

In the comparative-religion perspective, the allegorical and metaphorical material deployed by the prophet is better understood once its origins are properly identified. These origins dating back to the Old Testament or to pagan religions of antiquity are lost to modern interpreters. Initial readers (and perhaps the author himself) may have lost track of these sources as well, but the material was so well integrated that we can assume the final composition to have been fully comprehensible to its first-century audience. To elucidate the symbolism at hand, later readers and interpreters have much to gain from reconstructing the component parts of the composition and reflecting on the distinctive character and integrity of the final product. Origins that sunk into oblivion thus account for the 'strangeness' of Revelation in the eyes of modern readers.

The notion that visions of the New Testament Apocalypse were perfectly clear to their original audience finds another expression in the political-cartoon metaphor, a mode of representation evoked by exegetes to account for the symbolic character of John's writings. In order to be effective, the message conveyed to first-century readers required symbolic exaggeration. 'Frequently the situations depicted are deliberately exaggerated, and even made grotesque, in order that the message may be made plain ... The Book of Revelation uses the cartoon method more consistently than any other work of this order' (Beasley-Murray 1974: 16; see also Caird 1966: 6). Imageries unfolding in Revelation were designed to produce cartoon-like overstatements of current problems, combining conventional images of a world reflecting reality and yet larger than life. Since these conventions of caricatural language originate from a distant culture and historical context, students of the Bible must explore the author's conventions with a view to deciphering his allusions to history and principles of early Christian theology. 'There is cryptic reference to current affairs in bizarre allegories and symbols, sometimes decoded,' says Sweet (1990: 2), 'but for the most part obvious enough to the original audience, like our political cartoons. Some acquaintance with apocalyptic is indispensable for the serious explorer.'

A variation on the latter approaches to biblical analysis is to say that symbols will cease to create confusion and cryptic effects once they are recognized for what they are: means to convey coherent ideas. As L. Morris (1983: 20) puts it, Revelation was not written 'as a kind of intellectual puzzle (spot the meaning of this symbol!) sent to a relaxed church with time on its hands and an inclination for solving mysteries.' Rather, through his writings the prophet continually 'takes his readers behind the scenes,' repeating central ideas of Johannine theology: for instance, the notion that the future belongs to the Almighty, not to the Roman emperor. The ultimate power vested in God is a principle of permanent validity and is still relevant today. This is to say that 'John is an artist in words. We are to look for the meaning conveyed by each symbol in that symbol itself. It is a matter of indifference whether the symbols can be visualized or reconciled. That is not their purpose. *Their purpose is to convey ideas'* (21f.; emphasis added). The implication of this is that one must play John's game and translate his disconcerting imageries into intellectual principles – hence, 'convert into ideas the symbols he describes without troubling oneself about their incoherence' (Boismard 1968: 697).

The latter argument points to the continued importance of anagogical interpretation in contemporary biblical scholarship. Modern exegetes will insist that readers situate the text in its proper context, but once this is done there is still the question of how symbols relate to the circumstances surrounding the writing of Revelation and, more important, how metaphors can serve to express principles of Christian morality and theology. This is where anagogical reasoning comes in, converting intricate symbols into meanings of a higher conceptual order. While most exegetes are bound to use the anagogical method, some have explicitly prioritized this mode of interpretation. As Herder remarked more than two centuries ago, 'the book consists of symbols; and philosophers cannot endure symbols. The truth must exhibit itself pure, naked, abstract, in a philosophical way' (quoted in Fiorenza 1985: 184). If ancient imageries lack conceptual clarity for modern readers, it is incumbent upon the informed interpreter to show how *specific* symbols illustrate or typify general truths, thereby linking the *specie* to the *genere*, a method dating back to Tyconius and the Alexandrian school. According to Minear (1968: 233, 246) and Ellul (1977: 189), Babylon and Rome are thus mere examples of an archetypal evil force, symbols that stand for a demonic Power operating throughout the world and transcending all periods of history.

John's symbols will not lack intelligibility, provided that exegetes recover the initial meanings, sources, representational conventions, and immediate circumstances of the text. Alternatively, students of Revelation will restore the text's clarity by uncovering the general truths embodied in John's apocalyptic imagery. But the latter strategy – to look for permanent forces and principles transcending particular symbols and concrete events and characters of history – can lead to a rather different conclusion regarding the role of symbolling. In lieu of facilitating human understanding through graphic cartoons, telling examples, and vivid comparisons, symbols may be thought to serve the opposite function, which is to produce a text that moves beyond appearances of the visible world (Sweet 1990: 2). To some exegetes, signs of apocalyptic imagination are not designed to overcome but rather to reflect the problem that a prophet faces when speaking of things that cannot be described simply and logically – literally and rationally. John's message was never obvious from the start, and it is natural that he should have resorted to a language of cosmic scale to evoke realities that transcend the daily lives and immediate situation of his readership (Caird 1966: x–xi.). Visions of future events, supernatural forces, and universal principles will not let themselves be captured in a language of straightforward denotations and linear explanations. In the words of Charles (1920, 1: cvii), far from being literal or pictorial, John's symbols suggest 'to his readers what was wholly beyond the range of their knowledge and experience ... The appeal of such symbolism is made to the religious imagination. In this way it best discloses the permanent truth of which it is the vehicle and vesture.' This is to say that the prophet's 'experiences must ever be beyond the range of literal description. They can only be suggested by symbols.'

Modern exegetes who have applied the insights of structural semiotics or formal literary history to Revelation come to similar conclusions regarding the non-descriptive features of symbolic language, but they do so for entirely different reasons. In lieu of speaking to permanent principles of Church or world history, symbols are products of the order of language. They form a complex universe governed by codes or conventions that vary considerably from one culture, language, or literary genre to another, and that must be reconstructed through formal analysis. Without an in-depth study of the rules of composition and sign system deployed in Revelation, readers unfamiliar with the apocalyptic genre or code will be unable to make sense of John's imageries and their overall effects. To give one illustration of these effects, some exegetes claim that the literary devices and compositional forms used by John point to a text announcing the End and yet also playing havoc with linear rules of time–space organization, as if the End had already been brought to pass. Numerical series combined with anticipations, repetitions, interludes, and intercalations succeed in creating a tension between scenes of cosmic timelessness and the End-oriented movement of the entire book – between an End that is already realized and a final judgment that has yet to come (McGinn 1992: 14; Fiorenza 1985: 171ff.; Prigent 1981: 378f.). The apparent confusion of the apocalypse disappears once these formal effects and structural tensions are fully grasped.

Studies focused on the literary conventions of John's text will consider symbolism to be a central ingredient of the apocalyptic genre. According to Mounce (1977: 23), apocalypticism is characterized by 'the vision as a major instrument of revelation, concentration on the close of this age and the dramatic inauguration of the age to come, the unveiling of the spiritual order lying behind and determining the course of human history, the use of common apocalyptic motifs.' Symbolism is the ideal language to convey the latter visions. 'In giving free rein to the imagination, symbols of the most bizarre sort become the norm ... The extensive use of symbolism in apocalyptic literature may be accounted for in part by its subject matter (the close of this age and the dawning of a new age to come) and by the temperament of its spokesmen. It comes as no surprise that visionaries who specialize in the world to come feel compelled to resort almost completely to symbol.' While John rewrites past history as symbolic prophecies that have been clearly fulfilled (through events already known to the author), signs of future history are not easily interpreted; from this point on, 'prediction loses its clarity,' and symbols become all the more imperative.

Though less concerned with defining the apocalyptic genre, other scholars have argued that Revelation is essentially poetic, a text full of 'tensive symbols' partaking in 'the ambiguity, openness, and indeterminacy of all literature' (Fiorenza 1985: 186). Instead of being an obstacle to understanding John, literary imagination becomes an inherent feature of his text. As Beasley-Murray (1974: 23) puts it: 'John's visions of the end are those of an impressionist artist rather than the pictures of a photographer. For the most part they defy precision in application.' Likewise, Sweet (1990: 35f.) claims that 'a glance at other apocalyptic books shows that the genre is in its nature incoherent, with bewildering changes of scene and speaker, interjections, repetitions and inconsistencies. It works with pictures and symbols rather than a logically constructed argument.' Sweet adds that students of the Scriptures should generally prefer interpretations that 'seem impossibly difficult,' for 'we must beware of rewriting a text from another culture according to our canons of consistency. The first principle of good interpretation is to accept the strangeness of a text – try to tolerate loose ends and admit that understanding may at the moment be beyond us. It is only in this way that our perceptions can be enlarged – as with unfamiliar forms of art and music. On our view, allowing for the looseness of the genre, Revelation is an impressively coherent whole, and can be taken as substantially the work of one mind.'

To sum up, the *revelatory function* of John's apocalyptic symbolism is understood in one of four ways. First, exegetes may argue that symbols used by the prophet were fully intelligible to its original audience; primitive meanings can be 'revealed yet again,' provided that the original circumstances, sources, and conventions of the New Testament Apocalypse be elucidated. Second, biblical scholars may choose to treat apocalyptic symbols as telling illustrations of general principles of human history and Christian theology. Third, interpreters can claim that apocalyptic metaphors 'reveal' not so much a forgotten history as the mysterious nature of all things supernatural and transcendental that escape immediate human experience and understanding; the symbols make it plain that not all things can be made plain. Fourth, the symbolic arrangements of Revelation may be thought to follow precise rules of composition, literary codes, or conventions that are not entirely apparent, but that do operate effectively as means to convey particular views about history and the universe.

While these four views represent very different approaches to symbolism, they all share a basic assumption: although thickly textured, John's book is not an esoteric Revelation. Symbols of Revelation are always read in such ways as to reveal something. The imageries of Revelation express the meanings of an author or a culture, they reflect (on) the circumstances of a particular context, they betray the rules of a code or a genre in action, or they illustrate permanent truths and offer a glimpse of the infinite.

Fiorenza develops a different strategy. In her view, the imageries of Revelation should not be converted into propositional, esthetic, or logically coded expressions of constant truths, let alone a referential account of world history and events of the End. Instead she emphasizes the rhetorical function of John's apocalyptic imagination – not what symbols signify, but rather what they do to the reader, how they convince or motivate people to act in certain ways (1985: 187). To understand John's prophetic imagination, attention must be paid to the literary-historical context of Revelation, but also the multivalent meaning, emotive power, and mythopoeic musicality of the text at hand, a 'symbolic language compelling imaginative participation' (1991: 31, see 16, 19; 1985: 22, 25). Emphasis should thus be placed on the persuasive effects of symbolling. 'Insofar as scholarly interest is shifting from its preoccupation with rhetoric as technical device, style, and ornamentation to rhetoric understood as socio-political persuasion, the scholar pays renewed attention to how arguments are constructed and how power is inscribed in biblical texts' (1991: 21). Fiorenza goes on to argue that John's book combines three types of rhetorical speech: Revelation brings together the judicial language of defence and accusation (as in a court of law), deliberative words of persuasion and dissuasion (as in a political assembly), and epideitic expressions of praise and blame (as in a civil ceremony). These rhetorical modes are 'an active and fitting response' to the sociopolitical situations of John's time in that they seek to 'alienate the audience from the symbolic persuasion of the imperial cult' (1985: 6; see also 192).

While highly innovative, Fiorenza's analysis reproduces the common exegetic assumption that Revelation reveals something – in this case, a coherent strategy based on rules of rhetoric and a will to persuade. Her approach comes close to recognizing a fundamental rule of symbolling: in order to persuade readers to think and act in certain ways, symbols must be *alienated* from contending persuasions. Images must be manipulated in such ways as to exclude alternative usages that must be silenced because unspeakable. A new language that integrates alien imageries has nothing to gain from revealing its sources; little attention must be given to what must be rejected and forgotten. This is to say, *the will to convince is necessarily at odds with the will to reveal.*

Like many other students of Revelation, Fiorenza is well aware of the competitive, polemical, and manipulative aspects of symbolic rhetoric. She acknowledges that 'the symbolic universe of Rev. needed to appeal to common traditional cultic symbols in order to be *competitive*' (1985: 197; emphasis added). John 'does not freely invent his images and symbols but derives them from Jewish and Greco-Roman literature and tradition. By working with associations and allusions to very divergent mythic and religious-political traditions, he appeals to the imagination of his audience' (1991: 29). This means that the prophet 'achieves the rhetorical power of his work by taking traditional symbols and mythological images out of their original contexts and by placing them like mosaic stones into the new literary composition of his symbolic narrative movement' (31). But, like most exegetes, Fiorenza shies away from discussing the full implications of a language that takes symbols out of their context and assigns them to an alternative text. Instead she falls back on the traditional notion that Revelation derives much of its inspiration from the Old Testament. 'Although the open and multivalent images of Rev. have many overtones derived from Greco-Roman society and religion, the dominant tenor of its symbolic language is the cult of Israel' (1985: 197). After all John could hardly appeal to those cultic imageries he rejected as pagan activity and idolatry.

Early Christian Fathers used to think that Revelation had been written by Cerinthus, John's enemy. In a sense they were right. The author of Revelation brought his enemies and their cultic imageries into the service of Christianity. In his own way John had to cheat, which is what he did when he established the law of silence *vis-à-vis* the unutterable and then broke his own law by systematically appealing to alien cultic symbols. In order to be 'competitive' and 'persuasive,' the prophet had to trick pagan symbolism into doing something it was never meant to do: elevating Christ well above the Roman emperor, the spiritual above the physical, reducing motions of time and space (history, heavenly movements) to sign-manifestations of an immutable Spirit dwelling beyond the visible world. As all acts of language are, the schemings of Revelation were historically embattled from the start. The end-product was neither a mechanical copy of its source material nor an original creation that broke away entirely from its own origins. It was neither a coherent text that followed strict rules nor a confusing composition that had no rules whatsoever. It was neither pure Revelation nor absolute esoterism. The key to the New Testament Apocalypse lies somewhere between the overt and the covert, Logos and Chaos – in signs of what John insisted on never saying. In retrospect, it is not by accident, ignorance, or a lack of goodwill that the Apocalypse ('unveiling') has become Apocrypha ('hidden'), for a good deal of what John had to say concerned things and matters that begged to be silenced. To the rigorous and confusing silences of Revelation we now turn, with an emphasis on the ancient polemics and politics of astralism, and related imageries of star-signs appearing from the heavens.

4

Alpha and Omega

Prologue – The Veiling of Revelation (Rev. 1: 1–3)

The Book of Revelation is portrayed by John as an *apokalypsis*, the Greek term for 'disclosure.' The *unveiling* of past history and the end of time has fomented many literal inquiries into the exact semantics and intentions of John's writings. Against these restrictive approaches to Revelation, one should insist on the subtlety of the prophet's presentation of his vision, 'made known' (*semaino*) to him by the hand of the angel, an expression derived from the root *semeion*, 'a sign.' The metaphorical language suggested by this word implies a roundabout unfolding of the future conveyed through sign-manifestations of Logos, the word of God. The Apocalypse implies a 'bearing of records' (Gr. *martureo*, also 'martyr'), a vision couched in a thick rhetoric of allusive references and approximate similarity typical of the apocalyptic genre. In the words of Heraclitus, 'it neither states nor hides but merely indicates' (in Beasley-Murray 1974: 51). The obscure mediations and intimations of 'sign language' require a constant application of the 'like reserve': as in the Book of Ezekiel (where the word 'appearances' shows up more than twenty times), manifestations of God can be described only in the likeness of the appearances of what they really are. Nor can signs of the Verb be conveyed directly from God to humans, without intercession. Rather, they require a threefold chain of command: God 'appearing' and revealing himself via Jesus Christ, an angel, and a prophet–servant (Rev. 1: 1). This dense veiling of the Verb is much closer to the text's presentation of itself than any literal, unmediated expression of divine speech.

The deployment of evocative imagery in Revelation creates another temptation though: searching for meanings hiding from the human gaze.

Puzzled by John's tortuous symbology, readers may be tempted to unravel the secrets encoded in the Apocalypse with a view to 'seeing the Invisible' (Heb. 11: 27). Revelation may have torn back the curtain hiding the invisible and the future of this world, yet the prophet's imagery is so convoluted that it is bound to invite further uncovering. Against this deep-meaning approach, the interpretive strategy adopted in this book deals not so much with what the prophet is trying to convey as with themes and directions that are systematically avoided, shadow images that are never brought to light – in other words, the unspeakable and the illicit in lieu of the unspoken implications of the metaphor. The script reconstructed below is essentially un-signed, 'insignificant,' and unimposing, an astral counter-text that never imposes itself through sign-exposure. To be more precise, the unauthoritative text we are about to explore conjures up a pagan vision of heavenly spheres treated as divinities in their own right. The resulting script runs counter to John's notion that motions of the sky are phenomenal manifestations of an invisible Spirit, a concrete medium for sign-expressions of the Verb.

The Beginning of the Vision (Rev. 1: 4–20)

The Book of Revelation begins as a letter to the seven churches of Asia Minor, north and east of the island of Patmos, one of the Sporades in the Icarian Sea and apparently a penal colony of Roman proconsular Asia ruled by the emperor Domitian. This is where the Lord commands John, through a voice sounding like a trumpet on the Lord's Day, to write the things he has seen, those that are, and those that shall be. Through John, the seven churches are saluted by the Lord and the seven spirits present before his throne. In later chapters these spirits sent all over the world are likened to seven lamps burning before the throne of the Lord, and also the seven horns and eyes of the Lamb slain (Rev. 4: 5, 5: 6). The churches can also be assimilated to the seven golden lamp standards and stars spotted in the right hand of the likeness of the Son of Man (Rev. 1: 12f., 16).

The Son of Man is titled the faithful witness, the First-Born from the dead, the Ruler of the kings of the earth. His name is Jesus Christ, he whose blood freed humans from sins, the one who 'made us a line of kings' or priests to serve his Father, to be mourned by all. He is also portrayed as Alpha and Omega, the Almighty who holds the keys of death and of the abyss, with hair white as wool or snow, eyes as a burning flame, feet like bronze refined in a furnace, and a voice as the sound of the ocean. He has a sharp double-edged sword coming out of his mouth, a long robe tied at the waist with a golden girdle, and the facies of a sun shining with all its force.

L'Apparition du Fils de l'Homme, Beatus, Burgo de Osma (1086), fol. 23. Photo des Éditions Zodiaque, Abbaye de La Pierre Qui Vire, 89630 Saint Léger Vauban, France

At the time of John's writing, Asia Minor had replaced Palestine as the centre of the Christian world. Ephesus had succeeded Jerusalem in her capacity to represent the Church on earth. The prophet, however, was outside the New Jerusalem when the spirit possessed him 'from behind,' an event occurring on the Lord's Day. He was held captive in Patmos, across from coastal Ephesus. Although there were many churches in this area in John's time, only seven are mentioned. Paradoxically, the reduction of all churches to seven produces a vision of heptadic completeness (Farrer 1964: 62; Prigent 1981: 25). As pointed out by most commentators, the seven spirits hark back to Isaiah's sevenfold gifts of the Messiah (Isa. 11: 2) and to the seven-lamp candelabra and eyes of God as portrayed by Zechariah (Zech. 4: 2, 10).

Through the **seven churches** of Asia Minor, the septenary motif makes an early appearance in a text practically dedicated to it. The introduction ends with the first of seven beatitudes pronounced throughout Revelation (1: 3, 14: 13, 16: 15, 19: 9, 20: 6, 22: 7, 14). Also the revelatory expressions 'heard' and 'I saw' in 1: 10 and 1: 12 are repeated twenty-eight times and forty-nine times in the same book, respectively. But why should the number seven and its multiples be given so much attention? The answer is essentially calendrical. The septenary principle draws on ancient calculations of the lunisolar calendar and related festivities: the Sabbath, the New Moon, the Feast of (seven) Weeks, the Seventh New Moon, the sabbatical year, the Jubilee, and so on. The fact that the prophet's vision occurs on the Lord's Day reinforces this roundabout concern with the weekly foundation of time. Finally, the equation of seven angels with seven stars in Revelation 1: 20 points to the astral foundations of Near Eastern religions: the treatment of sky beings (planets, constellations) as guardians of individuals and territorial groups (Malina 1995: 258), and the cult of the seven planets led by the sun and the moon, all marching under the influence of the seven Pleiades and the two *septem-triones* of the northern sky.

The septenary motif is a product of ancient astromythology. This brings us to Hebrew divisions of time and the lunisolar calendar in the post-exilic period of biblical history (see Gandz 1970; Feldman 1978: 73f.). Briefly, the Hebraic year consisted of four seasons (determined by the equinoxes and solstices) and twelve unequal months, each of which began from the new moon (ocularly observed) and lasted twenty-nine or thirty days. A month was occasionally added after Adar (February/March), the last month of the ecclesiastical year, thereby adjusting the lunar period to the solar year and the agricultural cycle. Seven years in every nineteen had to be embolismic, lengthened by one month. While the sacred year began with the ripening of the earliest barley grain in March/April (Nisan), the civil year coincided with the arrival of rains and the sowing and ploughing season in the post-vintage month of Tishri (September/October, seventh of the sacred year). Each month was divided into four weeks according to the different phases the moon goes through about every seven days: the new moon, the first quarter, the full moon, and the last quarter. The week differed from its Greek or Babylonian counterpart in that it ran its course independently of the longer divisions of time. Finally, a day was from sunset to sunset, and consisted of twelve hours of daylight preceded by twelve hours of darkness. The night was in turn divided into three watches of equal duration, the first one starting at about 6:00 P.M. In daytime, the sun was said to be rising to the east, shining to the south, on the right hand of a person facing the east (so as to 'orient' oneself), and then setting 'behind,' to the west. While Pliny and Varro considered that the left hand indicated the east (Malina 1995: 92), ancient Jews equated it with the north, the hidden quarter of heaven.

Given these calendrical coordinates, it is understandable that the number seven should be given so much attention by followers of Balaam and by all Hebrews adhering to the septenary principle of the Mosaic law.[1] Every festival was connected in some way or other with this number. The law prescribed that a festival should occur every seventh day, every seventh month (Tishri), every seventh year, and also at the semicentennial end of a period of seven times seven years. The Pentecost was celebrated fifty days after Passover, at the end of the first grain harvest, seven full weeks after the sickle is put to the corn (Deut. 16: 9). The Passover and the Feast of Tabernacles lasted seven days each, and seven special convocations were to be held during the year. Animals to be sacrificed were very often seven in number, and so on.

Coming back to John's inaugural vision, several motifs confirm the prophet's preoccupation with calendrical motions of heaven and the solar implications of the seven spirits and churches of Revelation 1. The text thus speaks of the sun-faced, fiery-eyed, and flame-footed likeness of the Messiah. Also the Seer is said to be possessed by the spirit of God on the **day 'belonging to the Lord'** (Gr. *kuriakos*, Rev. 1: 10). The expression is evocative of official phrases denoting what belongs to Caesar, and also *Sebaste* days dedicated to kings or emperors in Egypt and Asia Minor. The term, however, also brings to mind the day of the sun (*dies solis*) as 'the day when the true and only *kurios* rose from death to the sovereignty of the universe' (Beasley-Murray 1974: 65). The expression refers to Sun-day, the day when the accession of Jesus Christ to the throne of God is celebrated, a resurrection feast that should be understood over against the emperor's day. Sweet (1990: 68) remarks that 'Christians may have called Sunday (*dies solis*) Lord's Day (*kuriake*) in reaction. Certainly Revelation presents Christ as true Emperor, in contrast with the Beast of ch. 13, and as sun (v. 16)'² (see Mounce 1977: 76; Charles 1920, 1: 23; Farrer 1964: 68f.).

Other signs of solarism can be found in the story of the deathly fall of Jesus Christ mourned by the whole world (Rev. 1: 7), his resurrection as first-born of the dead, and his subsequent ascension to stardom – to the supreme heights of Ruler of all kings on earth, above the lower regions of the earth (Eph. 4: 9ff.). What we have here is an edited story of the dying sun-god Tammuz, his estival and wintertime *descensus ad inferos* followed by his resurrection at springtime and ascent to heavenly glory, in the company of six other 'planets' commonly engraved on Roman imperial coins (Beasley-Murray 1974: 70). To the story of Tammuz we shall return later.

But of all signs suggesting an astrological plot, words that assimilate the churches of Asia Minor to **seven stars** in heaven (Rev. 1: 20) are the most telling. Little imagination is needed to see in these symbols the legacy of a seven-planetary system set in motion by the sun passing through the Pleiades at spring. The connection between church-stars and the wheels of lunisolar time is indirectly confirmed by the orderly, clockwise presentation of the seven churches of the New Israel, from the west coast (Ephesus) to northern lands (Smyrna, Pergamum), and then to the east (Thyatira) and the south (Sardis, Philadelphia, Laodicea) of Asia Minor. This circular trajectory is modelled after the circuitry of the sun moving from the west at dusk to the north at night, the east at dawn, and the south at noon.

The zodiacal implications of John's stellar imagery become all the more plausible when other attributes of the Son of Man are considered. The stars guiding the great wheel of time are placed in the right hand of an Almighty God portrayed as **the Alpha and the Omega**, the First and the Last (Rev. 1: 8, 16f.). These two-sided titles converge on two critical moments of the solar cycle: the equinoxes when the sun crosses the equator. When astronomically transposed, Alpha becomes the Hebrew *Aleph* that stands for Aldebaran, Taurus star ∂, Follower of the seven Pleiades, leading Star of Stars, the star whose heliacal rising used to mark the new year. Aldebaran was also known as the Star of the Tablet, or God's Eye (seven of them in Rev. 5: 6). In Babylonian mythology, the star stood for the great Nebo, the scribe of heavenly gods. Representations of this writer of the Book of Fate were common during the neo-Babylonian period (Cooke 1960: 104). At the time of the New Year festival, around the vernal equinox, Nebo revealed what the gods had in store for the coming year through his writings upon the tablets of Destiny. He was the god of writing and wisdom, the one without whom no plan is initiated in heaven.

In Ezekiel 9, Nebo appears as a scribe dressed in white and leader of seven spirits, an imagery echoed by the Son of Man in John. The scribe places a cross on the foreheads of the elect, thereby marking and protecting the faithful remnant of Israel. The gesture is reminiscent of the Passover story of the blood of the paschal lamb placed on the lintel of a house to save the household from the angel of death, a story commemorated at the beginning of spring, in the first month of Nisan (Exod. 12). John is now applying this springtime cross-mark and reading-of-the-book-of-destiny imagery to the seven-starred Passover Lamb, the Lord of Easter Sunday (Prigent 1981: 24f.).

But, while active at the New Year festival, Nebo also stood for the period of the year when days are shorter and nights are longer. As a wandering planet, the son and close companion of the sun-god Marduk (or Tammuz), Nebo was equated with Mercury, a planet that appears near the sun before sunrise and after sunset, just like Venus. Nebo was destined to fall with the dying sun-god, southward in the summer and westward in the late afternoon.[3]

Stories of the sun's yearly downfall brings us to the other side of the Living One – Omega as opposed to Alpha. In Hebrew, the last letter of the Greek alphabet becomes *tau*, which denotes the cross-shaped mark written on the foreheads of the elect in Ezekiel 9 (Cooke 1960: 106). The sign *tau* also took the place of the Scales in Jewish astrology, the seventh sign of the zodiac (an altar or censer in Euphratean astronomy, a motif appearing in Ezekiel 8 and 9; see Allen 1963: 273). The mark placed on the *forehead* of the faithful evokes the sun entering the Scales at the autumn equinox, a sun rising in telling direction: due 'east,' 'what is the front' (Heb. *qedem*). The cross-shaped Balance is exactly opposite from Taurus in the zodiacal wheel. The constellation rises about the seventh month of Tishri. This is a time of ploughing and sowing, activities heralding a season of darkness, the Day of Judgment, and the departure of the Lord from the Jerusalem Temple.

Like the sun in pagan mythology, God governs the alpha and the omega, the first and the last moment of cyclical time. In keeping with this synthesis, the *tau* letter brings together two critical moments of the yearly cycle: while it brings back memories of the Passover tradition and the springtime reading of destiny, the cross-mark written on the foreheads of the faithful also points to darker moments of the year, sombre events occurring at the end of time. The two-sided implications of this imagery are well reflected in the **double-edged sword** coming out of the Lord's mouth (Rev. 1: 16). As with the *tau* cross, the sword-tongue motif bears witness to God's word of justice, a retributive blade that can either protect the followers of Christ or be crossed with those who betray the one who died on the cross.

The connection between images of Alpha and Omega and the *t*-shaped cross of Jesus Christ and Nebo the scribe (Ezek. 9) used to be the object of conscious symbolic manipulation. As pointed out by Beasley-Murray (1974: 60–3), all three letters (*A, O, T*) played a central role in the ancient *Sator-Rotas* word square found in Pompeii, a puzzle that sheds light on the relationship between the alphabet and the order of time. The puzzle presents the same set of five words written both vertically and horizontally within a twenty-five-lettered square. According to one theory, Latin-speaking Jews and later Christians were inspired by Ezekiel's vision of the wheeled chariot and the team of seven cherubs and ink-horn scribe hailing from the north. They used the square to remind themselves that 'Arepo the reaper holds the wheels with care' and that a mark would be placed on the foreheads of the faithful to preserve them from judgment at the hands of the Grim Reaper (Rev. 14: 15). The cruciform letter *T* occupied the central position on all sides of the square, between the letters *A* and *O*, which stood for Alpha and Omega. Alternatively, the puzzle can be made to spell out 'Pater Noster' if arranged in the form of a cross, with the letters *A* and *O* standing out on each side of the introductory phrase of the Lord's prayer. In both readings, the cross lies at the centre of one's faith in a Father who stands as the First and the Last (Rev. 1: 17). The cross, I should add, evoked both the sacrifice of Christ and the basic heptadic and quadripartite measurements of ancient Semitic time and space, as represented by the four seven-lettered arms of the cross (with the letter *T* in the centre of each arm).

		A
		P
ROTAS	SATOR	A
		T
OPERA	AREPO	E
		R
TENET	TENET	A P A T E R N O S T E R O
		O
AREPO	OPERA	S
		T
SATOR	ROTAS	E
		R
		O

To sum up, visionary references to God the Alpha and the Omega, his Sunday visitation, his death mourned by the world, his resurrection and ascent from the lower earth, the seven stars and golden lamp standards in his right hand, the circular route of seven churches north and east of Patmos, all suggest thinly veiled astral and heliographic imageries that once played a central role in pagan mythology and imperial politics as well. From the beginning of Revelation, astromythology is both downplayed and recuperated by John. Through the rhetoric of metaphor, the prophet meets the powers of Sabaism and emperor-worship on their own ground.

Some have said of John's introductory verses that they contain the kernel of the Book of Revelation. This chapter adds credibility to this claim, though in a different perspective, with an emphasis on the astrological countertext of John's Apocalypse. Commentators such as Kraft (1974), Lohmeyer (1926), and McNamara (1966: 192–9) recognize the impact of astral mythology on John's imagery. In the words of Farrer (1964: 68),

just as the twelve stars (xii. 1) are the constellations marking the months of the year, so the seven stars are the seven planets naming the days of the week, Sun, Moon, Mars, Mercury, Jupiter, Venus, and Saturn. Christ embraces them in the span of his hand, because Sunday is his. Christ rose on the octave-day of Holy Week; he spans the week from Sunday to Sunday. And since the pattern of the week is printed upon all created time, and history itself is a week of ages ... the Christ of Sunday is the first and the Last, the beginning and end of God's creation (i. 17, ii. 8, iii. 14). It is of the highest significance in this connexion that the vision before us is a Sunday vision (i. 10). And in parallel with his mention of the seven stars St. John places the statement that Christ's countenance shines like the sun.

To our symbolical convention, it is an offence that Christ should be identified with the sun, and hold the sun among seven planets in his hand. It was no offence to John. The Virgin crowned with the Zodiac in xii is herself one of the twelve signs ... Stars were gods to the heathen, and angels to the Jews ...

Others are reluctant to grant astrology a central role. In his discussion of Revelation 1, Caird (1966: 15) argues that the use that John makes of signs of heavenly royalty 'was a direct challenge to the imperial myth of the divine ruler, and, since defiance of emperor-worship was one of the main themes of his vision, it is reasonable to suppose that the challenge was intended.' Caird, however, makes no mention of the role of heliolatry and the cult of stars in imperial politics. Likewise, Beasley-Murray (1974: 55) suggests that John's knowledge of the cult of emperors and planets 'is largely of archaeological value' compared with the Zecharian background which 'will have been determinative for him.' Having said this, the commentator goes on to say that 'even in John's day there were many who believed that the planets were gods, exercising a powerful and even fearful influence over the lives of men. From this it was an easy transition to make of them a symbol of the political power exercised by the Roman Caesars over the world ... When John declares that the seven stars are in Christ's right hand, he is claiming that the sovereignty over this world resides not in the Caesars of Rome but in the Lord of the Church' (70).

Prigent (1981: 26f., 30, 61n) doubts that John had the planets or any other precise group of stars in mind when he used the seven-star imagery. Also, he supports Goodenough's (1958: 175) argument that the star appearing over the Torlonia shrine should not be identified with the Messiah; the connection is too specific. What Prigent omits to mention, however, is Goodenough's clear endorsement of the astral implications of the seven lamps of the Jewish candelabra: 'Cumont's long insistence upon the astral significance of the seven lamps of the menorah goes very well with this interpretation, where the flaming menorah is three times in the center of the heavenly ceiling.' Finally, in spite of his sceptical attitude towards astralism, Prigent (1981: 26n) concedes in a footnote that Revelation borrowed from Jewish tradition the planetary symbolism and the notion of a correspondence between rituals and heavenly phenomena.

Charles (1920, 1: 12, 25, 30, 33) is also of two minds about the pagan underpinnings of Revelation. The exegete recognizes that the seven stars may be the seven planets, yet he goes on to say that 'in due time the source of these conceptions was wholly forgotten as well as the historical development involved.' In his view, John was entirely unconscious of the original connection between the seven-armed candelabra, the seven planets, and also the constellation of the Bear. He adds that the zodiacal-candelabra imagery explicitly discussed by Philo and Josephus is merely an afterthought of first-century Jewish writers.[4]

Charles applies the same reasoning to his discussion of Christ's descent into Hades. He notes that 'non-Jewish sources do not appear to have given birth to the Christian doctrine of the *Descensus ad Inferos.*' He none the less notes that the 'idea is in certain forms pre-Christian,' harking back to the descent of the Babylonian goddess Ishtar, Hibil Ziwa in the Mandaean religion, and the 'primitive man' in the system of Manes. The commentator concludes that the 'existence of these astral divinities Judaism did not question any more than in earlier times it questioned the existence of the tribal deities of the nations that surrounded Israel, *but in the interests of Monotheism, Judaism degraded these foreign deities into angels – subjects being in the service of Yahweh.*' The latter position is an integral part of the general argument developed in this book.

The idea that John may have forgotten or become wholly unconscious of the mythical past and pagan history of his own visions, an idea abundantly mocked by Lawrence (1974: 66–70), is an open question that can never be fully resolved. The parallels that exist between the metaphors of Revelation and ancient themes of astral religion are none the less striking. Practically all commentators have discussed elements of this pagan heritage. The fact that heathenish origins should have been forgotten or silenced in John's text is what we should be concerned with, as opposed to John's conscious intent, which can never be recovered (if it existed at all, without internal tension and some original obscurity). The thesis advanced in this book is that the language of Revelation uses a parabolic version of solarism and Sabaism to challenge the worldly powers that be and the reign of visible gods in heaven. As Lepsius (quoted in McNamara 1966: 193) once put it: 'Jesus, the Son of God, is raised to the throne of the Cosmos, the planet-gods who were worshipped by all the world are in his hand, the spirits of the stars have become his servants and have lost their right of sovereignty over the earth.' The celestial dominion is thus demoted to the 'outward appearances of the likeness' of Logos, a heavenly canopy of sign-manifestations of the spirit of Yahweh. Through a lavish deployment of metaphor – the particle *hos* denoting similarity ('as,' 'like') occurs some fifty-six times in Revelation – John's apocalyptic vision subsumes the rhetoric of imperial astrology under signs of the Verb.

Solarism and Circumpolarism

Revelation 1 produces many pointers favouring the supposition of a polemical connection between the language of the zodiac and John's vision of the End of Time. There is yet another imagery that can be interpreted in the light of primitive astronomy: the **right-hand** position of the seven stars, and the voice of the Lord coming from **behind** the prophet. Since the east is 'the front' (Heb. *qedem*), a sun-faced god speaking to the prophet 'from behind' would logically evoke the sun coming down to the west, with its right hand pointing to the south, as is the case with humans. As for the seven stars held by God, they would correspond to the Pleiades or Hyades lying to the south of equinoctial Aries, the Ram (father of the Passover Lamb). The overall scene can be observed on the western horizon either before dawn at autumn or at sunset in early spring. The composition confirms the equinoctial coordinates of a godly figure portrayed as the

Alpha and the Omega. Finally, the right-hand stars appearing to the south-west could be compared to John himself: the prophet is touched by what he becomes, that is, the right hand of the Lord (Rev. 1: 17). He becomes a messenger approaching the New Israel from behind – from the isle of Patmos situated southwest of Asia Minor.

But there are limitations to this zodiacal reading of the dexterous and rearward imagery of Revelation 1. For one thing, the right hand holding the stars and touching the prophet belongs to a godly figure who usually comes and faces the earth either from the eastern horizon (as with the sun and the Morning Star) or from the northern heaven, not from the west. The imagery of a sun-god arriving from the east or the north is all the more plausible as it tallies with seven stars appearing on the right-hand side of God. If appearing from the east, the right hand of a God passing through Aries points to the Pleiades, the Hyades, and also the 'hidden' north, the circumpolar crown, and the two septenary bears. Alternatively, the Lord could approach the earth from the north – hence, 'from behind' humans normally facing the south when orienting themselves (according to Pliny and Varro). Indications of God's northern origin are in keeping with other visions reported by John. Thus, if descending to Patmos from the 'upper north,' God's left foot would stand over the Icarian Sea and the right foot over the land of Asia Minor, as in Revelation 10. When seen at dawn in spring or at dusk in the fall, God making an appearance from his northerly abode coincides with the seven stars of Ursa Minor lying on the right hand side of Polaris. The scene is reminiscent of a fourth-century text of Mithraic magic portraying God holding the foreleg of a calf in his right hand, a figure representing the northern Bear (Kraft 1974; Ulansey 1989: 105f.). In this ancient text Mithras is seen descending from heaven, 'a god immensely great, having a bright appearance, youthful, golden-haired, with a tunic and a golden crown and trousers, and holding in his right hand a golden shoulder of a young bull: this is the Bear which moves and turns heaven around, moving upward and downward in accordance with the hour. Then you will see the lightning bolts leaping from his eyes and stars from his body' (quoted in Malina 1995: 70).

When seen from a northerly perspective, John's right-hand imagery is reminiscent of Babylonian New Year rituals. Ceremonial statues, presumably facing the northern crown of heaven, were made to raise their right hand to Nebo (vernal Aldebaran, galactic east, the Pleiades) while the left hand held a serpent or a scorpion (autumnal Scorpio, galactic west). At the beginning of the ritual, the sanctuary of Nebo was veiled to commemorate the sun's descent to the lower world, an event marking the autumn equinox. This ancient custom is now echoed in the veiling of the Cross during the period of Christ's death, immediately before his resurrection at Easter (Langdon 1931: 160, 316).

All the same, it is difficult to say which of these perspectives, zodiacal or circumpolar, offers the best parallel to John's inaugural vision of the Son of Man. Actually the question is of little consequence, for all of the scenarios noted above have two important things in common. First, they converge on events and themes of the vernal and autumn equinoxes. Second, they involve astro-religious imageries that formed an integral part of the imperial cult. This is true of the planets and the zodiac but also of the circumpolar stars. The latter were so closely related to the emperor that they could even mark his body. According to Suetonius (first half of second century), Augustus Caesar had spots on his chests and belly that were 'dispersed, for the manner, order, and number, like unto the starres of the celestiall beare' (Suetonius 1967: Augustus 80). Having said this, students of the Scriptures are likely to find the impact of solarism on revelation more plausible than the influence of circumpolarism. While most commentators are aware of solar-based religions of the Near East, none has examined the relationship between ancient myths of the northern heaven and symbols of the apocalypse. A northern view on John's astral metaphors has yet to be explored.

In chapters that follow, we shall see that bears of the north share many of the signs used by John to characterize the End of Time. *This is the time when the wrathful God portrayed as a Grim Reaper hails from the highest heaven, travelling in a seven-starred chariot supported or driven by four beasts, ploughing the earth and pouring the blood of evil creatures in his winepress.* Much of this autumn post-vintage scenery points to attributes and motions of the two circumpolar chariots, beasts, or ploughs. Like the throne of God, the two wheels of the north turn around the highest point in heaven. When rising due east of Polaris (together with the Morning Star appearing on the eastern horizon), the two bears signal the moment of truth brought at autumn. Both constellations comprise seven stars that can be reduced to a quadrilateral bier followed by three mourners; like the churches of Asia Minor, the stars are divided into four plus three. The stars can take the shape of oxen or ploughs driven by Boötes the Vintager, a constellation ascending at dawn in autumn. As with all agents of judgment, the bears or bulls of the north can either protect or punish: the creatures have been known to nurse the infant Jupiter, but also to menace the heavenly

Fold with their four-starred coffins and stormy character (kept in check by the vigilance of Arcturus). All of these associations tally with images deployed in John's vision of the End.

In retrospect, the Alpha and Omega imagery of a reaper 'holding the wheels with care' is to be understood against the background of a complex circuitry, a universe activated by several cosmic wheels: the ecliptic, the equator, and the two colures placed in a celestial vault whirling round the earth. Of all wheels moving in the sky, the zodiacal belt seems to be the most important. Accordingly, the Bible portrays the cosmos as being set in motion by a golden wheel called 'galgal or Mazzaroth in Hebrew, usually rendered the zodiac. The Jerusalem Bible, however, identifies Job's Mazzaroth as the Bear. The Hebrew 'galta, which is the Peshitta-Syriac Version's translation of Job's Mazzaroth, also stands for our wheeled wain (Job 38: 32; 2 Kings 23: 5; Feldman 1978: 71). Could it be that the universe is governed as much by wheels of the north as by constellations of the zodiac? Could it be that the two systems, zodiacal and circumpolar, are inseparable? After all, they are moving in synchrony and are guided by similar principles. Both circuits are led by bulls (seven oxen, Taurus) and by principles of fourness and sevenness, circularity and squareness: a quadrilateral coffin and three mourners revolving around the lodestar are synchronized with seven sun-led planets moving round the four quarters of time and space. Signs of reaping and ploughing at autumn point to a cosmos turning on a northerly axle that activates the great lunisolar pact – cosmic forces that can be turned against mortal creatures who break the pact through sinful behaviour.

The Crown of Heaven

Before we move on to the letters of Revelation 2–3, more should be said about the role of the northern heaven in ancient mythology. From Ezekiel (1: 4), we know that God approaches the earth from the north. In his discussion of this particular passage, Cooke (1960: 10) mentions that 'some would find an allusion to the Babylonian idea of the north as the home of the gods ... or to the north as the quarter from which trouble might be expected ... but Ezekiel would never connect a manifestation of Jahveh with pagan mythology.' Likewise Wevers (1969: 44) suggests that the 'north should not be pressed for esoteric meaning.' Wevers, however, goes on to say that this cardinal reference is 'appropriate in the light of the Jerusalem tradition situating Yahweh's holy mountain in the far north (cf. Ps. 48).'

The influence of 'pagan' mythology in Judaeo-Christian descriptions of the cosmos should not be underestimated. Briefly, the Semitic vision of the universe consisted of a solid heavenly dome constantly whirling around a celestial vault studded with fixed stars and wandering planets, and dividing the waters of above from those of below. Up until the Hellenistic period, the earth was thought of as a flat disk surrounded by a ring of water and floating upon the deep (see Feldman 1978: 102–4; Malina 1995: 4, 165–6).[5] Above the upper waters was the dwelling-place of God, inside heaven; there he sat throned on the vaulted roof or tent covering the circular earth (Gen. 1; Isa. 40: 22). The highest point of the dome was located in the *northern* quarter of the universe, which is only logical if we consider that the circumpolar north is the sole region of the vault that never 'falls into the deep.'[6] The heavenly tent covering the earth moved around the celestial pole, the point of entry of the *axis mundi* linking the centre of the earth to its heavenly roof (like a pole supporting a tent). About this northern axis Manilius once wrote:

Now where heaven reaches its culmination in the shining Bears, which from the zenith of the sky look down on all the stars and know no setting and, shifting their opposed stations about the same high point, set sky and stars in rotation, from there an insubstantial axis runs down through the wintry air and controls the universe, keeping it pivoted at opposite poles: it forms the middle about which the starry sphere revolves and wheels its heavenly flight, but is itself without motion and, drawn straight through the empty spaces of the great sky to the two Bears and through the very globe of the Earth, stands fixed ... this men have called the axis, since, motionless itself, it yet sees everything spinning about it. (1: 275–94)

Northern constellations revolved about the lodestar, once called Stella Maris, or Stella Polaris, the upper point of the celestial vault's axle (*Al Kutb al Sahamaliyy* in Arabic).[7] These constellations never 'touched the sea,' an expression used by Aratus, probably after the ancient Babylonian astrologers who inspired him via Eudoxus (Avienus 1843: 159). A Babylonian prayer to the polestar thus began: 'O star of Anu, prince of the heavens' (Langdon 1931: 94). As the father of all gods, Anu sat on a throne in the highest heaven, where he guarded the bread and water of eternal life.

But if the polestar is so high as to mark 'the hole in which the earth's axle found its bearing' (*Al Fass* in Arabic; Allen 1963: 450), how could it be located below the zenith, the highest point in heaven (directly overhead)? The answer to this riddle is simple: the earth rose in a northerly direction. To travel northward meant therefore to 'go up.'[8] If the north star appears to lie low, it is because the earth slopes upwards in its direction, via the heights of Syria (Heb. *Aram*, also for 'height'; Num. 23: 7), away from the lowland deserts extending to the south, between Palestine and Egypt. Just as the Babylonian and Canaanites thought of the north as the home of the gods, so did scriptural writers locate Yahweh's holy mountain far up in the north. This spatial imagery finds a telling echo in Ezekiel's description of Tyre (north of Judah) and 'the holy mountain of God' (Ezek. 28), a motif 'which ultimately stems from Babylonian mythology' (Zimmerli 1979: 120). Similar notions of the highest mountain on earth rising to the north can be found in the early Sanskrit book *Surya Siddhanta*, in mythical stories of the Norsemen, and even in the writings of Columbus and Chilmead (Allen 1963: 451f.). The Finns also believed that Polaris was situated at the top of the Heavenly Mountain.[9]

The Hellenistic period upheld most of these cosmographic notions save the shape of the earth, which became spherical from about 333 B.C.E., as reflected in Manilius's description of the *axis mundi*. While they still saw it as motionless and at the centre of the universe, Hellenistic people viewed the earth as a sphere surrounded by 'the seven planets (which include sun and moon), each moving in its own sphere, and these in turn are enclosed by an eighth sphere containing the fixed stars' (Scott 1991: 4). The cosmos known as the 'whole eight' thus became a global sphere encapsulating all stars and steadily rotating around the earth, one-quarter of which was inhabited by humans and entirely surrounded by water. While a few later thinkers such as Lactantius may have denied the globe concept, most agreed with Theon of Smyrna (early second century C.E.) that 'the entire cosmos is a sphere and the earth, which is itself a spheroid, is placed in the middle.' Theon described the celestial globe as 'turning around its immobile poles and the axis which joins them, at the middle of which is fixed the earth, and all the stars carried by this sphere and all the points of the sky, describe parallel circles, that is to say, circles everywhere equidistant, perpendicular to the axis, and drawn from the poles of the universe as centers' (quoted in Malina 1995: 47f.).

The north plays a pivotal role in all ancient conceptions of the cosmos, but it carries negative associations as well. In Hebrew, the northern quarter of the heavens is called the 'hidden' (*saphon*) in that the sun never shines in it and hides there night after night (assuming that it goes round the earth). Also to the north lies the seat of gloom and the origin of all Babylonian, Chaldean, Assyrian, and Median invaders of Palestine who came chiefly from upper lands by way of Damascus and Syria. In the same vein, readers of Ezekiel should recall the king of northern Tyre who fell from the holy mountain of God because of his countless sins (Ezek. 28). Calamities and winds of destruction are typically associated with this quarter of the earth, a region that provoked as much fear among Hebrews as did the circumpolar sky among the Egyptians and the ancient Chaldean astrologers who inspired the writings of Aratus.[10]

In short, all stars fixed to the celestial dome revolve about the highest sphere in heaven: a northern Polaris permanently fixed above the earth, a pivotal star that never descends to the horizon, let alone beneath it. On top of this highest point of the cylinder, axle, or axis 'round about which the primal wheel revolves' (Dante), there is the throne of God, and beneath it Mons Coelius. On the throne sits the Lord of the universe, an almighty *Polokrator* controlling the wheels and motions of the globe (Malina 1995: 72, 91). In keeping with this boreal vision of the highest heaven, paradise is a place that can be promoted 'neither from the east, nor from the west, nor from the south,' with the implication that the Lord's horns, arrows, and rays of lightning originate from the north, above the clouds and all moving planets. It is from this direction that signs of the heavenly life originate and judgment comes in due season, in the post-vintage days of autumn, with Yahweh 'holding a cup of frothing wine, heavily drugged,' to be poured out into the mouths of the wicked of the earth (Ps. 75.6; Isa. 14.12–14).[11]

Bears of the Northern Sky

Evocations of solarism and sevenness in Revelation 1 must be placed in their proper context: ancient perceptions of motions in heaven resulting in the sevenfold calculations of the Hebrew calendar, with a ritual emphasis on the spring and autumn equinoxes, the Alpha and Omega of yearly time. We shall see that the seven-star imagery and cognate motifs appearing in Revelation speak to Semitic religions based on the cult of the sun, the moon, and the seven planets marching through the zodiac, below and above the equator, under the leadership of the seven Pleiades rising to the east at spring and falling to the west at autumn. The same imagery, however, suggests a cosmos and a march of time governed by signs of the sunless north. Thus, when viewed from a northern perspective, the 'divine seven' take the form of Ursa Major. This age-old configuration of heaven involves an ox-driven chariot moving within the northern sky and pointing to major divisions in heavenly time and space. We now turn to a detailed reconstruction of the role of circumpolar stars in ancient astromythology, in anticipation of the light they shed on the cherubs and throne-chariot of Revelation 4–5.

The mythical significance of the Chariot, Lord of Heaven in Accadia (*Aganna*), should not be underestimated. This is the most conspicuous stellar formation in the northern sky. It comprises seven permanently visible stars that never travel beyond the horizon, towards the underworld nadir, at least not when seen above the forty-first parallel. In the words of Homer (fifth book of the Odyssey), the Great Bear is 'by others called the Wain, which wheeling round, looks ever toward Orion and alone dips not into the waters of the deep.'[12] The notion that Ursa Major 'wheels round' and 'never bathes in the ocean' alludes to an important feature of the constellation: its counter-clockwise movement around the polestar. When stars begin to appear at sunset in early autumn, the constellation can be seen landing on the northern horizon, below the North Star. Night after night, it moves gradually up towards its wintertime location around midnight, due east of Polaris, only to be turned upside down, close to the zenith, as the spring season arrives. Comes the summer, the formation undertakes its journey back to earth, to the northern horizon from its northwesterly station in heaven. At summertime, the sun and the nocturnal chariot are both going down yet towards opposite horizons: the south and the north.[13]

The overall circle drawn by the tail end of Ursa Major coincides with the outer limit of a circumpolar sky showing constellations that never 'touch the sea.' This huge sidereal **clock** of the northern sky can roughly indicate not only the time of the year, but also phases of the night, as reflected in ancient Mithraic texts and in the more recent writings of such English poets as Spenser (*Faerie Queen*), Tennyson ('New Year's Eve'), and Shakespeare (cf. the Carrier at the Rochester inn yard). The faint eye-testing Alcor, companion of Mizar (both in Ursa Major), played an important role in marking the March equinox among the Arabs about a thousand years ago. Arcturus, the Bear-Keeper often confounded with the She-Bear herself as he follows the curve of the animal's longish tail, was said by Hesiod (*c.* 800 B.C.E.) to rise about the middle of winter. The risings and settings of Arcturus show up in all classical calendars, including Ptolemy's. Ursa Major was used by the early Greeks in navigation and by ancient travellers guiding themselves through the deserts of Arabia. When landed on the northern earth, the constellation can mark the boundary between the East and the West; so thought Heraclitus of Ephesus about 500 B.C.E. Finally, the Talmud depicts this stellar creature as the guidepost of the world's north.

This constellation is by far the most famous of the stellar groups and appears in every detailed description of the celestial sphere reproduced on parchments, tablets, stones, and legends of the greatest antiquity. In North America, it is commonly called the Big Dipper, much like the Casserole of southern France. The two American Dippers find an echo in the Chinese ladle motif and in ancient biblical writings. The Hebrew word for north is *mezarim* (Job 37: 9), 'the scattering.' The same word can be read as the plural of *miser*, which denotes a **winnowing fan**, a long-handled wooden shovel used to throw up grain against the wind and to blow off the chaff. The word for north would thus evoke two long-handled fans, or the two 'dippers,' as perceived by the Hebrews (Maunder 1923: 263). In keeping with the 'scattering' motif, the north gave its Hebrew name to the summer wind that disperses the clouds and brings sunny weather, a wind blowing from the highest quarter of heaven (Job 37: 9, 22).

The Big Dipper designation is of recent origin when compared to **bovine** images such as the Thigh of Set, Bull's Thigh, or Fore Shank. In the centre of the Denderah zodiac, originally a ceiling in the Egyptian Temple of Hat-Hor (*c.* 34 B.C.E.), there is a foreleg to which the ancient *Book of the Dead* alludes as 'the constellation of the thigh in the northern sky.' This is the Thigh of Set, the fearful Egyptian god who flung Osiris into a coffin and was chained up by Isis (Boll 1914: 110). The same representation can be found on the kings' tombs and the walls of the Ramesseum at Thebes. Mithraic ritual texts, temple paintings, and iconographic representations of 'investiture' scenes link this bovine constellation to the seven gods called the Pole-Lords of heaven, guardians of the pivot and revolving axis of the vault of heaven. The bears are both symbols and instruments of Mithras viewed as a polar cosmocrator governing the motions of time.

Like the 'grain-winnowing fan,' the bull-thigh motif is in keeping with the Roman designation of our northerly constellation as seven oxen walking around the threshing-floor of the pole. Cicero and other contemporary writers made use of the Latin word *Septentriones* (*septem triones*) denoting seven ploughing oxen driven by Boötes the Ploughman, a term that became a synonym of the North Pole, the north wind, and the north in general. Since his heliacal rising coincided with autumn days of ploughing and grape picking, Boötes was also titled 'the Vintager.'

From the Vintager's Wheel and the Northern Team of threshing oxen (called the 'Seven Bulls' by the Persians) came the old English Plough title and the familiar terms of Cart, Wain, **Wagon**, and **Chariot**. Ursa Major was known towards our era as the Arctic Car (so, Aratus) or the Car of Egypt's Osiris, a chariot that lands right below King Cepheus and his polar Fold. According to the *New English Dictionary*, the expression 'Charles's Wain' confounds the great Charlemagne with King Arthur, hero of the

Round Table, who in turn evoked the star name Arcturus (and his circular Rove), Driver of the wheeled Wain. Teutonic nations knew this constellation as the *Wagen*, and the Scandinavians, as *Karls Vagn* (Thor's wagon). The Greek Aratus spoke of it as the Wain-like Bear, Romans as a *plaustrum* cart, and the scribe Ezra (fifth century B.C.E.) as *Ajala*, the Hebrew word for wagon. Arthur's Chariot finds another synonym in King David's Chariot, an expression used in Ireland and apparently introduced by the Christians. In France, the constellation became the Great Chariot, or *La Roue*, the Wheel, a term reminiscent of the biblical *'galta* motif.

To the ancient-chariot and seven-bull imageries can be added the **Bear** of Aratus, or Ursa Major proper, *Arktos Major* in Greek, from which we have the word 'Arctic.' The latter term stands for the north and is closely associated with the mountain bear country of Arcadia, northwest of biblical lands. The ursine figure may have originated from a confusion of two Sanskrit homonyms pronounced *Riksha*. In one gender, the word signifies a bear; in the other, it means a star, a bright thing that shines, after India's Seven Shiners, also referred to as Seven Bears, the Seven Bulls, or the Great Spotted Bull. But the heavenly bear image already showed up in a poem written in the year 270 B.C.E. by Aratus, who apparently copied Eudoxus, an astronomer of the fourth century B.C.E. reputed to have used findings of Akkadian or Chaldean astrologers made above 2000 B.C.E.

Dobh was the ursine name the stellar group got from Hebrew observers; it was *Dub* to the Phoenicians, and *Al Dubb al Akbar*, the Greater Bear, to the Arabians. Its prominent star *∂*, now called *Dubhe*, was *Thar al Dubb al Akbar* in Arabic, or the Back of the Greater Bear; star *ß* was *Al Marakk*, the Loin; star *y*, *Al Falidh*, the Thigh; and so on. As for the Hebrew word *'Ash* or *'Ayish* (Job 9: 9, 38: 32), it was 'Arcturus with his Sonnes' in the Geneva Bible, and 'Arcturus' in the Vulgate and the Authorized Version of King James I. With the Revised Bible of 1881-5 and the Jerusalem Bible, the latter translation was replaced by 'the Bear with her train'; the 'train' refers to the three tail stars. *'Ash* was also thought to apply to the square part of the constellation – hence, a quadrilateral Bier or Great **Coffin**, a title still heard in modern Syria. *Na'ash* was the term used for the whole constellation by Arabs of the Persian Gulf, who still speak of the three tail stars as Daughters of the Great Bier, or vengeful Mourners surrounding *Al Jadi*, the polestar deity who murdered their father, *Al Na'ash*.[14]

Manilius said of our two celestial *Arctoe* that they were rolling about the circumpolar Fold, yet in opposite positions, 'pursued as they pursue.' Unlike Ursa Major, however, Ursa Minor was referred to by the Arabs as

Al Fass, 'the hole in which the earth's axle found its bearing.'[15] The Little Bear's star *x,* which shared its 'Phoenician' name with the full constellation, is our North Star. This pivotal star used to be called *La Tramontana,* possibly because Mediterranean people saw it beyond their northern mountain boundary, as suggested by Allen (1963: 454).[16] The term *Tramontane* was also applied to the whole constellation, a configuration closely associated with *Mons Coelius* or Heavenly Mountain, where gods and the polestar once sat.[17]

The importance of the Great Bear and the boreal sky can be verified through ancient beliefs of Babylonian religion and mythology. Briefly, Anu was the 'great bull of heaven,' the highest god governing spring rains and all the heavenly constellations that marked the passing of time. Although his heavenly way comprised all stars located along the ecliptic, as a constellation he was placed in the 'yoke of the wagon star among the northern polar stars, about which the firmament revolves.' His son Enlil, titled earth-god and Lord of Winds, governed the astral band north of the ecliptic, known as the way of Enlil. He in turn was married to Ninlil, a mother-goddess pejoratively known as *'Ashtoreth* by the later Hebrews. Ninlil governed the 'polar band of the heavens' and was identified with the constellation *Margidda,* that is, Ursa Major, the Wagon Star (Malina 1995: 84; Jacobsen 1976: 95–9; Langdon 1931: 14, 94, 109, 305, 317).

In chapters to come, we shall see that key images of Revelation invite comparison not only with solar deities of the ancient Near East, but also with dippers, fans, oxen, ploughs, wheels, chariots, coffins, and bears sighted in the northern sky. Biblical characters behaving like creatures of the northern crown will be shown to play roles ranging from models of celestial glory to forces of evil and agents of divine wrath. While they can serve godly functions, sevenfold formations of the north can be ill-natured. Just as there is some confusion about the actual gender of our two circling constellations (are they she-bears, nymphs, nurses, or long-tailed he-bears each named Arctus and Ursus?), so there is considerable ambivalence in regards to their attributes, benevolent or malevolent. Although the object of worship and ritual sacrifice, the Thigh of Set was linked with malignant Set himself, his evil associates of circumpolar darkness, as well as their Greek counterparts, the giant Typhon and his fierce winds of destruction. In *King Lear,* Ursa Major is portrayed as a lecherous beast, an animal reputed for its savageness; its behaviour is reminiscent of the Bear Race of wild Arcadians and descendants and dogs of Lycaon, who gave their names to the constellations and set an example for Lacaon's daughter Kallisto. To these negative associations can be added Aratus' remark that the Bears are continually announcing forthcoming storms. The Larger Bear was especially feared by dwellers along the Nile, a fact that takes us back to basic principles of solar mythology: the constellation's ascent at dawn coincided with the heliacal rise of Sirius and the death of the sun-god at summer (Allen 1963: 123).

In Revelation, the terror that creatures of the northern sky used to inspire reaches new heights. John's vision of the End activates the many anxieties associated with these creatures. But the language deployed by the Seer conveys an even deeper angst: the fear of actually naming or acknowledging a heathenish pantheon that must be ignored and silenced at all costs. This is to say that the New Testament apocalypse does two things simultaneously. On the one hand, it tempts readers into probing star-gods for answers to the riddles posed by John's symbolism. On the other hand, it displays the Endtime sufferings that await those who dare succumb to the temptation. In the chapters that follow I examine these paradoxical effects of Revelation with a dialogical method that eschews the hermeneutic strategies reviewed in chapter 3. The approach will stray from the beaten tracks of anagogy, teleology, and genealogy, interpretive traditions at odds with a postmodern philosophy that questions the pursuit of essences, final ends, pristine origins, and root forms of cultural history. Thus my aim is to pay attention to the parallels that lie between astrological and apocalyptic imageries without attaching universal meanings or forms to metaphors of the apocalypse; reading into the Scriptures literal signs of things to come; or, what is even more tempting, arguing that astralism provides the original code, intentions, and context that once inspired the Book of Revelation.

5

The Seven Churches of Asia

The language of Revelation is largely metaphorical in that it constantly transfers to some words the sense conventionally attributed to other words. But why the transfer? Why must the word of God be revealed or disclosed through such convoluted symbolism? In an attempt to answer this question, Thompson (1990: 8) claims that the function of John's prophetic language is to unify the world into an organic whole, 'stitching earth to heaven, the present age to the coming age, local conditions to suprahuman processes, animals to divinities, and fire to water.'

In the process of nesting or extending the environment through metaphors and homologues nothing is left behind. Minor local issues do not drop out as the seer moves to global and cosmic environments; rather, they are taken up into the cosmic. Everything – local, global, animal, vegetable, mineral, divine – keeps its own place as it is taken into a larger unified system or ordered world. The metaphorical language of myth gathers up the scrap of the world and presents them as parts of a whole. (6)

The oneness of the world is played out in a forum of infinite likeness. Thompson's notion of comprehensive unity achieved through myth is in keeping with most conceptions of the rhetoric of metaphor. This imagery of harmony, however, does not do justice to the powerful ways of the metaphor. Things can never be united without cutting something away, displacing it, and leaving it behind. If anything, the allusions of metaphor are suited to the task of moving meanings in dispute from one realm of language to another, displacing some signs towards the foreground, while pushing others into the background. The allegorical attention paid to enemies of the Church in Revelation is a case in point. Through metaphor, the

Seer refers indirectly to the sins of heliolatry and the imperial cult prevailing under Domitian, both of which are antithetical to the Church. While adapted to Hellenistic and oriental culture surviving under Roman authority in Asia Minor, John's letters written to Jews of the diaspora show great restraint in evoking 'heathen' belief systems and the rule of Rome. The author prefers to allude to astromythology and Rome in the guise of an older representation of evil, Babylon. In lieu of being discussed openly, paganism and events in his own days are addressed through visions of heaven and the End of Time.

Revelation derives point and force from its condemnation of current enemies of the Church but also its ability to reconcile the teachings of Christ with fragments of 'pagan' symbology. The strength of John's vision comes from its polemical import – its ability to silence the enemies of the Church while harnessing their attributes and institutions to the service of Christ. As with other chapters of Revelation, the letters to Asia Minor are a convoluted exercise in 'polemical parallelism.' The end-product is an allegorical tract employing the form of ancient royal or imperial edicts (Aune 1990) and permitting the Church to recuperate all the powers usurped by enemies of the Church: Roman emperors and their stellar allies dwelling in heaven.

Ephesus

The epistles to the seven lamp standards or churches of Asia Minor and their pastors or heavenly guardians concern the conduct and destiny of each church, using the conventional language of astrological geography to introduce each city, with one 'angelic star,' heavenly guardian or sky servant per locality (Malina 1995: 258; cf. Treatise of Shem and 1 Enoch 86: 1–3, 88: 1). The letters proceed in an orderly fashion, in a clockwise direction, beginning with the city closest to the penal isle of Patmos. Ephesus, apparently the most important church in Asia Minor, is reproached with having less love for God. The Ephesians, however, earn praise for their resistance to the heretical teachings of the **Nicolaitans,** a name referring to the Gnostics who, apart from worshipping the seven planet-rulers of the cosmos (Arnold 1989: 8, 11, 46), abhorred the material world of the flesh or simply treated it as of no matter to the spirit, allowing licence with no spiritual consequence. Alternatively, reference to Nicolaitanism may be an allusion to the cult of Balaam (Rev. 2: 14f.; see Charles 1920, 1: 52). As argued by Hemer (1986: 91f., 94, 104), Jews in exile probably directed this reproachful name against followers of Christ. Christians in turn rejected it as a misrepresentation of Paul's precept of liberty and battle against Jewish legalism.

Paradoxically, Ephesian resistance to heresy is expressed through a language influenced by 'pagan' mythology. Although echoing symbols found in the Old Testament, images used in John's letter to Ephesus can be understood against the background of Ephesian religious beliefs. For instance, John's **tree of life set in God's paradise** (assimilated to the cross of Christ; see Gal. 3: 13) had an analogue in the Ephesian palm-tree motif and the tree shrine dedicated to Artemis (Hemer 1986: 42f., 46, 52). The great port city of the western coast was well known for its temple of the goddess Artemis, whose fertility cult had merged with that of the mother-goddess of the Middle East (Beasley-Murray 1974: 73). As the Asian counterpart of Diana the Roman huntress, she was known as 'Diana of the Ephesians,' a goddess twice discredited in the New Testament: in the Acts of the Apostles (19: 24–35) and the apocryphal Acts of John (43).

Artemis was the Greek goddess of the moon, Apollo's twin sister. She was an Asian divinity of conception and birth, adored in Palestine under the name Ashtoreth, the consort of Baal and faithful companion of the sun falling or dying in the summer season. She resembled other ancient underworld goddesses such as Persephone, the Phrygian Cybele, and the Babylonian Ereshkigal (Arnold 1989: 24, 26, 58, 88, 125, 169). Artemis was identified with the Greek sorceress Hecate, goddess of the moon, the earth, and the underground realm of the dead. Like Ishtar and Lilith (Isa. 34: 14), Hecate was a kindred spirit of the demoness Lamashtu, who kept close company with fearsome dogs and wolves. The goddess and the canine beasts in her train evoked the dog days of summertime Sirius (in the Greater Dog) and the stellar bears or Spartan Dogs of the north, evil creatures associated with humans engaging in sorcery and menacing the Church and the flock of Ephesus.[1]

Given her connection with the estival solstice, Artemis was thought to have put Orion to death after his pursuit of the Pleiades. The goddess survived the demise of two constellations that marked the vernal equinox and that were created by God together with the Bear and the morning star. In other words, she was equated with the constellation Virgo, associated with the summer solstice, the sun in Leo and the dog days of Sirius (as in Ovid's *Ars Amatoria*). Signs of the zodiac were prominently displayed around her neck, showing her superiority over the heavenly powers controlling fate. Her cult thus reflected the widespread and well-attested first-century beliefs in astral spirits prevailing among the 'pagans' and Jews of Ephesus and western Asia Minor, beliefs now challenged by

John through the powers vested in Christ (Arnold 1989: 17, 21, 28f. 46, 66f, 123, 128f., 155).

Smyrna

Smyrna is beset by false Jews forming the **synagogue of Satan**, after the manner of the false apostles acting as ministers of Satan in Ephesus (2 Cor. 11: 15, Rev. 2: 2, 9). 'Assemblies of Satan' probably alludes to synagogues of the Jewish diaspora dedicated to syncretic cults involving Graeco-oriental elements of sun-worship centred on Zeus or Jupiter, the god from whom 'fell' the Ephesian Diana (Isa. 14: 12, Acts 19; 35). Smyrna witnessed the cruel execution of Polycarp the Christian, who denounced state religion and the worship of the Roman emperor. Although she is to endure a period of tribulation and testing, Smyrna must not fear such sufferings and shall not be hurt by the second death at the hands of the judging Lord. In keeping with this picture of a city of suffering rewarded in the afterlife, the name Smyrna was expressive of myrrh, a substance used in rituals of weeping and burial nourished by hopes of resurrection (Hemer 1986: 76).

A few words should be said about the **crown of life** promised to those who are tested and 'prove victorious' when faced with persecution. Apart from being an emblem representing the physical aspect of Smyrna's buildings on the rounded top of the hill Pagos, the crown (*stephanos*) was a token of priesthood, festive joy, military victory, athletic prowess, and civil merit. According to Charles (1920, 1: 58f.), however, the crown may also have been derived from the sun-god and other heavenly beings wearing crowns of light or nimbuses. A speech given by Aelius Aristides (second century C.E.) on the occasion of the restoration of Smyrna following an earthquake suggests yet another astrological interpretation. Aristides wrote: 'I think, if the image of any city ever deserved to appear in the heavens, as they say the crown of Ariadne and other representations of rivers and animals are found among the stars and are honoured by the gods, that the emblem of this city ought to win the contest' (quoted in Hemer 1986: 73).

The crown of Ariadne, known to us as Corona Borealis, brings us back to ancient stories of the sun-god, Venus, Diana, and Virgo falling in the summer. To begin with, the Northern Crown is sighted in the highest quarter of heaven, a circular crown-like space containing the future 'paradise' or garden promised to Ephesus, from the Persian word *pairi-daiza*, for a round-shaped park surrounded by a wall. Corona Borealis was thought of as Cybele drawn by lions, with Leo preceding her; the goddess appeared with a necklace on Smyrnian coins (Ford 1975: 396). Classical Latin writers apparently associated the constellation with Proserpina – the Chaldean Phersephon, from *Phe'er*, 'Crown,' and *Serphon*, 'Northern.' Her Greek counterpart was Persephone, who stood for Virgo or Diana in the Attic dialect (Allen 1963: 177, 460).

The constellation Virgo is closely connected to issues of idol food. From Aratus's *Phenomena* we know that Virgo took refuge in heaven, near Boötes the Ploughman, because of people of the Bronze Age who ate flesh of the ploughing ox. In keeping with this imagery, the Northern Crown may have formed in the earliest astronomy the right arm of Boötes the Ploughman. Another name for the Northern Crown is the dish called Kasah Sheketch in Persian, a plate to serve such idol meat as the nearby Egyptian Thigh of Set, the Northern Oxen, or Plough. The imagery tallies with evocations of food sacrificed to idols in Pergamum and Thyatira (Rev. 2: 14, 20) and with the observation that the constellation rose at dawn in the late summer season, just before humans set the plough to work. Given these sinful associations, the platter should be broken, as is the case with the heavenly crown and the pagans of Thyatira condemned to be 'shattered like earthenware' (Rev. 2: 28; Allen 1963: 176). Just as the celestial crown or dish is situated outside the circumpolar sky, so too heathens eating idol food are to be expelled or excluded from the future paradise. The Thigh of Set that feeds their appetite is likely to be transformed into a quadrilateral coffin followed by three mourners, a coffin prefiguring the 'bed of tribulations' inflicted upon the northern church of Thyatira (Rev. 2: 22).

Pergamum

Although confronted with heresies, both Ephesus and Smyrna had generally followed sound doctrine. By contrast, the cities of Pergamum and Thyatira sheltered followers of heathen cults. The former city was famed for its school of medicine and was the 'Lourdes of the ancient world' (Charles 1920, 1: 60). She owed this reputation to her god *Asklepios Soter*, a coiled snake on a pole whom people of every origin came to see with hopes of being healed (as in Num. 21: 8–9). This divinity, known as *Pergamus deus*, represented a threat to the soteriological doctrine of spiritual healing and salvation through Jesus Christ (Hemer 1986: 85). Pergamum's great acropolis was all the more threatening to early Christians as it was the centre of the imperial cult in Asia Minor; a temple dedicated to Rome and Augustus had been built in 27 B.C.E. There sat the gigantic temple of Zeus Soter, built on a high hill with an altar overlooking the plain below. It is against this background that John accuses the city of sheltering the high seat of Satan the Serpent and the followers of Nicolaus and Balaam. The principal sin committed consisted in **eating food sacrificed to idols** and 'going a whoring' with false gods (see Num. 25: 1, 31: 16), on a lofty site substituted for the holy throne and mountain of God rising to the north (Ps. 48: 2, Ezek. 28).

Pergamum took pride in her cult of Zeus and Athena, the protectors of the city during the Attalid period. The Greek pantheon, however, seemed to have been superimposed on Anatolian figures of Dionysus and Asklepios, the Greek namesakes of the Asiatic bull-god and the serpent-god (Hemer 1986: 81). All of these divinities were assimilated to stellar creatures of the sky. Balaam was closely linked by early Christians to Simon the magician, the cult of stars, and the Magi of Persia. Asklepios (whence our word 'scalpel') also had a referent in heaven – namely, Ophiuchus the Serpent-Holder. The classical Hyginus (*c.* 1 C.E.) united this constellation with the neighbouring Serpens, also called the Serpent of Aesculapius (Acts 8: 9–24; Sweet 1990: 89, 97). These serpent signs located in the vicinity of autumn Scorpio tally with John's explicit evocation of **Satan** the snake. They reinforce *all other previous allusions (Virgo, the dog days, Corona Borealis, etc.) to the sun-god marching south, below the celestial equator, towards the post-vintage days of wintertime darkness and final judgment.*

But how does this astromythical symbolism connect to the **double-edged sword** coming out of the Lord's mouth (Rev. 2: 12, 16)? This intriguing motif has been interpreted by most commentators as another case of 'polemical parallelism' pitting the teachings of Christ, Ruler of the kings of the earth, against the imperial cult of the Roman emperor Domitian, who proclaimed himself *dominus et deus.* It evoked the power over life and death vested in the 'right of the sword' (*ius gladii*) granted to the senatorial governor of Asia, the proconsul residing in the provincial capital of Pergamum. But when combined with images of Christ the warrior (Rev. 2: 16), the sword image suggests another polemical parallel involving, not emperors, but rather characters of heaven competing for godly attributes. To be more precise, the sword belongs to a constellation that stands in conflict with Virgo, Ophiuchus, and Serpens: the late-spring Orion, to whom we now turn.

Orion is located on the opposite side from Scorpio and the Serpent-Holder. While he appears at dawn before the dog days of Sirius, his evening appearance is associated with the dreaded storms of winter. The Babylonian counterpart of Orion is Gilgamish, Nimrod in Hebrew mythology, the founder of Babylon, a hunter *armed with a sword and bound to the sky for his rebellion against Jehovah* (Gen. 10: 9). Since this giant of the sky comes right after Taurus, deposing it from its vernal throne, as it were, the warrior was considered to be responsible for Taurus's legendary death and quartering that produced the northern Thigh formation (Ursa Major) weeped by Ishtar. Artemis, the Greek counterpart of Ishtar and Virgo, was the one who in turn put Orion to death. In keeping with the eternal cycle of months and seasons, the demise of the bull formation at the hands of Orion killed by Virgo gave way to the heliacal rising of Scorpio and the two serpents at autumn. The triumph of darker forces was eventually followed by the resurrection of the sun-god passing once again through Aries and also Taurus, the bull-god that played a key role in Pergamese religion. Tradition has it that **Antipas**, the bishop of Pergamum and 'faithful witness' of the Lord (Rev. 2: 13), was burned in a brazen bull under Domitian.[2]

When translated into Christian symbolism, signs of spring resurrection point to Christ the Lamb slain, the Alpha and Omega governing the wheels of time. The Messiah triumphs over death at the time of the vernal equinox, which is when the sun enters the Ram, father of the Lamb. All indications are that it is at this time of the year, when the sun starts its ascent above the celestial equator, that the **manna** promised to the faithful in Pergamum fell from heaven. Manna is the opposite of the unclean idol food (consisting of sacrificed bullocks, rams, lambs, goats, etc.) denounced in John's letters to the churches. As shown below, the calendrical circumstances of the sacred manna food tie in directly with the cycle of seasons and related stories of solar resurrection.

The word manna is akin to the Sumerian *ma-nu*, a sacred plant connected with the tamarisk and date palms and with the water, the bread and the plant of birth and life. In Jewish tradition, manna was eaten during the wanderings of Israelites in the desert, which is where the elect were exposed to the temptations of Balaam. The journey is commemorated every year at the Feast of Tabernacles or Festival of Tents, in the seventh month of Tishri, about the autumn equinox, when days of darkness and the 'early rains' began. While memories of Israel's forty-year journey across the wilderness used to be celebrated at fall, they were also incorporated into springtime festivities that came with the arrival of the 'later rains' in the month of A'dar. This is a cold and rainy part of the year when hail is frequent. The period now coincides with the forty weekdays preceding Easter – hence, the Lent (from Anglo-Saxon *lencten*, 'the spring'), a period of fasting and penitence modelled after the trials and temptations of Jesus in the wilderness.

The association of manna with the Passover tradition and the spring harvest of barley and wheat is confirmed in the Book of Exodus, chapter 16. The food of heaven is ground and baked, treated as a substitute for bread or wheat, and collected at dawn, just like grain harvested at the beginning of the year (Deut. 8: 3; Ps. 78: 24; Wis. 16: 20f.). As with frost in spring and wheat in summer, the food dissolves when the sun grows hot. It appears together with quails, birds known to keep close company with the sun as they fly northward in March, across Egypt and the Holy Land, to return southward in September. Twice the normal amount of manna was gathered on the 'sixth day' of the week, which could mean either Friday (Lat. *Veneris dies*, the day of Venus the Morning Star) or the sixth month of the civil year (A'dar). Both moments in time are connected to the spring equinox, marked, as they are, by hail falling from the sky and the Lent period ending with the death of Christ on the cross. All of these vernal indicators are reinforced by Joshua's notion that manna stopped falling on the 'morrow of the Passover' (15 Nisan), a time when Israel was given access to the new corn of the land of Canaan (Josh. 5: 12). Finally, in John's letter to Pergamum, manna is clearly a symbol of immortality, a comment that applies to food from the tree of life (Rev. 2: 7) but also to Christ on the cross, the Lord who resurrected at Easter and became living bread sent from heaven (John 6: 51). Thus the manna imagery prefigures the bread of the Eucharist celebrated on Sun-day (1 Cor. 10: 3ff.; Prigent 1964: 21), holy bread that was part of the vernal Paschal Supper tradition, to be accompanied by wine harvested at the other end of the year, just before the autumn equinox.

Similar astro-calendrical implications can be found in the biblical concept of redemptive naming. In John's letter to Pergamum, the bread of Christ entails a new life and a **new name** engraved on a stone (Rev. 2: 17). A close parallel lies between the granting of a new name, the letter *tau* used by Jews to represent the Divine Name, and the protective mark of the cross written on the forehead and echoing the blood of the Passover lamb (Exod. 12, Ezek. 9: 4ff.). In the Christian tradition, the act of 'sealing' or 'writing the name of God' on his servants, terms made explicit in the letter to Philadelphia, implied ownership, authentication, and protection leading to salvation.[3] The symbolism was extended to baptism, which signified death in Christ, a ritual 'in which a man took on himself the Name, and acknowledged Christ's ownership' (Sweet 1971: 148; cf. Mounce 1977: 116f.; Prigent 1964: 23; see Rom. 6: 3ff.).

The Christian cross and the sealing of God's name can be represented by the cruciform *tau* letter which, from a calendrical perspective, stands for the two equinoctial moments in yearly time. As shown in the previous chapter, the last letter of the Hebrew alphabet (the equivalent of the Greek Omega) stood for the Balance evoking the autumn equinox. But the letter also played a key role in the Passover tradition celebrated in the first month of Nisan. The double equinoctial implications of the *tau* seal or name applies to manna as well. While associated with the spring equinox, the miraculous foodstuff was received during Israel's wandering in the wilderness, as commemorated in the seventh month of Tishri, a time of the year characterized by shortages of grain food. Both manna food and the *tau* seal are tied to the onset of spring and the autumn equinox, the Alpha and the Omega governing the order of time.

Few modifications are needed to convert manna and the letters and names of divine fate into the '**stone** with a new name on it' promised to the faithful witnesses of Pergamum. We know that manna came in the form of small round seed resembling the hoar frost and that precious stones fell with the bread of manna in the desert (Joma 8). The notion that bread and stones are interchangeable is confirmed in the ancient practice of using white *tessera* stones as tickets to bread and festivals (Mounce 1977: 99f.). When combined with stones used for writing, the miraculous manna food also leads to ancient stories concerning the ark of the covenant and the two testimonial 'stone tablets' given to Moses on Mount Sinai. In the epistle to the Hebrews, it is said that, when Jerusalem was taken by the Chaldeans, Josiah hid the golden pot containing the heavenly manna together with the tables of stone, the ark, Aaron's rod, and the holy anointing oil. All treasures were to be restored to Israel in the days of the Messiah (Heb. 9: 4).

Apocryphal writings of the Old Testament suggest that the ark, the stone tablets, and the pot containing manna were hidden underground in Mount Nebo, the 'high place' from which Moses saw the promised land and where the prophet died (2 Macc. 2: 4ff.; Deut. 32: 49, 34: 1). The mountain is situated due east of Jerusalem, in the land of Moab, whose king **Balak** and daughters once persuaded the Israelites to eat food sacrificed to idols and practise immorality, in accordance with 'the counsel of **Balaam**' – a story made explicit in the letter to Pergamum (Num. 25: 1ff., 31: 16; Rev. 2: 14). The location is all the more suited for the burial of the stone tablets as the mountain evokes the divine Nebo, Babylonian god of writing (Isa. 46: 1, 48: 1). While he appeared as a heavenly scribe in Ezekiel, the Babylonian Nebo was represented by the Greek Alpha or Hebrew Aleph – hence, Aldebaran, Taurus star ∂, Leading Star of Stars, and also the Star of the Tablet. Readers are reminded that Nebo was the one who read the Tablets of Destiny at the New Year festival, thereby predicting the fate of humans throughout the coming year. Since the scribe was thought to accompany the sun-god in his journey to the lower world, he was associated with the autumn equinox and darker moments of year. Accordingly, the scribe had it in his power to write the *tau* cross on the foreheads of men, the last letter of the alphabet marking the autumn equinox. In his own way, Nebo stood for the Alpha and Omega of the Babylonian order in heaven. Memories of this ancient deity and the writing symbolism assigned to him are particularly well adapted to Pergamum, which boasted a library of more than 20,000 volumes and where parchment was apparently invented (Mounce 1977: 95).

The equinoctial duality of the solar cycle conveyed through signs of manna and letters of the alphabet finds another echo in the double-edged imagery of *two stones* used for the writing and reading of humans' fate, good or bad. While the bread and the mark of God were opposed to unclean food and the sign of the beast, the white stone and the stone of Zion standing for the Saviour contrasted with the stumbling stone cast by Balak before the children of Israel (Rom. 9: 32; 1 Pet. 2: 8; Rev. 2: 14). Similarly, the white *tessera* stone showing a name 'known only to the man who receives it' was one of a pair consisting of white and black stones used as voting ballots, amulets to influence one's luck, or pebbles to draw lots in criminal cases. The imagery is a variation on stones and tribal names that covered the breastplate of the high priest. It also echoes the testimonial Urim and Thummim placed into the pouch of the high priest's ephod, or the two stone tables of the covenant kept inside the ark.[4] As Ford remarks,

it might be possible to connect the taw of salvation or preservation with the judicial proceedings involving the *Urim* and *Thummin*, the objects, probably sacred lots, by which the priests gave an oracular decision in the name of Yahweh. These were set into the breastplate of the high priest (Exod. 39.8–21) but originally were small stones of the same size or shape but with different marks on them, such as *aleph* and *taw*, respectively the first and the last letters of the Hebrew alphabet. In judicial proceedings the decision *aleph* would mean guilty ('*rr*, 'to curse') and *taw* innocent (*tmm*, 'to be blameless'). (1975: 122f.)

Beasley-Murray contends that the white-stone motif is so many-sided that it is virtually impossible to determine the intention of the author of Revelation (1974: 89). But the difficulty involved in eliciting precise meaning from the stone symbol stems not from its many-sided implications. The problem comes rather from the danger of letting the stone imagery admit to a cult of nature performed through ritual divination. The material presented above suggests that the symbols deployed in the letter to Pergamum

competed with pagan imageries such that some of its implications, especially those of astrological import, had to be forgotten or simply silenced.
John's exercise in polemical parallelism requires that heathenish usages of
signs of divinity – godly attributes usurped by evil humans and false gods –
be obliterated from the surface text.

Repression achieved through silence is not enough though. John's task is
considerably more complex. Although in direct conflict with pagan practices, his prophecies are an attempt at 'recomposing' the lunisolar and stellar rhetoric that served the imperial rule, reappropriating it to the exclusive
benefit of the Son of Man and his Father dwelling in heaven. Wittingly or
not, John reclaims the language of astromythology through simple evocations of Christ the warrior, his sharp double-edged sword, stones used for
writing, and the manna bread falling from the sky. All of these signs converge on God's command over the Alpha and the Omega of cyclical time,
or life and death embodied in the equinoctial beginnings and endings of
solar motions in heaven. Given this rewriting of Sabian mythology, spiritual salvation can no longer be achieved through offerings made to the sun-
god Tammuz or the Phoenician Eshmun, the snake-holding god of healing
(= Adonai, Yahweh; see Langdon 1931: 74–7). Nor can immortality be
attained through Zeus or Asklepios the snake-healer, the Serpent-Holder,
and kindred spirit of two other ancient serpents regulating the wheels of
time: the Water-Snake spanning from one node to another, and the constellation Draco marking the North Pole. Redemption can be attained through
Christ alone, heir to the Serpent sent by God to punish and heal Israelites
wandering in the wilderness (Exod. 21: 4ff.). In an effort to foreclose
humans' debt to nature, John's words to Pergamum demote visible spheres
of heaven to mere metaphor.

Thyatira

Thyatira is accused of tolerating harlotry practised in the name of Jezebel
(2 Kings 9: 22). The lady was swept through by the 'adultery of eating
food which has been sacrificed to idols.' To use Aratus's imagery, she
behaved like humans of the Bronze Age, who ate the flesh of ox, a crime
that led Virgo to leave the earth and take refuge in heaven, near Boötes.
Jezebel followed the Nicolaitan doctrine proclaiming that idols are
devoid of any powers and that animals sacrificed to them may be eaten
without defiling the Christian spirit. While Nicolaitanism was resisted in
Ephesus and had a limited impact in Pergamum, it was overtly indulged
in Thyatira.

The local patron god of this church was Apollo Tyrimnaeus, who played an important part in the imperial cult and was represented by a bronze statue, a material used to describe the Son of God in the letter to Thyatira (Rev. 2: 18). Like the bronze figure, the unusual 'Son of God' designation of verse 18 was 'set against opposing religious claims or against a syncretic attempt to equate the person of Christ with deities recognized by the city' (Hemer 1986: 116). The Son of God stood against Apollo and the emperor, both of whom were acclaimed as sons of Zeus. The cult of Apollo incorporated Anatolian rituals dedicated to the city goddess and consort of the Greek sun-god – namely, Artemis Boreitene, known to the Romans as Diana or Virgo (Hemer 1986: 118). Apollo and Artemis were probably honoured on the occasion of festivities and banquets organized by the local guilds, with the implication that its Christian members were pressed to eat meat sacrificed to the current idols. The condemnation of **Jezebel** in 2: 20, possibly a nickname for a self-proclaimed Thyatiran prophetess, reflects John's repudiation of syncretic cults involving the worship of earthly rulers and their heavenly allies. The original Jezebel was a model of infidelity and wickedness, and her Thyatiran counterpart stands accused of following in her footsteps. She too incited followers of the Lord to commit fornication and eat food sacrificed to false gods resembling the Canaanite Baal and his consort Astarte (1 Kings 16: 31ff., 21: 25f.).

Towards the end of the letter, John brings in the **Morning Star** to oppose the rule of pagan gods and false prophets teaching the **deep things of Satan** (Rev. 2: 24, 29). Most commentators see in these words an implicit reference to astrology, the goddess Ishtar and the planet Venus, an emblem of sovereignty since Babylonian times and an integral part of the imperial and military symbolism of Rome (Beasley-Murray 1974: 93f.; Prigent 1964: 25). This polemical reformulation of pagan imagery allowed the prophet to redirect the attributes of 'light-bearing' Lucifer, 'son of the morning,' towards the service of God. As Morning Star, Christ is empowered to conquer the 'bright star' that stood not only for Satan, but also for the northern kings of Babylon and Tyre situated in Phoenicia, the kingdom whose gods Jezebel promoted in Israel (Isa. 14: 12ff.; Ezek. 28: 12ff.). But God's repossession of the ancient 'morning light' title also implied a repudiation of the astral pantheon, reducing the godly planet to mere analogy. This twofold strategy – deploying the natural language of Sabaism while subjecting it to a higher rule, the logocentric – permitted a full substitution of God for all lights shining above. As made clear at the end of Revelation, the messianic Jerusalem that John envisaged no longer needed the sun or the moon for light, 'since it was lit by the radiant glory of God and the Lamb was a lighted torch for it' (Rev. 21: 23). In the words of Ignatius, 'a star shone in heaven brighter than all the stars ... *whence all magic was dissolved* ... the ancient kingdom [of Satan] was pulled down, when God appeared in human form to bring a new order of everlasting life' (in Sweet 1990: 97; emphasis added).

In his battle against the cult of visible spheres in heaven, God can be counted on to 'shepherd' (Gr. *poimainein*, 'rule, destroy,') pagan nations 'with an **iron sceptre and shatter them like earthenware**' (Rev. 2: 20, 22, 27f.). A shepherd protects and rules over his flock with an iron rod, a club that can inflict considerable suffering. The same staff, however, can generate new life and be used to engrave the name of a founding tribe. It can be equated with 'Aaron's rod that grew the buds' and that was placed in the Holy of Holies, together with the golden pot containing manna and the stone tablets of the covenant (Num. 17: 1–9; Heb. 9: 4f.). The royal rod or sceptre ties in with the star of Jacob motif (Num. 24: 17; Jer. 23: 5; Zech. 3: 8; Farrer 1964: 76) and with earlier signs recorded in the letter to Pergamum (sword, manna, stone, name).

The rod is all the more powerful as it serves the principle of life and death reigning over the seasonal motions of bodies in the sky.[5] If assigned to a shepherd dwelling in heaven, the staff belongs to Arcturus, known to the Chaldeans as the Guardian Messenger, the Shepherd of the Heavenly Flock, or the Shepherd of the Life of Heaven. Arcturus rose at the time of the autumn equinox, about mid-September. The star shared its name and attributes with its constellation, Boötes the Herdsman. Boötes guarded the circumpolar fold, drove the Oxen of the Wain, and heralded the grape harvest and the season of ploughing. He is closely associated with the northern sky or crown of heaven and has often been confounded with Cepheus, a shepherd dressed in royal robes, with one foot on the pole and the other on the solstitial colure (Allen 1963: 93–101, 155ff.).

The right arm of Boötes was once formed by Corona Borealis, a heavenly configuration resembling the crown mentioned in the letter to Smyrna. We have seen that the Northern Crown evokes Semitic representations of paradise and the wreath of thorns worn by Jesus. The formation also points to stories of Virgo, Cybele, and Astarte falling in the company of the sun-god, towards the season of wintertime darkness. In John's message to Thyatira, the semicircular group of stars assumes its Persian shape, a *Kasah Sheketch* earthenware 'broken to pieces like clay vessels.' The potter's ware may have been destroyed with the rod that Yahweh once employed to crush *shepherd and flock, chariot and charioteer, ploughman and team* (Ps. 2: 9; Jer. 51: 20ff.). The Persian dish deserves to be destroyed as it may have been used to serve idol food, such as the neighbouring Thigh of Set (Ursa Major, the Plough, the Chariot).

Given their 'pagan' associations, the dish and the thigh should both suffer the same fate: the idols should be turned against their own worshippers. While the dish should be shattered, the northern Thigh of Set should be converted into a **sickbed**, a funeral bier or a coffin, as opposed to Jezebel's banquet couch or adulterous bed. In his letter to Thyatira, all is as if God had transformed the northern Thigh formation (mourned by Ishtar) into a bed of tribulations, to be inflicted on Jezebel and her Thyatiran followers residing in the north (Rev. 2: 22; see L. Morris 1983: 72; Jacobsen 1976: 201f.). The destructive action of Ursa Major seen as a coffin is indirectly confirmed by another calamity imposed on Jezebel: the lady's infidelity is so reproachable that the Lord will see to it that her **children die** (v. 23). Commentators tend either to pay no attention to such details or to treat them as conventional phrases that add little to the text (Cooke 1960: 62). And yet the imagery is loaded with references to lessons of astromythology and the agricultural calendar. The threat of women being deprived of children is congruent with a scene of humans facing the danger of famine, or losing their seed sown at autumn. More important, we learn from Ezekiel (5: 17) that, come the End of Time, children will be robbed by beastly creatures. What animals could these be? Could they be the 'two she-bears [that] came out of the wood and savaged forty-two of the boys' (2 Kings 2: 24)? The latter animals appeared to Elisha while in Bethel, north of Jerusalem, a town where people worshipped the golden calf. Alternatively, could it be the bear that young David killed (1 Sam. 17: 34f.) and that stood for a pagan empire (Dan. 7: 5; Rev. 13: 2), a creature that became particularly ferocious when robbed of her cubs (2 Sam. 17: 8; Prov. 17: 12; Hos. 13: 8)? Or could it be the ursine constellation that rises in the company of summertime Leo (around the time of the grape harvest), just like biblical bears usually appearing in the presence of lions (Prov. 28: 15; Lam. 3: 10; Dan. 7: 4f.; Rev. 13: 2)?

These questions can be answered in the affirmative. All indications are that our seven-starred bears/bulls of the north are kindred spirits of the Moabite Molech (or Ashtar-Chemosh) and also the seven child-snatching *sedim* of Semitic mythology, false gods to whom children were apparently sacrificed, much to the horror of Israel.[6] These bull-like animals had much in common with the child-slaying demoness of Sumerian origin called Lamia by the Greeks, or Lilu (from Sumerian *lil*, 'wind-demon'), Lamashtu, and Ishtar by the Babylonians. Another name assigned to this evil woman was the 'sword which shatters the head' (see Ezek. 5: 1ff.). She was Lilith to the Hebrews and the Christians, an evil spirit frequently mentioned in Jewish mythology. Readers are reminded of Lilith's association with wild beasts in Isaiah (34: 14) and her legendary encounter with Elijah, the prophet who saved a child from being devoured by the demoness. Hebrew legends describe Lilith as the mother of all demonic *sedim*, the first wife of Adam (before Eve), a stealer of children, and the one who tried to harm Mary before she gave birth to Jesus.

The countertext of the Thyatiran message is profoundly astrological. Sweet recognizes a direct connection between words used in this letter and the teachings of Gnosticism, sorcery, and astrology. In his view, it is 'difficult for a modern Westerner to appreciate the place of magic and astrology in a world felt to be dominated by hidden and hostile powers' (1990: 92). Although insightful, Sweet's comment about humans' attraction towards 'the hiddenness of sorcery and astrology' is somewhat misdirected and is better addressed to the teachings of John, not to paganism. Far from being an occult practice, the cult of stars and planets was an open secret and a generalized phenomenon throughout biblical lands. Moreover 'pagan' religion was based on faith in teachings of the natural 'sphere.' It paid homage to the *visible* bodies of gods and goddesses dying and resurrecting in heaven, all in due season and in accordance with the perceptible laws of nature. In its own way, the Book of Revelation recuperates the latter language while also reducing it to silence. It hides the gods of nature from the reader's gaze, to the benefit of *faith in the hiddenness of Logos*.

On the whole, John's writings to the churches of Asia Minor reproduce Paul's twofold battle against Judaic legalism and pagan libertinism. On the one hand, the prophet is constantly echoing and reapplying Old Testament imagery and phraseology but without ever actually quoting the Scriptures. John's reluctance to repeat words of the Old Testament illustrates the Pauline rejection of 'legalism with its exaltation of trivialities and Pharisaical insistence on codes of rules' (Kiddle 1940: 33f.). On the other hand, Revelation is also an attack on antinomianism, on the notion that faith should be placed above and separated from the precepts and prohibitions of moral law. John preaches against using the Pauline concept of freedom to justify a liberal view of Christian accommodation and assimilation to the urban culture of pagan rituals and emperor worship (Hemer 1986: 14, 92, 123; see Thompson 1990: 123; Theissen 1982).

Two important qualifications should be added to this widely accepted reading of John's repudiation of both the Nicolaitans and the Pharisees of this world. First, the contrast between legalism and libertinism should not be overdrawn. Both 'perversions' of faith in the Lord had one thing in

common: a devotion to ancient imageries and ritual paraphernalia conveying an astrological view of the world, a belief system centred on the calendrical motions of life and death experienced by earthly and heavenly bodies
alike. Second, the immorality of 'pagan' religion should not be exaggerated.
Chapters 2 and 3 of Revelation denounce in no uncertain terms the per-
verse ways of Christians who succumb to harlotry and sorcery promoted
by Jezebel. The prophet is intolerant of libertarian morals based on the cult
of nature and carnality in life. It is to be expected from John that competing
religions be associated with satanic evil in its purest form. But readers
should bear in mind that John's language is essentially an exercise in
polemical parallelism. His task is not to eliminate contending religions and
morals but rather to reformulate age-old teachings of the death and resurrection of the sun-god within a logocentric perspective, casting naturalistic
imageries in a new metaphysical mould.[7]

Sardis

The letter to Sardis includes two key motifs that can be understood in the
cultic setting of ancient astrology. The first consists of **white robes**, garments of everlasting light worn by the elect in the tent-like home and kingdom of the future heaven (2 Cor. 5: 1ff.; Prigent 1981: 65). The celestial
implications of the body-and-garment-of-light symbolism are self-evident.
The second image involves a **Book of Life** containing the names of the
faithful. It holds promises of a heavenly life for those who refrain from
indulging in acts of divination, worshipping gods made in the image of the
golden calf, a kindred spirit of the leading Taurus and the seven bulls of the
north (Exod. 32: 32f.; Ezek. 13: 9). The Book of Life is akin to civil registers
used in Asia. But it is also reminiscent of the Babylonian tablets of destiny
stolen from the female dragon of the sea and worn on the breast of the sun-
god Marduk, to be written and read by Nebo at the New Year festival. At
one time the tablets were thought to be kept in the underworld realm of
Arallû. This was the place of judgment and of no return, inhabited by the
seven devils of Babylonian mythology and ruled by Ereshkigal, a name
closely associated with Hecate, Artemis, and Persephone (Jacobsen 1976:
56f., 178f.; Beasley-Murray 1974: 98).

Other elements of Smyrna's religious background reinforce some of the
astrological themes implied in previous letters to Asia Minor. Although
disguised under Hellenic appearances, the public image of Sardis represented on coinage involved local deities of Anatolian inspiration. According to Hemer (1986), Cybele, Artemis to the Greeks, was the principal

goddess. She was attended by eunuch priests called *Galli*, possibly echoing the seven *Gallû* demons or chthonian bulls of Babylonian and Assyrian mythology. As death-goddess and guardian of the grave, Cybele resembled Persephone and the earth-goddess who gave her life, Demeter, mother of Dionysus (the god of vegetation and wine commonly shown on Sardian coins). The nature-goddess typically appeared with lions, travelling in a car drawn by two winged serpents; the scene brings to mind Virgo keeping company with Leo and Hydra (the Water-Snake) at summer, followed by two other ophidian constellations rising at autumn (Ophiuchus and Serpens).

The nature religion of ancient Anatolia generated stories of rejuvenation involving serpents sloughing their skins. A new life could also be achieved by humans drinking or bathing in the blood of a sacrificed bull, rituals harking back to the death of Antipas of Pergamum burnt in a brazen bull. These immortality rituals and related myths were part of the cult of Attis, a cult that revolved around the cyclical decline and revival of the sun-god and his female consort dwelling in heaven. Cognate stories and coin illustrations spoke of bulls standing before altars surmounted by coiled serpents, and also Heracles (alias Hercules) burnt in effigy or dragging a humped bull. Other stories implicating a Nimrod-like giant struggling against a serpent converged on *yet another vision of the autumn sky*: Hercules adjoining Boötes and slaying Hydra, with one foot planted on the twisting Serpent's head.[8]

In his discussion of the letter to Sardis, Thompson (1990) mentions an archaeological find of a synagogue with furnitures showing elements of Jewish culture combined with Roman and local Lydian designs. The lion motif commonly used throughout biblical lands provides a good example of the complex mixture of Jewish and Gentile iconography in the Sardian find. Kraabel's understanding of this so-called syncretism phenomenon is that 'the Sardis Jews are not simply "reusing" the lion-statues in their synagogue, but actually associating themselves in some way with this traditional Sardis image.' Jewish accommodation to Anatolian culture reflects 'the expressions of self-confident Jewish communities, existing in Asia Minor ... These are bold acts, not timid ones, and should not be misrepresented as "syncretism" or "apostasy" simply because they appear strange in the twentieth century' (Kraabel 1978: 23f., in Thompson 1990: 141).

Judging from his words to the seven churches, John's reaction to religious integration in Asia Minor was more negative than Kraabel's. Still, Kraabel's comment concerning the vitality of a Jewish culture adapting to Sardian traditions could be applied to John himself. The rule of cultural accommodation can be extended to a Christian Apocalypse that makes more concessions to Gentile symbolism than John and his commentators will care to admit. John's prophetic writings show considerable adaptability. In his own way, the prophet succeeds in connecting one idiom to another, effecting a compromise between distinct traditions with a view to translating the teachings of Christ into local rhetoric. But the Book of Revelation goes beyond a simple combination of different belief systems. The powers of speech exercised in Revelation betray, not a strategy of simple accommodation, but rather one of complex rhetorical domination – luring an adversary language to serve the ruling Verb.

Philadelphia

Although once more allusive and elusive, the language and symbols used in the next letter fit naturally into a Sabian pattern and derive point and force from it. Consider first the **door and key** of vv. 3: 7f., symbols befitting a city known as the 'gateway to the east': Philadelphia was located along the post route from Rome via Troas and continuing eastward, up onto the great central plain. The city was at the junction of trade routes leading to Mysia, Lydia, and Phrygia. It was founded by Attalus II *Philadelphus* of Pergamum, who, some say, entrusted it with a mission to promote Hellenistic culture in Asia Minor. The connection between an 'open door' and new missionary opportunities in Asia Minor is made explicit in the writings of Paul to the Church at Corinth (1 Cor. 16: 9; 2 Cor. 2: 12; see L. Morris 1983: 77f.).

But there was also a cosmographic counterpart to human-made doors and gateways constructed on earth. In his capacity as 'the gate of the sheepfold' and 'the door to the Father,' Jesus the good shepherd is depicted as holding the key to the House of David, after the manner of the four Levites and chief porters in charge of the temple. To this Davidic key are added the keys to the underworld placed in God's possession. The keys give the Davidic Messiah the power to rise from Sheol, as if he were coming back through the door drawn on Phrygian graves (Hemer 1986: 205; see Arnold 1989: 58). They give him the power to cast and lock the dragon into the bottomless pit and to open the future kingdom of the heavenly court to the elect.

A Montanist promise is made to the faithful in Philadelphia that they shall be pillars supporting the Lord's everlasting sanctuary established on earth. As with Old Testament laws written on the door posts and gates of Israel, their names shall be inscribed on pillars of the sanctuary together with the name of God and his city, the 'new Jerusalem which comes down from my God in heaven' (Rev. 3: 12). The city shall have twelve gates, a number corresponding to the apostles and the tribes of Israel, but also the twelve stellar doors or lodging-houses successively entered by the sun-god marching through the sky.[9] In retrospect, the heavenly door composition is well suited to a church acting as keeper of 'the gateway to the east.' I am referring to Philadelphia, but also the gateway to Eden (Gen. 3: 24), the door that Yahweh goes through when moving in and out of the Jerusalem Temple (Ezek. 10: 19, 11: 1). To the east lies also the gateway that the sun crosses when moving into the heavenly throne-room at daybreak (Jacobsen 1976: 204).

According to Josephus, high priests used to open the Temple doors on the eve of Passover, in the hope of final redemption, a tradition preserved in the paschal celebrations of the early Christians (Prigent 1964: 34f.; 1981: 79). But the door motif can open on to darker events. We know from Old Testament prophets that retribution comes with the opening of floodgates in heaven (lasting five months) or the blowing of a wind of tribulations hailing from the east (Gen. 7: 11–24; Isa. 27: 8; Jer. 4: 11f.). The first association suggests the pouring of rains that comes at fall and returns at spring. The easterly-wind motif points in the same direction: the Lord's departure and judgment occurring in the post-vintage days of autumn (Rev. 14: 19f., 19: 15). This is the season of satanic Babylon, the harlot who makes all the population of the world drunk with the wine of her adultery and fornication (Rev. 17: 2, 18: 3). The season of sowing and making wine belongs also to Bacchus, or the Greek Dionysus, a central deity of ancient Philadelphian history.

This brings us to the question of **wine** production in Philadelphia. According to Hemer, the city was characterized by a precarious agricultural economy and depended heavily on viticulture.

The volcanic soil was unusually suitable for vines, but too little wheat was grown, and the city may have suffered during periodic famines. It is argued that Rev. 6.6 refers to Domitian's edict against vines in AD 92, a measure which may have been intended as a drastic means of increasing corn production, but which hit Philadelphia with exceptional severity because of its dependence on viticulture. The act violated a code observed even by a conquering enemy: it was unprecedented in a patron. *The character of Christ (v. 7) may be set against disillusionment with the imperial god.* (1986: 175, cf. 158f., emphasis added)

Hemer shows how the faithfulness of Christ evoked at the beginning of the letter stood in contrast with the unreliability of imperial patronage, as illustrated by the disastrous effects of the Roman edict to which Revelation 6: 6 may allude.

In a Philadelphian perspective, the god of wine would have every reason to retaliate the injuries of Rome. This can be done with the assistance of evil satyrs and other attendants of Bacchus or Dionysus, demons that Eratosthenes (second century B.C.E.) used to equate with the centaur-like Sagittarius adjoining Scorpio and reigning over beasts (Manilius 2: 265f., 4: 384; Rev. 18: 2). From a Christian perspective, however, judgment executed by creatures of darkness is acceptable on condition that it be carried out on behalf of the Lord. To use the Dionysian language, God alone can crush his enemies like jugs of wine, treading evil forces like grapes in a wine press, destroying them as a thief (Rev. 3: 3) or a jackal attacking the unguarded vintage. What is more, only the Messiah can redeem the faithful by pouring his wine-like blood, allowing the vine of Israel to attain the blessings of the good life in heaven, the kind that humans enjoy under a vine and a fig tree.[10]

To the followers of Jesus in Philadelphia, Christ should be substituted for Dionysus. He should also replace the Nabataean Dusares, the sun-god and patron of fertility who was given birth in late December by the virgin Earth-Mother, the Greek underworld goddess Core. As Langdon points out, what we have here is a reflection of the Babylonian myth of Tammuz and Ishtar: 'There is a wide syncretism here in this Arabic religion, composed of Babylonian, Greek, and Egyptian elements; and beyond all doubt the Nabataeans possessed an elaborate cult of Tammuz and Ishtar, of Osiris and Isis, of Dionysus and Basilinna, the equivalent of Proserpine-Core, in which this deity was represented as a youth, son of the Mother-goddess, who was reborn yearly in midwinter and who died in the summer' (1931: 18f.). Langdon adds that the mother-goddess figure corresponds to the North Semitic Ashtart and the Greek Tyche depicted as Fortuna holding a cornucopia, with a turretted headdress and an infant at her feet. Coins showing representations of Fortuna have been found in Ephesus, Philadelphia, Laodicea, and the neighbouring Hierapolis. In Sardis she was Artemis or Cybele. Pergamum had her own Tyche as well (see Jacobsen 1976: 47–63; Hemer 1986: 138, 238n47). The connection between these female divinities and the solar and agricultural calendar is confirmed in Jacobsen's discussion of the Babylonian myth of Dumuzi and his sister: 'Grain was harvested in the spring and brewed and stored afterward. The grape was harvested only in the autumn and was made into wine then. It is this difference in the time of death and descent that the myth takes as its theme to explain in terms of timeless happenings in *illo tempora*. When Dumuzi of the beer disappears underground in the spring or early summer, his sister, the wine goddess, seeks him disconsolately until, by autumn, she herself descends into the earth and finds him there in the netherworld' (1963: 62).

We know that God's control over the grapes and winepress of autumn lends itself to expressions of wrath directed against those who take too much delight in fruit of the vineyard. The same imagery, however, can be used to express **love,** as in verse 9 – hence, the Love Feast held around the spring equinox. The theme of brotherly love is an integral part of Philadelphian history, a legacy of the family who founded the city – namely, Eumenes II, king of Pergamum, and his brother Attalus II, known as Philadelphus, 'lover of his brother.' The proverbial solidarity of these two rulers was celebrated on coin-types representing two identical young men or twins suckled by a wolf (Hemer 1986: 155). When placed in the sky, the iconography coincides with Gemini, an ancient constellation which Jews claimed for Simeon and Levi jointly, the *Teomim* Brethren. The Gemini formation rose at spring, immediately after the signs of Aries and Taurus. The season was marked by the Passover and the Christian feast of brotherly love, involving the sharing of the bread and wine of the Eucharist. Gemini used to be identified as Adam and Eve, but also Castor and Pollux, the morning and evening star forming the figurehead of the Alexandrian ship on which Saint Paul and his companions embarked as they sailed from Malta to Rome (Acts 28: 2). Gemini was considered the house of Mercury, a wandering planet acting as herald of the gods, protector of commerce, god of eloquence, and guide of departed souls to Hades. This imagery was so familiar to the early Christians that, when in the inland province of Lycaonia, east of Phrygia, Paul's eloquence earned him the name of Mercury (Hermes), a title shared by Nebo, the Babylonian god of writing (Acts 14: 12.)

Laodicea

Manifestations of Bacchanalian joy expressed at autumn or love celebrated at spring are close to being made explicit in the letter to Laodicea, a city in a Phrygian province sought for its pleasant wines and baths (Hemer 1986: 183). 'Look,' said the Lord, 'I am standing at the door, knocking. If one of you hears me calling and opens the door, I will come in to share his **meal,** side by side with him' (Rev. 3: 20). The supper in question is the Eucharist, the Lord's Supper and supreme sacrifice, which stands as 'the key not only

to the letters but the whole book as the epilogue indicates (22: 17, 20)'
(Sweet 1990: 106). The words to the last church of Asia Minor are an invitation to the marriage supper of the Lamb, an event announced by a bridegroom knocking at the door of his beloved, as in the Song of Songs (Song 5:
1ff.; Matt. 25: 6, 26: 29; Rev. 19: 9). Jews interpreted the bridegroom's invitations in the Song as Yahweh seeking out Israel during their honeymoon
period in the desert (Hos. 2: 14ff.). Similarly, Christians viewed the Love
Feast as the Lord being wedded to his bridal Church at the End of Time.
From a calendrical perspective, themes of hymenean communion were
connected with both equinoctial seasons. While Israel's departure from
Egypt and journey in the desert was commemorated at fall, the Song was
read in the Passover season, a time of the year when the Messiah was
expected to 'come.' The latter term originates from the ancient Aramaic
marana tha formula and is often used by John to evoke Easter celebrations
and the eucharistic liturgy (Feuillet 1975: 214; Prigent 1964: 37f., 42).

In Laodicea, relations between gods, the cycle of seasons, and hopes of
resurrection revolved around non Judaeo-Christian deities such as *Men*,
the Carian god of medicine later identified with Asklepios (Ophiuchus),
snake-healer and father of Hygeia. The city had her own Tyche, a Virgo-
like lady of affluence holding cornucopiae. Local mythology also spoke
of an infant who was born yearly in midwinter and died in the summer.
Echoes of these divinities can be found in John's tacit reference to the
cornucopian wealth, the eye ointments, and the hot medicinal waters of
Laodicea and the neighbouring Hierapolis (Rev. 3: 16–18).[11]

Ford (1975: 419) makes mention of archaeological discoveries comprising a statue of Isis, reliefs of Ganymede, and the victory of Theseus over
the minotaur. The goddess Isis, also worshipped in Thyatira, used to be
equated with the dog days of Sirius and the circumpolar Dragon (Allen
1963; 123, 208; Hemer 1986: 247). Ganymede is a beautiful Phrygian youth
of Greek fable, carried to heaven by an eagle and made cup-bearer to the
gods; Manilius described him as the Waterman, or Aquarius, preceded by
Aquila, a rainy-season character well suited to represent an area reputed for
the hot baths of Hierapolis and the cold waters of Colossae. As for Theseus, he was cast as the heavenly Hercules standing between Draco and the
Serpent-Holder. With the assistance of Ariadne (the adjoining Corona
Borealis), he slew Minotaur, a half-man, half-bull creature assimilated to
Centaurus situated below Libra. All of these fabled characters and stellar
representations converged on a central theme of Semitic mythology: the
death of a sun-god heading south of the celestial equator, falling under a
yearly spell of darkness and rains.

But the sun-god never falls in vain. Like the rains of winter that fall to feed the earth, the sun-god's estival descent is a vital requirement of the cycle of life. Although opposed to cultic expressions of faith in nature, the supreme sacrifice of the Son of Man partakes in the calendrical regulations of life and death affecting the godly spheres of heaven and earthly creatures alike. A failure to comply with the sacrificial exigencies of Nature threatens not only the universal order, but also human hopes of resurrection. Immortality is achieved by humans who propitiate and emulate gods falling and rising, disappearing and reappearing in their heavenly abode. Christ the Morning Star is no exception to the rule: he too must descend to the lower regions of the earth before he can rise from the dead in due season (Eph. 4: 8f.). The Son of Man must suffer the fall if he is to ascend to new heights at Easter (from *Eastra*, the Anglo-Saxon goddess of spring). Imageries deployed in John's letters to Laodicea and other churches of Asia Minor are subject to the ascetic teachings of the lunisolar order dressed in a logocentric garb.

The fall can be converted into an offering towards the renewal of life: gestures of sacrifice are a requirement of life that lasts. The blessings of life (grains at spring, grapes at autumn) must be earned through ascetic conduct (offerings of bread and wine) lest humans lapse into sin and suffer another Fall. To use the culinary code, humans who eat idol food instead of imitating Christ sacrificing his own flesh will not be invited to the Lord's Supper. Rather, they will be reduced to meat in a burning caldron, flesh to be vomited by God and devoured by fowls of the sky (Rev. 19: 17f.). Likewise, those who drink wine in lieu of pouring their blood for Christ shall not be saved by the blood or wine of the Eucharist. Instead they shall bleed to death; they shall be crushed like grapes in a winepress and be made to drink the full wine cup of the Lord's anger (Rev. 16: 19).

Signs of health and bodily functions can be used to convey the teachings of Christian asceticism – the notion that good things are obtained only when renounced. Instead of 'thirsting for what is right,' longing for the life-giving waters of Christ (Matt. 5: 6; John 7: 37f.), Phrygians indulging in the **hot** baths of Hierapolis and the **cold** waters of Colossae shall leave a bad taste in the mouth of God; the Lord will **spit** them out and condemn them to never quench their thirst in heaven (John 6: 35; Rev. 3: 15ff.; 7: 16). Likewise, the eyes of humans who take pride in their own medicine and visible gods (the eye-salves of Laodicea, the sun and the lights of heaven) will be closed. Unless they place a blind trust in the Spirit of the Lord, the 'ultimate source' of God's visible creation (Col. 1: 17f.; Rev. 3: 14), these humans shall be made **blind**. Because of their faithlessness, they shall never see the New Jerusalem lit by the radiant glory of God and the Lamb. Instead of their eyes being cured with a paste made with God's spittle, evil-eyed humans shall be spat out of the Lord's mouth (John 9: 6; Rev. 21: 23).

In the letter to Laodicea, the lessons of Christian morality are also expressed through sartorial metaphors. Lovers of the world who value their riches and fine clothing, as do the Laodiceans, are pitiably poor and shamefully **naked** in spirit. Come the End of Time, they shall be stripped of their wealth and deprived of the white robes of heaven (Rev. 3: 18). Finally, ascetic reasoning can be expressed by way of sexual analogy: in lieu of preserving the virginity (Rev. 14: 4) of a bridal Church wedded to the Lord, unfaithful men and women who indulge in fornication shall be deprived of God's hymenean love and lose their children as well.

In retrospect, the easternmost city of Laodicea poses the greatest threat to the Church's struggle against enemies of the Lord. As in Genesis, expulsion from the garden of the tree of life is executed in an eastward direction, towards the sun at dawn, with a flaming sword held by the Lord and his angelic cherubs (Gen. 3: 24; Rev. 1: 16; 2: 12). While dwellers of western-most Ephesus can hope to be fed from the tree of life in paradise, the luke-warm Church of Laodicea is in danger of being thrown up by the spirit of Eden, never to share the Lord's meal again (Rev. 2: 7; 7: 16; 20). A Phrygian city that takes pride in her banking institutions, her medical school, her soothing waters, and her clothing industry deserves to receive the severest condemnation and warnings from the Lord. Laodicea is guilty of seeking the good life through worldly measures (e.g., eye-salve) that do not con-form to ascetic usages (faith in the unseen). Ephemeral joys will bring misery (blindness, a great darkness) in lieu of the blessings of heavenly sal-vation (granted in the light of God). Love of this world achieved without repentance and godly 'reproval' (Rev. 3: 19) should not be expected to last.

Christian morals preached by John preclude the teachings of antinomi-anism, or the Nicolaitan notion that humans may rejoice in the consump-tion of food and sex without harming the Spirit. As suggested above, such conduct can only lead to a chain of events going by contraries: a bed of orgiastic abandon turning into a funeral bier; idol-food eaters that God can no longer stomach; stars and lofty creatures rising above and against God, only to suffer a great fall, and so on. Tensions between needs of the body and the life of the spirit can be resolved through self-denial only. Hesitancy in sacrificing the body to the spirit will produce at best middle-of-the-road compromises resembling the neither hot nor cold – mediocrity in lieu of true ascetic mediation. The letters to the seven churches reiterate the foun-dations of Judaeo-Christian asceticism: the good life shall be secured only by those who renounce it. In spite of etymological claims to the contrary, the Nicolaitans shall never be 'conquerors-of-people,' for conquerors can prove **victorious** only by virtue of their sacrifice. Those who refuse to wear Jesus' crown of thorns are given due warning: come the End of Time, they shall not be granted the crown of eternal life, victory, and glory in heaven (Rev. 2: 10f., 4: 4, 6: 2, 12: 1, 14: 14).

Beyond the Letter of the Law

The style of John's letters to the seven churches is secular, giving us little foretaste of the cosmic tableaux deployed in later chapters of Revelation. A closer reading of these letters, however, reveals a broad range of astromythical imageries that set the scene for John's visions of the End of Time. Metaphors used in Revelation 2–3 must be situated against the religious background of Roman emperor-worship and belief systems revolving around the cult of stars and the signs of heavens about to be displayed at length by the Seer. These metaphors reinforce the heliographic implications of John's Prologue and initial call to prophesy (Rev. 1). Evocations of the Morning Star, the Book of Life, a new name engraved on stone, manna, and the blessings of wine and love converge once more on a seven-starred solar system ruled by a godly figure acting as the Alpha and the Omega, the First and the Last of cyclical time.

The solar symbology is apt to suggest the rewards promised to the faithful. But it can also be used to put the churches on guard against the temptations of idolatry and announce the trials awaiting those who fail to repent. Given their intent to warn, the letters shift from memories of a solar pact between God and humans to signs of a downfall occurring at summer, or the trials of the End of Time arriving in due season: the darker days of the year that begin at fall. The plot thickens as allusions are made to constellations associated with the sun-god marching south, towards the post-vintage days of wintertime darkness and final judgment. Signs of impending darkness include Virgo (the Ephesian Diana), Corona Borealis (the crown of Smyrna), the sword-holding Orion, and Satan the Serpent (the 'right of sword' and the snake-healer of Pergamum). The letter to Thyatira contains words moving in the same direction: towards Arcturus, a shepherd holding an iron rod and rising at autumn, and also the sickbed or Coffin of the northern heaven, a constellation responsible for the death of children falling at the hands of kindred spirits of Lilith and Jezebel.

For the moment, John shows discretion when speaking of heavenly manifestations of the hereafter. Compact symbols and metaphors are substituted for highly textured stories of the lunisolar calendar and mythical motions of the heavenly spheres. The caution shown by John in spelling out the astromythical underpinnings of his letters to Asia Minor is in keeping with his repudiation of Judaic legalism and Christian antinomianism, both of which gave free rein to expressions of lunisolarism. The Seer refrains from paying full attention to ancient measurements of time that governed ritual laws of the Old Testament and observances of pagan calendars alike. Having reduced the language of time in heaven to mere metaphor, the prophet can turn astral gods into sign-appearances heralding the End of Time and the triumph of the invisible Creator over his visible creation. Through the rhetoric of phenomenal likeness, John undertakes a logocentric recuperation of all those sacrificial exigencies of life illustrated by divine motions of the sun, the moon, and the stars.

The letters to the churches are a subtle attack against idolatrous investments in the deceitful signs of pagan religion. As Pilch (1992: 126) remarks, the letters exhibit such 'intense concentration of vocabulary related to deception and lies' as to suggest a religious situation marked by 'a disturbing degree of inauthenticity, misrepresentation, defamation, lies, deceit, denial, delusion and the like.' We have shown that the glorification of *false appearances* has much to do with the cult of perceptible stars and planets usurping the powers of the invisible Lord in heaven, practices that John struggles to denounce and silence all at once. Paradoxically, the Seer cannot repudiate these illusory appearances without resorting to 'an extremely heavy overlay of appearance' (Malina 1995: 259) of his own, using metaphors to misrepresent and hush up the unspeakable gods of ancient paganism. In the end, lies can hardly be fought without denials of another sort.

6

The Chariot of Fire

From a scene on earth, John's vision shifts in Revelation 4–5 to a higher plane, a throne-room involving the whole cosmos. We now turn to the Sabian countertextuality of this complex throne-room composition, starting with memories of the Old Testament that inspired John's description of the cherubs and the throne of God: to be more specific, Ezekiel 1 and 10.[1] Analyses that follow will show that the writings of Ezekiel and John pursue two complementary objectives: abolishing the cult of nature (sun, moon, stars) while also recuperating the powers of astromythology under the rule of God who reigns in heaven. Astrological imageries are not simply abandoned or denounced by the prophets. Rather, they are converted into metaphorical evocations of the 'appearances of the likeness' of the true Lord. Through visions of the Chariot of God, the story of the sun-god and his female consort (Tammuz and Ishtar) is revised in phenomenal disguise, that is, rehabilitated through the rhetoric of worldly 'appearances' and things made in the likeness of the Great Beyond.

Solarism in Ezekiel

In the Month of Tammuz (Ezek. 1: 1–3)

Ezekiel's first prophetic vision and commission from God came to pass in the fourth month of the thirtieth year, or in the fifth year of the captivity of Jehoiachin, King of Judah, in 593 B.C.E. As noted by Cooke (1960: 3, 7) and Greenberg (1983: 39), there are still some doubts as to what the thirtieth year originally meant.[2] The calendrical reference corresponds to one of five things:

1 a later insertion by a scribe based on his own reading of history in Ezekiel;[3]

2 an important event that occurred thirty years prior to 593 B.C.E. (e.g., the discovery of the Book of the Law in the eighteenth year of Josiah, c. 621);

3 a particular era (e.g., the foundation of the neo-Babylonian Empire by Nabopolassar in 625 B.C.E.);

4 the thirtieth year of the current Jubilee period (consisting of seven times seven years, a period ending in the fiftieth Jubilee year); or

5 the prophet's age (Alexander 1976: 12).

Given the vagueness of the text, it is unlikely that the question of the exact meaning of this date will ever be resolved. In any case, as pointed out by Zimmerli (1979: 167), priestly calculations of Old Testament chronology are largely obscure. This should not stop us, however, from exploring broader cultural evocations that can be elicited from the 'thirty year' motif. To begin with, the date is congruent with the beginning of Ezekiel's priestly office announced in verses 1–3; we know from the Old Testament that a priest started his public ministry at the age of thirty (Num. 4: 3, 23, 30, 35, 47). The number of years required of a man to accede to priesthood is all the more significant as it evokes ancient lunisolar calculations of time. When interpreted in cyclical terms, the date suggests a new era emerging under a new moon marked with the raising of the year to the full monthly power of thirty. Thirty times twelve (or thirteen) months of about thirty days each should bring *an extraordinarily new moon*. Accordingly, Ezekiel's vision occurs at the beginning of the lunar month and in the fourth month of Tammuz (June/July). This is when the new moon begins to grow in size and nocturnal duration as it accompanies the sun's southward journey towards the celestial equator. As if to confirm the prophetic importance of the number thirty, the Book of Ezekiel ends with a New Jerusalem temple comprising thirty rooms and cells (Ezek. 40: 17, 41: 6, 46: 22).

The biblical number thirty is typically predicated on signs of fertility, might, and wealth: in other words, a man's adulthood, his children, his soldiers, and precious objects (golden bowls, pieces of silver). On the negative side of things, however, the same figure can be assigned to days of weeping, a mourning period that tallies with the darkness that marks the end of a lunar month.[4] This brings us to the other date mentioned in verse 1: the fourth month dedicated to the mourning of the sun-god Tammuz, mid-June to mid-July (Greenberg 1983: 40). According to Cooke (1960: 4), by the end of the pre-exilic period numbers rather than names were used to designate the months; Babylonian names came into fashion only later, in the post-exilic literature. Ezekiel's knowledge of Akkadian deities and related rituals is none the less confirmed in a later passage, where the prophet describes the sight of women in the Temple weeping for Tammuz (Ezek. 8: 14).

Tammuz was worshipped throughout Semitic lands and connected with licentious festivals. His cult was informed by a rich, pan-Semitic mythology revolving around the sun-god's estival descent to the lower world, beneath the failing summer waters of the Euphrates. Tammuz was god of the sunshining sky and the green earth, the divinity of pasture and flocks, corn, and subterranean waters. The solar deity perished in the hot summer season, which is when the sun begins its downward journey in heaven and when the air is still, the heat intense, and much of the country parched, dry, and hard. He died every summer, when at the peak of his heavenly flight, and then in autumn, when departing to the underworld, south of the celestial equator. There Tammuz became 'the wanderer on the plains of the lower world,' or Lord of the Dead, also called Nergal or Enlil. He was Bel to the Akkadians (cognate of Hebrew *Baal*, 'lord') and the head-god Marduk in Babylonian mythology, a pagan deity known as Merodach among the Hebrews (Isa. 46: 1; Jer. 50: 2, 51: 44; see Jacobsen 1970: 95f.; 1976: 73; Kramer 1961: 124–6; Langdon 1931: 75–7, 180, 336–51).

Memories of a dying sun-god inevitably led to stories of vernal resurrection (as in Ezek. 33–48). Year after year, Tammuz returned from his wintertime sojourn in the deep to cover once more the earth with corn and the pasture of life. Plants fed by spring rains and buds bursting in due season announced his return to the upper world. The deity thus stood for a youthful, kingly sun, and for prolific vegetation as well. He was the Healer *par excellence*, one who knew the secret of life after death. Dusares, his Nabataean counterpart, was believed to be reborn in December, when the sun begins its upward march towards the north. By and large, however, the sun-god's return was celebrated at the beginning of the year, at the time of the spring equinox heralding the sun's moving above the celestial equator, towards the northerly vault of heaven. The well-known Adonis of Gebal and the Phoenician god Eshmun shared in this central cult of Tammuz that spread throughout the Fertile Crescent from Babylonia/Assyria to Palestine/Syria.

The story of Tammuz cannot be told without mentioning the great goddess Ishtar, the virgin Earth-Mother (the Moon, Venus, Virgo) that stood as his mother, sister, wife, and mistress, also known as Ashdar, Innini, Nintud, Aruru, or Ninlil in Semitic lands. She was the Queen of Heaven and goddess of Fate, Sex, Love, and Fertility. She wept over the death of Tammuz and, *like the moon, Venus, and Virgo following in Leo's footsteps*, she descended to the lower world to recover him, thereby setting an example for all women bewailing the death of the fertility-god during the month of Tammuz (Wevers 1969: 69; Jacobsen 1970: 30; 1976: 138–41, 201f.; Kramer 1961: 96–8, 121f.; Langdon 1931: 256ff., 326ff.). To her story we shall later return.

A vision occurring in the month of Tammuz announces a time of mourning and wailing, a period of climatic, economic, and ritual darkness. The timing of Ezekiel's revelation also points to the cause of sombre days to come: religious obscurantism expressed through heliolatry. Evocations of the Tammuz sun are a prelude to the prophet lamenting the sins of Judah, or the sight of women wailing for Tammuz at the entrance of the north gate of the Jerusalem Temple, a scene followed by men facing the east, bowing towards the sun, from the inner court of the Lord's Temple (Ezek. 8: 14–17).

The place where Ezekiel received the word of God is another indication of cultic sins about to be committed. The word of God was addressed to the prophet while among the exiles on the bank of the river Chebar, in a colony located near Nippur. The identity of the Chebar canal is obscure (Greenberg 1983: 40). Cooke (1960: 4–5) suggests that the river sprang up from and flowed southeast back into the Euphrates; it was called the Euphrates of Nippur and the River Nile by the Sumerians and the Arabs, respectively. As for Nippur, it was a major Babylonian centre for the cult of the Earth-Mother Ninlil and her brother-husband Enlil, god of the Earth and the Sun. It is precisely this cult of the dying sun and his weeping wife (otherwise known as Tammuz and Ishtar) that Josiah fought against when he destroyed the sun's chariots at the entrance of the Jerusalem Temple, and also which Ezekiel evoked when writing about the sins of Israel, possibly in the thirtieth year after Josiah's covenant with God.

The cult of Tammuz implied the deification and worship of earthly kings, a practice denounced in no uncertain terms by Ezekiel in his dirge over the King of Tyre (Ezek. 28: 1–19; Jacobsen 1970: 150; 1970: 86f.; 1976: 114). Even more menacing, however, was the deification of celestial bodies associated with these pagan kings. More than anything Tammuz was a product of Semitic heliolatry. According to Langdon (1931), the divinity had many titles, one of which was Star of Heaven, or the Heavenly, 'He of the Bright Eyes.' The Akkadians spoke of him as the shepherd guarding the gate of the great Anu, who was the Creator of heavens and the sky-divinity who fathered all gods. He was killed, according to the Harranians, by a king who refused to worship the seven planets and the twelve signs of the zodiac. His cult, of Sumerian origin, was taken up in Holy Gebal, the sacred city of West Semitic religion and the principal centre of sun-worship in Phoenicia.

Semitic religion began essentially with the deification of sun, moon, and Venus. Connotations of heavenly height are thus embedded in Semitic terms used for god (and placed at the end of Ezeki-el's name), such as the Akkadian Ilu, the Canaanitish El, the Hebrew Eloah, the Aramaic Elah, and the Arabic Ilah. Ishtar, the Syrian 'Lady of the Sea' and consort of El, was consistently identified with Venus. She was the Queen of the Stars, the goddess of Fate worshipped in all Semitic cults, including Nippur's, where she took the form of seven Mother-goddesses. She stood as the female principle or daughter of Anu in the highest heaven and daughter of the Moon, whose cult found favour with the kings of Judah before the reign of Josiah. The Hebrews knew her as the shameless Ashtoreth or detestable Asherah, the idol worshipped by Solomon and the whole of Israel following the death of Joshua.[5]

To sum up, trouble brews in a scene where the sun begins its summer fall towards the Babylonian deep, followed by faithful Venus, Virgo, and the moon. The male sun and his female consort are descending in a southeasterly direction, just like Ezekiel exiled from the land of Judah (situated northwest of Nippur) and the river Chebar flowing towards the Persian Gulf (Zimmerli 1979: 119). A scene occurring in the month of Tammuz at the end of a thirty-year period is loaded with signs of heavenly darkness and human sorrow, trials that are amply described in the Book of Ezekiel. The vision invites sorrow over the sun-god's death suffered in the summer season. More important, it announces the great ordeal that will afflict men and women who lament the fall of heavenly spheres treated as gods.

The end of a thirty-year period, however, can generate signs of better days to come (as in Ezek. 1, 33: 21–48: 35) – hope for a new moon and the solar body resurrecting at spring. In spite of the forthcoming darkness, there is a glimmer of hope: a period of darkness may give way to the brighter days of redemption attained through paschal sacrifice. Ezekiel's calendrical superscription conjures up the vision of a new kind of ascent: the rise of a Davidic nation to sacrificial glory, the sort of glory associated with a new moon and with God's ministry on earth granted at the beginning of the manly age of thirty.

North Wind and Solar Throne (Ezek. 1: 4–5)

Ezekiel's vision starts with 'heaven opening' and the throne or chariot of

Yahweh appearing in a cloud coming from the north, with light around it and fire emitting flashes of lightning. The throne is supported by four living creatures moving below a vault gleaming like crystal; the animals are winged and wheeled and their faces are turned 'to the four quarters.' When transposed from moments in time to locations in space, a vision occurring in the month of Tammuz is congruent with Ezekiel's evocations of fiery heat and bright light coming from the heavenly north. The cloud of fire starts moving down from the north just as the sun reaches its northernmost position on the ecliptic. This is a time of the year when the sky is clear and winds blow from the northwest, winds that 'scatter' (Heb. *mezareth*, 'the scatterer, the north') the clouds from the sky and bring the 'golden splendour' of sunny weather (Job 37: 9, 22).

A wind blowing from the northern vault of heaven and the holy mountain of God carries negative associations as well. As the 'hidden' quarter of the universe, the one where the sun never shines, the north inspires fear. In biblical terms, the north points to the seat of gloom, the origin of all invaders of Palestine and the rule of sinful Tyre (Ezek. 28). These negative aspects of the septentrional sky coincide with Ezekiel's vision of a windstorm blowing from the north in the month of Tammuz. The storm is none the less an anomalous sign: the bitter blasts of Boreas (Manilius 5: 67ff.) that bring cold storms and lightning in Palestine and the Euphrates Valley usually occur in the darker period of the year. But the scorching sun in Tammuz is heading in the same direction: the summer scene announces the death of the sun-god heading south, below the celestial equator, towards the autumn equinox and rainy days of the year. So is Ezekiel's chariot of fire descending from the north, with the cherubs flying down to the earth in the midst of a cloud. Both the sun and the Lord of Heaven are travelling in a southeasterly direction, from Israel to Nippur, to reveal themselves to Ezekiel exiled in Babylonia.

This brings us to widespread associations of Yahweh with the Semitic sun-god and his kingly chariot drawn by four animals, a symbolism that gives way to four chariots in Zechariah (6: 1ff.). The 'solar chariot' motif is found among the ancient Persians and the Assyrians, who spread it to the Hebrews under the royal title of Yahweh 'who sits enthroned on the cherubim' (covering the ark of the covenant of the Lord.).[6] Josiah banished this heliocentric imagery erected at the entrance to the Jerusalem Temple (2 Kings 23: 11). Admittedly Ezekiel does not use the 'solar chariot' motif when describing 'the fiery-wheeled throne,' yet the motif must have been familiar to him as part of both Yahweh's list of titles and the architectural design of Solomon's Temple (Cooke 1960: 12). As pointed out by Hollis

(1933), the temple was planned in such a manner that the eastern gate of the temple area could let the morning rays of the equinoctial sun enter directly from across the Mount of Olives, into the Holy of Holies, thus making possible the entrance of the Glory of Yahweh and the ritual enthronement of the deity as king. A coin of Gaza dating from the fourth century B.C.E. shows the Hebrew deity as a sun-god sitting on a winged wheel – hence, 'the one who rides on the sky and guides the chariot of the whole cosmos,' as Philo used to say. According to Langdon (1931: 43), 'Yaw of Gaza really represents the Hebrew, Phoenician and Aramaic sun god *El, Elohim,* whom the monotheistic tendencies of the Hebrews had long since identified with Yaw' (see also Gordon 1961: 205f., 211f.). In keeping with this solar imagery, the God of Heaven reveals himself in high places and in the midst of fire.

The evidence presented above suggests that Ezekiel's inaugural vision can be read in the light of the ritual departure of the Glory of Yahweh occurring at the time of the summer solstice, a moment of the year marked by the dethronement and fall of the sun-god heading south. These days of scorching heat coincided with the sun's entrance into Leo (in Ezekiel's age) and the ascent of Sirius at dawn, or the star ∂ in the constellation Canis Major, commonly known as the Dog Star (after the larger group). Sirius gave its title to the 'dog days' in July and August, or the *canicule* in French, from the Latin *dies caniculariae*. The Babylonians and ancient Egyptians used the heliacal rising of this brightest star in heaven to determine the length of the year. The Temple of Isis, erected about 700 B.C.E., was oriented towards Sirius when it was known as Her Majesty of Denderah. Its worship had begun, however, long before its prominent appearance on the square zodiac of Denderah. The Hebrews knew it by its Egyptian name, Sihor, which meant the Nile Star, possibly because the constellation bathed in a Milky Way called the Heavenly Nile.

Like estival Tammuz, Sirius was, to use Homer's words, the brightest 'but sign to mortal man of evil augury.' Manilius's description of Sirius spoke of a sign of heaven that brought opposite effects to the world, those of harmony and war, peace, and destruction:

No star comes on mankind more violently or causes more trouble when it departs. Now it rises shivering with cold [evening rising in January], now it leaves [evening setting in May] a radiant world open to the heat of the Sun: thus it moves the world to either extreme and brings opposite effects. Those who from Mount Taurus' lofty peak observe its ascending when it returns at its first rising learn of the various outcomes of harvests and seasons, what state of health lies in store, and what measure of harmony. It stirs up war and restores peace, and returning in different guise affects the world with the glance it gives it and governs with its mien. Sure proof that the star has this power are its colour and the quivering of fire that sparkles in its face. Hardly is it inferior to the Sun, save that its abode is far away and the beams it launches from its sea-blue face are cold. In splendour it surpasses all other constellations, and no brighter star is bathed in ocean or returns to heaven from the waves. (1: 394–410)

Langdon has shown the mythical connections between Sirius, Saturn, and the god Ninurta, the Babylonian morning sun, brother and lover of the Earth-goddess Astarte or Ashtoreth. In Babylonian mythology, Saturn opened the gate of sunrise to the sun-god Shamash. Scriptural references to these male deities suggest that they were part of Canaanitish religion and had a direct impact on the cult of Yahweh. In the Book of Amos, accusations are lodged against Samarians for worshipping Kawain, from the Akkadian *kaimanu*, 'the steady star,' the name for Saturn. The planet was associated with the Hebrew Kiyyun and the equally detestable Siccoth, Rephan, and Chiun: 'Sikkut is a corruption of the popular name Sakkut as god of sunrise, and Kiyyun is a false vocalization in Hebrew for Kaywan, as the Septuagint Raiphan for Kaiphan proves' (Langdon 1931: 135; see 61, 317, 341; on Saturn in Greek mythology, see Malina 1995: 88). The Succoth–Benoth idol mentioned in the Second Book of the Kings was in turn identified with the constellation Zarpatinum or Zarbanit – hence 'Our Lady' Virgo – titles that were current in the periods preceding and following the rise of Christianity. She was the wife of Marduk and lover of Tammuz and Adonis (2 Kings 17: 30; Amos 5: 26; Acts 7: 43).

The Image of Jealousy (Ezek. 8)

Old Testament stories of the fall of Jerusalem are modelled after the sun's southward march commencing in the month of Tammuz. This is confirmed by the dating of Ezekiel's next vision, which comes a year later, in the sixth month of 'good-for-nothing' Ellul, a time of the year when the wind blows chiefly from the northeast and the heat is still intense, though the sun has started to decline. As argued below, the vision offers a clear expression of sins of solar-worship.

While sitting in his house with the elders of Judah, the prophet is taken up between heaven and earth by a lock of his hair. According to Cooke (1960: 90), from this passage is borrowed the apocryphal story of Habbakuk's transportation in Bel and the Dragon. The prophet's encounter with a fiery-loined spirit shining (Heb. *zohar* in the Massoretic text, 'of the sky') in heaven brings him to the northern door to the holy place of the Jerusalem Temple. The door to the north, a direction emphasized three times in the text, is the gate from which priests usually approached the brazen altar placed in the inner court, on a higher level than the rest of the temple enclosure. There, to the north of the altar gate, Ezekiel sees the seat of the Image of Jealousy that will cause Yahweh to bring judgment to Israel and abandon the temple completely, not to return until the millennium.

At the entrance of the north gate, Ishtar-like women weep for Tammuz and the loss of earthly fertility. In the myth of Tammuz, the north connotes death: 'the summer solstice, which brings the annual death of the god, brings the sun to its farthest point north of the equator' (Cooke 1960: 96).[7] As already mentioned, Tammuz was the Sumerian–Babylonian god of the dying summer vegetation whom women lamented and whose name was given to the fourth month by Jews after the Babylonians. 'In the cult drama of the death of the god and lament for him, celebrated at the end of spring, the loss of the god, the waning of the power for new life in nature, is counteracted by mourning and lament' (Jacobsen 1970: 100; cf. Kramer 1969). The god can be traced as far back as 3000 B.C.E., and his rite was probably imported into Judah from Mesopotamia (Greenberg 1983: 171). His sister and wife was called Ishtar in Akkadian, Asherah (2 Kings 21: 7, 23: 6) or Ashtoreth (Astarte) in the Old Testament, Lady of the Sea and consort of Baal or the Canaanite god El. His summertime reorientation towards the underworld, beneath the celestial equator, was mourned by Ishtar, who went down to bring him back to vernal life. Like the Egyptian god Osiris, the god embodied 'a hope of resurrection and a return to material life' (Cooke 1960: 96). The Syrian counterpart of Tammuz was Adonis, a title for which both Yahweh and Tammuz competed. In the words of Origen, 'he who is called Adonis among the Greeks is said to be named Thammouz among the Hebrews and Syrians' (in Cooke 1960: 97).

Like Tammuz, Ezekiel undertakes a journey to the underworld: 'He next took me to the entrance of the court. I looked; there was a hole in the wall. He said, "Son of Man, break through the wall." I broke through the wall; there was a door. He said, "Go in and look at the filthy things they are doing inside." I went in and looked: all sorts of images of snakes and repulsive animals and all the idols of the House of Israel drawn on the wall all around' (Ezek. 8: 7–10). The prophet goes inside to witness seventy elders of Israel worshipping the beasts and creeping things pictured on the walls. To this scene is added the sight of twenty-five men spotted between the temple's east-oriented porch and brazen altar, with their backs turned on the ark of alliance and the Holy of Holies. The men are facing and worshipping the sun towards the east, which is where the sun-god rises every morning and on the first day of spring. Yahweh has every good reason to be jealous of Tammuz, a visible sphere in heaven usurping the divine attributes of the invisible Lord. Women are bewailing the fall of Tammuz at summer when they should be mourning Yahweh's departure from Jerusalem and the Holy Temple.

Zimmerli rejects the suggestion that late summer-solstitial celebrations and a comprehensive cultic event associated with the departure of Yahweh lie behind the four sins of Ezekiel 8. As for the Image of Jealousy set up at the outer gate, the exegete claims that it should not be equated with the former Asherah image erected in the temple area and removed by Josiah. Nor should we see in the twenty men appearing in the Greek Version a numerical reference to the sun-god Shamash of Babylonian theology (Zimmerli 1979: 238f., 243). In his discussion of Tammuz, however, Zimmerli recognizes that the use of his name in Ezekiel 8 was 'a consequence of the inclusion of Palestine in the Assyrian sphere of influence in the eighth and seventh centuries B.C. Through the Assyrian rulers, and even more through the communities from the East which were settled in what had once been the Northern Kingdom, the Tammuz figure set foot in Palestine and was given a place in certain city circles of Jerusalem.' The commentator adds that women lamenting a dead god on the threshold of Yahweh's sanctuary signalled, not the end of Yahwism, but rather something that was supplementary to it. Faith in Yahweh 'completely lacked this aspect of pious sympathy with the deity in the rhythm of nature, oscillating from life to death and then from death back to life. Did it not therefore call for some supplementation here?' – supplementary imageries that offended the prophet's feeling for cultic purity (Zimmerli 1979: 242f.).

Similar hesitations are reflected in Zimmerli's interpretation of men bowing to the east, towards the sun (Ezek. 8: 16). On the one hand, the author disagrees with commentators who recognize in this scene elements of Assyrian star-worship (2 Kings 21: 5) or echoes of a solar cult built into architectural designs of the Jerusalem Temple. On the other hand, Zimmerli sees evidence of a solarized version of Yahweh-worship under Egyptian influences mediated by Phoenicia.

In the period of weakening and relaxation after the reform these tendencies [sun- and star-worship] must have reasserted themselves under Jeohoiakim, whether we now think of them as established from the Assyrian period, or trace them back to Solomon, or even beyond this to reckon them as influences of the Canaanite Baal religion. Further to this it is also possible, *and even probable*, that here these ritual features were not regarded in the minds of those who practiced them as a betrayal of the Yahweh faith, but rather as elements of a *possible solar interpretation of Yahweh*. (Zimmerli 1979: 243f.; emphasis added)

This solarized expression of Yahwism did not imply a return to religion as practised under Manasseh – hence, the reintroduction of nature-worship into the Jerusalem Temple (contra Wevers 1969: 69; Cooke 1960: 92, 99; Greenberg 1983: 203). Solar imageries none the less met with the disapproval of Ezekiel, who, unlike Jeremiah, spoke of his times with a concern for the cultic purity of faith in Yahweh. According to Zimmerli (1979: 245), the abominations evoked by Ezekiel reflect, not the abandonment of beliefs in Yahweh, but rather what the prophet saw as impure expressions of true faith under pagan influence.

But in what way were the underworld abominations discovered by Ezekiel connected to the cult of sun, moon, and stars? What did these abominations consist of, and why were they so repulsive? In an attempt to make sense of the reptiles and animals carved on the walls, idols possibly of Babylonian or Egyptian inspiration (cf. Greenberg 1983: 169), Zimmerli (1979: 240) suggests that hybrid creatures endowed with anomalous features tend to be given pejorative attributes in the Old Testament. These include aquatic creatures without scales and fins, birds that do not hop on two legs, small lizard-like creatures, and so on. Although interesting, this typological argument is vague and does little justice to the richness of ancient ophidian symbolism. Snakes appearing in the context of a journey to a place of darkness (Ezek. 8: 10, 12) are loaded with mythical implications. In the Old Testament, Yahweh is addressed as Adonai,[8] My Lord, a designation which the Phoenicians equated with Eshmun, the god of healing identified with the serpent. As pointed out by Langdon (1931: 78), 'both Tammuz and his mother bore the title *ama-usungalanna*, "mother-great-serpent of heaven," that is the serpent deity who emanated from the Heaven god Anu.' Langdon adds that the serpent evoked the generative powers of the Earth-goddess and her dying son in Sumerian, Babylonian, and West Semitic mythology. A closely related biblical motif is the brazen serpent set upon a pole by Moses to heal human beings bitten by serpents. Other relevant attributes of the serpent include fire (reflected in the Akkadian *Shahan* title) and the secret of immortality: witness the story of the serpent and the tree of life in the garden of Eden, or the Semitic legends of a snake casting its skin and stealing the plant of rejuvenation (Jacobsen 1970: 29; 1976: 36f., 207; Langdon 1931: 89f., 151, 177ff., 183ff., 226ff.).

The sun Tammuz and the serpent have much in common. For one thing, the sun is as deadly as a poisonous serpent: the solar body burns everything to death at summer, a period of the year when it suffers a downfall affecting the whole earth. But the sun also emits a vital flow of heat and light. Like a serpent that loses its skin without ever dying, the solar body falls at night and at wintertime, only to rise to a new life at dawn and in early days of spring. Both creatures are thus Janus-faced: while they can kill or consume life when fully erected, they also know the secret of life after death.

The sun and the snake not only resemble each other, but also keep close company in heaven. According to Langdon (1931: 77f., 90, 164, 178, 345, 349; cf. Jacobsen 1970: 17f., 29, 324n8; 1976: 44, 60, 211), Tammuz used to be identified with Orion, the faithful shepherd of heaven, but also Ningishzida, a name for Hydra. The dying sun-god was originally called Mighty Serpent Dragon of Heaven (*Ushum-galanna*) and is related to a family of eminent stellar snakes comprising the Water-Snake (Hydra) spanning the equator almost from node to node, the Serpent touching the equator at one node, and the circumpolar Dragon that marked the north pole. The ascending and descending nodes of the sun's visible path, above the equator in the spring and below in autumn, are still symbolized by the Dragon Head (Ω) and the Dragon Tail ($\mho$), respectively. Heavenly serpents point to the never-ending story of the cycle of life and death suffered in due season: the periodic fall of the solar body followed by its resurrection at dawn and spring.[9]

The Four Wings of Chronos (Ezek. 1: 6–28)

A close reading of Ezekiel shows how elements borrowed from astrological religions were not simply silenced or condemned by the Old Testament prophet. Rather, images of Sabaism were recast in a different mould, disguised as outward manifestations and sky servants of Yahweh. Although concerned with the purity of faith in Yahweh, the writings of Ezekiel were not immune to expressions of naturalism. Like the solarized Yahweh imageries he denounced, Ezekiel's visions converged on a conflictive and co-optative, adversative and assimilative relationship between Yahwism and Sabaism.

In the centre of the summertime cloud blowing from the north, Ezekiel saw what seemed four animals. Each creature is described as having a human form, with four faces turned to the four quarters: more specifically, a man (listed first), a lion to the right, an ox to the left, and an eagle (listed last). The animals had oxen-like hoofs glittering like polished brass, and four wings spreading upward, two that touched and two that covered their bodies, with human hands showing from underneath. They all went straight ahead and never turned as they moved; they went forward, four ways, unswervingly. When they halted, their wings folded down, and when they left the ground their wings sounded like rushing water, the voice of Shaddai, the noise of a storm or a camp.

Flaming torches darted between the animals, with lightning flashing and streaking from the fire. The creatures ran to and fro like thunderbolts. Beside each creature there was a wheel on the ground glittering as chrysolite. All four wheels seemed to be working inside another wheel; their rims were enormous and had eyes all the way around. The spirits of the animals were in the wheels, and the creatures never moved or left the ground without them. A vault gleaming like crystal formed an arch extending over their heads and wings. Above this vault could be seen a sapphire throne and the glory of Yahweh sitting on it – a man-like being that shone like bronze, with fire extending from his loins upward and downward and a bright rainbow all around him. Ezekiel heard a voice speaking from the throne, and soon afterwards the prophet was taken up by the wheeled animals and brought to Tel Abib, to the exiles beside the river Chebar.

The facial description of the four-faced creatures portrayed as cherubs in Ezekiel 10 suggests a configuration of constellations that matches the scene of a hot sun rising together with stormy Sirius 'who brings fire upon the entire universe' (Manilius 5: 17; 5: 206–33).[10] Each heavenly ministrant has the face of an ox to the left and a lion to the right (from the spectator's point of view; see Cooke 1960: 14). Likewise, a morning sun looking west at the time of the heliacal rise of Sirius is flanked by vernal Taurus on the viewer's left side, and estival Leo on the right; the spectator is facing the east as prescribed by custom (Gen. 14: 15; Job 23: 9).

In Ezekiel's fifth vision of glory, the generic term 'cherub' is substituted for the ox, and comes first in the listing of faces (Ezek. 10: 14). The bovine animal is granted a leading role. In keeping with this, all creatures have calf-like hoofs, with the implication that they can follow the guiding steps of Taurus along the ecliptic circuit. The ox is the wheeled creature that keeps the cycle of seasons spinning. Taurus came first in the early Hebrew zodiac and was designated by *A* or *Aleph*, the first letter of the alphabet. It marked the vernal equinox from about 4000 to 1700 B.C.E., a period of great astronomical achievements, and was probably not deposed from its leading position until the sixth century B.C.E., when the equinoctial sun appeared just below Aries' brightest star, Hamal. Near the 'crouching bull' came the constellation Auriga, also known as the Charioteer, who 'lifts his team [of four] from

ocean and wrests up from the downward slope of the horizon where icy
Boreas lashes us with his bitter blasts' (Manilius 5: 67ff.; cf. 1: 362). Ezekiel's
cherubs are reminiscent of the pivotal role of Taurus in the ancient zodiac and
of winged bulls and solar chariots in Assyrian and Babylonian mythology.
The bovine creatures also hark back to the Egyptian cult of the bull-god
Osiris (the counterpart of the Sumero-Babylonian Tammuz) and the Semitic
worship of golden calves (Exod. 32: 1ff.; Deut. 9: 16; 1 Kings 12: 29).

But what about the other two faces? According to Boll (1914: 35) and
Malina (1995: 99f.), the eagle-faced cherub points to Pegasus, the midheaven winged horse that stood as the Babylonian Thunderbird, leading
star of equatorial Anu. An equally plausible representation of this cherub
lies in the constellation of Aquila, known to the Hebrews as *Nehr*, an
Eagle, Falcon, or Vulture. Its bright star Altair set on the northwestern
horizon just as Sirius rose with the summer sun, at the other end of the
Milky Way. Its heliacal rise occurred when the sun had entered the sign of
scorpion at autumn; in Abraham's day, Scorpio was actually represented
by an eagle. All is as if visible Altair were allowed in this summer-morning
vision to stand for the invisible Antares, the last star on the fallen tail of the
Milky Way, to the extreme opposite of rising Sirius.

There is, finally, the human face. Boll and Malina equate this cherub with
the Scorpion-Man of Babylonian mythology, a stellar creature guarding
the gate of the sun in the west. As suggested by Maunder (1923: 167), however, this face could also be linked to Aquarius, the Man bearing the water-
pot and rising with the sun at the time of the winter solstice. Aquarius was
thought in Euphratean astronomy to control the celestial Sea inhabited by
Capricornus (Sea-goat), Pisces, Pisces Australis, Cetus (Whale), and Eridanus (River) (cf. Manilius 4: 384f.). These constellations lie on the southern
hemisphere of a summer sky divided into two halves by the galactic path.
They represent the time of the year when the sun is rising, from the short-
est day of the year to the longest, a period ending with the rise of Sirius. A
nocturnal sky showing these constellations is a reflection of days that are
no longer, a heavenly panorama that precedes the morning rise of Sirius
and that produces the sound of 'rushing water' (Ezek. 1: 24) when set in
motion. All constellations of the celestial sea are made to move along with
waters of the Milky Way and those above the heavenly vault, in anticipation of the rains and storms of a winter season yet to come.

Winged cherubs and their like in Egypt and the Near East have combined a bull's or a lion's body with the face of a man or an eagle, or a
human body with the head of an eagle. Although four-headed representations of rams and the god of the north wind have been found in Egypt,

four-faced gods seemed not to have existed in Mesopotamia before Ezekiel (see Zimmerli 1979: 125). Ezekiel's vision can therefore be credited for bringing all of these creatures together in a single, four-faced expression of the complete cycle of seasons. Lofty representatives of the four seasons are placed on each side, north and south, of the Milky Way as it appears immediately before sunrise, at the time of the summer solstice. Much like Manilius and other observers before Christ, the prophet used key stars and constellations of the galactic pathway to distinguish and also unite the two heavenly spheres and the four corresponding spaces in astronomical time, those of a four-winged Chronos (Cooke 1960: 23). And in the same breath, discreetly but effectively, Ezekiel pulled together the emblems of the four principal tribes of Israel: a lion for Judah's camp, a man and a river for Reuben's, an eagle and a serpent for Dan's, and an ox for Ephraim's. The composite Israelite body could thus be exalted in the manner of a man standing above all creatures, an ox above all domesticated animals, a lion above all beasts, an eagle above all birds, and the integrated circuitry of the universe above all divisions in space and time. 'All of them have received dominion ... Yet they are stationed below the chariot of the Holy One' (Midrash Shemoth R. 23; see Cooke 1960: 14; Wevers 1969: 45; Beasley-Murray 1974: 117; Greenberg 1983: 56). Ezekiel's preoccupation with promoting the unity of the chosen people (resolving tensions evolving especially along the north–south axis) is confirmed in a later chapter, where the Lord is said to transform the two separate sticks or kingdoms of Ephraim and Judah into one (Ezek. 37: 15–28).

Still, this picture of cosmic unity is undermined by signs of the sun-god falling in due season. Death awaits this Near Eastern sun-deity divided into two parts, the upper and the lower halves, possibly as a reminder of the calendrical duality of the solar body moving above or below the celestial equator (Ezek. 1: 27; see Zimmerli 1979: 122). In Ezekiel, the heavenly chariot comes down and ceases to fly for a while; in a similar vein, the word *solstice* denotes a sun standing still, which is what the sun appears to be doing in early summer before it changes its course, from north to south. The sun is about to plunge into a period of darkness, which means that the Glory of Yahweh is on the point of leaving the temple through its eastern gate, only to return at a later time (Ezek. 11: 23, 43, 44).

On the Darker Side of Light

A summer-solar reading of Ezekiel's cherub and chariot hailing from the north has certain limitations. Unlike Yahweh's wheeled throne of fire, the visible sun dips below the horizon at night. Also it 'folds its wings down' only when it sets to the west, not when it prepares itself for an easterly or northeasterly take-off at dawn. The sun is never accompanied by four-corner formations all at once, nor can it lift up without forcing all constellations to disappear from sight. Furthermore, the sun never travels in the northern heaven, let alone above the zodiac or the celestial vault. Finally, the chariot or wheeled-throne motif carries connotations of kingly glory, not of mourning and death.

Instead of being pictured in diurnal colours, Ezekiel's vision of a starry chariot might be more intelligible if situated against a nocturnal sky. Celestial bodies differ from one another in glory: 'There is one glory of the sun, and another glory of the moon, and another glory of the stars' (1 Cor. 15: 41). But while solar coordinates are once removed from the surface text, the influence of stellar configurations are twice removed from the reader's sight, confined, as they are, to a backstage of forces evolving at night. All is as if the dimmer aspect of stars and the moon had been overshadowed by a triumphant solar force and a fixation about the heliacal rise of constellations entered and eclipsed by the sun.

Beneath the scene of a flaming sun rising at dawn, readers of Ezekiel 1 can detect faint signs of the action of the moon and Venus. As already mentioned, Ezekiel's vision occurs at the beginning of the lunar month Tammuz, when the rising moon assumes the shape of a two-horned creature reminiscent of the Bull heading the yearly cycle. A crescent moon appearing in its first quarter follows close behind the dying sun-god, heading towards the nether world of wintry darkness, which is the central theme of the epic of Tammuz and his female consort. The story of a horned cow descending into the lower world features a sensuous goddess called Ishtar (Isis, Innini, Ashtoreth, etc.) engaged in a loving quest for her son, brother, or husband named Tammuz. Ishtar was better known as Venus, daughter of moon, the brightest wandering star, Queen of Heaven, faithful companion of the sun. As Venus, Ishtar acted as mediator between day and night by virtue of her periodic appearance at dusk and dawn. She was the goddess of Fate governing the lunar cycle and related calculations of ritual time.

Ezekiel's description of the Lord's sapphire throne echoes the story of Venus's descent to recover her lost god. The goddess undertook her journey by putting on 'the beauty of her figure' – hence, ornaments and a necklace of lapis lazuli, stones the colour of the precious sapphire. In keeping with this symbolism, Babylonians pictured Venus as seven goddesses, or a star with seven rays, a septenary motif engraved on the sapphirine seals of ruling kings.

This astrosolar imagery, however, runs counter to the Yahwistic tradition. Only Yahweh can rise as the morning star, sit on the throne of God, and walk amid red-hot coals. Venus and the cherub called Lucifer, the light-bearing king of northern Tyre, cannot usurp God's throne with impunity – without being condemned to another fall (Ezek. 26–8). The same fate awaits the star Venus appearing on the morning of estival Tammuz. The star was bound to follow in the footsteps of the estival sun-god and suffer a great fall immediately after peaking in heaven. To the Romans the story was that of *Venus cum Adone*, or Venus falling into the Euphratean deep with her son Cupido, a cherub otherwise named Adonai (= Yahweh), or Tammuz the son of Ishtar. The latter duo became synonymous with Pisces, the constellation that culminated when Sirius rose to the east, carried Venus and her boy out of the Euphrates, and became the lady's station in heaven (Manilius 4: 801).

Ezekiel's vision creates a twilight scene emerging at the dawn of a troubled summer day. While hiding all astrological references from the surface text, the material presented above suggests a thickly textured combination of lunisolar and zodiacal aspects of the universe. This mixture of diurnal and nocturnal coordinates of the sky, however, does not account for the prophet's imagery of a chariot descending from the north. Although the solar throne may rise to the northeast at summertime, it never actually journeys to the northern sky. Why would the northerly quarter of the universe acquire so much importance if 'hidden' and never visited by the sun during the day?

This brings me to a riddle that lies in the background of Ezekiel's cherub scene. The riddle concerns a celestial formation that

- appears as a four-wheeled chariot surrounded by a multitude of starry eyes;
- stands for and descends from the 'windy north' (Heb. *mezarah*);
- never falls into the deep, goes in all four directions yet forward, without ever changing its circular course;
- functions like a *galgal* wheel working in a larger circumpolar wheel, revolving in synchronism with the *Galgal Hammazaloth*, the zodiac in Hebrew.

As in Ezekiel, this wheeled configuration

- is oxen-hoofed;
- faces a lion and a bull to its immediate right and left, respectively;

- lands to the north at summertime (as Sirius rises in the company of a scorching sun) and then ascends to the east at autumn;
- guards the highest heaven defined as a circular court and its Fold.

Finally, our mysterious formation

- touches down on the northern horizon at summer, at the bottom of the crown of heaven, and then ascends to the east at autumn;
- lands below a throned king who has one foot on the celestial pivot and the other on the solstitial colure, with a rainbow-shaped Milky Way spanning the sky above his head;
- serves as a four-faced Coffin attended by female mourners;
- is a car driven by Tammuz (i.e., Osiris), whose wife weeps the death of vernal Taurus (cf. Allen 1963: 435; Jacobsen 1976: 201f.);
- announces storms and the cruelty of infidels hailing from the north.

The creature in question is the Great Bear. In the words of Clement of Alexandria (c. 150–215), the pagan philosopher turned Christian theologian, 'undoubtedly these golden statues with six wings each indicate either the two Bears, as some would have it, or rather the two hemispheres of the earth' (quoted in Malina 1995: 92). As with other astromythical interpretations presented in this book, the case that can be made for a circumpolar reading of Ezekiel's chariot-throne motif is essentially cumulative. Many of the similarities listed above are points of little individual significance. Collectively, however, they add up to a striking parallel between the Seven Bulls or Great Chariot of the north and the cherub and wheeled-throne composition of Ezekiel. Not that mythical stories of northern stars constitute the 'real meaning' lurking behind Ezekiel's throne scene. Rather, the point is that the text betrays *a tricky question that the prophet has every reason not to answer*. Given the similarities between the scriptural plot and its astromythical counterplot, why must the parallel never be made explicit? Why doesn't the Seer make any direct reference to well-known stories of stellar and lunisolar divinities dwelling in heaven? The answer to this question is simple: however familiar they may be, imageries that speak to the cult of nature cannot be preserved in their pagan form. They can serve the cause of Yahweh only if transformed and adjusted to faith in the Spirit that lies beyond the visible spheres.

To conclude, notions of ancient astrology may account for the intriguing scene of four cherubs moving forward four ways without ever turning, each with one wheel 'inside another' and with four faces turned to the four quarters. According to Cooke (1960: 17), it is probably 'a mistake to picture the wheel as bisecting each other at right angles ... for one revolved beside each Creature ... and the four Creatures stood in a square, as is implied by the position of their outstretched wings ... and of the central fire.' Rather, the prophet was simply 'looking at the whole group from an angle, because he could see all four wheels at the same time; seen from this point, they would appear to be revolving one within another ... Like the living creatures ... they had no need to turn in order to face the particular direction taken.' Although reducing the complex to the simple, Cooke's alternative explanation strays from the vision. When taken literally, Ezekiel's composition remains intriguing and difficult to account for. But when situated against the background of ancient Semitic astrology, the scene becomes familiar. Notions of winged bodies distributed *at right angles* in a heavenly square and moved by wheels operating inside other wheels – one colure within another, the ecliptic within the celestial equator, the solar chariot within the zodiacal wheel, the wheeled Wain within the circumpolar circle, all 'spheres' within the celestial dome or tent – represented basic principles of primitive astronomy. In Ezekiel's vision, the cherubs are a synthesis of the fourfold divisions in heavenly space, and the four of them form a team rolling on the four wheels (equinoctial, solstitial) of time.

Fire from the East (Ezek. 10–11)

Ezekiel 10–11 involves another intervention of the heavenly cherubs and their mobile chariot. The man wearing linen clothes is told from the sapphire throne above the vault to go in between the wheels under the cherubs, to fill his hand with the coals of fire from between them, and to scatter them over the wicked city of Jerusalem. The man does as he is told and receives the coals from the hand of one cherub. The four creatures, each one-wheeled, four-winged, and four-faced, are said to be stationed on the right (southern) side of the temple and then to lift and pass through the east gate of the temple, with the glory of the Lord hovering over them. The cherubs take pause at the east gate to the entrance of the temple. Before leaving the temple, the cherubs utter words of doom (dispersal outside the city, death by the sword) against twenty-five men indulging in feelings of false security; the men think they are safe inside their walls, like meat in a pot is safe from fire. In reality their city-pot has already been filled with the meat and corpses of those they have slain; the men have behaved with the same cruelty shown by the heathens surrounding them. After promising repatriation and a new covenant to the exiles, the glory of Yahweh leaves

Jerusalem; it rises and pauses on the mountain to the east of the city, the Mount of Olives overlooking the city across the Kidron valley (Zimmerli 1979: 252; Wevers 1969: 80; Greenberg 1983: 191). The scene ends with Ezekiel being lifted up by the spirit and taken to the Chaldean exiles, presumably through the northern route of Syria and then in a southeastward direction, towards the colony on the banks of the river Chebar.

The initial sight of the cherubs, chariot, scribe, and messengers of destruction coming into Jerusalem and the temple area implies a northerly view. The cherubs and the mobile throne eventually proceed to their 'bright-southern' position inside the temple (Ezek. 10: 3, 5), opposite to the site of cultic sins reported in Ezekiel 8.[11] Later they move and rise to the entrance gate and the Mount of Olives, in the direction of *mizrah* ('rising'), the east. The eastern gate, elsewhere called 'the gate of the Lord' (Ps. 24, 118: 19–20), faced the 'front' (Heb. *qedem*, also 'the east') of the temple, letting rays of the equinoctial sun enter the building at dawn. Its location permitted the glory of Yahweh and his ark to enter the temple at the beginning of the ecclesiastical year at spring, followed by its departure at the start of the civil year in autumn (Ezek. 43, 44). From their eastern position, both the cherubs and the Lord finally transport themselves and the prophet to the land of Chaldea (*up north* and then) towards the southeast.

The overall trajectory of these heavenly spirits, from north to east to southeast, converges on recollections of the solar body departing from its summertime apogee in the northern heaven, passing through the eastern equinox, and then moving towards its wintry position at dawn – rising low in the southeastern sky. Logically, this general movement away from the northern sky, towards the right and the south, tallies with the cherub motif replacing the bull face ascribed to the left and the north in an earlier scene (Ezek. 1: 10).

We know that the cherub motif introduced in chapter 9 originates from the Akkadian *karibu*, a term denoting the winged, human-headed bulls sighted at the entrance of temples and palaces and interceding before higher gods (Cooke 1960: 112; see Greenberg 1983: 182; Jacobsen 1976: 229). These spirits usually numbered seven and were associated with stellar bears, bulls, or chariots of the north. Like cherubs supporting the Lord's mobile throne, the beasts or wheeled chariots of the northern sky comprised four principal stars (followed by three cubs or mourners). But the septenary cherub team also points to the Pleiades, a constellation that could be reduced to six plus one (the Lost Pleiad), which is how Ezekiel's angels of doom appear in the prophet's vision. The Pleiades were closely tied to Taurus and their appearance from the sun indicated the approach of harvest at springtime, around the time of the seven-day Passover feast, when seven bulls were sacrificed (Ezek. 45: 18ff.). As with Aldebaran, the Star of the Tablet that stood for the scribe Nebo, their setting in autumn marked the other equinox and the time for the new sowing, in the *seventh* month of Tishri.

In short, heptadic calculations are a legacy of the seven-planet solar system, the weekly phased lunar order, the guiding constellations of the Pleiades (Amos 5: 8), and the two Chariots or teams of bulls moving within the circumpolar sky. The importance of sevenfold figures is made evident in Ezekiel's description of the future temple (based on a vision received around the vernal equinox: Ezek. 40: 1) and in other passages as well.[12] We shall see that figures of sevenness are reinforced elsewhere in the apocalyptic literature, such as in John's vision of winged beasts and spirits evolving in heaven.

Other relevant names for ursine constellations of the north include 'the scatterings,' which is what Ezekiel's second vision of doom is about (Ezek. 12: 14, 13: 13). There is also the Hebrew *'galgal* Wheel motif, which Ezekiel confounds with the cherubs themselves and which is synonymous with whirlwinds, wagons, and chariots of destruction.[13] It is from between the wheels of the mobile throne that the scribe leading the six angels is given the fiery coals to be scattered over the city of Jerusalem. To the *'galgal* wheels of heaven may be added the saucepan motif: a *Casserole* or Dipper filled with 'meat' – hence, grain to be winnowed or a bull's thigh, another term for Ursa Major. The *Casserole* (or *la Roue*) becomes a hot caldron when seen landing on the northern horizon early on a hot summer morning, with the sun rising to the northeast. The scene may be pictured as a quadrilateral bier stationed to the north, separating east from west, after the fashion of the brazen altar in the Lord's Temple, the place of sacrificial fire approached by the messengers of doom (Ezek. 9: 1f.).

Seasonal motions of wagons and wheels of the northern sky are in keeping with the movements in space described in Ezekiel. Both the prophet and the linen-clothed sacrificer enter the Lord's house through the northern gate and then are brought to the eastern door as they go out and 'up from the earth.' The cherub-driven chariot follows the same path as it accompanies the glory of God, which ends up standing upon the mountain, 'on the east side of the city' (Ezek. 1: 4, 8: 3, 9: 2, 10: 19, 11: 1, 23, 43: 4). These motions correspond to the trajectory of the sun rising to the northeast at summer (17: 10, 19: 12). The trajectory also coincides with the early summer morning scene of a Great Chariot moving from north to east, and then up towards the zenith as the autumn approaches, the season of expiation and final judgment.

The boiling caldron or cooking pot standing for the city in Ezekiel 11 can provoke contradictory sentiments of security and danger. People living inside a city are as safe inside their walls as meat in a pot. Ezekiel, however, reinterprets the proverbial saying to mean the opposite. As made clear in 24: 3ff. (also 22: 17ff. 43: 19, 45: 18f.), the event of a siege is comparable to cooking or heating up a pot, with the contents of the caldron (cuts of leg and shoulder meat) standing for the population inside the city enclosure. Because of the evil practices of rulers, the city walls will no longer protect its dwellers, but rather will hold them together for slaughter and a purge.

The *Casserole* or Thigh of Set can serve contradictory functions as well. As a Bear it may keep an eye on the northern Fold menaced by Orion. But the stellar bear can also act as a nocturnal jackal or a false prophet (Ezek. 13: 4) threatening God's Fold, as was commonly thought on the Nile. Alternatively, the constellation can serve the cause of judgment, punishing the infidels whose fate is reflected in God's Eye, a designation that fits not only Aldebaran and the scribe Nebo, but also the polestar about which the Seven Bulls constantly revolve. In keeping with this retributive imagery, Ezekiel's vision of the future conveyed by the scribe is written under signs of cruel darkness and destruction by fire, images that point to the estival descent of both the sun-god and Mercury, towards the south and the season of obscurity. This sombre vision is written in the form of oracles against sinful nations such as northern Tyre, a Phoenician land that was once an example of richness and perfection and that used to be located on a holy mountain guarded by a cherub (Ezek. 28: 13f., 40: 2; Gen. 3: 24). Phoenician signs of strength and pride are destined to rebound on the city of Tyre, a people walking amid red-hot coals, to be destroyed by the guardian cherub and wheeled wagons and chariots of fire hailing from the Babylonian northeast (Ezek. 26: 7ff., 28: 12ff.). Evil nations shall be punished as their weapons and beastly representatives are turned against them.

In retrospect, cherubs stationed at the eastern gate are made to follow in the footsteps of creatures whom God once placed at the eastern gate of the Garden of Eden, with a flaming sword in their hands to keep fallen humans out of paradise, away from the tree of life (Gen. 3: 22–4). The fury of the guardians of heaven awaits the chosen people of Israel condemned to bear the weight of their debauchery and to be destroyed by their own evil image: a lofty beast of the north called Phoenice or Ursa Phoenicia, a wheeled formation of mighty chariots and wagons marching from Babylon (Ezek. 22: 31, 23: 24–9). Beasts of the north will be sent to rob children and attack the flock of Israel (Ezek. 14: 12–20, 34: 1–16, 36: 38, 39: 2). Likewise, the cherubs' wrath will be turned against their own inverted image, the wicked prince of northern Tyre. The creatures can be expected to oppose Lucifer, an anointed cherub who once walked on the holy mountain of God, till he tried to rise above, and therefore against God, only to be immediately judged, destroyed by his own fire, and thrown like ashes to the ground (28: 11–19). In the end the most evil crime of all shall be punished: the abuse of identity between the sacred and the profane, the invisible and the visible, God and humans (22: 26, 28: 2, 44: 23). As in Isaiah (46: 1ff.), judgment awaits all those who dare equate Yahweh with lofty formations and false gods rising in the sky.

The Flight from Hiddenness

According to Zimmerli, the cultic sins witnessed by Ezekiel at the entrance of the inner court met a strong human need, which is to express sympathy with nature and to bring the phenomenon of death into the world of religious feeling. By clinging to the rhythm of the withering and blossoming of nature, worshippers of the sun-god Tammuz compelled the Lord to strike a partnership with humans in the sense of sharing their mortal condition. Like his own creation, the Creator became subject to natural alternations between life and death. Human beings stood to gain from this partnership: as long as they propitiated and emulated the sun-god created in their own image, they could maintain their own hopes of rebirth. By introducing faith in nature within the Holy Temple area, sin disguised as piety 'enters into the proximity of the divine abode.' Blasphemy results from prayers to the sun, for it is through the fear of death and *the cult of visible spheres in heaven* that humans maintain their 'flight from the hiddenness of God ... The power of what is preeminently visible, the sun, here leads men, standing before the very sanctuary of God, to turn their backs on him. Inside the sanctuary they stand amidst lies, however much they veil their lies from themselves with a beautiful solar temple-theology and liturgy' (Zimmerli 1979: 252). Men are guilty of turning their back on the Lord, reluctant as they are to look at a God so 'unnatural' as to be invisible to humans.

Because of their sinful conduct, Israel, Tyre, and idols rising in heaven shall be cast into the pit like proud trees hurled down to Sheol (Ezek. 28: 8, 31: 15, 32: 18). The fate awaiting false gods and their followers finds another allegorical expression in Ezekiel's tale of the dying crocodile applied to Egypt. The Pharaoh, the 'young lion of nations,' the dragon or fearsome crocodile dwelling in waters of the Nile and the primordial sea, is to be extinguished at the same time as the sun, the moon, and the stars are dimmed and covered with clouds (Ezek. 32: 1–8). The resulting darkness is worn like garments of mourning that point to the day of Yahweh and the weeping of Tammuz. The battle between Yahweh and the Egyptian crocodile echoes the Babylonian account of Marduk catching the primeval dragon of chaos in his net and making the canopy of heaven from the stretch-out skin of *Tiamat* (Jacobsen 1976: 178f.).

As suggested by Maunder (1923: 209), Egypt, the crocodile, and Job's satanic dragon named Leviathan are all one and the same. Job describes the eyes of the dragon as eyelids of the morning; the sun coming out of the sea is likened to the reddish eyes of the beast emerging from the water. Given this sun–crocodile association, the slaying of Leviathan and Ezekiel's crocodile brings about total darkness and the sufferings of a great downfall (Job 3: 1–10; Ezek. 32: 17ff.). This is logical, given all ancient associations between the eye motif and the light stemming from the sun and the stars (as in Manilius 1: 132ff.). Finally, the association of crocodile with the 'young lion of nations' suggests a link with the southbound sun passing through estival Leo.

Zimmerli (1979: 159f.) argues that the tale of the crocodile and the Babylonian story of Tiamat differ in some respects, such that we cannot say with certainty whether one story echoes the other, as is generally assumed. Nor can the luminaries fading out be read as a reference to circumpolar Draco being extinguished by Yahweh. Given these comments, Zimmerli can be suspected of 'fleeing from the hiddenness' of Ezekiel's text. The commentator's reluctance to probe the hidden meanings of Ezekiel's vision is understandable: it coincides with the prophet's effort to reduce the cult of heavenly bodies to silence, demoting the astral pantheon (Leo, Dragon, etc.) to mere zoological metaphor. The exegete is faithful to the language of 'approximate similarity' deployed in Ezekiel, an anti-Sabian rhetoric that shows restraint in the parallels to be drawn between immutable spirits and visible bodies moving in heaven (Zimmerli 1979: 122).

Ezekiel is none the less faced with a fundamental riddle: how to speak of stellar and lunisolar idols while condemning them to silence? The answer is simple: he must speak of the unspeakable with utmost discretion. Although central to Ezekiel's vision of sins committed in Jerusalem, Israel's stargazing debauchery is never entirely exposed. Contrary to what the prophet says in Ezek. 23: 29, acts of 'shameful whoring' are too shocking to be fully disclosed; uncovering the naked truth would be too much of a concession to the unutterable. While explicitly denounced, widespread stories of Tammuz and other Semitic gods of his like must be given as little attention as possible – hence, forgotten, as Yahweh commands.

There is more to repression, however, than one discourse (Yahwism) conquering all contending imageries (naturalism) simply by way of silence.

Acts of repression also depend on a language's capacity to recuperate signs of the unthinkable to its own advantage. In the apocalyptic context, signs of the lunisolar system can be made to serve God in one of three ways. The first strategy consists in inflicting upon worshippers of the sun, the moon, and the stars all those trials experienced by the heavenly spheres suffering death at fall. A period of darkness affecting the solar body can thus be used as a sign of tribulation heralding the day of Yahweh. If turned against themselves, forces of darkness fulfil a divine purpose: punishing the infidels in due season. But there is another way, less negative, to conquer the Sabian language. Faith in the Spirit can be promoted through the blessings of Nature ruled by the heavenly spheres. Although glorifying the supranatural, Yahwism must promise to the elect the eternal transients of life and death governing the visible world. Just as the falling sun is destined to rise from the deep and the dead, so too Israel can count on being raised from the grave at the beginning of the sacred year, about the vernal equinox (Ezek. 37: 1–14). While the wicked are to be punished like their own pagan gods turned into agents of destruction, the elect are to be granted the blessings traditionally accorded to heavenly idols: an afterlife beginning at spring (see Ezek. 20: 8, 21: 23–32). If rewritten in the female gender, the story consists in the star of Israel falling in the company of the Queen of Heaven she resembled and whorishly adored. The demise of Israel is then followed by repentance and reinstatement. The queenly nation ends up being restored to her former glory, after the manner of Ishtar (Venus, the New Moon) rising every year in the company of the sun-god heading towards the month of Tammuz.

The third measure that can be applied towards the subsumption of enemy forces lies in the deployment of strategic metaphors. As Greenberg points out, Ezekiel conveys sign-manifestations of the Lord through the rhetoric of similarity, that is, in the likeness of the appearances of images that are not to be confused with the substance of his vision. This language of comparative 'likeness,' a buffer idiom associated with the 'colour' metaphor (Heb. k^e'en), 'is an aspect of the desire to be faithful and exact while indicating consciousness of the visionary nature of the event.' This implies not 'a reservation with respect to looks but with respect to substance,' an 'unwillingness to commit oneself to the substantial identity of the seen with the compared' (Greenberg 1983: 52f.; cf. 43, 167). The latter comment points to a central feature of logocentric discourse: the insuperable distance that lies between the invisible Spirit and his perceptible expressions. Greenberg's point is insightful, but it leaves out another equally important feature of Ezekiel's use of comparative phraseology: the prophet's unwillingness to equate the appearances of God with the full descriptions of 'pagan' divinities. Through metaphorical parlance, foreign mythical material is disassembled and recomposed in such ways as to produce 'resemblances' that are highly evocative, yet never fully recognizable.

Greenberg himself is reluctant to delve into the foreign parallels of Ezekiel's symbolism at any great length. While he recognizes that certain motifs such as references to the north may have symbolic meanings (the seat of God, the source of misfortune), the exegete tends to prefer more mundane lines of interpretation. The north wind of Ezekiel 1: 4 thus points to a real sandstorm blowing in July over the whole of Iraq, a common occurrence for the season (Greenberg 1983: 42, 51, 201). In his discussion of fourfold divisions and animal symbols in Ezekiel, the author recognizes the supplementary influence of Egyptian mythology, Babylonian literature, and the iconography of Western Asiatic cultures. He none the less adds that Ezekiel 'was too much concerned over the purity of Israel's worship ... to have imported into it images drawn directly from the pagan sphere.' Although necessarily based on familiar imageries, the visions he saw were 'so new as to exclude for the prophet the possibility that he was merely drawing out of the stock of memory a sight that his heart craved' (Greenberg 1983: 58, cf. 169). The exegete ends up replicating the prophet's polemical ambivalence *vis-à-vis* the 'pagan sphere,' without offering new insights into the squaring of the circle – into the impact or 'textual immanence' of influences that are squarely 'transcended' by the prophet.

John's Throne-Room Vision (Rev. 4–5)

In his description of the wheeled throne of God, the writer of Revelation draws heavily on the Book of Ezekiel. Several details of John's chariot imagery none the less stray away from the Old Testament. The astromythical implications of Revelation 4–5 change accordingly. In John's text, a door in heaven opens on to the sight of the Almighty Spirit looking like a diamond and a ruby. The Spirit is seated on a throne surrounded by

- an emerald-like rainbow;
- twenty-four elders also throned, dressed in white robes, prostrating themselves before God, and throwing their golden crowns in front of the throne;
- four six-winged creatures with many eyes and the faces of a lion, a bull, a man, and an eagle, all of them worshipping the everlasting Creator day and night;

• a multitude of angels, about ten thousand times ten thousand.

Lightning is seen and thunder is heard from the throne. Before the throne, there are seven burning lamps or spirits of God, and a sea of glass resembling crystal. A loud angelic voice is heard asking who can open or loose the seven seals of a scroll held in the right hand of the Almighty. The text specifies that no man in heaven, on earth, or under the earth is worthy of opening and reading the scroll. As the prophet weeps, one of the elders announces that the Lion of the tribe of Judah, or Root of David, has triumphed and will open the scroll and the seven seals. The latter appears between the throne and the elders, in the shape of a slain Lamb, with seven horns and eyes, standing for the seven spirits God sent out all over the world. The redeeming Lamb comes forward to take the scroll from the One sitting on the throne. He is given praise for his sacrifice by all living things in Creation and witnesses of the throne scene, especially the animals and the elders holding harps and golden bowls scented with the prayers of the saints.

The Lamb and the Lion

The scene is clearly reminiscent of Ezekiel's vision of the throne and the creatures supporting it. The universe is governed by a throne resting on top of a stellar vault whirling above the flat circular earth, a tent-like firmament separating the waters of above from those of below (Gen. 1: 7, Ps. 104: 3, 148: 4).[14] The vision incorporates a fourfold division of seasonal time and heavenly space, as expressed through four cherub-like creatures and their zodiacal reflections (Beasley-Murray 1974: 117f.; Farrer 1964: 91f.; Prigent 1981: 86 ft.). The scene, however, is dominated by a Passover Lamb echoing the sign of the Ram, as opposed to Ezekiel's encounter with God in the summer month of Tammuz. The Ram was associated with the Jewish month of Nisan, as confirmed by Josephus's claim (first century C.E.) that the liberation of his people from Egyptian bondage occurred when the sun was in Aries, in the first month of the sacred year. The month was *Nisanu* to the Assyrians, with Aries representing the sacrifice of a ram on the altar.

As *Princeps zodiaci*, Aries was commonly thought to rule over the head. Its ability to overcome the winter and rise above waters of the sea is reflected in the words of Manilius: 'a pale Sun swims upward from the icy waves and begins by slow degrees to blaze with golden flame as it attempts the rugged path where the Ram heads the procession of the skies' (2: 940ff., see also 2: 456, 4: 744ff., 5: 32ff.; see Malina 1995: 101f.; Boll 1914: 44).

Columella, a first-century Roman writer, spoke of this constellation as Athamas, father of Phrixus, who fled on the back of the Ram together with Helle, the sister who fell off into the sea, where she drowned. At the end of his journey, Phrixus sacrificed the ram. According to Allen (1963: 76), Athamas is the Roman version of the youthful Euphratean sun-god Tammuz Dumuzi, 'the Only Son of Life, whom Aries at one time represented in heavens, as did Orion at a previous date' (see Manilius 4: 744ff.). Other titles of the golden-fleeced Ram (Hebrew *Teli*) include the *Princeps juventutis*, appearing on a coin of Domitian, and the King of Gods, shown at Thebes with ram's horns. Aries was known as Ammon in Egypt and Jupiter in Rome. It was also the Euphratean Scimitar, a sword to protect the kingdom against the Seven Evil Spirits or Tempest Powers.

The slain Lamb symbology carries the legacy of Aries (Boll 1914). Christ the 'little lamb' (Gr. *arnion*, dim. of *aren*), however, is the docile *alter ego* of the powerfully loined Ram. He is the son, not the Almighty Father. As such, his imagery cannot be equal to 'that of power, force, control, and conquest' (Malina 1995: 101).The twofold presentation of the leader of the heavenly flock, meek and powerful, gentle and wrathful, implies that Christ the lamb must be slain if he is to rise to power and turn into the seven-horned ram. Like David, Christ is portrayed as a vulnerable lamb that grows into a ram struggling against hostile beasts and bringing the whole cosmos under his sway. When transposed to the sexual domain, this dual representation of God conveys a particular view of human morality. Unlike the phallic and demonic Scorpio entered by the sun at seedtime, about the autumn equinox, the spring lamb represents a meek, immature, tender-fleshed animal, less than one year old, without permanent teeth and horns. As such he can bear the sin of humans and, by right of self-sacrifice, accede to the light and the glory of his Father in heaven – to the power of the many-horned Ram communing with his bridal nation at the End of Time (Chevalier 1990: 39f.). Paradoxically, through the pouring of his blood, the Passover lamb can become the conquering warrior-lamb, the champion of God's flock, a creature fearsome as a dragon and powerful as the Lion of the tribe of Judah (Rev. 5: 5, 5: 9; Farrer 1964: 92). In other words, the Lord's victory lies in his sacrifice: his martyrdom is a 'guarantee of final redemption from archetypal Egypt and Babylon' (Sweet 1990: 131).[15]

John's Spirit appears under the sign of vernal Aries, but is also cast in the light of summertime Leo. While Aries is connected to the equinoctial east, fearsome Leo evokes the northernmost sun that begins to fall, towards the storms and darkness of the winter season. In Egypt, Leo was the House of the Sun and was coloured red and green (Allen 1963: 252), colours that coincide with John's description of the Lord (sardius) and the rainbow cloud (emerald) encircling his throne. The Lion was the sign of Judah, as made explicit by Jacob in Genesis (49: 9). Euphratean astronomers knew the constellation as the Shining Disc, which precedes Bel, the patron god of Babylon; Bel of Babylon was the title given to Marduk, and also Adonis, a title applied to Yahweh. Leo's titles and attributes include the Iranian Scimitar, the Akkadian Sceptre or Great Fire, and the Assyrian Fiery Hot.

For the time being, signs of spring resurrection prevail over summertime motions of solar apogee and descent. The throne-room vision is slanted towards a scene of vernal enthronement, a time of the year when potentates ascended their thrones (Beasley-Murray 1974: 110). This is a far cry from Ezekiel's moving throne associated with the month of Tammuz. The problem raised by this solar composition remains none the less the same: given the cyclical nature of all forms of life, no one can rise to glory without sacrificial trials. To resurrect at spring, all living bodies must experience the fall of death from summer to winter.

Harp, Altar, and Crown

A solar interpretation of Revelation 4–5 does not hinge on the appearance of the Lamb and the Lion alone. Other stellar indices of darker days to come include the throne-altar and the **harps** or lyres given to the elders. The sound of a harp or lyre can be as promising as music of the spheres. Like Cicero, Theon of Smyrna used to think that 'the seven spheres give the seven sounds of the lyre and produce a harmony because of the intervals which separate them from one another' (quoted in Malina 1995: 105). But the musical instrument can also be disquieting, especially if it is associated with Lyra, a constellation anciently identified with Ishtar (Langdon 1931: 317). Briefly, Lyra used to be placed in the beak of a Swooping Vulture (the nearby Aquila). It lies on the opposite side of Aries and Taurus, along the Milky Way, close to the circumpolar sky. In its own way the *seven-stringed* Harp is the inverted image of the seven Pleiades, which the Arabians and Jews used to put on the rump of Aries. The two formations border on opposite sides of the circumpolar fold and the Milky Way. Unlike the Pleiades, the Harp mounts to the sky at dawn after the rise of Libra and Scorpio at fall. The Harp thus evoked the autumn equinox. The constellation was also described by Aratus as the Tortoise or Shell discovered by Mercury, a kindred spirit of the Babylonian god of destiny and writing (Nebo) dressed in white, just like the twenty-four elders holding the lyres in Revelation 5. The association between the Harp and the writings of Fate is made more direct on the Borgian globe, where Lyra appears as a *Scroll*.

The golden **bowls** of incense held by the elders point in turn to the celestial altar known as Ara, also a Censer, the *Mundi Templum* or the Golden One in the Temple. Some saw in this constellation the Altar of Noah evoking the covenant between God and all living creatures. The alliance was sealed with offerings burnt on an altar, with the smoke rising above Ara, towards the highest heaven, northward through the flame-like Milky Way (Boll 1914: 32f.). The solar pact was also sealed with a rainbow appearing in the clouds, another motif made explicit in John's throne-room vision (Gen. 8: 20–9: 17; Ezek. 1: 28; cf. Maunder 1923: 181f.; L. Morris 1983: 87; Sweet 1990: 117f.; Caird 1966: 63). Notwithstanding these covenantal associations, the altar and the rainbow can herald a season of judgment (Ford 1975: 71). Signs of ill omen may emerge from Ara and Lyra, two constellations that stand near Aquila and the wintry sting of Scorpio. Although apparently eternal, the Noahic covenant hangs over human heads with the same menacing frailty that Aratus once assigned to Ara. Confirmation of this weaker and sombre aspect of the stellar altar is found in Libra, the equinoctial Balance which Euphratean astronomers represented as an altar or censer held in the claws of Scorpio. The Greeks eventually cut off the altar from Scorpio's claws and turned it into Libra; this occurred about 237 years before Christ. Persians placed the autumn Scales in one hand of a human figure, with the other hand grasping a lamb (Malina 1995: 163; Allen 1963: 61ff., 273f.).

Another neighbouring constellation is Corona Borealis, a northerly crown anciently portrayed as Persephone or Cybele drawn by lions, as shown on Smyrnian coins. The kingly or queenly head covering is a befitting image for the circumpolar 'crown of heaven' and for John's vision of the heavenly throne-room. In Revelation 4, however, the **crowns** of glory placed on the heads of the elders are thrown before the Lord's throne and the Lion of Judah. The gesture is a reminder that the kingly crown is a poor substitute for the wreath of thorns worn by Jesus. The scene is reminiscent of Corona Borealis (a broken platter, to the Persians) falling below the northern horizon as Leo rises to the east at dawn, before the days of vintage and ploughing.

Variations on a Heptadic Theme

On the bright side of the text, the **seven seals and stars** held in the right hand of the Almighty carry with them the sweet influence of the vernal Pleiades. Since these stars are directly connected with Aries and navigation, they can serve the same function as the rainbow, which is to remind humans that God protects them against another Flood, saving the world from trials that would bring the solar order and the Noahic pact to a tragic end. Cognate representations of the Pleiades include a flock of birds, in most cases doves, emblems of peaceful existence and reconciliation with God (Gen. 8: 8, 10). Another common figure is that of a hen with her chicks, an expression used by Matthew and Luke with reference to Christ; Aben Ragel and other Hebrew writers thus imagined the Pleiades. The Starry Seven rising in the company of the seven planets thus signalled the vernal resurrection of the sun-god and Christ the Hen. Finally, the Pleiades evoked abundance among the Babylonians, presumably because of their appearance at harvest time.

The Pleiades' influence may none the less be bound to a more sombre season. According to Hesiod, the evening setting of the Pleiades coincided with the new sowing at autumn. There were also speculations about the impact of their midnight culmination. The event may have given rise to the cult of the dead, which is at the origin of our All Hallow Eve, All Saints' Day, and All Souls' Day. While Hippocrates thought their midnight culmination brought the spread of diseases and death, the Egyptians used the event to mark the feast of the Egyptian goddess Isis, sister of the sun-god Osiris. Finally, Aratus associated the Pleiades' acronical rise with the arrival of winter and the pouring of rain – hence, the flood; according to the Talmud, the Deluge was caused by the Lord taking two stars out of the Pleiades.

A darker reflection of the Starry Seven can be seen in their 'half-sisters' located in the same part of the sky: the seven Hyades, stars that Ovid, Manilius, and Pliny associated with storms and rains (attending their morning and evening setting in May and November). Other stars resembling the Pleiades include the circumpolar Bear, a creature that can bring about the rule of evil or the End of Time. The two heptadic formations are similar in so many respects that the Pleiades have been called the Chariot or Wagon, as in the late-antiquity writings of Hesychios. Given this resemblance, a hen with her chicks can easily turn into a child-killing she-bear, a beast as ferocious as Christ exercising wrath over his children at the End of Time.

Ancient connections between **stars** of the north, the **eye** motif, and a throne-vision that speaks of humans' **fate** written on a **scroll** tally with the imagery deployed in Revelation 4–5. They bring back memories of the fate of humans lying in the hands of Nebo, the Babylonian god of writing represented as Aldebaran, the Star of the Tablet or leading Star of Stars. The scribe acted as God's Eye. He was the royal star, *Alpha* in Greek or *Aleph* in Hebrew, a letter associated with the sun going through the Pleiades and Taurus, rising to the east at spring. But Nebo's mark also resided in the *tau* cross, a letter that stood for Libra entered by the autumn sun. Seven stars appearing at spring are thus a mirror reflection of the bear or the plough revolving around the North Star, defined as God's Eye, a constellation set in motion in darker days of the year, in the season of judgment. The plough invites the Easter Lamb to act wrathfully, turning himself into a northern reaper, a ploughman, a vintager, or a bier inflicting great sufferings on dwellers of the earth. Although portrayed in vernal colours, John's heptadic star imagery is a prelude to the rise of a seven-horn beast resembling the harlot Jezebel and the whore of Babylon.[16]

On the whole, John's throne-room scene betrays the influence of a planetary system guided by the Pleiades on the trail of Aries, an enthronement imagery harking back to the seven stars appearing on Babylonia's scroll-like, cylinder seals. But the composition also carries undertones of the sun's passage through summertime Leo and its southward fall towards Libra and Scorpio. These motions coincide with the rise of a fearsome seven-starred beast, plough or chariot residing in the highest quarter of heaven, the north. Forces or destruction (opposed or subservient to God) lurk behind the seven churches, stars, horns, eyes, and spirits of God.

Twenty-Four Elders and Four Living Creatures

We now proceed to the twenty-four elders and the four living creatures surrounding the throne, posted outside the four gates of the sky, after the 'four angels standing at the four corners of the earth' (Rev. 7: 1). As argued by Gunkel and Zimmern, the living creatures are of Babylonian origin and correspond to the four wings and quarters of heaven and the four seasons of yearly time. Irenaeus, Saint Augustine, and others associated these animals with the Four Evangelists (Charles 1920, 1: 122ff.). The creatures resemble Ezekiel's cherubs (lamps, eyes, stars, planets) save that each has one face and six wings in lieu of four, for a total of four faces and twenty-four wings. They have no wheels, they are not sighted beneath the throne, and they are not gathered in the same heavenly location or at the same gate. Although the throne is suffused with colours of the rising sun, the creatures are not actually supporting it, such that they can no longer head in one direction all at once, forming a moving war-throne or sun-chariot, as in Ezekiel.[17]

Apocalypse, Cod. 8, f.89a Beatus, Spanish, 233465. Rylands Library, Manchester, Great Britain; Foto Marburg/Art Resource, New York

These alterations brought to Ezekiel's cherub imagery allow the animals to spread round about the throne, taking each of the twenty-four elders under their wings, as it were. The protection offered by the winged animals is a timely one in that it coincides with

- a twenty-four-hour wheel divided into four periods of six hours each;
- the twenty-four star-gods of the Babylonian pantheon, with twelve to the north of the zodiac and twelve to the south, as reported by Diodorus of Sicily, c. 20 B.C.E. (Malina 1995: 93f.; Gunkel 1895: 302–8; Zimmern 1903: 633; 2 Enoch 4:1);
- the twenty-four decanal hours borrowed from the Babylonians and further developed in the Hellenistic period, decans synonymous with elders and council members in Israel (Malina 1995: 94–6; see John 11:9);
- the twenty-four orders of priests and Levites taking turns at the temple, each serving for one week at a time and twice a year (1 Chron. 24: 4ff., 25: 1; see Charles 1920, 1: 132; Ford 1975: 72f.); and,
- the twelve patriarchs (stellar sons of sunlike Jacob and his lunar wife led by the lion cub Judah) joining the twelve apostles to form the twenty-four names written on the foundation stones and gates of the New Jerusalem (Gen. 37: 9ff., 49: 9; Isa. 11: 1ff.; Rev. 12: 2, 21: 12ff.; Feuillet 1976: 459; Prigent 1981: 85).

After Charles (1920, 1: 131), commentators tend to emphasize the connection between John's elders and the priestly order of the Old Testament, 'for the points in common between the two can be explained within Judaism.' Parallels between apocalyptic visions of spirits driving heavenly throne-chariots and Babylonian star-gods regulating the wheels of time should not for all that be dismissed as purely coincidental. As pointed out by Charles (1920, 1: 150), John's evocation of 'everything that lives in the air' (Rev. 5: 13) may very well refer to the sun, moon, and stars, for the 'Jews attributed a conscious existence to these luminaries.' Moreover, a lunisolar calendar shared by most Semitic cultures (based on quadripartite, heptadic, and duodecimal divisions) pervaded all Judaic institutions. The Levitical order itself was organized along chronological lines, on the basis of a rotation of weekly duties spanning the year. The twenty-four equal parts of the Hebrew day, a decanal system of Babylonian origin and adopted by the Greeks, were divided into day and night, each consisting of twelve 'ocular' hours (Heb, *shaah*, 'look, glance'). The twenty-four priestly orders of Judaic tradition were thus inspired by measurements of time reflecting the bright-eyed planets and fixed stars evolving in heaven.

The notion that heavenly patterns exist for the unfolding of time and history on earth is made explicit in Jewish apocalyptic literature and the Scriptures.[18] If one applies this principle to Revelation 4–5, twenty-four elderly decans or council members surrounding the heavenly throne could be likened to a Fold of planets and stars revolving around the polestar, flying on the wings of time. As starlike spirits, the elders would commence their yearly journey by going through a door consisting of Seven Stars, or the Pleiades opening like the 'heavenly tablets' and sealed scrolls of human destiny, to be read at spring. This is the appropriate time for the Lord to accede to his throne, after the manner of Marduk in the Babylonian creation myth (Charles 1920, 1: 138, 143; Sweet 1990: 123). All of these stars would revolve like day and night, and like the weekly and seasonal quarters of the month and the year. Finally, the heavenly Fold would form a circle placed around the Lord coloured sardius and jasper, after the first and the last of the twelve tribal gems fixed to the breastplate of the high priest (Exod 28: 17–21).

Some commentators see in Revelation 4–5 the fulcrum of the whole book, the principal framework into which all subsequent visions dovetail, and rightly so (Beasley-Murray 1974: 108). The two chapters offer a global spectacle of stellar, lunisolar completeness, a celestial staging of all divisions of spaces and spells in time. The throne-room scene owes much of its imagery to the lunisolar pact affecting the normal regulation of the wheels and works of Chronos. The throne and the heavenly formations are none the less viewed synchronically, as if they were brought to a standstill, swayed by an Ancient One portrayed as both the 'Head of Days' and 'the Sum of Days' (Dan. 7: 9; 1 Enoch 46: 1f.; 47: 3; Charles 1920, 1: 113). Since they are harnessed to a Spirit standing above time, cherubs can no longer be equated with wheels set in motion as in Ezekiel. Having severed their ties with the order of time, John's four animals siding with God can be freed from the four-starred Bier of the North and spread round about the Lord's throne, something Ursa Major can never do.

Dramatic events to come are offset by the absence of movement in the sky. The text covers all four seasons and quarters of heaven, such that the universe can stand still, if only for a while. The text brings together stones representing the first and the last tribes of Israel, the youngest and the oldest. While **sardius** (named after Sardis) is as red as the blood and wine of Christ, and his wrath exercised at autumn (through the crushing of grape), **jasper** evokes the purity, whiteness, and brightness of the paschal Lamb resurrecting at spring. When combined, the two colours embody the hopes of saints 'who have washed their robes and made them white in the blood of the Lamb,' to use John's imagery (Rev. 7: 14).[19] In Exodus (28: 18), the two precious stones are mediated in the middle by the green emerald, which represents the Lion of the tribe of Judah; when tied to the rainbow motif, the colour emerald becomes a token of the Noahic pact guaranteeing solar continuity through time (Mounce 1977: 134). In the same spirit of unity, the text speaks of heaven, earth, and water, a tripartite conception of the universe originating from Babylonian mythology (Rev. 5: 3; Charles 1920, 1: 139). Finally, John's vision brings together the three levels of a heavenly Trinity comprising the One Sitting on the Throne (north), the seven spirits (Pleiades, east), and the Lamb or Lion of Judah (south). The composition harks back to the Babylonian trilogy of ecliptic Anu, the northern way of Enlil, and the southern way of Ea (Malina 1995: 84; Langdon 1931: 94).

The synthesis may very well suggest the end of all divisions in space and time. As Malina (1995: 52, 80f., 152) notes, the door opening in heaven at the beginning of the throne scene allows the Seer to accede to the other side of the heavenly vault, thereby reuniting the inside and outside realms of the sky dome. As in 1 Enoch 14, the visible and the invisible are no longer separated, with the implication that immortal souls can climb to the summit of the universe and see everything from God's perspective, standing, as they do, 'upon the back of the world,' to use Plato's words (in *Phaedrus*).

Although synthetic, John's throne-room vision is none the less slanted towards signs of paschal resurrection celebrated at springtime. The vernal mood of Revelation 4–5 tallies with the purpose of the book, which is to announce the 'newness' of hymns and names, heaven and earth, the holy city and the whole of creation. All of reality is transformed by Christ, who offers the world a fresh start (Rev. 2: 17, 3: 12, 5: 9, 14: 3, 21: 1, 5). Indices of a universal afterlife, however, are expressed through a rhetoric that remains elusive. The language used by the Seer is so indirect that doubts can be cast on the vernal coordinates of John's throne-room vision. Signs of the spring equinox could always be read as a prelude to starlike spirits falling in the summer and dying at fall. As argued in the previous chapter, a door that opens in heaven (as in Rev. 4: 1) and that planets can go through (1 Enoch 33–6, 72) will give access to the paschal throne, provided that it be placed to the east or the north. But the same door could also lead to the sight of the Lord departing from his temple in due season – the sun entering northernmost Leo, and then heading east and south, towards the gateway of the autumn equinox.

While never made explicit, indices of darker days to come can be read into Revelation 4–5. For one thing signs of death are part of a *biblion* document made fast with seven seals and used as a testament among members of the Church (Zahn 1924: 393ff.). Also a heavenly throne appearing near the earth can be suspected of falling towards the earth's environs for purposes of judgment (1 Thes. 4: 16f.; Rev. 4: 2; H. Morris 1983: 85). A scene of this kind evokes the downfall of the solar body at summer and other stellar motions that do not augur well for 'dwellers of the earth' rebelling against the Lord (Caird 1966: 129). Motions observed in the northern sky are particularly important in this regard. From scriptural references to heaven and from Ezekiel's chariot vision, we learn that the Lord's seat of judgment and war-throne can be located to the north. Thus we can expect the Lord's throne and seven star-spirits to approach the earth somewhere from the north, as if following in the footsteps of David's Chariot approaching the circumpolar horizon. When the dreaded Ursa Major reaches this lower atmospheric position, the seven stars of Ursa Minor appear on the right-hand side of the Spirit dwelling above Polaris and facing the earth. The scene matches the right-hand position assumed by the seven stars of the Lord and the seven-sealed scroll of the seven-horned Lamb (Rev. 1: 16, 5: 1). This conjunction of northern constellations coincides with a rainbow-cloud of lights or stars of the Milky Way appearing above the two Bears (Rev. 4: 3, 6). All of this can be seen at dawn in the spring season as the sun recovers from its southern fall. This view of the sky would be reassuring were it not for the fact that the same heavenly scenario reappears at a darker time: at sunset in autumn, on the eve of the season of judgment.

In other words, there are two possible readings of John's throne-room imagery: one suggesting a cosmic breakthrough (vernal), and another conveying (autumn) signs of an apocalyptic breakdown. In reality, given the severe tone of the epistles to the churches situated east and north of Patmos, the text can proceed in the calamitous direction only. We know that victory over the seven-horned Beast and wicked forces in its train will come at the Endtime: God and the twelve tribes of Israel shall triumph. But we also know that the ending can come only after a great judgment, a flood of tribulations as harsh as the cold, rainy days of winter experienced at the end of every year. Redemption comes in due season, after all sorts of trials resembling the Flood and the waters of wrath that once covered the earth, only to be rebuked by God who re-established the fixed laws of the luni-solar system through the Noahic Covenant (Gen. 9: 8ff.). The bitter implications of the book-roll about to be opened have yet to be assimilated by enemies of the Lord and his followers alike.

John recasts the battle of Genesis in a prophetic mould. The **sea of crystal-like glass** and lightning proceeding from the throne (Rev. 4: 5f.)

brings us back to the sight of a floor-like firmament separating the waters of above from those of below, with God imposing 'limits they must never cross again, or they would once more flood the land' (Ps. 104: 7ff.; Malina 1995: 93). The Noahic covenant passed between God and his children included a promise that the earth would be replenished and that solar alternations of day and night, summer and winter, would continue forever. God not only set bounds to oceanic motions, but also gave orders to the morning and sent the dawn to its post.[20] Likewise, Mesopotamian myths of creation portrayed God defeating the dragon of the sea and imposing order on chaos. Old Testament stories of the exodus spoke of God using waters of wrath to destroy the enemies of Israel; the Lord thus conquered the ancient dragon and dried up the waters of the Abyss (Isa. 51: 9f.). The dragon of the sea stands for Satan, the prince of Tyre, or the king of Babylon (Rev. 12: 7ff., 13: 1; see Isa. 14: 12, 27: 1; Ezek. 28: 12f.).

The origin of this [sea] symbol is to be found in the Babylonian creation myth. There we are told that Marduk, the god of light and order, went to battle with Tiamat, the primaeval ocean monster, goddess of darkness and chaos, and, having killed her, split her body into two like a flat fish and made heaven out of one half and earth out of the other. From the Ras Shamra tablets we know that this myth was current also in Canaan, where the part of Tiamat was played by Lotan (Leviathan), the seven-headed monster. In the biblical account of creation in Genesis 1 the pagan story has been demythologized in the interests of a thoroughgoing monotheism, but traces of its original shape remain in the victory of light over chaos, in the name Tehom (the Deep) which is a recognizable variant of Tiamat, and in the separation of the waters above the firmament from the waters under the earth. Elsewhere in the Old Testament other echoes of the myth are found: there are references to Yahweh's primordial victory over the ocean monsters Rahab and Leviathan ... and to the creative act of power by which he confined the rebellious waters of the sea within their prescribed limits. (Caird 1966: 66)

Through creation and alliances with his people, God triumphs over chaos and the fusion of waters of above and below. But the Flood could always return, either to punish evil humans or to test the faith of followers of God. Since covenants can be broken through sin, the Lord may choose at any time to set aside the regulations imposed on the sun and the deep, and to punish sin by a local flood or a falling darkness (Schiaparelli 1905: 2, 40), *signs of the winter season deployed on a larger scale*. In the same way that Marduk's struggle against Tiamat was re-enacted at every New Year Festival, God's battle against Satan was constantly repeated in the Scriptures. When need be, the afflictions of chaos can be reactivated; at God's command, they can recoil on agents of evil. An obscured sun, a surging mass of water, and a flood of destroyers are typical expressions of biblical judgments befalling a wicked nation.[21]

Flood-like tribulations may also serve to put humans' faith to the test. Persecution and troubles suffered by the faithful are like another Red Sea, a 'barrier which the redeemed must pass in a new Exodus, if they are to win access to the promised land' (Caird 1966: 65).[22] When humans pass the test successfully, all seas disappear from their sight, as in the heavenly Jerusalem (Rev. 21: 1). Come the End of Time, oceans shall give way to waters of cleansing, redemption, and regeneration flowing from God's throne. Faith thrives on the waters of baptism springing from Solomon's 'Sea,' a caldron or bath placed inside the temple and used for ritual washing (1 Kings 7: 23ff.; 2 Chron. 4: 6; 1 Peter 3: 20f.; Rev. 22: 1). When viewed calendrically, bitter waters turned into living springs point to a winter spell feeding into the cycle of life – hence, the 'early rains' falling at autumn and the 'latter rains' at spring – equinoctial waters vital to agriculture and the regeneration of life on earth (Jer. 5: 24; Unger 1957: 908f.).

Of Silences and Lapses of Memory

This completes our discussion of Revelation 4–5. Readers should note the dramatic change that occurs as one moves from the letters to Asia to the throne-room vision (Charles 1920, 1: 102). In lieu of the troubles and threats faced by the seven churches, we now have heavenly manifestations of peace and glory, with no reference to church affairs or cultic sins committed against the Lord. A similar shift will soon follow, this time in reverse, towards a cosmic version of the woes suggested in the letters to Asia Minor. Revelation 6 is about to portray the Lamb breaking the seven seals, a gesture resulting in four catastrophes followed by three.

Before we delve into the first trials of Judgment, something should be said about these compositional shifts, leaps that are not as erratic as they may seem. In previous chapters, we saw that John's inaugural portrayal of Christ and reproaches addressed to the churches contain allusions to ancient stories of star-gods dying and resurrecting in heaven. Despite their worldly focus and their negative tone, signs deployed in the prologue and the letters lend themselves to visions formulated on a cosmic scale. Revelation 1–3 anticipates the exalted imagery deployed in the throne-room scene of Revelation 4–5. But while ecstatic, the throne-room vision prefigures in turn the sufferings of darker days to come; the woes announced in the letters are by no means forgotten. John's vision of the throne 'contains' (conveys, withholds) signs of 'what is to come in the future' (Rev. 4: 1), hints of woes hidden from the surface text.

Although different, the prologue, the letters, and the throne-room vision convey similar recollections of the past, and create similar fears and hopes of the future. They also have in common silences and lapses of memory concerning their astrological inspiration. What Isaiah says of the future Jerusalem applies to John's treatment of idols of primitive astronomy: '*the moon will hide her face, the sun be ashamed,* for Yahweh Sabaoth will be king on Mount Zion, in Jerusalem, and his glory will shine in the presence of his elders' (Isa. 24: 23; emphasis added). Through convoluted symbolism, the author of Revelation hides the stellar gods and puts them to shame. As a result, John avoids speaking of God in terms that are too clearly reminiscent of pagan deities; stellar manifestations of the Lord shall not be confounded with God. John's use of analogy in his description of heavenly spirits represents an effective way of keeping false gods at a distance from his vision. But the powers of false gods are not simply excluded from John's prophetic discourse. Rather, they are demoted and recuperated through metaphor: star-gods are downgraded to the rank of subservient followers, messengers, and attributes of the Lord dwelling above the heavenly spheres.

Commentators have noted John's tendency to avoid a detailed anthropomorphic portrayal of the One Sitting on the Throne (Charles 1920, 1: 115). The same comment can be extended to other natural codes deployed by the Seer, whether zoological, cosmographic, or astrological: all of them are explored in the vaguest possible terms. While the Son of Man *is in the likeness* of the Morning Star and the paschal lamb, no mention is ever made of a real lamb or the constellation Aries, let alone Venus and the sun-god rising to the east. The prophet borrows imageries from ancient conceptions of the universe, yet he reduces all worldly languages to sign-manifestations of God's will. Signs, attributes, and titles of natural gods are diluted and manipulated at will, all in the interest of monotheism and logocentrism. The 'newness' of God's Word can be unveiled through older modes of speech on one condition: that an everlasting veil be thrown on cults of the heavenly spheres and ritual observations of Sabian time – traditions at the root of John's metaphors.

Instead of reflecting on the reasons for John's silences and lapses of memory, commentators of Revelation share with the prophet a reluctance to spell out the astromythical underpinnings of his language. The impact of Sabaism on apocalyptic literature is underemphasized. When discussing the sea motif, L. Morris (1983: 89) suggests that cosmological interpretations be rejected, in that 'such views give John's language a precision he himself does not give it, apparently of set purpose. He does not say *before the throne there was a sea* (as AV), but "there was as it were a sea" ... Again John's reserve about heavenly things is to the fore. He is not giving an exact description but speaking in symbols.' Similarly, Charles (1920, 1: 131) argues that the parallels between the twenty-four elders and the star-gods of Babylonian mythology are 'no more than a coincidence; for the points in common between the two can be explained within Judaism.' Possible references to the story of Marduk in the Babylonian creation myth are dismissed on similar grounds (with some hesitation though): 'our author has no consciousness of the existence of this myth, even if in the above form it ever existed. *Some elements of the picture, however, do appear to go back to a heathen origin*' (Charles 1920, 1: 143; emphasis added). Charles adds that Gunkel himself has admitted that John may have lost conscious memory of the Babylonian origin of his imagery.

Beasley-Murray and Mounce are of the same view as Charles. Although the astrological interpretation of John's throne-room vision is an attractive theory, there is still 'no evidence at all that Jewish apocalyptic knew of an angelic order of twenty-four in heaven' (Beasley-Murray 1974: 114 ft.). As Mounce (1977: 135) puts it: 'no exact counterparts [of the Babylonian star-gods] are to be located in Jewish literature.' Caird (1966: 64f., 68) is also in agreement. He recognizes the highly malleable, kaleidoscopic quality of John's symbols, he admits that the four living creatures of Revelation 4 'may well have had their ultimate origin in the study of constellations,' and he states that we need have 'no hesitation in accepting the evidence that the [Babylonian] creation myth was one of the major sources of John's symbolism.' All the same, he asks 'did John intend his readers to see here a reference to the stars, or was he merely copying from Ezekiel? All we can say is that the creatures have no astrological significance which is consistently developed in the rest of the book.'

To paraphrase Caird, the fundamental question is whether John takes over details from earlier prophets and mythologies 'which are used simply for their associative value or are intended by him to convey some precise symbolic idea.' Most commentators have adopted the former position: given the lack of precise details and explicit references to pagan star-gods, one should not read pagan mythology into Revelation (e.g., Prigent 1981: 30).[23] The exercise can, but should not be, done, for the two sign systems do not fit at all points, as if they should. Although open to criticism, these conclusions are a credit to John's verbal artistry. *Wittingly or not, his task consisted precisely in avoiding undue precision – subverting naturalism in the interests of Logos and through the vagueness of metaphor.*

7

Seven Seals and Four Trumpets

The first chapter of Revelation abounded in solar images of God. John's vision began with evocations of the sun-faced, fiery-eyed, flame-footed likeness of the Messiah. The text alluded to the Lord's death and solstice-like descent to the underworld. It also spoke of God's Sunday visitation and resurrection, an event celebrated at springtime and centred on the Messiah's ascent to heaven and enthronement as Ruler of all kings. Indirect references to the equinoctial aspects of the divine included the Alpha and Omega title assigned to the Living One and the circular route of the seven church-like stars (seven planets, Pleiades, Bears of the North) sighted in God's right hand.

With the throne-room vision of Revelation 4–5, propitious solarism triumphs. God's throne-chariot is no longer associated with the month of Tammuz, as in Ezekiel. Rather, the seven-star and Passover Lamb imagery bring signs of springtime resurrection to the foreground (Prigent 1964: 78f.). While appearing in vernal colours, the Lord also stands above the order of time. The motions of heaven are arrested as the heavenly vault opens and the twenty-four elders and four living creatures spread around the heavenly throne. Both effects of timelessness and vernal resurrection converge on the glory of God's final victory over forces of evil (Prigent 1964: 73). Darker days to come are none the less conveyed through astrological pointers such as of the lion of Judah (Leo), the temple altar (Ara), and the harps (Lyra), and crowns (Corona Borealis) of the elders. Given these pointers, the seven planets and Pleiades guiding the wheels of time may give way to nocturnal forces that are less reassuring: that is, the seven-starred Lyra and Hyades ascending at autumn, in conjunction with heptadic coffins, bears, bulls, chariots, or ploughs of the north rising to power on Judgment Day.

This brings us to Revelation 6, a chapter that offers full-blown heavenly expressions of the warnings signified in earlier visions. The chapter begins with four horsemen whose colours and attributes are variations on the autumn stories of Sagittarius, Orion, Libra, and Scorpio. Their southward appearance is well suited to a vision of martyrs rising from beneath a heavenly altar, or souls ascending from Ara. The riders usher in the darker period of the year, a 'little season of rest' about to turn into in a nightmare. Unless humans are faithful to God, the Noahic pact can come to naught and stars fall like figs blown by a hot sirocco wind hailing from the south. The lunisolar order can collapse as the celestial vault sutured by the Milky Way turns black as sackcloth and disappears like a scroll rolling up. If humans put faith in the heavenly luminaries in lieu of the white robes of the saints, God will cause star-gods to turn against their foolish worshippers: 'inhabitants of the earth' shall perish where they have sinned. 'Evil must be allowed to run its course and work its own destruction' (Caird 1966: 145). As in 1 Enoch,

Many of the chiefs of the stars shall make errors in respect to the orders given to them; they shall change their courses and functions and not appear during the seasons which have been prescribed for them. All the orders of the stars shall harden (in disposition) against the sinners and the conscience of those that dwell upon the earth. They (the stars) shall err against them (the sinners); and modify all their courses. Then they (the sinners) shall err and take them (the stars) to be gods. And evil things shall be multiplied upon them; and plagues shall come upon them so as to destroy all. (80: 6–8)

This is to say that, come the Day of Judgment, 'neither the joyful spheres of the circular zodiac, Aries, Taurus, and Gemini, nor those stars, regulating time, which appear with these in heaven, in which you, wretched one, have trusted much, will profit you' (Sibylline Oracles 13: 69–74).

Images of the End continue in Revelation 8 as the luminaries are silenced in heaven for half a year, echoing the great stillness that came before the primordial chaos. The first four trumpets sound the 'day of blowing,' in the seventh month of Tishri, the season of repentance and judgment. This is the time for Ara to tilt over the world like an altar or censer pouring coals and fire on the earth. John's southward, summer-to-winter vision of forthcoming events is reinforced by four woes modelled after the plagues of Egypt: the burning of vegetation, a mountain of fire thrown into the deep, a desert wormwood star dropped into rivers and springs, and a great darkness invading the sky. To these images of the sun falling to the south is added an eagle flying in 'midheaven,' the zenith of the sun (Beasley-Murray 1974: 159). The bird evokes the destructive powers of Aquila keeping company with Leo and the Serpent-Holder, signs of the hostile god of summer heat and winter darkness. As argued below, a scene involving a predatory fowl, a serpent, and a censer joining in the southern sky and spanning one-third of the universe can also take us back to ancient stories of the Water-Serpent, the Raven, and the Cup.

Like a lull before the storm, Revelation 7 offers a pause. The chapter reverts to the equinoctial blessings of John's throne-room vision, in anticipation of the glorious afterlife promised to followers of the Lamb. The elect receive protection from angels holding back the four winds of destruction, the Lord spreading his sky-tent or exodus shelter over the world, and a vernal Nebo-like angel rising to the east with the seal of the living God in his possession. The scene lays out a fourfold and twelvefold view of the universe, a lunisolar order ruled by the Passover Lamb and the Noahic pact. Words of sevenfold praise, palms in the hands of the saints, white robes washed in the blood of the Lamb, a list of tribes where Dan's name is deleted, springs of living water that counter the hunger and thirst suffered by the martyrs, all converge on manifestations of the spring and autumn equinoxes. As we shall see, the text paints in glowing colours the blessings of a New Jerusalem ruling over the world after the end of time.

Six Seals Opened (Rev. 6)

The Four Riders

Revelation 6 features four horses empowered to kill 'by the sword, by famine, by plague and wild beasts.' The first horse summoned by one of the four living creatures is coloured **white** and mounted by a rider holding a **bow**, receiving the victor's laurel **crown**, and going from victory to victory. One constellation of the southern sky fits the description: Sagittarius, with its arrow aimed at the Scorpion's heart. In it there is a crown called Corona Australis (the Southern Wreath, to Ptolemy) and the archer's bow. Cuneiform inscriptions designate this archer and centaur-god as the Giant King of War – hence, the fearsome Sumerian Nergal, a deity of the summer-to-winter sun, 'a formidable agent of death and pestilence, lord of the grave, and judge of those that die' (Langdon 1931: 135; see Jacobsen 1976: 227f.; Unger 1957: 417). The Second Book of Kings (17: 3) mentions this mythical figure elsewhere known as Light of the White Face. The stellar group was associated with the month of November/December and winds from the south or southwest. The white horse mentioned by Zechariah stood for the west (Charles 1920, 1: 156).

Boll (1914: 91) and Malina (1995: 125f.) argue that the first rider points to Leo, a constellation crowned with kingly attributes and rising in the company of the Bowstar (Canis). The month and year of Leo were apparently associated with 'a manifestation of wild animals' and 'multiple damage to fields.' But there is another formation in the sky, directly opposite the Archer, which represents a great god of war, a hunter and his bow, the autumn season, and the southwest. I am referring to the Giant Orion, cut in half by the celestial equator and standing south of the ecliptic, a character known to chase the Virgin Stars (Pleiades) to the west and the deep just before the heliacal rising of Sagittarius. To the Hebrews, Orion was the rebellious Kesil, who later became Gibbor the Giant. Gibbor was kindred spirit of the primeval giants born from the union of fallen angels and daughters of humans, bastards to whom Gabriel gave a sword to cause strife among them (1 Enoch 88: 2; see Charles 1920, 1: 165).

When seen as Orion, the first horseman becomes the second rider: a great **swordsman** mounted on a bright **red** horse, sent to 'take away peace from the earth and set people killing each other' (Rev. 6: 4). Stormy Orion was renowned for his mighty sword and a powerful right arm called Betelgeuse. In the eyes of Ptolemy, ruddiness was characteristic of this leading star, a colour evoking ideas of war and carnage. Zechariah connects the colour with the east, a direction that tallies with Orion's equinoctial location immediately below Taurus. According to Malina (1995: 122), however, ancient representations of Virgo offer a better parallel: like Hecate, the lady used to be seen as a sword-bearing figure that was generally peaceful but that brought about much violence when associated with thunder, an earthquake, or a darkened sun.

Be that as it may, both Virgo and Orion are closely connected to the wheat motif. As the place of rest of the Egyptian sun-god Osiris, Orion was titled Smati-Osiris, the barley-god. This brings us to the third seal and horseman summoned by the third animal. The horse is **black**, the colour of the hidden quarter of the world where the sun never shines (Zech. 6: 6). The rider holds a pair of **scales** evoking the scarcity of **corn and barley** and a concern for sparing **oil and wine** in difficult times. A voice is heard saying 'a ration of corn for a day's wages, and three rations of barley for a day's wages, but do not tamper with the oil or the wine' (Rev. 6: 6). In this scene, the barley-god turns into an agent of famine (Charles 1920, 1: 156). When calendrically transposed, the symbolism recalls the vision of a Messiah coming in the post-vintage season of autumn, a time of the year characterized by the scarcity of bread and the abundance of vintage (available at high costs; see Ford 1975: 107f.; Charles 1920, 1: 168; Farrer 1964: 100).

Given these connotations, the black horse would logically point to Libra, the Scales, Aratus's dim sign of the fall equinox (Boll 1914: 85ff.; Farrer 1964: 100; Malina 1995: 122f.). Spanning September and October, the Balance ushers in a period of darkness, days of wine making, ploughing, and sowing. It also brings back memories of wanderings in the wilderness. Boll relates this third rider to an old belief predicting famine for any year standing under the sign of Libra: 'the grain harvest will be bad but the olive and vine will yield plentifully' (see Beasley-Murray 1981: 133). A year in Libra portends a rise in price measurements affecting the grain harvest. As mentioned in an earlier chapter, the Balance was represented by the Hebrew letter *tau*. It conveyed the notion of the proper measuring of commodities but also time and seasons: 'For He has weighed the age in the balance, and with measures has measured the times, and by number has numbered the seasons: neither will He move nor stir things till the measure appointed be fulfilled' (4 Ezra 4: 36ff.). Revelation 6 uses this rule of proper measurement to remind us that the final resurrection will come in due time only, when the tally of those destined for martyrdom is completed (Rev. 6: 11; 1 Enoch 47).

The Balance can be converted into a scorpion or its claws, as in the writings of ancient Greeks. The substitution gives us the fourth horse, a deathly **pale** beast mounted by a rider called **Plague**, with **Hades** following at his heels. Scorpio's wind was located to the southwest. Situated between Libra and Sagittarius, the constellation was equated with the autumn equinox, which marked the decline of the sun towards the lower world. The chthonian imagery applies to John's fourth rider, a horseman called Plague and followed by Hades, *Sheol* in Hebrew – the subterranean abode where the dead are confined till Judgment Day. Concerning the latter duo, Malina reports a pairing of deities

... (e.g., already in the Canaanite tradition of Ugarit: Gupanu-and-Ugaru, the messengers of Ba'alu, traveling in pairs ... ; also Kotharu-and-Khasisu; Zizzu-and-Kamathu, and finally the personal attendants of Athiratu/Ashera, Qidshu-and-Amruru). In the religious traditions of the eastern Mediterranean, the god Muth (Ugaritic: Mot = Death) was born of Kronos in pre-historical times; 'the Phoenicians call him Death-and-Pluto' ... 'Pluto' and 'Hades' are the same, both being personifications of the cosmic Abyss at the southern edge of the orb of the earth ... John mentions Death-and-Hades also in 1: 18 and 20: 13–14. (1995: 123–4)

In the writings of Vettius Valens and Nechepo-Petosiris, the Scorpion is explicitly connected to Hades and the plague motif. Comets appearing in this constellation portended a plague of reptiles, insects, and locusts; so thought Pliny. Scorpions were associated with wild beasts as well, a motif made explicit at the end of the fourth seal (Ford 1975: 103). Finally, Scorpio's colour was brown, after Zechariah's sorrel horse heading south (Zech. 1: 8, 6: 2–7, 7: 8; Allen 1963: 364; Charles 1920, 1: 162f., 168). Another rendering of the word for sorrel is pale yellow, a hue that matches a southward sun weakening at autumn.

On the issue of colours, we know from Ptolemy (*Tetrabiblos* 2: 89f.) that Saturn, Jupiter, Mars, and Venus used to be assigned the attributes of blackness, whiteness, redness, and paleness or yellowness, respectively. Ancient texts show how colours, planets, zoomorphic constellations, winds, and cardinal directions were correlated in complex ways. The resulting typologies, however, were so variable as to preclude their systematic application to John's horsemen composition. There is ample evidence to confirm Malina's insightful notion that Revelation 6 *begs to be read* against the background of ancient Mediterranean predictions based on zodiacal twelve-year cycles known as the *dodekaeteris*, a widely practised divination system where consecutive years are ruled by successive zodiacal constellations (Malina 1995: 119–28). The first-century Treatise of Shem is a Jewish illustration of this particular formulation of ancient astrology. But the question as to whether the Leo–Virgo–Libra–Scorpio scenario is to be preferred over the Sagittarius–Orion–Libra–Scorpio interpretation can never be truly resolved. John's imagery is not sufficiently precise or explicit enough to permit a positive, unambiguous identification of astral codifications governing his text. This is not to say that comparative analyses of astromythology and the Apocalypse serve no purpose. After all the issue is not so much what astral code John adopted as to what reasons he had for *not making full use* of the contemporary astrological implications of his own imagery. While the symbols deployed by the prophet are an invitation to astrological speculation, students of Revelation should recognize that John had good reason not to accept his own invitation.

Four Woes Followed by Three

The four horsemen appear to be riding on the wings of Sagittarius (Leo?), Orion (Virgo?), Libra, and Scorpio. Together they cause winds of retribution to blow from the southwest, round about the dreaded days of the winepress, a period of ploughing and sowing. Unlike the horses of Zechariah 6 or the cherubs and winds of wrath of Revelation 4 and 7, John's four messengers of destruction do not proceed from the four corners of the earth or seasons of the year, as was thought by Zimmern. Rather, they all slide into the same place and 'clearly belong together' (Charles 1920, 1: 162–4). Instead of ruling over the entire world, they are given 'authority over **a quarter of the earth**,' to use John's words (Rev. 6: 8). The horsemen all slide into the same quarter of the year as well: the sun's descent suffered at fall.[1]

The autumn, southwest implications of John's four-rider scene are well suited to a vision received on the isle of Patmos, southwest of the Christian churches of Asia Minor. In its own way, this meridional imagery announces the fifth seal – martyrs and witnesses of God appearing beneath an **altar** in heaven (Charles 1920, 1: 173f.). This brings us to the stellar formation called the Altar, a southern asterism (Aratus 429) situated beneath Scorpio, at the bottom of the Milky Way. Ara is a reflection of the Jewish altar of burnt offering, a constellation that barely appears on the southern horizon, the lowest of all four quarters of the sky. Given its lowly position, the Altar is apt to conjoin themes of heavenly sacrifice, earthly martyrdom, and subterranean death. Martyred souls dwelling in the chambers of Sheol can hope to rise to glory like smoke ascending from Ara the Censer, towards the northerly throne sited in the highest heaven and reached via the Milky Way. In the words of Manilius (1: 755ff.), martyrs beneath the altar are like 'the souls of heroes, outstanding men deemed worthy of heaven, freed from the body and released from the globe of Earth.' These souls 'pass hither [through the Milky Way] and, dwelling in a heaven that is their own, live the infinite years of paradise and enjoy celestial bliss' (see Charles 1920, 1: 173; Boll 1914: 32f.). Deserving souls receive the same rewards as stars rising in heaven and the sun marching north, ascending to a new life granted at spring. Saintly catasterism is substituted for 'pagan' cults of solar emperors and the stardom of defunct Caesars translated to heaven.

The fifth seal ends with souls crying for their blood to be avenged by God. The martyrs receive the resurrection bodies, white robes or 'garments of light' (Ps. 104: 2; 1 Enoch 62: 16) they deserve. They are requested to **rest a little season** until after the fall of all tribulation saints. Charles (1920, 1: 187) assimilates this request to another story where the saints cannot sit on their thrones or receive their crowns till the Beloved has returned from his journey to the underworld. In calendrical terms, the 'little season of rest' evokes the darker period of the year, or the sun's *descensus ad inferos,* a journey preceding the sun-god and the paschal lamb resurrecting at spring.

Ancient conceptions of the heavenly vault sutured by the Milky Way can shed light on yet another seal, the sixth. Manilius's vivid portrayal of the firmament is worth quoting at length:

And just as the rainbow describes its arc through the clouds, even thus the white track marking the vault of heaven lies overhead; and it draws the gaze of mortals upwards, as they marvel at the strange glow through night's darkness and search, with mind of man, the cause of the divine. Perchance, they wonder, the firmament is seeking to split into separate segments; with the slackening of the framework cracks are opening and admit new light through a split in the ceiling: what would men not fear might befall them, when they behold the great firmament damaged, and hurt done to heaven strikes their eyes? Possibly the skies are coming together and the bases of two vaults meet and fasten the rims of celestial segments; out of the connection is formed a conspicuous scar marking a suture of the skies, and transformed by its dense structure into ethereal mist the compressed seam causes the foundations of high heaven to harden into a solid joint. (1: 710ff.)

The fears expressed by Manilius are made real in the sixth seal. When opened, the seal provokes a violent earthquake: 'the sun went as black as sackcloth; the moon turned red as blood all over, and the stars of the sky fell on to the earth like figs dropping from a fig tree when a high wind shakes it; the **sky disappeared like a scroll rolling up** and all the mountains and islands were shaken from their places' (Rev. 6: 12–14; emphasis added). The sky folds like 'a papyrus rent in two, whereupon the divided portions curl and form a roll on either side' (Charles 1920, 1: 181). The seam that joins the celestial vault comes apart, causing an earthquake, the darkening of sun and moon, and the downfall of stars. The scene amounts to a total breach of the Noahic pact, a prelude to the End of Time and music of the heavenly spheres.

The regularity of the heavenly bodies is not unshakable. 'When, then, the sun and moon and stars forsook this order, the end of the world was at hand' (Charles 1920, 1: 181). Men who worship false gods such as the planets, failing to view them as signs subserving the Lord who created all things, are given due warning: unless they cease idolizing the stars, they will throw the bodies of heaven back into chaos. They will upset the entire universe, for they and their idols are changing the 'order of nature' (see Ford 1975: 111). Woes caused by the sixth seal add up to a collapse of the lunisolar order and all measures of mediation between day and night, heaven and earth. Patterns of creation inscribed in the celestial writ are foreclosed with the seal of the Lord as heaven is forced to depart like a 'scroll when rolled.' Horns and mountains of worldly power are shaken by

Vision céleste et sixième sceau, Beatus, Gérone (975), fol. 131. Photo des Éditions Zodiaque, Abbaye de La Pierre Qui Vire, 89630 Saint Léger Vauban, France

winds of divine judgment. The apparently stable edifice of islands, mountains, and 'high places' located above the nether world caves in, forcing
people of all classes, seven of them, to bury themselves in caves and among
rocks.

The scene takes place in days of the declining sun-god, from the summer
solstice to the autumn. This is the time for **figs** to fall (July/August) and the
sun to travel south, setting in old age to the west, towards the darkness of
winter. We have seen that the four horses appearing under the first four
seals are under the same spell of a southwesterly fall. All is as if the horses
brought with them a hot sirocco wind hailing from the southern desert and
giving vent to God's wrath directed against mountains and rocks, the
earth's greenery, and all enemies of true faith. Stars are made to fall like
unripe figs blown by a gale coming from the lowest quarter of the earth.
The calamity reflects ancient notions of 'a heavenly tree with the stars as its
fruit and the sirocco which casts them to the ground' (Charles 1920, 1:
181n, 192n; Mounce 1977: 161; Isa. 34: 4).

These catastrophes are accompanied by the darkening of sun, suggesting
an eclipse of the leading sphere of heaven (Beasley-Murray 1974: 130; see
Mark 13: 24f.). The sun and the moon go into eclipse as the moon is at or
very near one of its two orbital nodes, crossing the apparent path of the
sun. These points of intersection have been marked for ages by the Head
and the Tail of the Dragon, which stand for the ascending and descending
nodes of the solar path, respectively. The draconic symbols originate from
serpent-like creatures of the sky such as Draco, which used to mark the
poles of the equator and the ecliptic. Mention should also be made of
Hydra, the Water-Snake extending along the equator, with its head and tail
pointing to the two equinoctial nodes. It is against this astral background
that an eclipse was understood as a dragon devouring the sun or the moon.
As in Job's lament over his birth, a great darkness in heaven ushers in the
appearance of a draconic beast called Leviathan.

Signs of an impending darkness can also be assigned to a particular
period of the year, the autumn. A sky going as **black as coarse sackcloth**
(Rev. 6: 12) results from the sun entering the sign of Scorpio escorted by
Libra and Sagittarius, with Orion chasing the Pleiades to the west. Similar
tropes apply to the Day of Judgment. Come the End of Time, the leading
stars and planets, both seven in number, will defect from the highest
heaven, towards the west at night and the south at autumn. A great darkness will fall on God's creation, sparing only those who have seen the light
stemming from the other side of the vault. Those who are faithful to the
Father of Lights shall put off their garments of flesh. In lieu of being cov-

ered with black sackcloth, they shall receive **white robes**, clothes of light worthy of immortal souls dwelling above the vault (Caird 1966: 86; Charles 1920, 1: 184, 186). These garments will replace luminaries of the natural order, lights that will no longer be needed in the messianic Jerusalem (Rev. 22: 23f.).

Luminaries as we know them are all the more perishable as humans tend to confound them with God. 'Inhabitants of the earth' who worship the lights of heaven in lieu of God shall perish together with their own heavenly idols falling on earth. Star-gods will be turned against their own worshippers. The sun and the moon will go into eclipse, and the sky will roll up and vanish. God will thus remove the temporal veil obstructing humans' grasp of the Everlasting Spirit dwelling above the vault (Rev. 20: 11). At the same time the Lord will bring down all the 'high places' exalted by 'men of pride' (Isa. 2: 12ff.). He will crush 'the armies of the sky' commanded by earthly emperors who seek to rise above, and therefore against, God. When treated on par with God, the natural order laid out in heaven is bound to fall apart, together with those who put their faith in it. 'The moon will hide her face, the sun be ashamed, for Yahweh Sabaoth will be king on Mount Zion, and his glory will shine in the presence of his elders' (Isa. 24: 21ff.).

The anti-Sabian message is fundamental to Revelation. But why should it be covered with convoluted imagery? Why is it that John evokes constellations and planets descending on humans instead of simply denouncing star-gods that are offensive to God and do not even exist? *Why should the Apocalypse not be allowed to explain its own symbolism, in conformity with most commentators' expectations of prophecies and visions that are truly 'revealing' of John's intentions and God's will* (Mounce 1977: 153; Prigent 1981: 109n, 111)? The answer to this question has already been sketched out. First, one central task of Revelation consists in demoting all celestial pantheons: stellar allies of worldly emperors are reduced to what they are – inferior spirits endowed with visible bodies and subserving either God or his enemies. By paying no attention to the cult of nature, John abolishes the rhetoric of star-gods dying and resurrecting in heaven. Second, powers vested in forces of heaven are recuperated by the Spirit manifesting his will through world history. By distorting stories and lessons of pagan mythology, transforming its protagonists into agents and heralds of Logos, the Seer co-opts the Sabian code into serving the rule of God. The code in question, however, imposes real constraints. Although freeing himself from overt expressions of astral religion, the prophet does not modify his sources at will, as some commentators suggest (so Mounce 1977: 152).

The Lull before the Storm (Rev. 7)

The worst has yet to come; six seals have been broken. The seventh must wait till the seal of the living God has been delivered, via the seventh chapter. Visions of future trials are thus held up in Revelation 7. But signs of darker days to come are scarcely forgotten; they are simply kept in abeyance for a while, before the last seal is opened. Once again the text performs a counter-march, towards imageries of Revelation 4–5 and related sounds of godly praise and churchly glory. The interlude serves an important narrative purpose. Memories of the throne-room vision played out in Revelation 7 set the scene for events of a radically new future: the final day when the faithful shall triumph against the forces of evil.

The intermission allows an angel ascending from the east to command angels of the four winds and corners of the earth not to blow over the land, the sea, or the trees, till twelve thousands from each of the twelve tribes be sealed on the foreheads with the name of the Almighty. The same mark of protection is granted to tribulation saints from all over the world, martyrs with palms of victory in their hands and robes made white in the blood of the Lamb. They all assemble in a scene of praise (sevenfold) and worship before and round about the throne and the Lamb, serving God day and night in his heavenly sanctuary. Martyrs are told that in the end they will suffer no more thirst, hunger, or sunheat. The One Sitting on the Throne shall spread his tent over them. The Lamb shall feed them and act as their shepherd, guiding them to springs of living water.

We have seen how the four horses of Revelation 6 evoked the sun declining towards darker days of the year, moving from the summer solstice to the autumn equinox and the winter spell. Logically, a pause in a story that speaks of the end of the world should produce a shift in time, towards the sun rising to the east at spring (Prigent 1981: 119). The shift is suited to the appearance of an otherworldly scribe dressed in white, empowered to seal the foreheads of the faithful with God's mark of protection, as in the Passover tradition and Ezekiel 9. Eastertime signals the triumph of Aries and God's eye reflected in the Star of the Tablet, *Aleph* in Hebrew. As already mentioned, the star in question is Aldebaran, a sign of the New Year identified with the Babylonian deity named Nebo, the god who used to reveal humans' fate written on the Tablets of Destiny.

The vernal spell ruled by Nebo and the paschal Lamb is a time of relative plenty and beneficial rains (Heb. *malqosh*), a season when the greenery of the earth comes back to life. To use John's imagery, this is a time when humans are exempted from **hunger and thirst**, afflictions typically experienced at summer, under the heat of the sun. The Lamb resurrecting at spring embodies the fountain of life, the inverted image of sweat and tears exuded by humans in pain. **Springs of living water** satisfy humans who thirst for God and the teachings of the Spirit (John 4: 14; Rev. 7: 17).

In Jewish thought God commonly manifests himself at dawn and at Eastertime, when the sun rises due east. In this direction lie the messianic 'Dayspring' or Morning Star, the gateway that God goes through as he enters the Holy Temple, and the origin of the wise men who followed the rising star of Jesus.[2] When observed at spring, the eastern horizon shows the seven planets heading north, with the morning sun passing through the seven Pleiades. These heptadic formations echo John's sevenfold doxology (Rev. 7: 12): 'Praise and glory and wisdom and thanksgiving and honor and power and strength to our God for ever and ever.' As praise is given to the Lord, malevolent forces of the four corners of the earth are kept in check (see 1 Enoch 74, 34: 3). The narrative wards off evil from the north, the dark quarter of the universe ruled by imitations of God's sevenfold perfection: for instance, Dan's tribe, a northerly people traditionally reproached for bringing Satan and the darkness of idolatry into the world.[3] Accordingly, the tribe is deleted from John's list. By contrast, the Saviour is said to spring from **Judah**, the first tribe listed in Revelation 7.

With the sweet influence of the Pleiades rising at spring comes the Noahic Covenant safeguarding the universe against another Flood. Angels hold back the waters of the Flood so that Noah and his family can enter the ark (1 Enoch 66: 1f.). The Noahic alliance or solar pact struck between God and humans mean that circles of stars (ecliptic, equatorial, circumpolar) formed around the Lord's throne can be counted on to regulate the march of time and the alternation of seasons. Similarly, John's angels standing at the four corners of the earth show restraint so that God's servants can be protected against his wrath. Moreover, Revelation 7 offers protection to concentric ranks of spirits standing around God's throne: the four angels, the twenty-four elders, the four living creatures, and martyrs adding up to the square of twelve tribes multiplied by ten times the square of ten (Rev. 7: 4–11; see Charles 1920, 1: 211; Farrer 1964: 106).

Although on a larger scale, the numerical rapport between tribesmen and the elders (144,000/24) corresponds to the sixfold ratio of elders to the four cherubic animals forming the innermost circle of heavenly spirits. Our six-winged creatures are surrounded by twenty-four elders encircled by a total offspring of 6,000 times their numbers. Four is twice multiplied by six, and then taken a thousandfold. This throng numerous as the stars of heaven (Gen. 15: 5) follows the same quadripartite and duodecimal principles that govern Judaic society, the lunisolar calendar, and basic themes of Babylonian cosmogony (1 Enoch 82; Charles 1920, 1: 203f.; Ford 1975: 125; Malina 1995: 121). The universe is ruled by numbers that are not of little concern to John or his readers, as Charles would have it (1920, 1: 200f.). Rather, John's *universal order*, a spiritual Israel formed without distinction of race, nation, tribe, or language, combines Judaic notions of tribal-remnant theology with measures of ancient astrology. As elsewhere in Revelation, signs of pagan cosmogonies and the Old Testament Israel are piled up and metaphorically adjusted to the twelves tribes of the New Jerusalem, the Church of Christ, and the Israel of God.[4]

The new order is led by a two-sided figure, a **Lamb** simultaneously weak and powerful. Great strength lies in demonstrations of meekness: the Lamb's position of leadership in the solar universe hinges on the spirit's vulnerability and willingness to accept his own downfall. The Good Shepherd accedes to sovereignty by accepting to be treated as lamb sent to the slaughter, a sheep dumb before its shearers (Isa. 53: 7). The imagery expresses the Christian principle of victory by sacrifice. On the astrological plane, it implies that the power vested in the equinoctial Ram stems from his offspring, a Passover Lamb slain for the sake of the faithful whose robes are whitened in the blood of the Saviour. The pouring of the **blood** of Christ and the martyrs empowers the seven-horned lamb to act wrathfully, causing a scene of vengeance and retribution performed at fall. Scarlet-coloured sinners and blood-like grapes shall be crushed at autumn, the season of Judgment (Gen. 49: 11; Isa. 1: 18). The paschal Lamb may deliver the flock and rise to glory, provided that plans of self-sacrifice and punitive retaliation be carried out – trials modelled after the downfall of the solar body moving from spring to summer and the autumn equinox.

Other chapters delve into the implications of a spring-to-autumn fall at great length. For the moment, John is primarily concerned with long-term steps needed to protect the faithful against the darkness of evil and the harshness of sombre days to come. These measures comprise the **seal on the forehead** of God's servants, a cruciform *tau* letter that stands for the autumn Scales, the rite of baptism (Prigent 1981: 120), and the teachings of dying with Christ. Signs of providence also include a check on **winds** blowing from the **four corners** of the earth. As Charles (1920, 1: 204) notes, the corners should not to be confused with the four quarters or cardinal points of the compass. In 1 Enoch (34, 76: 1–4), winds proceed from twelve portals, four of which are beneficial, while the other eight are noxious. 'For according to Jewish conceptions the winds that blew from the four quarters, i.e. due north, south, east, and west, were favorable winds, whereas those that came from the angles or corners ... were hurtful.' Given these coordinates, the corner winds evoke the solstices. Their diagonal location coincides with the morning and evening positions of the sun heading northeast and northwest at summer, southeast and southwest at winter (cf. Malina 1995: 166).

The **palm** leaves held in the hands of the followers of Christ (Rev. 7: 9) also serve to protect the faithful against the End of Time, everyone's last winter of discontent. Under favourable conditions, trees can stand for solid leaders and pillars of faith on earth (Ford 1975: 115f.). Instead of their star-like fruit being shaken down, good trees that grow tall can withstand hot winds of destruction and preserve the unity of heaven and the world below (the sea, the deep, the south, the wilderness), as in Revelation 7: 1. These comments apply particularly well to the palm tree, a motif that reinforces promises made to the faithful. Palm trees provide not only protection from the burning sun, but also roofing material and highly valued food (dates). They grow in perennial freshness in almost desert-like conditions, those suffered by Israel during the exodus. These properties account for the use of palm trees at the autumn Feast of Tabernacles, a ritual commemorating Israel's wanderings in the desert (Lev. 23: 40). It is on this sacred occasion that the Lord makes himself visible, **spreading his tent** or tabernacle over humans, sharing his Shekinah dwelling (Gr. *skenosei*) with his people, images echoed in Revelation 7: 16.[5] Isaiah (4: 6) spoke of this exodus shelter as a heavenly canopy giving 'shade by day from the heat, refuge and shelter from the storm and rain.'

As pointed out by Ford (1975: 128), the Feast of Tabernacles finds another echo in the **springs of living water** promised in Revelation 7. The wellspring ties in with the 'early rains' (Heb. *yoreh*) falling in the seedtime month of Tishri. It also tallies with the Light of God being substituted for the luminaries in heaven, lights that weaken at autumn. The substitution allows the redeemed to worship God in times of darkness.[6]

In Revelation 7, the Seer anticipates all of the blessings provided by the two equinoxes, moments of the year that govern the cyclical regeneration of a twelvefold universe. Having received these reassurances, John's readership can expect a great calm to come after the final storm of God's wrath. But trials have yet to be suffered. Revelation 7 creates no more than a calm before the storm, a glimpse of future blessings in the midst of chaos.

The Seventh Seal and the First Four Trumpets (Rev. 8)

The seventh seal can now be opened. The seal prepares us for the judgments of the seven trumpets that come in response to earlier prayers of the martyrs (Rev. 6: 10). The seal is broken, followed by half an hour of silence in heaven.

Next I saw seven trumpets being given to the seven angels who stand in the presence of God. A large quantity of incense was given to him to offer with the prayers of all the saints on the golden altar that stood in front of the throne; and so from the angel's hand the smoke of the incense went up in the presence of God and with it the prayers of the saints. Then the angel took the censer and filled it with the fire from the altar, which he then threw down on to the earth; immediately there came peals of thunder and flashes of lightning, and the earth shook. (Rev. 8: 2–5)

The **angel** holding the censer could be Michael, the guardian of Israel in times of tribulation. He is one of the principal mediators between God and humans, an archangel traditionally placed on the right hand side of God and qualified to officiate at rituals involving sacrificial and devotional offerings to God (Charles 1920, 1: 225f., 228; Ford 1975: 131). Being nameless, the spirit could also be assimilated to the Nebo-like character of Revelation 7, the angel appearing to the east with the seal of the living God in his possession.

While Nebo's chief assignment is performed at spring, he was also empowered to reveal the sombre fate of humans, a task reflected in the scribe's close association with the sun declining in the darker half of the year. In John's vision, this two-sided profile of Nebo gives way to two angelic characters appearing separately, before and after the seventh seal. While one angel transmits signs of divine protection, the other initiates God's final sentence by setting the world on fire (Rev. 7: 2f., 8: 3–5). Eschatological manifestations of high-ranking angels can go one of two ways: towards the renewal of life at spring, or the sufferings of judgment at autumn – hence, trials at the end of the year. Whether blissful or wrathful, the Great Day disclosed by the seventh seal of Revelation 7 belongs to the Lord showing himself in the equinoctial days of the month of Abib (seventh of the civil year) and Tishri (seventh of the sacred year).

Depending on the text, the implications of Tishri can be stressed at the expense of vernal Abib. The movement from the sixth to the seventh seal reflects this strategy. While Revelation 7 can be read against signs of paschal resurrection, the scene of the seventh seal followed by seven **trumpets** is slanted towards the 'day of blowing.' The latter falls on the seventh New Moon (Tishri) and denotes the Feast of Trumpets ushering in the second half of the sacred year (Farrer 1964: 112). Trumpet blasts are typically heard on the first day of the seventh month which brings about a season of repentance and judgment, a time when the Lord judges the material world and his moral creation.

In the levitical code Tishri 1 is called the first day of the seventh month and has no connexion with New Year. It is rather the first day of the great penitential season which culminates ten days after in the Day of Atonement (Ezek. xlv. 20). It is in fact the Day of Judgment. In the Talmud (*Rosh H.* 16a) the Mishnah declares that, while God judges the world at Passover in respect of produce, at Pentecost in respect of fruit, and at Tabernacles in respect of rains, Tishri 1 is the day when he judges all mankind. (Caird 1966: 109f.)

Horns (Heb. *shophar*, 'ram's horn') of the vernal ram could have been used to sound the day of resurrection – hence, God's victory, his accession to the throne of the greatest King, and the beginning of a new order. Instead of this, the horns are now blown to herald the conclusion of an era, the approach of a massive gathering, the onset of a great battle, and a summons to general repentance. As in the writings of Ptolemy (*Tetrabiblos* 2: 90–1), the horns can be turned into calamities sent from heaven: trumpet-shaped and bowl-shaped comets afflicting the earth. In accordance with Judaic tradition, trumpets announce a final exodus preceded by a new series of plagues (Beasley-Murray 1974: 152ff.).

The seventh seal opens on to the equinoctial sun falling below the celestial equator. The hour has come for the sun to be quietened for *half a year*, as it were. Accordingly, the seal brings about a period of **silence in heaven for about half an hour** (Rev. 8: 1). The text has reached a midpoint of no return – as if the seventh seal had been placed halfway between Alpha and Omega, Aleph and Tau, the Beginning and the End. The broken seal acts as an overture to the seven trumpet blasts and the unfolding of the second half of Daniel's seventieth week. As night is falling at the end of the first half of the year, trumpets sound the hour of darkness and mix with evocations of the semicentennial 'trumpet blast' called *yobel*, for 'Jubilee.'

The seventh seal and the half-hour silence that follows allow God to receive the incense of Israel and the suffering saints and to listen to their prayers aimed at vengeance (Rev. 6: 10; see Charles 1920, 1: 224). The silence thus initiates the Lord's 'great hour,' which the second Book of Esdras pictures in two parts: a return to the seven-day period of silence or stillness that existed at creation, followed by the destruction of everything that is corruptible (2 Esdras 6: 39, 7.29ff.; see Rissi 1966: 3–6). The pause evoked by the Seer is akin to the night or winter that precedes the re-emergence of light, or the daily sacrifice of incense-offering that comes before the 'dayspring.' John's half-hour silence is 'the first dark half of God's great eschatological hour, to be followed by the other half, the bright new creation' (Beasley-Murray 1974: 150; see Ford 1975: 136; Sweet 1990: 159). It brings about trials reminiscent of the primordial chaos and the Egyptian punishment, judgments of darkness followed by a bright new age.[7]

Alternatively, the silence may be the last hour of the night marking a transition to a new start.

In the previously cited *Testament of Adam* we read: 'The twelfth hour is the wait-ing for incense, and silence is imposed on all the ranks of fire and wind until all the priests burn incense to his divinity. And at that time all the heavenly powers are dis-missed' (1: 12, OTP). A like pause of silence occurs in the *Testament of Pseudo Apollonius of Tyana* where at the twelfth hour of the night 'the orders of the sky and the fiery orders pause' (CCAG VII, 179, 7–8). In these traditions, this pause takes place at the time of incense, just as in Rev. 8: 3. (Malina 1995: 136)

Other symbols deployed in Revelation 8 are indicative of a narrative moving in synchrony with a sun-god travelling south. The composition offers a southward look on the universe, a downward view directing our attention to Ara, the **altar** or **censer** sighted in the lowest sky. The seven-trumpet series begins here, on the site of the heavenly altar standing in front of the Lord's throne.[8] Charles (1920, 1: 27) notes that, from the end of the first century B.C.E., the souls of the redeemed were thought to ascend directly to heaven, as opposed to going first to Hades after death. This belief appears to be confirmed by images of prayers and a cloud of incense going up from the altar in Revelation 8. The scene, however, carries the leg-acy of an older eschatological tradition: the altar of the deceased is placed on the lowest horizon, near the southern entrance to the nether world, with the implication that the souls lying beneath it are still in Hades.

The connection between the constellation Ara, the Day of Judgment, and the trials of winter has already been discussed. Ara, also known as the Censer, used to be located within the claws or near the sting of autumn Scorpio. The claws were eventually separated from Ara and replaced by the Scales, a formation called the Fire by the Hindu astronomer Varaha Mihira (c. 500 C.E.), probably after the Greek altar motif. Scorpio rising to the southeast at dawn marks the beginning of Ara's upside-down climb to the southern sky, a movement observed throughout the winter. The scene of an altar tilted above the earth coincides with **fire** thrown from the sky, punishing all those 'inhabitants of the earth' who are at home in a world of moral darkness. The imagery tallies with John's first-trumpet vision of hail falling from heaven, a sight reminiscent of winter storms damaging crops in Palestine (Jude 12; see Ford 1975: 138).

The First Four Trumpets and the Soaring Eagle

The first four comet-like trumpets produce calamities affecting the earth, the sea, the rivers, and the sky. They bring about

- hail and fire, mixed with blood, dropped on the earth, burning a third of the earth, the trees, and the grass;
- a great mountain set on fire and dropped into the sea, turning a third of the sea into blood, killing a third of the living things, and destroying a third of the ships;
- a huge wormwood star in flames falling on a third of all rivers and springs, making them bitter and poisonous;
- the blasting of a third of the luminaries (sun, moon, stars), with their light going out for a third of the day and the same at night.

In accordance with the heavenly low altar scene, the reader's attention is now veered off the equinoctial east, round to the southern aspects of a sun falling in due season, from summer to winter. Signs of destruction associated with the 'deep south,' and therefore the abyss (Malina 1995: 143), comprise the scorching sun in Tammuz and the burning of vegetation. They include the destruction of water by a falling body bitter like the wormwood plant – hence, the absinthe growing in desert places (Heb. *midbar, negeb*; Gr. *notos*, 'the south') and apparently 'falling under the control of poisonous Scorpio' (Malina 1995: 140). Waters of the sea turning red as blood evoke in turn the effect of volcanic eruptions or a falling rain filled with particles of fine red sand blowing from the Sahara lowlands. As if to confirm their southern orientation, the trumpets cause disasters modelled on the plagues of the southern land of Egypt (Caird 1966: 113). Finally, the trumpets cause the sinking of a great mountain resembling the southern kingdom of Babylon, as pictured in the Sibylline Oracles (V: 158ff.; see Beasley-Murray 1974: 155ff.).

John's southern-oriented narrative is about to make lengthy references to scorpions, snakes, and birds of prey. Before we say more about the first four trumpets, mention should be made of the concluding imagery of Revelation 8: an **eagle** flying in the zenith, where the sun stands at midday, announcing the last three trumpets and related troubles (Rev. 8: 13; see also

Apocalypse of St John: The Angel of St John and the Seven Stars, twelfth century. PF2200, Arquivo Nacional da Torre do Tombo, Lisbon, Portugal; Giraudon/Art Resource, New York

14: 6, 19: 17). On the celestial plane, Ara and Scorpio are sighted in the immediate vicinity of Serpentarius and Aquila, the equatorial Serpent-Holder and the Eagle. While Pliny attributed 'much mortality by poisoning' to the Serpent-Holder, Aquila was the archetype of birds of ill omen. The eagle was a large, strong, flesh-eating bird that flew swiftly, soared high, nested in inaccessible rocks, sighted its prey at great distance, and fed her young on human blood (Deut. 28: 49; Job 39: 27–39; Prov. 23: 5). It tortured Prometheus by preying on his liver. As a constellation, it kept close ties with fearsome Scorpio. From the Jewish-Aramean Targum, we know that Aquila and Scorpio were ascribed by the Hebrews to Dan's tribe, from which the Serpent was destined to spring.

An eagle appearing in midheaven at night brings to mind the culmination of equatorial Aquila and the heliacal rising of the Pleiades in the train of Aries. The scene is a prelude to the creature swooping down on inhabitants of the earth, falling from the sky as the sun passes through Leo. This is the time of the year when the solar war-god (a lion-headed eagle in Sumero-Babylonian mythology) falls to the south, towards the desert, the place where the eagle brings the sun-clothed woman in Revelation 12. When reascending to the east at dawn, Aquila signals the disappearance of the Pleiades to the west and the triumph of darkness over light. In keeping with these summer and winter motions of Aquila, Leo, Scorpio, and the Serpent-Holder, *the eagle appearing in Revelation 8 brings about an immediate darkening of the sky and the onslaught of lion, scorpion, and snake-like beasts* attacking the earth (see the fifth trumpet). The parallel between the two scripts, the astrological and the eschatological, is striking.

Like the sun, the Eagle goes both ways: it soars high but then swoops low. As in Hosea 8, a swooping eagle accompanied by trumpet blasts acts as a harbinger of God's judgment and the conclusion of an age. The ambivalent attributes of the Eagle are verified in Langdon's discussion of its Babylonian counterpart, a commentary worth quoting at length:

The eagle, therefore, was the symbol of the Sun-god as the spring and morning sun, victorious over the powers of darkness and the underworld through which he passed nightly ... Like all Sun-gods, however, Ninurta was also a twin god, and hence one of the most common Sumerian names for him was 'god-Mash,' the twin god, expressing his two original aspects as god of the sun above and below the equator, the beneficent spring sun, and the hostile god of summer heat and winter's cold. It is true that to Nergal was latterly assigned the character of the hostile phases of the sun, and Ninurta received the propitious powers of that luminary, but he also retains in many minor aspects traces of the ancient duality. The two names of Mash are Umunlua and Umunesiga, apparently 'Lord who gives plenty' and 'Lord the cruel.' (1931: 115–16; see also 6off.)

While the bird-shaped Ninurta is associated with vernal storms and the pouring of spring rains, 'the subsiding of the flood and the lowering of the water table as the summer lengthens corresponds to Ninurta's being cast into the pit' (Jacobsen 1976: 133).

In Revelation 8, the aquiline motif leans heavily towards darker days of autumn and winter. As pointed out by Farrer (1964: 117), the bird brings to an end a series of cherubic emblems mapped on to the seasons (reversing the order of Rev. 4: 7): the estival Lion of Judah appearing in Revelation 5, the paschal lamb in Revelation 5 to 7, the watering angel in Revelation 8, and then the autumn eagle and scorpions in Revelation 8 and 9.

Riddles of Sevenness, Fourness, and Threeness

The **three** final woes announced by John's eagle are reminiscent of the three bright stars of Aquila (∂, β, γ) that form the eagle's head and that received many titles in ancient astrology. More important, the last woes are part of an overall division of the seven trumpets into four and three more, a scheme that is not as artificial as Charles claims. The first four epistles to Asia Minor and the four initial seals broken in Revelation 6 stood out against the entire heptadic series. What we have in both cases is a septenary rule broken into a quadripartite series, followed by a triad.

The progression entails a movement from higher to lower scales of time. The overall principle of sevenness runs across all calculations of the Hebrew calendar, from the weekly cycle to the full centennial period. It also presides over the comings and goings of the sun-led planets, the Pleiades, and the two Bears circling in heaven. When applied to the cosmos, the number four also comes with its own letters of nobility, but of a lower, yearly and subyearly order. It marks the completeness of the four seasons, the quarters of the earth, and the lunar periods in the monthly cycle. The number can be brought down to the lowest notches in time: hours in a watch held at night or in the daytime. As for ternary calculations, they come last and are of the lowest order. To the Chaldeans, the Egyptians, and the Greeks, the month was made up of three Decans comprising ten days each. Just as there are three points of the compass, the sun must visit each day (the east at dawn, the south at midday, the west at dusk), so the night can be divided into three watches. The number three is absent at higher levels of the Hebrew calendar.

Sevenfold movements proceeding from fourness to threeness suggest premonitory visions evolving from colder to hotter series of events – to the 'last hour' of human history. The end-result is a cumulative storage of narrative angst. As night is falling at autumn (in the month of Tishri), a trumpet sounds the hour of darkness. A period of darkness begins with the first four-hour watch – hence, four trumpets equaling **one-third** of the night. Correlatively, the quatuor of Revelation 8 sounds the downfall of a third part of God's material creation. One-third of all luminaries, the earth, the greenery, and the creatures of the water are destroyed by fire, drowned in a sea of blood and darkness, or wasted away because of a wormwood falling from heaven (Rev. 8: 7–12). The scene of the four trumpets is brought to a conclusion by a loud voice, a piercing screech, or brays of great harshness to come: three more woes have yet to fall on God's moral creation. In the Talmud, the first nighttime watch also ends with a cry identified as the brays of a hungry ass.

As with the half-hour silence, the fact that destruction should be limited to one-third of everything gives inhabitants of the earth an opportunity for repentance. If humans pay no heed to the warning, as will be the case, the subscript will store up wrath for the Day of Judgment (Ezek. 5: 1–5; Rom. 2: 5). Calamities will affect the entire world, including the elect. For those who are faithful, however, days of darkness will mean a new exodus. Trials of the End of Time will lead up to the scene of God delivering the martyrs, a prelude to the final darkness of the new Israel's pilgrimage to heaven on earth.

The Serpent, the Raven, and the Censer

Revelation 8 echoes the seasonal motions of the Serpent-Holder, Ara, Scorpio, and Aquila. But the chapter can also be read against the background of another astrological composition involving a serpent, a predatory bird, and a censer-like vessel of tribulations. All three formations can be seen joining in the southern sky, spanning one-third of the universe, and rising at dawn in the solstitial company of both Leo and a four-starred Bier followed by three stellar mourners. I am referring to *Hydra et Corvus et Crater*, or, as Ovid wrote, the Cup and the Raven riding on the Water-Snake. Hydra used to cover nearly one-third of the equatorial belt about 4,700 years ago. The constellation took about seven hours to cross the meridian. The snake's head and tail practically marked the equator from node to node and were associated with eclipses of solar and lunar bodies devoured by the dragon (Maunder 1923: 158, 198f.). The creature was sometimes represented with three heads and was worshipped at the time of the summer solstice. Ancient Euphratean astrologers knew it as the source of the fountains of the great deep and a representative of the dragon Tiamat. Because of its southern location, Hydra dominated one of the three Babylonian 'ways of heaven,' the lower Way of Ea. A comet appearing in this constellation signalled the spreading of poison over the world (Allen 1963: 247–9).

The effects of Hydra creep into Revelation 8: the darkening of luminaries in heaven, the falling of a mountain-like star, the poisoning of inland waters, and the limitation of all disasters to one-third of the material universe. In the tail of Hydra comes also the rise of summertime Leo followed by autumn Scorpio, mirror images of John's fifth-trumpet locusts endowed with scorpion stings and lion teeth. The notion that Hydra hides under the biblical serpent figure is verified in the scriptural expression of the 'one crossing like a bar,' a possible allusion to the Water-Snake stretching along the equatorial line (Maunder 1924: 203). As for the poison secreted by the serpent, it used to be equated with the animal's gall, a term also designating a plant bitter like the wormwood. Thus a poisonous wormwood star falling on earth suggests a heavenly snake pouring its bile over the world. As in Jeremiah (9: 15, 23: 15), mortals indulging in sin are fed with a mixture of wormwood and water of gall.

On Hydra's back, there is the Raven (Lat. *Corvus Corax*), a bird that fed on seed and fruit. The raven, however, was also a black-plumed predator, a carrion-eater, an unclean creature of evil portent that Greek and Roman myths associated with Hades (Prov. 30: 17; Isa. 34: 11; Luke 12: 24). The bird is like a vulture, another rendering of the Greek word *aetos* used by John – hence, an agent of doom hovering over corpses and associated with military invasions and trumpets sounding the alarm (Deut. 28: 49; Jer. 48: 40; Hos. 8: 1). When transposed in heaven, the raven becomes the Great Stormy Bird of the Desert, a seven-starred constellation fixed in the low southern sky, condemned to everlasting thirst by Hydra guarding the ten-starred cup of Crater. It was the struggle of the gods against the giants that sealed the bird's unfortunate fate. As for Crater, the Jews knew it as a cup and the Greeks as an earthen vessel to store blood-like wine. Caesius assimilated the constellation to the Cup of Christ's Passion. With John's seventh seal, however, the sacrificial cup is turned against enemies of the Lord. A vessel emptied of its sacrificial contents and poured over the world augurs ill for Babylon, a city that Jeremiah once described as a golden cup in the Lord's hand (Allen 1963: 179–84).

The eagle or vulture appearing after the fourth trumpet sounds like the hungry ass that brays at the end of the first four-hour watch of the night, an ass anciently associated with Cancer and the Raven. The raven and the ass appear together on a coin of Mindaon. In many ways, the Raven riding with the Cup on the tail of the Water-Snake inspires more fear than the

Eagle, the Altar, and the Serpent. Unlike the Eagle, Corvus cares not for its young and never acts as an agent of deliverance. It keeps company with Crater, a pale reflection of the southern vessel-shaped Ara. It escorts a treacherous snake freed from the grip of any god resembling the Serpent-Holder stepping on Scorpio, or Hercules on Draco. Given these attributes, no mercy is ever shown to the Raven. The bird must suffer everlasting thirst, a far cry from ancient legends of the eagle conquering the serpent and ascending to heaven, in search of the plant of life counteracting the poison of death (Kramer 1961: 126; Langdon 1931: 166–74). Finally, the contrast between the two stellar triads involves a real opposition. One team rises at the expense of the other: the heliacal rising of the Water-Snake followed by the Raven and the Cup presupposes the Eagle's fall to the west.

The Raven appears after Leo in the summer season when figs are ripe. It was known as the Fig Bird who returned to the god Apollo with Hydra in his claws. The legend tells of the carrion-bird's lie about his failure to fetch a cup of water and his loitering at a fig tree till the figs were ripe. The creature is thus apt to bring about Isaiah's or John's vision of heavenly stars falling on earth like figs cast to the wind.

Signs of the Raven converge on the sun's descent to the south, or the sun passing through Leo and preparing the way for Scorpio. These movements coincide with the rise of the seven stars of Ursa Major east of Polaris. As in Revelation 8, four woeful signs (the Bier) followed by three (the Mourners) herald a great darkness, an eclipse caused by seven Devils invading the vault of Heaven (Jacobsen 1976: 123; Langdon 1931: 106). Come the End of Time, the sacred seven (the sun-led planets with Aries, the Pleiades, and the Hyades in the forefront) shall be overthrown from the high north.

As the seven trumpets are blown, the heptadic principle is turned against God's material creation, with a measure (one-third) of restraint. The limitations placed on the seven woes, however, only add to the narrative anxiety storing up in the reader's imagination, towards the final delivery of John's apocalyptic crescendo. The afflictions sounded by the four initial blasts proceed by cosmographic progression, from the horizontal land/sea duality to the mediatory plane of rivers going down and spring waters rising to the earth. With the fourth trumpet the narrative springs up from inland waters to heaven. Next comes the eagle flying high overhead, a prelude to evil forces descending on inhabitants of the earth. As in the legend of Etana, the ascent of an eagle is followed by a deathly fall. In the long run, however, readers can count on a broad-winged bird standing in the sun to deliver the faithful from evil and eternal death (Exod. 19: 4; Deut. 32: 11; Rev. 12: 14; see Ford 1975: 140).

The Forgotten and Reasons to Forget

The Book of Revelation is clear about the prerequisites of an afterlife in the New Jerusalem: access to heaven is to be found through self-sacrifice. For those who enjoy the bright life, feasting without fasting, sins will fall on their heads. The sky and the whole of nature will recoil on worshippers of Nature. Revelation 8 reaffirms a basic rule of anagogical reasoning, of morality expressed through convoluted imagery: *humans shall perish where they have sinned*. The rule of proportional retribution – 'tit for tat punishment,' as Malina (1995: 191) puts it – implies that evil shall return with venom to cause its own destruction. A blazing mountain-star falling from heaven thus causes the 'day star' (Venus) and the 'high places' of Babylon to fall, polluting the sea and destroying her commercial empire.[9] 'When Babylon's star drops from the zenith, Babylon's ruin is at hand' (Caird 1966: 115). Come the End, evil humans shall be forced to eat worm-wood (Heb. *laanah*), the bitter fruit of idolatry, and the wrath of God (Deut. 29: 17f.; Jer. 9: 14f., 23: 15). Like Adam and Eve, Babylonian 'inhabitants of the earth' behave self-destructively, poisoning their own springs of life through self-idolatry.

The opposite fate awaits those who follow the sacrificial ways of the Son of Man. Power will be given to those who renounce it. The incense or prayers of the saints will turn into coals of fire falling from the heavenly altar, destroying their enemies dwelling on earth. The death of the faithful shall thus be avenged, and their souls shall benefit from the very things (water, winds, fire, the luminaries) that God uses to punish wicked humans.

The martyrs will triumph in the company of a slain Lamb acting as a powerful ram, a Morning Star rising to glory in heaven. Planets and stars will be harnessed to God and turned against Sabian enemies of the Lord. To paraphrase Isaiah (14: 12ff.), rulers of the earth and their heavenly allies who aspire to climb up to the heavens and set their throne on the Mount of Assembly (in the recesses of the north), above their rival the Most High, deserve to be hurled down into Sheol. When faced with these crimes, the Almighty retaliates through agents of destruction resembling his own enemies. His will is fulfilled through evil forces turned into subservient angels and spirits of retribution. The Lord has it in his power to harness all the figures of ancient astrology to his own logocentric rule.

When situated against the latter teachings, scriptural details such as the half-hour silence and the restriction of woes to a third part of God's material creation are not as arbitrary as they may seem. Actually, our analysis

Warning Angels and the Fall of Babylon (Apoc. 14: 6–13). Commentary on the
Apocalypse by Beatus de Liebana. Spain (Leon), *c. 950* CE. M.644, f.176v. The
Pierpont Morgan Library, New York; Art Resource, New York

departs from Beasley-Murray's approach (1974: 157f.), where 'it is the intent of the prophecies, not their detail that is important.' The implication of the exegete's argument is that cosmogonic imageries should not be taken too seriously, for 'astronomy is less important than the thing signified.' Likewise, Mounce (1977: 178) argues against pressing John's visions into well-defined patterns that produce a perfectly logical apocalypse, a contradiction in terms. Caird (1966: 106) is of the same view: a septiform pattern or some other chronological or arithmetic framework should not be imposed on the whole of Revelation.

In a sense, these scholars are right. Their conclusion concurs with John's position regarding naturalism: *star-gods and related idols should by all means be forgotten.* But the question, mine at least, is how to put into words rules applying to things that should be forgotten and silenced, if not through recollections of language? The answer to this riddle is to be found in the allusions, indiscretions, and insinuations of biblical symbolling. Through anagogical reasoning, dreamlike signs convey moral intents that are never spelled out or fully justified. Clarity of purpose would defeat the central task of Revelation, which is to downgrade the natural order of bodies and signs to mediations of an immaterial, atemporal God ruling the world 'from outside.' Stars are lowered to the status of material entities, poetic metaphors, agents, or sign-manifestations of God. If they are conscious beings, they are without clear astrological identity. From gods they become vaguely defined creatures either judged by the Lord or forming an anonymous array of warriors and hosts serving the Almighty in heaven.[10]

Creatures of heaven rebelling against the Creator and spreading the sins of astrology are at the origin of both the Fall and the Flood. From the sky came the fallen angels, who, in the manner of Satan 'the primeval serpent' (Lucifer, the Morning Star, Rev. 12: 9), committed the original sin of seducing the daughters of mortal humans, producing the unnatural offspring of giant demigods known as Nephilim (Heb. *naphal*, 'to fall'). From the moment they were created, these 'sons of God' violated the ruling order, a crime that resulted in the worldwide judgment of the Flood (Gen. 6; Num. 13: 33; see Ford 1975: 147). The fallen angels failed to keep their place in space, in the realm of the spirit, well above the earth and the carnal flesh. With this crime came also the discovery of astrology: the angels crossed cosmic boundaries by revealing the secrets of the sky to the women with whom they defiled themselves (Malina 1995: 150, 189). The angel Kokabel taught them 'the signs of the stars,' Shamshiel 'the signs of the sun,' and Shahriel 'the signs of the moon.' They 'made known the eternal mysteries which were kept in the sky, so that the experts among the sons of man should practice them' (1 Enoch 6, 8: 3–4, 9: 6–8). They did as if humans could be as knowledgeable as God, usurping his place on the other side of the vault. Oblivious to the will of God, the angels ignored not only everyone's place in space, but also their own place in time. They are the stars that 'have transgressed the commandments of God from the beginning of their rising because they did not arrive punctually' (1 Enoch 18: 14–16). The timing of the stars is an integral part of God's government of the universe, and heavenly beings that do not comply are bound to be dislodged from their privileged positions in the cosmos.

While an integral part of Revelation, the latter conversation with astrology is never spelled out by John. In the final analysis, the Book of Revelation thrives on the confusion, vagueness, and arbitrariness of detail. John's intent lies neither in signs that do the hiding, nor in signs that are actually hidden. The truth of Revelation lies rather *in the act and sign of hiding* – in the relationship between the said and the unsaid, the text and the countertext, the textual body and the spirit of the Verb.

8

The Last Three Trumpets

In Revelation 9, scorpion-tailed locust demons rise from the abyss, forming a cloud of smoke covering the sun and sky and hurting unsealed humans for a five-month period. The demons have golden crowns, human faces, lion teeth, and the wings of horses and chariots of destruction. In the analyses that follow, we shall see that these evil creatures hark back to the Babylonian Epic of Creation featuring the sun-god Marduk conquering the dragon of chaos and forming the canopy of heaven with the dragon's skin. On the astrological plane, the text will be shown to elaborate on the wrathful summer-to-winter aspect of Revelation 6 and 8. The story centres again on the sun-god passing through Leo and Scorpio and journeying through a five-month period of rains and darkness, a season of repentance and judgment, followed by his ascent above the equator and resurrection at spring. The season tallies with John's southeastern outlook on the future, as confirmed through evocations of locusts from the desert, sulphur from shores of the Dead Sea, a heavenly altar resembling Ara, and four angels stationed at the Euphrates. This imagery is accompanied by evocations of serpents, scorpions, lions, centaurs, and other beasts of the southern sky. Although subserving the dragon, all of these creatures are unleashed against followers of the Beast. Judgment is once more brought through self-destruction: God turns emissaries of the bottomless pit against their own master.

To the five-month motif John adds calculations of threeness and fourness. Two trumpets and two announcements combine with a four-horned altar and four angels of wrath to bring about three plagues and to destroy a third of humanity. Trials of Judgment Day follow the ternary and quaternary divisions of the night, or three watches of four hours each. The composition uses phases of the night to plot woes of the great darkness heralding the End of Time. To complete these calculations, John applies figures of tenness to the satanic army released under the sixth trumpet, a numeric symbology prefiguring the beastly statue of Revelation 13.1. The decimal figure goes back to the story of Dan's composite monument (Dan. 2), a bear-footed beast showing ten king-like toes and horns of worldly power rebelling against the Highest in Heaven.

Revelation 10 speaks of a scroll of bittersweet revelations to be digested by the Seer and prophecies to follow. As argued below, the roaring-lion and mighty-giant imagery of this chapter point again to the dog days of a midsummer sun heralded by the giant Orion, Nimrod in Hebrew mythology. This is the time for the solar god to rise and fall as it passes through Leo, heading for the darker days of winter. The estival implications of this material tally with the vision of a mighty sun-faced angel appearing south of the isle of Patmos, with his right foot in the (Red) sea and the left on the land (Egypt, Rome). The chapter allows the Lion of Judah and his followers to take full control over the solar imagery and prepare their attack against the evil forces portrayed in autumn colours in Revelation 9. The struggle over forces of the solar pact governing the universe is already fixed, in favour of the Father of Lights. The cosmos is forever governed by a godly lamb identified with the sun in Aries, a lion roaring at summer, or seven claps of thunder echoing the full planetary system and constellations of the circumpolar north. Mysteries of the world's future are revealed like a roll of astral secrets unfolding in heaven. Most of these secrets concern the firmament of the first creation, the fate of which is to disappear like a scroll rolling up at God's command.

Images of scrolls, scorpions, and five-month spells are also found in Ezekiel 2–7, chapters that inspired John's vision of the End. In these chapters, the Old Testament prophet performs several intriguing oracles. Among other things he mimics the siege of Jerusalem by lying on his left side for a period of 5 months (150 days) and then on the right for 40 days. We shall see that these numbers can be related to the story of the Flood in Genesis and the rainy season that lasts from October to the spring equinox. Much of this symbolism originates from the period of the year that begins with the early rains of autumn and that ends with the later rains falling before Easter. Other signs deployed in Ezekiel's pantomimes (iron pan, bread-dung, hair cut and scattered, scales) have calendrical or astromythical implications that reinforce the autumn aspect of the trials and tribulations of Judgment.

Our analysis of this chapter ends with a brief reading of the two witnesses and last trumpet woes of Revelation 11. The narrative alludes again to signs of the hot summer sun falling upon evil humans while passing through Leo, heading south, towards signs of final autumn tribulation affecting the lower portions of the cosmos, including the outer court of heaven. The discussion will revolve mostly around narrative images of God's measuring rod, fire burning the earth, waters locked up in the sky, and a period of trials lasting three and a half years – the darker half of the End of Time, the winter of everyone's discontent.

The Fifth and Sixth Trumpets (Rev. 9)

As the fifth trumpet blows, a star angel holding the key to the shaft leading to the Abyss descends from the sky and releases an army of locusts that form a cloud of smoke covering the sun and the sky. With stings in their scorpion-like tails, they are empowered to hurt the unsealed humans for a period of five months. The demonic locusts cannot satisfy the death-wish of humans tortured by them, nor can they harm any fields, crops, or trees. The locusts resemble horses armed for battle, with golden crowns on their heads. They have human faces, women's hair, lion teeth, a body-armour like an iron cuirass, and wings sounding like chariots and horses charging into battle. Their emperor is the angel of the Abyss, called Abaddon in Hebrew, Apollyon in Greek.

The sixth angel appears next and is accompanied by a voice coming from the four horns of the golden altar in front of God. The voice commands the angel to release the four angels chained up at the river Euphrates. The time has come for one-third of all humans to be destroyed by twice ten thousand times ten thousand riders wearing breastplates coloured flame, hyacinth blue, and sulphur yellow. The demons' horses have heads of lions, snakelike tails, and mouths spitting fire, smoke, and sulphur. Those who escape these plagues continue to worship devils and their inanimate, handmade idols of gold, silver, bronze, stone, and wood. They indulge in murder, witchcraft, fornication, and theft.

The **abyss** or deep pit (Heb. *tehom*) inhabited by the archetypal serpent denotes the chaos of waters which once covered the earth and were later confined to the shores of the earth. The abode of the damned and of enemies of God has been closed and sealed and is accessible through a shaft.[1] As Charles (1920, 1: 239) notes, the abyss evoked by John stands as 'the preliminary place of punishment of the fallen angels, of demons, of the Beast, and the false Prophet, and the prison for 1000 years of Satan.' As a fiery Sheol or Hades, this nether-world prison prefigures the hellish Gehenna, the 'lake of fire' where the wicked suffer the 'second death' through eternity. This sealike reservoir of limitless evil had its ana-

Cinquième trompette, Beatus, Gérone (975), fol. 156 v. Photo des Éditions
Zodiaque, Abbaye de La Pierre Qui Vire, 89630 Saint Léger Vauban, France

logue in heaven and will no longer exist in the future Jerusalem (Rev. 4: 6, 15: 2, 21: 1).

The monster-in-the-pit composition harks back to the Epic of Creation. The Babylonian story (Heidel 1951; Langdon 1931) is of Akkadian origin and centres on the defeat of the dragon of watery chaos at the hands of the sun-god Marduk, a battle between light and darkness from which the whole world sprang. Sumerian myths identify the male dragon as the storm-bird Zu or the serpent Mushussu subdued by the older sun-god Ninurta. In the Epic, both the bird and the serpent are subservient to Tiamat 'the bitter ocean,' a female sea-dragon, serpent, or flame-belching lion with wings, bird talons, and a body covered with scales. Similar Assyrian designs show Marduk conquering a serpent monster, a scorpion-man, or a winged lion (sometimes combined with an eagle head). The Sumerian Mushussu was represented with the body and head of a serpent, the forefeet of a lion, the hind legs of a predatory bird, a tail ending with a scorpion sting, a two-horned crown, and a lock of hair hanging behind the head. The creature inhabited the bitter waters of the salt sea – a-ab-ba in the old Sumerian idiom.

The story claims that the union of the salt sea (tiamtu, 'female bearer') and the underworld freshwater sea (apsu, 'male engenderer') put an end to the great void that came before the act of creation. From the admixture of these waters emerged the logos of life contrasting with the earlier chaos of darkness. Chaos used to be inhabited by monstrous followers of Tiamat, creatures with heads of dogs, goats, or bulls; fish tails; and the feet and bodies of hippocentaurs. Through the mingling of the waters of above and below, the gods of order were called into existence. These divinities banded together against Tiamat and her husband, Apsu, the freshwater sea that became the abode of Ea and the birthplace of Marduk, the sun-god and hero of the Epic.

Marduk was Janus-headed, four-eyed, and four-eared. He struggled against Tiamat, using among other things the Plant of Extinguishing Poison and the four winds created by Anu, father of all gods. Tiamat responded by summoning her dragon monsters, eleven in all, led by Kingu, to whom she had given the Tablets of Fate. Marduk made a net to enmesh the dragon, and called upon the four winds to prevent her escape. Once trapped, Tiamat was put to death by the raging Imhullu wind blowing through her mouth and into her belly. An arrow shot by the sun-god tore her belly and rent her heart. Beasts in the train of Tiamat attempted to flee but were ensnared and imprisoned in the lower world as gods of lower-sky constellations. Marduk took back the Tablets of Fate from Kingu's breast and then split the skull and severed the arteries of Tiamat. The north wind carried the creature's blood to a hidden place, possibly the Red Sea. The victorious sun-god proceeded to make the canopy of heaven, using half of the dragon's stretched-out skin; he used the other half to form the earth. He put the stellar watchmen in charge of the canopy and confined the rain-waters above the vault. He made Heaven for Anu, the Earth for Enlil, and fixed the subterranean freshwater sea for Ea.

The Babylonians identified Mushussu with the constellation Hydra, the Water-Snake. The Marduk-Tiamat conflict gave rise to winged representations of the monster appearing as a sphinx, a unicorn, a human-headed animal, or Pegasus the heavenly horse. Beasts in the train of Tiamat included Ugallu the Great Lion (Leo), Uridimmu the Gruesome-lion (Lupus), Giurtablili the Scorpion-man (Sagittarius), and Kulilu and Kusariqqu the Fish-men (Aquarius, Capricorn).

As elsewhere in Semitic lands, all things on earth were thought to have their counterparts in heaven. The fifth tablet of the Epic of Creation contained astrological tablet motifs such as Marduk stationed west of Leo, near Cancer, with his star above the head of Hydra before Leo. The sun-god was reputed to have fixed the year, the constellations in the sky, the easterly and westerly gates of the sun, the motions of the moon, the twelve zodiacal signs in the ecliptic way of Anu, the stellar decans (three per month), the equinoctial nodes, the southern stellar band of Ea, and the northern way of Enlil. Marduk's temple was located in the star of Babylon or the configuration Iku, a constellation that included Aries and Cetus. Iku marked the New Year and the related festivities and prayers recited in a northerly direction. The Epic of Creation was modelled on the story of the sun's victorious ascent above the equator and his resurrection at spring. The religious history of Summer, Akkad, and Babylonia is full of references to the cult of the dying sun-god Tammuz and hopes of life renewed at the vernal equinox.

In Revelation 9, the Seer witnesses a variant of the primordial conflict between sun-god and dragon. The struggle is between the sons of light and forces of darkness, a great battle reflected in visible formations and cyclical motions of the heavenly spheres. The rise of demonic locusts from the fiery lake of the nether world is expressly associated with the darkening of heaven and the luminaries and with **scorpion tails** torturing humans for a period of **five months**. The imagery can hardly fail to evoke the *five-month period it takes the sun to reach the vernal equinox after its passage through the late-October sign of Scorpio.* In the words of Martindale,

men-scorpions and men-horses ... were common in Babylonian imagery, and these

centaurs have scorpions' tails. In the Hellenistic Roman period, this composite figure had also passed to Egypt, and stood as a symbol for the zodiacal sign Sagittarius, or the archer ... It further appears that in hellenistic calendars locusts appear in
the zodiacal sign of the scorpion, and since from then to the end of the year there
are five months, it may be that St. John's 'five months', a reckoning found only here
in the Apocalypse, may imply that this 'plague' is to last to the end of the symbolic
year of the world's endurance. I add that Sagittarius was known as 'diadem-wearer',
and represented very often with long hair, and so in an ancient treatise are centaurs
described. (in Ford 1975: 152; see also Farrer 1964: 118; Boll 1914: 68f.)

In his discussion of Revelation 9, Malina (1995: 145) reaches the same
interpretive conclusion. He too considers that the five-month scorpion
imagery points to the 'final zodiac signs of the annual cycle. In other
words, the locusts are to afflict men till the end of the year.' He goes on to
cite a passage from Nechepso-Petosiris showing an explicit connection
between locust activity and the sun in Scorpio: should the sun 'be fully
eclipsed in Scorpio ... there will be many murders in Syria, Cicilia, and
Libya and there will be many locusts.'

The five-month, pain–affliction attribute of the scorpion-tailed locusts
could perhaps be explained as a reference to the life cycle of the winged
insect, which lasted from early spring to the end of the summer season.
Against this interpretation, readers should note that natural swarms of
locusts never last more than a few days, that the spring season marks the
triumph of life over death, and that the surface text precludes the summertime devastation of the earth's greenery. We are entering a period dominated not so much by the blazing heat of the estival solstice as by the forces
of darkness echoing the Flood, a rainy spell characterized by the 'waters
prevailing upon the earth an hundred and fifty days' (Gen. 7: 24). As in
Gehenna, the tortures inflicted by creepers moving in darkness are an integral part of a life cycle that can never be fully terminated, not even for those
who seek full death (Rev. 9: 6).

The connection between locusts, the cold season, and the Day of Judgment is made explicit in 1 Enoch 76, a passage where the insects come
down on the earth together with rain, frost, and snow. This combination of
zoological and calendrical motifs is confirmed in Joel's portrayal of a locust
army led by God at the end of time, an apocalyptic vision that inspired
John. Joel speaks of trumpets sounding the alarm and announcing the day
of Yahweh, the sun and moon growing dark, and the stars losing their brilliance. The scene includes expressions of gathering, mourning, fasting, and
repenting. The symbology belongs to the seventh month of Tishri, a time

of the year marked by the Feast of Trumpets, the Day of Atonement, and the Feast of Tabernacles. The month represents a time of holy convocations, expiation, and penitence heralding a five-month period of rain and darkness. Joel's vision ends with prayers answered by God tabernacling with his people. Locust plagues are then compensated by God, who 'has given you the autumn rain, since he is just, and has poured the rains down for you, *the autumn and spring rain as before.* The threshing floor will be full of grain, the vats overflow with wine and oil.'

The spatial implications of the scorpion–locust composition reinforce the calendrical underpinnings of Revelation 9. Like the sirocco wind, locust plagues invaded Israel from a south or southeasterly direction, or the arid wasteland that separates Palestine from the land of the Euphrates and the Tigris. Vast numbers of these insects rose with the wind in the morning, like a cloud obscuring the sun. Scorpions had in common with these locusts that they were associated with botanical death, the desert, and the south. Accordingly their celestial representation was fixed in the lowest sky, the *southern* quarter ruled by Scorpio. Like locusts, Scorpio can at best fly low. In short, John assimilates the sun entering the sign of southeastern Scorpio to the morning appearance of a locust cloud ushering in the darker half of the year.

Although cryptic (and for good reasons), John's language is unmistakably astrological. To paraphrase Charles (1920, 1: 253), this is a clear case of apocalyptic Judaism and Christianity depending on eschatological mythology. On the grounds that too many connections have to be assumed, Prigent (1981: 141–3) rejects the latter interpretation. This is surprising if we consider that only one connection is needed to complete John's locust composition. A metaphor overtly linking scorpions to Scorpio would suffice. But, given John's predilection for expressions of approximation and likeness, and the fit between his text and contemporary astromythology, it is understandable that John should not spell out the latter connection, if only allegorically. In restrospect, what needs to be explained is not the intended meaning of the scorpion motif as much as John's silence, his refusal to mention the 'nearly obvious' – the lunisolar and astral countertextuality of his imagery. Paradoxically, Prigent (1981: 148) provides us with an answer to this riddle: through his writing, John busies himself imposing a barrier between Christianity and the belief systems of the 'pagan' world.

Southern constellations in the vicinity of Scorpio have a direct bearing on John's vision of scorpion-tailed, centaur-shaped, long-haired, winged locusts with lions' teeth and golden crowns above their human faces.[2]

Readers are reminded that stellar reflections of bitter-sea Tiamat and the monsters in her train were fixed in the southern sky. They comprised the centaur, a mythical figure given to much wine and often appearing as a medicine man. The latter attributes may allude to Centaurus (between Hydra and the Southern Cross) rising at dawn in the post-vintage days of autumn, in the company of the Serpent-Holder identified as Aesculapius, god of healing (Ford 1975: 145). A kindred formation of the southern sky is Sagittarius, the horse-bodied Archer located not too far away from Scorpio, on the other side of the Altar (Manilius 5: 339–63). Ancient representations of these heavenly centaurs were endowed with lion heads and serpent tails, as in Egyptian art, or with powerful wings and scorpion tails, a Hellenistic and Egyptian 'remnant of an older Babylonian conception in which Sagittarius and neighboring Scorpio were fused.' The Scorpio-Man was in turn portrayed 'with a human torso, animal lower body, lion-footed and scorpion-tailed ... The bow carried by Scorpionman was said to derive from the fangs of Scorpio' (Malina 1995: 145). At the foot of Sagittarius stood a crown-shaped, seven-starred wreath that the creature apparently dropped while playing; so thought Hyginus.

The southern heaven is also the dwelling-place of the Water-Snake of the great deep, and the Raven, the 'stormy bird of the desert' riding on his mother Hydra. To these constellations could be added Lupus flying near Centaur, and Judah's southbound Leo[3] with a mane prolific as a woman's hair (as in the Egyptian Androsphinx sculptured with the head of adjacent Virgo). Other members of the draconic host, most of them either rainy or aquatic, include Capricorn, the fish-tailed, two-horned sea-goat, known anciently as the Southern Gate of the Sun and the Ocean Storm. Mention should be made of Aquarius, who controlled the heavenly Sea inhabited by Cetus (the Sea Monster), Delphinus (Leviathan to Caesius), and Pisces Australis. The sea motif points in turn to the River Eridanus (the Nile, the Euphrates, the Red Sea) ruled by Pisces, a constellation portrayed by Manilius as fish that 'fill the flood.' Finally, we have the two dogs, especially the greater one that used to be called the 'watch-dog of the lower heavens' and that contained the Egyptian god Sirius, the Dog Star worshipped as the Fair Star of the Waters and a midsummer sign of evil portent. All creatures mentioned above have in common that they swam in the sea either south of the ecliptic, in the company of the demonic Water-Snake, or south of the equator, pointing to darker days of the rainy season.

Manifestations of the sixth trumpet involve similar creatures: flame-belching horses with heads of lions and tails of snakes. The three plagues that come out of their mouths include the corrosive **sulphur** found on the desolate shores of the Dead Sea (or Sea of the East), a substance usually combined with storms of fire and lightning to express the wrath of God (Gen. 19: 24; Rev. 9: 17, 14: 10). John's vision thus maintains a southeasterly outlook on future history. Menacing forces hailing from the south and the equinoctial east are reinforced by the sound of an angelic voice emerging from an **altar** in heaven, a formation normally located east of the Ark and the Lord's Temple, but also in the southern sky, *right below autumn Scorpio*. The voice comes in response to the prayers and cry for vengeance heard from the martyrs and the altar in earlier scenes (Rev. 6: 9f., 8: 3f.).

The voice commands the sixth trumpeter to release the **four angels** chained up at the river **Euphrates**. As in the Epic of Creation, the Lord makes use of four angelic wings or winds to unleash hordes of fire-breathing demons resembling Leviathan, the sea-monster (Job 41). These spirits hark back to the four-corner angels holding back the winds of destruction in Revelation 7, save that they are agents of retribution stationed to the Babylonian east, on the other side of the Arabian desert. Although different, both angelic quaternions serve to express the will of God, whether it be through manifestations of providence or signs of wrath. Also, four spirits assigned to the river Euphrates could be stationed at the four corners of Babylonia, or even the whole world, provided that the Euphratean empire be made to stand for the *lowest, southernmost sphere* of heaven. I am referring to the celestial counterpart of the deep or nether Sea, or the complete circle of meridional constellations listed above. When read in this light, John's sixth-trumpet vision is reminiscent of the Deluge brought by 'angels of punishment who are prepared to come and let loose all the powers of the waters which are beneath in the earth' (1 Enoch 66: 1).

The Euphrates flew south and marked the *southeastern* limit of the Roman Empire. Beyond it throve the rival power of Parthia. Jews and Christians expected Ezekiel's Gog prophecy to be turned against the Roman Empire and the pagan world and to be fulfilled by Parthian and Median squadrons of horsemen wearing bright plate-armours (1 Enoch 56: 5; Ezek. 38, 39; Amos 7: 1). But the Euphrates extended to the north of Palestine as well. It rose in Armenia; passed through Assyria, Syria, Mesopotamia, and the city of Babylon; and then flew into the Persian Gulf. The river served as a natural boundary and the main axis of the Babylonian Empire. Sometimes referred to as 'the flood,' this great river of Asia conjured up visions of diluvian invasion – hence, 'floods of enemies' (Isa. 8: 5ff.) rising from the east and south, and marching in from the north, by way of Damascus.[4]

The same spatial coordinates apply to real **locusts** originating from the southeast and yet marching from the mythical north and the land of Gog.[5] The winged insects are reminiscent of the plague that devastated Egypt, a nation equated with the sea-dragon and inhabiting the southern land of the River Nile (Ps. 89: 9ff.; Isa. 30: 7, 51: 9f.; Ezek. 29: 3; see Maunder 1923: 20ff.). The swarms came from the arid east and were eventually thrown into the Red Sea, *southeast of Egypt*. Malevolent evocations of the high north and the deep south are thus brought together through manifestations of the deadliest enemy of God: Satan the dragon, Lord of the bottomless pit. In Revelation 9, however, these forces are turned against themselves, to the detriment of wicked followers of the Beast. In conformity with the rule of judgment by self-destruction, emissaries of the bottomless pit are turned against their own master. They join battle with God against Leviathan. The arch-enemy is Rahab, the great sea-dragon whose head God once smashed on the waters, reducing the monster to a subservient creature controlled by God (Ps. 74: 13; Isa. 51: 9; Rev. 12: 9). John calls this angel of the Abyss Abaddon and **Apollyon**, a name evoking the rule of destruction (Gr. *apollumi*, 'to destroy') and the universal graveyard of Sheol, Hades, and Death. The name also suggests an attack on the Roman emperors who regarded themselves as the incarnation of Apollo, a supreme deity represented by the locust symbol (Beasley-Murray 1974: 162f.).

This completes our discussion of the spatial, astral, and calendrical underpinnings of key images of Revelation 9: the abyss, the dark sky, the scorpion and snake tails, the horses, the lion teeth, the locusts and the five-month pain they inflict, their crowns, the golden altar, the burning sulphur, the idols, and the four Euphratean angels. Before we turn to Revelation 10, however, something should be said concerning figures of threeness, four-ness, and tenness appearing under the penultimate trumpet, the sixth. Calculations of threeness can be linked to ancient divisions of the night. The first four trumpets sounded the end of one of three watches, or the first watch of a great darkness falling on **one-third** of the material creation. The fifth and sixth trumpets followed by two angelic announcements mark the passage of another four-hour watch. As a result, one-third of the human race is killed by plagues involving hordes of demons (Rev. 9: 13, 18, 10: 1). Satanic creatures plaguing the life out of humans who are without God's seal bring the narrative closer than ever to the hour of midnight, the dreaded hour when the first-born of all unsealed households in Egypt were put to death (Exod. 11: 4).

In Jewish tradition, the two hours that come after midnight complete the second watch that ends with the bark of a dog. This is the animal that did not even bark at Israel while the first-born of Egypt were being killed

(Exod. 11: 7f.). The unclean animal heard at night has a direct bearing on our reading of Revelation 9. For one thing it is reputed to eat human flesh and blood and will be excluded from the kingdom of heaven, just like the fortune-tellers, fornicators, murderers, and idolaters they associate with.[6] Dogs are so cruel and vile as to evoke the hour of the beast and the reign of prostitution and harlotry, themes converging on the devil, the sea-monster, and the bottomless pit (Deut. 23: 18; Ps. 22: 20; Prov. 23: 27). On the astrological plane, dogs keep close company with southern Hydra: witness the two stellar Dogs and also Sirius, the Dog Star of the Nile worshipped by a pagan nation equated with Rahab (Ps. 87: 4). The animal barking at the end of the second watch is therefore a kindred spirit of the demons and the **three plagues** of Revelation 9. It too harks back to the primeval serpent and the nocturnal sea-monster dwelling in the lowest heaven, a three-headed Water-Snake stretched out below three signs of the zodiac: Cancer, Leo, and Virgo.

The idea that woes may proceed through the quaternary phases of the night finds another confirmation in the horns of the golden altar and the angels stationed at the Euphrates, both of which are four in number (Rev. 9: 13f.). We have seen how Ara, a constellation rising with autumn Scorpio to the east and the south, can be substituted for the altar of burnt incense usually placed east of the Temple. The voice that comes from this altar and commands that four angels be released from the Euphrates could belong to a cherub stationed at the eastern gate of the Lord's heavenly temple, as in Genesis 3 (v. 24) and Ezekiel 10 (v. 19). Alternatively, the voice could come from a **four-cornered altar** converted into a sacrificial deathbed, a Bier consisting of four stars ascending east of Polaris in the morning at summer. The heliacal rising of this Coffin, otherwise portrayed as the long-tailed She-Bear of the north, is a prelude to days of Atonement and Judgment. The estival scene coincides with Draco rising from the northern horizon, and Leo, the Dog Star and the Water-Snake re-emerging from below the eastern horizon.

In Revelation 9, animals harnessed to the northern Plough have gone wild, as it were. From seven oxen that are castrated yet productive they have turned into seven 'strong ones' (Heb. *abbir*, 'bull, horse') pulling coffins, wains, and chariots of destruction (Ps. 22: 12; Isa. 34: 7; Jer. 8: 16, 47: 3). Beasts of burden ploughing the earth at autumn have become emissaries of death: fearsome bulls, war horses, and also the lion, the king of predators with a mane prolific as a woman's hair. This hostile conversion of our *Septem Triones* team, from good to evil, accounts for the number of demons evoked by John, a figure harking back to Daniel's description of kingdoms on earth. In John's vision, the horsemen riding on the backs of the beasts are **twice ten thousand times ten thousand**. Although the figure may be simply idiomatic, it can also prefigure a seven-headed, bear-footed beast walking on four legs, a creature marching on twice the decimal number of kinglike toes and horns assigned to Daniel's composite statue. The toes and horns are worldly kingdoms to be destroyed at the End of Time (Dan. 2: 41f.; Rev. 13: 1). John's narrative will soon deploy other signs that confirm this interpretation of the numerical scheme appearing under the sixth trumpet. For the moment we turn to the conversion of our seven oxen into a roaring lion and the seven thunders heard in its train (Charles 1920, 1: 261).

Eating the Small Scroll (Rev. 10)

Now that the six trumpets have been sounded, a mighty angel can make his appearance, in a manner that resembles Gabriel but also the wrathful Lamb, Christ, the Lion of the tribe of Judah, the Root of David (see Dan. 8: 16, 9: 21, 12: 7). The angel descends from heaven, wrapped in a cloud, with a rainbow over his head, a face like the sun, legs as pillars of fire, his right foot in the sea, and the other on the land. The Seer has returned to earth and hears the angel shouting as a roaring lion, seven thunderclaps uttering secret words, and a heavenly voice telling the prophet not to put them in writing. The angel lifts his right hand to heaven and swears by the everlasting Creator of heaven, earth, and sea that the mystery and secret intention of God shall not be delayed any longer and shall be fulfilled at the sound of the seventh trumpet. Finally, the prophet is told to take the unsealed book or small scroll (*biblaridion*) out of the angel's hand and to eat it up, which he does. The effect is one of sweetness to the mouth but bitterness to the belly. The Seer also receives a command to continue prophesying, this time about all parts of the world.

In lieu of being foretold through a direct vision, things to come are written in the scroll. According to Charles (1920, 1: 257f.), the scene acts as a prelude to the first part of Revelation 11, which consists in a short proleptic digression about the two witnesses of the true Lord under the future reign of the Beast in Jerusalem. Narrative logic would be sacrificed for the nonce; continuity is broken so as to briefly announce the future Jerusalem of Revelation 11, a vision that is so abridged as to be practically unintelligible. By contrast, Mounce (1977: 205) views the intermission as a literary device that allows John to instruct the Church regarding its role and destiny during the final period of world history, which is to bear witness to Christ till her last breath (Beasley-Murray 1974: 168). L. Morris (1983: 136) adds that the prelude serves the same function as the interlude between the sixth and the seventh seals: 'In both cases the effect is to set off the seventh visitation as particularly important. We are all keyed up for the climax but it does not come. We are kept in suspense.'

Prospective accounts of the scroll scene can be supplemented by a retrospective rendering of Revelation 10. Our reading of the fifth and sixth trumpets centred on the autumnal, southbound implications of scorpion-tailed demons emerging from the deep. Signs of the fall equinox were shown to herald the winter season, a spell accompanied by allusions to the dog days of a midsummer sun falling as it passes through Leo. The **roaring lion** figure appearing in Revelation 10 reinforces the imagery of a solar downfall occurring under Leo. The narrative is thus shifting to the earlier moment of the estival solstice, when the sun's descent begins. But the point of this flashback is to allow God and his spirits to recover full control over the solar imagery, at the expense of evil forces ruling over the darkness of winter. Logically, godly forces must ascend to the sky before they can be brought down against enemies of the Lord. As with Jesus on the Mount of Transfiguration (Matt. 17: 2), they must attain climactic heights of the summer sun if they are to **come down** on evil forces risen against the Most High.

The antagonism between the Lamb and the Beast consists in a struggle over forces of the solar pact governing the universe. In Revelation 10, God wins the battle. An angel of God comes down from heaven, with a face resembling the sun, legs of fire, and a voice powerful as a lion's roar echoed by seven thunderclaps. The imagery suggests the sun in fiery Leo leading the seven planets (Boll 1914: 22). The combination of sun and cloud naturally produces a rainbow, an effect that confirms the great Noahic pact by virtue of its ability to conjoin heaven and earth and mix masses of light and water in heaven. Humans are thus protected against another Flood, a great darkness emerging from the deep to destroy all flesh (Gen. 9: 13f.; Eccles. 43: 11f.; Ezek. 1: 28). Pacts, however, are always two-sided: they can create unity when respected, but they can also be broken. The same two-sided principle rules over the angel's right hand and the scroll it holds. Just as words of revelation can taste sweet and yet be bitter when swallowed, so the raising of the right arm can denote either the protection obtained from a sacred oath (taken before a judgment seat and attested by *seven* witnesses or animals sacrificed) or threats of the accusing hand pointing at the guilty (Deut. 32: 40; Sweet 1990: 178).

Ancient attributes of Leo implied a similar paradox. Since it marked the highest and the hottest manifestation of the sun in heaven, Leo stood for the House of the Sun (Lat. *Domicilium Solis*) and was an emblem of fire and heat. We know from Pliny's first-century writings that the Egyptians worshipped this zodiacal creature whose heliacal ascent coincided with the rise of the great River Nile, marking a critical moment in the yearly cycle. Its strategic position right above the Water-Snake is reflected on the planisphere of Denderah, where the constellation is shown standing on an outstretched serpent. It is also echoed in John's glorification of the Lion of Judah, the leading tribe of Israel whose heir is called upon to overpower the primeval serpent (Rev. 5: 5, 7: 5).

But there was a retributive side to Leo's character. Even when portrayed in a divine light, the creature possessed destructive powers resembling those of his demonic foes. The scorching heat of Leo was an integral part of the death story of a green earth withering at summer. With it came the decline of the sun-god, a downward movement equated with *one of two things:* either a celestial body descending on creatures of the earth, or the demise of the solar sphere heading south. The latter scenario suggests the sacrificial fall of a deity subjected to a life cycle implicating the Creator and his creation alike. In the end, however, both scenarios have similar effects; a 'lion in fire' implies the downfall of the principal luminary of heaven and the green life it feeds. A scene of this sort can be made worse with sounds of thunder; when appearing in conjunction with the sun in Leo, thunder announces sedition and death. John's conversion of the sun-led Seven into bursts of thunder does not bode well.

The imagery of Revelation 10 is all the more unsettling as it may associate the Lion with the seven beasts of the circumpolar sky (Ursa Major, Ursa Minor), animals that can upset peace in the highest heavens. This astral lion–bear connection is made evident in the sky, with the Lesser Lion taking its place between the She-Bear and Leo. In Euphratean astronomy, Leo was called the Shining Disc, which precedes Bel, a patron god closely related to the Plough Oxen of the north (Allen 1963: 253). The same connection is confirmed in several passages of the Scriptures where the two animals appear together. Finally, the verb used by John to denote the roaring of lions (Gr. *mukaoami*) applies to the mooing of cattle and the bellowing of oxen (Mounce 1977: 208).

The zodiacal lion and the northern bear share something else that puts them in a class analogous with the primeval serpent and the great dragon: tails drawn out of proportion, even when absent from the animal's natural anatomy. A large appendage extending from the trunk can easily connote potency beyond measure, or Eros let loose. When freed from the exigencies of sacrifice, long tails will be deployed at the peril of the living flesh. The moral of a powerful body tailed by its own evil image applies to Leo and its tail star, known as Deneb, a luminary diametrically opposed to Regulus in position but also in character: unlike the royal 'heart of the lion,' Deneb was thought to portend misfortune and disgrace.

The bittersweet-scroll scene betrays a meridional outlook on the world, a solar body at the height of its estival power, yet falling to the south. Revelation 10 contains several details that are congruent with this interpretation. They include the angelic **pillars of fire** which once accompanied the people of Israel into the wilderness, under the scorching sun of the desert (Exod. 14: 19, 24). There is also the descent of both the Seer and the light-bearing angel to earth, a movement that ties in with motions of the estival sun (Charles 1920, 1: 258, 262). More important, there is the intriguing imagery of the **right leg in the sea and the left on the land**. John's vision of an angel with a scroll in his hand is to be read against the background of the prophet's ministry among the seven churches of Asia and his exile on the shores of the isle of Patmos (Beasley-Murray 1974: 169). The prophet's concern with the fate of Jerusalem and the rise of demons held back at the river Euphrates implies that he is looking south of Patmos for signs of the final hour and the End of Time, signs conveyed by the angelic likeness of the *sun in Leo*. Logically, a sun-like spirit looking at John from his midday position south of the Aegean should be able to put his right foot in the Great Sea (or the Red Sea) and his left foot on the land of Egypt or Rome. In his own way, John's solarized angel resembles the sea-serpent Lahmu, a lower world 'calamity' appearing in the Babylonian Epic of Creation with his left foot treading the earth (Langdon 1931: 291). The direction which the sun is now heading for, west at night and south at winter, suggests that the dualities of light and darkness, heaven and earth, land and sea are not about to be resolved.

The southern, summertime aspect of Revelation 10 is reinforced by the **mighty giant** trope applied to the angel standing astride the land and the sea. As noted by Beasley-Murray (1974: 170), John's angel can be likened to Gabriel, whose name is related to the Hebrew word *gibbor*, 'a mighty man.' The same Hebrew name was attributed to Orion, Nimrod in Hebrew mythology and Gilgamish to the Babylonians. As already mentioned, Gilgamish was the hunter who brought Taurus down (producing the northern Thigh formation) and rebelled against Jehovah, a crime that caused him to be bound to the sky under Orion's name. Armed with a sword, Orion was a kindred spirit of the primeval giants to whom Gabriel had given a sword to cause strife among humans. The stellar giant was cut in half by the celestial equator and stood south of the ecliptic. He appears before Sirius, on the opposite side from Scorpio and the Serpent-Holder, between Taurus and Leo. When rising in the morning, Orion announces the dog days and heliacal rise of summertime Sirius, eventually giving way to an evening appearance associated with the dreaded storms of winter. Given these calendrical coordinates, our 'inconstant' giant of the sky acted as a substitute for the summertime Tammuz and stood for the Hebrew *Kesil* or *Kislev*, the stormy month of November/December. All in all, God's control over solar images means that the falling motions of Revelation 10 can be assigned to Orion and the Lion of Judah coming down on forces of evil.

Catastrophes to follow will reach the same proportions as those of 'the sky disappearing like a scroll rolling up' (Rev. 6: 14). Paradoxically, the opening of the scroll in Revelation 10: 2 implies the *foreclosure* of the celestial Writ and former laws of the universe governed by the sun-led Seven. The foreclosure is likely to last for a while, till the world is reconstructed anew. The firmament viewed as 'what is spread out,' after the Babylonian image of the skin of Tiamat used by Marduk to construct the vault of heaven, is on the point of being transformed by God's second Act of Creation. Readers are about to witness a new *scroll unrolled like an unskinned Serpent still alive* – a roll of secrets deployed like events unfolding in the sky (Mounce 1977: 212).

Scrolls, Scorpions, and Five-Month Spell in Ezekiel (Ezek. 2–7)

John's fifth and six trumpets speak of four heavenly creatures, scorpions, Babylonian invaders, a bittersweet scroll, and a five-month spell, all of which invite comparison with the Old Testament visions of Ezekiel. The comparison is all the more interesting as the summer-to-winter orientation of Revelation 9–10 is amply confirmed in Ezekiel 2. This is where the prophet falls before the Lord only to be entered by the celestial spirit, put back on his feet, receive knowledge, and 'see the light.'

He said, 'Son of man, I am sending you to the Israelites, to the rebels who have turned against me [to Ezekiel's exiled countrymen living beside the river Chebar, vv. 11, 15]. Till now they and their ancestors have been in revolt against me. The sons are defiant and obstinate; I am sending you to say, "The Lord Yahweh says this." Whether they listen or not, this set of rebels shall know there is a prophet among them. And you, son of man, do not be afraid of them, do not be afraid when they say, *"There are thorns all around you and scorpions under you."* (Ezek. 2: 1–6; emphasis added)

Ezekiel faces the prospect of dwelling in a land of thorns and **scorpions** crawling beneath him. The prophet or Son of Man approaches a desolate land as he rises in the company of a scorching sun at the height of its summer power (Rev. 1: 1), moving closer than ever to the 'hidden' quarter of heavens, the darker north. The scene coincides with the fall of Scorpio sinking below the horizon just before the heliacal rise of Orion and the sun in Tammuz (mentioned in Ezekiel 8). The arachnid dwelling in southern areas of both the earth and the sky reminds human beings of the paradox of a summer sun at the pinnacle of its flight yet journeying through a world of excessive heat and growing darkness. The scorpion inspires fear as it evokes a land of heat and desolation and the sun-god declining after the summer solstice and the autumn equinox.

The light seen by Ezekiel brings sweet knowledge (Ezek. 3: 3; see Rev. 10: 10) transmitted through a roll of writing. But the light also conveys the heat and bitterness of words of judgment pronounced by God against sinful Israel. Ezekiel eats the scroll and acquires a new tongue, a prophetic voice possessed by the Verb. The prophet is told that God will make him as defiant, obstinate, or hard-headed as the Israelite rebels (Ezek. 3: 7). The expression used here is 'a harlot's brow' or 'hard of forehead' (Zimmerli 1979: 138; Greenberg 1983: 69). It suggests a pushing ox or ram (Cooke 1960: 39), animals that mark the vernal equinox and that are diametrically opposed to the Scorpion figure standing for the rebels (Ezek. 2: 6). The prophet is then taken up by the spirit at the sound of a 'tumultuous shouting' and the noise of the wheels and wings of the ox-footed cherubs. Ezekiel goes to Tel Abib, the dwelling-place of the rebellious exiles beside the river Chebar. He stays there for seven days and is appointed by God as sentry to the House of Israel.

The prophet's flight to Tel Abib implies an upward–downward paradox. On the one hand, the Lord, the House of Israel, and her prophet have departed from Jerusalem and risen to the country of Chaldea, a foreign land located east of Palestine and typically reached by way of north. This occurs at a time of the year when both the sun in Tammuz and the Chariot of David or 'wain-like bear' are rising to the northeast at dawn. In keeping with these movements in space, Ezekiel is driven to Tel Abib, a mount situated to the northeast of Nippur and the nearest centre of sun-worship along the river Chebar. Cooke points out that Tel Abib is the Hebrew form of a Babylonian word denoting 'the hill of the storm-flood,' a common designation for a mound covering an ancient city or a sandhill produced by the action of wind and water (Cooke 1960: 42–3; see Wevers 1969: 51; Zimmerli 1979: 139; Greenberg 1983: 71). On the other hand, an ascent performed under the sign of Tammuz is weighed down by forces of gravity. First Ezekiel is made to 'sit' among exiles beside waters of the low-land river, spending a week there, as if he were suffering from a state of depression (Ezek. 3: 15). He then rises to small heights only, that is, a sandhill or mound in the valley, in 'the wide plain of Babylonia, with mountains in the distance' (Cooke 1960: 46). The Son of Man has not really left the lowlands and banks of Chebar and can hardly be said to have risen above his fellow men. Further narrative conditions have to be met for the prophet to be turned into a true watchman standing on the walls and over the House of Israel.

While in Tel Abib, Ezekiel is commanded to get up and go out into the valley. He does as he is told and prostrates himself before the glory of Yah-weh, which enters him and causes him to stand up. The spirit orders him to go shut himself alone in his house, away from rebels in exile, and then to lie down, bear the sins of his people, and perform a prophetic simulation of Israel's sufferings under the siege of Jerusalem. The tension between motions of rising and falling is not easily resolved. The exiled prophet has yet to find a way of both joining and rising above a fallen people. After prostrating himself, the prophet stands up, yet he heads in the direction of the lower plain, and then secludes himself in his house and **lies down**, after the manner of Israel falling apart under Babylonian rule.

Why should the prophet be made to move upward and downward almost simultaneously? The answer to this riddle lies in Ezekiel's dual task. The rise of a Babylonian enemy to the northeast weighs him down, in anticipation of the sufferings that will befall the House of Israel (Greenberg 1983: 125–7). The Son of Man, however, has in common with enemies of the chosen people – Chaldea and the Babylonian sun-god Tammuz – that he must serve as an instrument of God's wrath against idolatrous Israel. He must therefore be allowed to rise up to this vengeful occasion and mount up a decisive offensive against sanctuaries, incense altars and idols situated on mountains and **high places** of cultic malpractice (Ezek. 6: 3ff., 16: 16, 18: 6). The sites in question, those previously condemned by Josiah, involve 'sun-images' and colourful tents resembling the celestial vault that shelters the many star-gods of pagan cults (Isa. 40: 22; see Zimmerli 1979: 186).

God orders Ezekiel to perform a ritualized siege of Jerusalem within his house, a prefigurative scene followed by prophecies directed against the mountains of Israel. The prophet mimics the siege of Jerusalem (Ezek. 4: 1–3, 7, 5: 5–10) and lies bound for 190 days, first on the left side and then on his right (40 days), gestures evoking the exile of Israel and Judah, respectively (4: 5–8). He then eats food that is coarse, unclean, and scanty, a ritual signifying scarcity during the siege and pollution during exile (4: 9–17). Finally, he shaves his head and beard and burns or scatters the hair, thereby simulating the destruction of the ungodly, their dispersion, and judgment at the hand of God (5: 1–4, 11–16).

The siege enacted in Ezekiel 4 involves the building of trenches, mounts, battering-rams, and camps. The Seer also makes use of an intriguing **iron pan** acting as an impenetrable wall placed between the prophet and the city (Ezek. 4: 1–3). Signs of an imminent attack originating from Chaldea are placed under the aegis of an even more destructive agent: the sun Tammuz ascending to the northeast of Palestine and heading southeast, towards the wilderness of Arabian plains, the desert that lies like a hot 'pan' or 'blazing caldron' between Judah and Chaldea. Just as fiery arrows are thrown above the ramparts of a besieged city, so too invaders of Israel must rise above the flat, pan-like plains or caldron of the Arabian desert. Fiery arrows and swords of famine and desolation are prophetically drawn from the latter direction, creating an empty wasteland 'from the desert to Riblah' (in Syria on the Orontes), from the south of Palestine to the northernmost point of the country (6: 14). Because of her infidelity, Jerusalem is to fall at the hands of Chaldean invaders. Israel is to be dispersed and perish by fire, sword, famine, and plague, with Jerusalem being reduced to a Babylonian brick made of clay dried in the sun of Tammuz and covered with a map of Jerusalem (4: 1; see Zimmerli 1979: 161; Greenberg 1983: 103).

The iron pan points to a land of burning heat, the outcome and origin of an invasion mounted from Chaldea and the desolate south. The cooking utensil is all the more evocative as it suggests a motive for Israel's punishment: infidelities committed from within her house. The household instrument is a saucer-shaped pan or flat griddle that was used for baking, as in the preparation of *minhâ* cakes offered to the Moon, Queen of Heavens, and other false gods (Lev. 2: 5, 6: 14, 7: 9; see Cooke 1960: 51). The *hin* measure to weigh Ezekiel's daily ration of water taken with his bread or cake was also used to prepare the oil and wine accompanying the *minhâ* offerings (Ezek. 4: 11, 45: 24, 46: 5–14; Num. 15: 4–7, 28: 14). Moreover, an iron pan used in the preparation of cereal offerings resembled a *teraphim,* a household god serving oracular functions. A *teraphim* was occasionally hidden under the sacrilegious oak tree (Ezek. 6: 13) together with other idols such as the nude figurine of Ishtar, the goddess of Love and Harlotry (Gen. 35: 4). When seen against this ritual background, the pan becomes an obstacle or 'barrier of sin,' to be placed between the prophet and his people indulging in pagan cults (Cooke 1960: 51; Greenberg 1983: 104; see Isa. 59: 2).

Contrary to Zimmerli's understanding of 'sign-action' (1979: 155), Wevers (1969: 54) and Greenberg (1983: 122f.) contend that Ezekiel's pantomime is meant to convey to an audience a prophetic oracle or prediction (of Jerusalem's siege) that stirs hopes and fears of the future but that should not be confused with pagan magic designed to bring about an event. This reading of rituals enacted by Ezekiel is in keeping with the surface text. But it does little justice to the influence of astrological religion on the prophet's imagery, magical actions, and pagan rituals otherwise denounced by Ezekiel (Greenberg 1983: 122). Similar comments apply to the intriguing symbolism applied to the exile of Israel and Judah in verses 4: 4–8. God said,

4. Lie down on your left side and take the sin of the House of Israel on yourself. I am making you bear their sin for as many days as you lie there. 5. I myself have set the years they will sin at a hundred and ninety days; during these you are to bear the sin of the House of Israel. 6. And at the end of these days, you are to lie down again on your right side and bear the sin of the House of Judah for forty days. I have set the length for you as one day for one year ... 9. You are to eat it [bread] for as many days as you have been lying on your side, a hundred and ninety days. (Ezek. 4: 4–9)

The ritual performed by the prophet is an oracle inspired by elements of Semitic cosmography. In Hebrew left means north and right south; when orienting themselves, humans turn their faces towards the rising sun (Gen. 14: 15; Job 23: 9; Zimmerli 1979: 166; Greenberg 1983: 105). While the left connotes the northern sky and the sun's immediate past, the right points to future time, that is, the south where the morning sun has yet to go. The two directions allude to events that have befallen Ephraim or Israel to the north and that have yet to befall Judah to the south. These associations are confirmed by the dating system used by Ezekiel. In the Septuagint Greek Version, the period of 190 days shows up in verses 5 and 9 (as in the Jerusalem Bible quoted above). But the number 150 appears in verse 4, to which can be added the 40 days of verse 6. The two figures add up to 190 days or years, starting with the deportation of the northern kingdom by the Assyrians in 734 B.C.E. Israel's captivity was gone, and 40 years for Judah were still to come (starting in 587 B.C.E.; see Cooke 1960: 53; Zimmerli 1979: 167).

A period of 150 days is also mentioned in Revelation in connection with the fifth trumpet announcing the sufferings caused by scorpion-tailed locusts rising from the abyss, winged demons endowed with the power to injure human beings for five months (9: 5, 10). As in Ezekiel, John's reference to a period of 150 days is part of a vision that speaks of scorpions, lions, chariots, and fire appearing on the Day of Yahweh, a day of darkness, not of light (9: 2, 8f.; Amos 5: 18). We have seen that the imagery is unmistakably astrological. The period corresponds to the length of the winter or rainy season extending from late October to mid-April and the spring equinox, for a total of five months. A great darkness begins as the sun enters the sign of the Scorpion, immediately after the autumn equinox occurring in the seventh month of Tishri, the month of Atonement and Judgment (Beasley-Murray 1974: 153).

There is one other passage in the Old Testament where the number 150 is combined with 40: the story of the flood which 'lasted forty days on the earth,' heavy rains and waters that 'rose on the earth for a hundred and fifty days' (Gen. 7: 4, 12, 17, 24, 8: 3, 6; cf. Green 1983: 106). The five-month period has already been accounted for. But what about the forty days of diluvial rains in Genesis and the same period of trials imposed on Judah in Ezekiel? Could it be that this shorter spell evokes memories of wandering in the wilderness (Amos 2: 10, 5: 25; Num. 14: 33; Luke 4: 2, etc.)? Could the forty days correspond to the Lent commemorating Jesus' fasting in the desert, a period that coincides with the pouring of 'later rains' (Heb. *malqosh*) immediately before Easter and the arrival of spring? If so, the pantomime and oracle used to predict the fate of Israel and Judah would conjure up a vision of wintry darkness and flood-like tribulations, a spell lasting five months and ending with forty days of fasting and wandering, all before the spring equinox (as in Ezek. 29: 11–17).[7]

There is more. Ezekiel's forty-day fast occurs in the thirtieth year. The same combination of numbers applies to Jesus, who spent forty days in the wilderness at the age of thirty, and also David, who acceded to the throne when he was thirty and reigned as long as Solomon, Saul, and Jehoash, that is, forty years.[8] All of these add up to seventy years, which is the span of Israel's servitude. It is also the length of a normal life that 'lasts for seventy years,' beginning with thirty years of youth followed by forty years of kingship, priestly ministry, or a generation of grown men (Zimmerli 1979: 166).[9]

Ezekiel is commanded by God to eat meagre portions of unclean food. The food consists of a barley cake baked over dung (Greenberg 1983: 107), a sign of starvation and pollution to be endured during the siege and the sufferings of Judah and Israel in exile (Ezek. 4: 9–17). The earlier implication of idolatrous cake offerings conveyed through Ezekiel's iron-pan motif is now reinforced by images of 'bread-dung' associated with the cult of sun, moon, and stars. Food that tastes like excrement is tied to the

Hebrew word *gillulim*, a favourite term for idol in Ezekiel and a pun on *gelalim*, 'dung pellets' or 'dung-idols.' The idols in question are worshipped in those 'high places' condemned by Ezekiel, an expression translated as 'pillars to the sun' by Jewish commentators (Wevers 1969: 60). In a similar vein, Ezekiel 7 assimilates idols made of gold to human secretion (in particular a woman's menstrual flow; see Zimmerli 1979: 208).

The compromise suggested by God, that the prophet eat cake baked over dung from a cow in yoke (Heb. *baqar*) instead of human excrement, is an allusion to cheap barley bread that served as a Jealousy Offering (to the priest cursing a man's unfaithful wife, Num. 5: 15). Since it embodies the good life (produced through fermentation), bread can also be an obstacle to a life free of sin. In biblical parlance, while women are expected to avoid the sweet bread of deceit and idleness, humans must ritually avoid the leaven of sin. Moreover, no one should live by bread alone, a food substance eaten in secret by depraved women preaching that unlawful pleasures are sweeter than lawful ones. Ideally bread should be used for charity. Failing this, humans shall not be saved from eating the bread of affliction, as in the day of the final harvest (Deut. 8: 3; Prov. 9: 13ff., 22: 9, 31: 27; Isa. 30: 20; Matt. 4: 4; 1 Cor. 5: 6ff.). The notion that it should be cow dung alludes again to the price to be paid for an adulteress or a false prophetess, the opposite of a young heifer that has no fault or blemish and that has never been yoked (Num. 19: 2; Hos. 3: 2; Ezek. 6: 9; 13: 19). The bovine motif is also in keeping with Ezekiel's vision of the ox-driven Chariot of Yahweh and common representations of Ishtar and other figures of the heavenly pantheon.

In his last oracle (Ezek. 5), Ezekiel uses a sharp blade to cut hair from his head and beard, and then scales to divide the hair in three parts: one part to be set on fire in the centre of the city, another to be tossed around the city with a sword, and the remainder to be scattered to the wind. The ritual prefigures trials to be suffered by those who do not obey the laws of surrounding nations and the rule of Yahweh. The trials include plagues, starvation, exile, death by the sword, and children robbed by wild animals.

The pantomime is reminiscent of a ritual performed on the evening of the 15 Nisan, the first month of the religious year (March/April). The ritual involved three men cutting barley grown in Palestine and without manure, exposing the grain to fire and the wind, and using the flour as a 'first fruit' oblation to Yahweh. Given the sinful conduct of Israel and Judah, the narrative transforms this offering into a sign of sufferings brought by way of Judgment, in the seventh month of Tishri, around the autumn equinox (Unger 1957: 350, 355). Manifestations of mourning (moaning, baldness, sackcloth) are suited to this time of the year, which is when lunisolar idols of silver and gold (Ezek. 7: 16ff., 27; Ps. 115: 4; Acts 19: 24; see Unger 1957: 415) are destined to fall; to be more precise, from the month of Tammuz till the sun-god and his female consort rise again at spring.

The oracle does as if Orion – the sun-god Tammuz, the Barley-God of Egypt, the Hebrew Kislev or giant Gibbor – had been turned into a famine-god, as in Revelation 6 (Charles 1920, 1: 156). Southern Orion was a warrior equipped with a mighty *sword*. While he announced the dog days and heliacal rise of summertime Sirius, his evening appearance marked the approach of winter and its attendant storm. The astrological and calendrical underpinnings of Ezekiel's oracle are further reinforced by the prophet's use of **scales** to allocate the forthcoming trials. As pointed out by Zimmerli (1979: 173), 'division, numbering, and weighing are all acts of judgement' (Dan. 5: 26ff.). On the astrological plane, measurements point to Libra. The Balance is opposite Taurus in the zodiac and stands for the equality of day and night, or the autumn equinox. Apparently of Chaldean origin, the constellation once formed the Claws of the Scorpion. Euphratean astronomers represented it as an altar or censer, images that appear in Ezekiel 6: 4ff. and 8: 11. We have seen that in Jewish astrology, Libra was represented by *tau*, last letter of the alphabet. It stood for a time of the year that marked the Day of Yahweh and the End of Time. John resorts to the same symbolism in his description of the third rider in Revelation 6: 5; as in Ezekiel, the Balance evokes the scarcity of grain food and a concern for sparing oil and wine in difficult times (see Beasley-Murray 1974: 133).

Other autumn motifs deployed by Ezekiel include the 'injustice flourishing' in a period of vintage heralding the Day of Yahweh (Ezek. 7: 7, 10) and also the judgment of unfaithful Israel in the post-vintage days of the winepress (Rev. 14: 19ff.; Zimmerli 1979: 207; Cooke 1960: 78). Mention should also be made of the sound of trumpets (v. 7: 14) blown in the Seventh New Moon, on the occasion of the Feast of Trumpets. Finally, there is Ezekiel's emphasis on questions of commerce and law, both of which have been associated with the Scales since the greatest antiquity (Ezek. 5: 6f., 7: 12ff.). In the words of Manilius,

balancing night with the length of the day when after a year's space we enjoy the new vintage of the ripened grape, the Scales will bestow the employment of weights and measures and a son to emulate the talents of Palamedes, who first assigned numbers to things, and to these numbers names, fixed magnitudes, and individual symbols. He will also be acquainted with the tables of law, abstruse legal points, and words denoted by compendious signs; he will know what is permissible and the penalties incurred by doing what is forbidden. Under no other sign would Servius more fittingly have been born, who in interpreting the law framed legislation of his own. Indeed, whatever stands in dispute and needs a ruling the pointer of the Balance will determine. (4: 205ff.)

The cosmic implications of a vision of Judgment inflicted on the Day of Yahweh are made clear in the prophet's announcement of an End 'coming for the four quarters of the world' (Wevers 1969: 62; Zimmerli 1979: 203). Likewise, restoration of the dead will come from the four points of the compass, or the wings and winds blowing through Yahweh's breath (Ezek. 37: 9; Cooke 1960: 399–400). But until then, the four quarters of the universe shall serve to disperse the unfaithful children of Israel (Ezek. 5: 10ff., 6: 8). Out of the four cardinal directions, the north can be expected to play a special role. People blown to the winds like wicked chaff separated from grain are likely to suffer the action of *mezarim*. The Hebrew word stands for the north and the action of 'scattering' performed by 'winnowing fans,' the ancient Hebrew names given to the two Bears, Bull, Chariots, or Ploughs treading the 'threshing floor' of the circumpolar sky. The fans are substitutes for oxen and also instruments to feed animals that will till the ground at the time of Judgment, at the beginning of the rainy season (Isa. 30: 24).[10]

The four pantomimes executed by the prophet are primarily concerned with the punishments that God has in store for the children of Israel who disobeyed his law. While the trials of judgment are described in detail, two things remain in the dark: the precise crimes committed by the unfaithful, and the secrets associated with God's manifestations in heaven and on earth. The first question has already been answered through a close examination of bread baked in an iron pan and cooked over cow dung, idols of gold and silver, altars and high places of mourning. All these motifs point to ancient practices of lunisolar worship condemned throughout the Old Testament. The imagery is a prelude to Ezekiel's witnessing the sight of women weeping for Tammuz at the north gate of the Jerusalem Temple, 'filth practiced here by the House of Israel' (Ezek. 8: 6). As for the second question – what meanings can be granted to obscure manifestations of Yahweh? – one should consider what the Talmud says about Ezekiel's reluctance to expand on the figure of God and his throne chariot: 'there is another heaven, which is found over the heads of the creatures, for it says: and above the heads of the creatures there was something like a platform, like awesome crystal. This much it is permitted to you to say, but to speak further is not permitted to you, for it says in the book of Ben Sira: *Seek not after that which is hidden from you, meditate not upon that which is veiled from you*. Apply yourself to things which are permitted to you, and do not concern yourself with mysteries' (in Zimmerli 1979: 124–5; emphasis added).

But why should these secrets be left unexplored? Could it be that discretion regarding the mysteries located on the other side of the heavenly vault, the place where God dwells, betrays a fundamental interdiction? Could the virtues of modesty and ignorance concerning the cosmos betray a taboo on equating the two sides of the vault: the visible and the invisible, the astrological and the spiritual, bodies moving in a finite sky and the immutable God dwelling in infinity, above and beyond the material sphere (see Feldman 1978: 212f., 218)? The fallen angels have paid dearly for their violation of this heavenly secrecy pact. In a Yahwistic perspective, an abuse of identity between the two realms is to be feared above everything else, for it amounts to a treatment of physical entities as cultic divinities. This is precisely the fear that haunts most of God's visible manifestations, especially those appearing in heaven *at the End of Time*. Although pitched on a cosmic scale, with a formidable deployment of all the forces of heaven, the Day of Judgment cannot afford to reinforce humans' cultic attitude towards star-gods governing the motions of Time. If anything the End should confirm the triumph of a Spirit *ruling from outside the boundaries of Time* – hence, a new order that will clearly transcend the seasonal motions of sun, moon, and stars, all transient features of the Noahic pact.

In the apocalyptic literature, the fear of cultic naturalism is countered through repression; stories of the astral pantheon are best forgotten. Efforts to reduce Sabaism to silence, however, are not enough. The law of Yahweh stands more to gain by turning stellar imagery to its own advantage, conquering the powers of astromythology in the realm of language. Signs of tribulations announced in Ezekiel – scorpions and scales, a spell of 150 days to the left followed by 40 to the right, people dispersed to the four winds – become the site of a Sabian language simultaneously silenced and recuperated by the Verb. Idols of gold and silver die in harness as they are put to work and destroyed all at one stroke.

The Two Witnesses and the Seventh Trumpet (Rev. 11)

In the prophetic-ministry and seventh-trumpet scene of Revelation 11, John continues to steer his narrative course to signs of autumn judgment, as in Ezekiel 2. The first part of Revelation 11 anticipates the future reign of the antigod in spiritual Jerusalem, diverting the attention from the satanic empire of Rome. In the words of Charles, 'for the moment the steady progressive current of our author's thought has been checked, and he has here turned aside into a backwater, but with 11.14 we return again into the main current' (1920, 1: 282). This reading accords with the surface flow of events. But it ignores the development of narrative symbology. When read astrologically, Revelation 11 does not stray from the bittersweet-scroll scene, which implied a wrathful sun god falling upon mortals while passing in Leo. Although shifting to the future reign of the Beast, Revelation 11 maintains the summer-to-winter orientation that prevailed in previous scenes and explores its implications even further.

The chapter begins with the prophet receiving a rod-shaped reed to measure the temple of God, the altar, and the worshippers. The angel instructs him to omit the outer court of the Gentiles, who shall take over the holy city for a period of 1,260 days, that is, 42 months or 3½ years. The prophet learns that two witnesses of the Lord shall be given the power to lock up the waters of the sky as long as they are prophesying. They shall turn water into blood, strike the world with plagues, and consume their enemies with fire coming out of their mouths. The two witnesses are wearing sackcloth and are like olive trees or candelabra standing before God. Their testimony will last as long as the siege, after which they shall be killed by the Beast emerging from the Abyss. Enemies from all over the world shall rejoice over their death. Their corpses shall lie for three days and a half in the main street of the Great City responsible for the crucifixion of Christ. The city in question is Jerusalem turned sinful, but also Rome identified with Sodom and Egypt.[11] God will then breathe life into the two martyrs and make them rise to heaven in a cloud, in full sight of their frightened enemies. The vision ends with a violent earthquake and the collapse of one-tenth of the city, killing 7,000 human beings. God-fearing survivors give glory to the Lord.

The Lord's right arm, his double-edged sword coming out of his mouth (Rev. 1: 16), and his bittersweet words of Revelation are two-sided: all of them offer promises of protection and warnings of punishment at the same time. The rod-like reed given to the prophet conveys the same mood of retributive ambivalence. In the hands of a shepherd, the **measuring-rod** made of sweet cane can be converted into a rod for counting or protecting the flock. An illustration of this imagery lies in the twelve rods of the tribe princes of Israel, emblems placed in the tabernacle before the ark of the covenant (Num. 17: 1–9; Ezek. 20: 37). When applied to Gentiles of the outer court, however, the rod cannot serve to count or protect them, since they know no measure in the eyes of God and do not count among his flock. In their case, the rod motif should be used for punishment, striking a weak nation like a weed 'shaken in the water' or by the wind (1 Kings 14: 15; Prov. 10: 13). Measures are to be taken against evil conquerors of the holy city.

According to Arnold, ancient spells and magical texts made frequent use of dimensional terms (breadth, depth, length, height) combined with images of divine light and brightness, as in Ephesians 3: 18. Interestingly, 'a number of alleged parallels to this expression have been found in a variety of sources including the Jewish Wisdom Literature, Jewish-Hellenistic cosmic speculation, Gnosticism, other Jewish texts identifying the heavenly cubic form of Jerusalem, and Stoic writings' (Arnold 1989: 90). The symbolic object of these narrative preoccupations with measurements vary greatly, from an expression of power to a representation of the love of God, his manifold wisdom, his holy city, his heavenly inheritance, or the cross of Christ. Although valid in their own right, these interpretations of objects of measurement should not preclude a discussion of the origins of measurements of time and space – namely, mathematical studies of motions of the heavenly spheres.

Consider the **outer court** occupied by the Gentiles. Where should this court be located? We know that the real temple and the city itself were in ruins when Revelation was written, which precludes a literal, down-to-earth reading of our passage. In any case Revelation 11: 19 places the **sanctuary** of God in heaven (11: 19), with the implication that divisions on earth reflect configurations in the sky. Logically, this sanctuary would lie in the highest sky, the northern crown of heaven, with the outer court lying below, to the south, close to the earth. By extension, the peripheral court left unmeasured and unsealed by the Lord could be likened to the southern band of stars, or the Babylonian way of Ea. These spatial connections tally with the suggestion made in the letters to Asia Minor, that the New Jerusalem is to be found north of the real Jerusalem. By contrast, the city's deviation from true faith, Sodom's rejection of God's messengers, Egypt's oppression of God's people – all are so many *southern* illustrations of a City of Destruction or universal Vanity Fair portrayed on a world scale.

In heavens, the outer court of the south is the abode of the draconic host governing the darker and rainy half of the year. This brings us to another key imagery of Revelation 11: the absence of rainfall. The notion that the two witnesses can lock up the sky so that it does not **rain** during their ministry has both historical and astrological implications. On the historical plane, we know from Josephus that the invasion of Jerusalem by Titus or its destruction by the King of Babylon in the days of Zedekiah were preceded by a famine of water, a sign of imminent trials. The fountain of Siloam and other springs located *outside* the city dried up almost completely (Charles 1920, 1: 285). The same menace is now turned against evil enemies expelled from the centre of the Great City, never to profanate the Lord's sanctuary again (Dan. 9: 26. 11: 31ff., 12: 11f.).[12] On the astrological plane, the narrative does as if the scorching heat of the sun in Leo was meant to last as long as humans continued to indulge in idolatry. God will not allow the rains of autumn to come to the rescue of earthly vegetation and all the life forms it feeds.

Rains arriving in the month of Tishri, the seventh, are of vital importance as they soften and prepare the dry ground for ploughing and the sowing of wheat and barley. The two witnesses appearing before God and the last trumpet, also the seventh, have the power to stop rain from falling during the days of their testimony. They can cause the earth to dry up completely, beyond the normal estival drought, as if consumed by **fire**. The text extends the plagues of summertime famine into the darker half of the (seventieth) year (cf. Charles 1920, 1: 279, 289). It does so through two witnesses or lamp standards,[13] two pillars of fire that stand for the legs of the mighty angel: their bodies contain enough fire (and the oil of olive trees) to destroy their enemies. It should be noted that the **plagues** inflicted by the two witnesses are modelled on those of Egypt (Exod. 7: 14ff., 11: 10), suggesting a meridional outlook on the future, in keeping with the southward march of the estival sun.

The period of **three and a half years** during which the Beast and the Gentiles shall reign over Jerusalem reinforce the autumn colours of Revelation 11, a season that ushers in the second half of the year. As most commentators note, the three-and-a-half-year period corresponds to the last half of Daniel's seventieth week, a prelude to the Second Advent of the Wrathful Lamb (Dan. 7: 25, 9: 24ff., 12: 7). This is the last half of the seven years that will put an end to half a millennium consisting of seventy times seven years. The half-millennium period is ten times the lapse of a Jubilee that ends with a 'trumpet blast,' as in Revelation 11: 14. In keeping with these calculations, the text mentions that the wicked shall rejoice at the death of the two witnesses for three and a half days; this is a short period compared with the three and a half years that the ministry of the witnesses shall last and that the woman shall be nourished in the wilderness (Rev. 11: 3, 12: 6–14).[14] The imagery none the less confirms the interchangeability of days, weeks, and years.

The 'week' drawn on different scales is divided into two halves, as if they formed a single unit composed of day and night, or the brighter and darker days of the year. The first half ends with the last intervention of two septenary groups of angels (seals and trumpet series), on the fourteenth moment of a monthlike cycle, midway between the beginning and the end. The same scheme applies to the Feast of Tabernacles, which occurs after the fourteenth day of Tishri, the month that begins with the Feast of Trumpets and that breaks the sacred year into two parts. It is on this day of the year that trumpets sound the sombre days of atonement and final judgment – the beginning of a winter season that originally lasted three and a half months; so thought the Babylonians (Moffat 1951: 416; cf. Charles 1920, 1: 279f., 289n).[15] All in all, the three-and-a-half-year motif points to a dual principle operating at all levels of the lunisolar calendar: the daily, the weekly, the monthly, the yearly, the centennial, and the millennial.

While the two witnesses are empowered to inflict great sufferings upon the pagans, both of them are fated to die at the hand of the Beast rising from the fiery deep. The seal of the Lord offers protection against spiritual assault, not against physical pain and death. Fire from the Abyss must be turned against the two witnesses if they are to follow in the footsteps of the Lord dying, resurrecting, and ascending to heaven from the Mount of Olives. After being killed and exposed for half a week, in the city where the Lord gave his last breath, the witnesses are given the breath of divine life and made to rise to heaven. Resurrection comes after sacrificial sufferings, penitence, and mourning. Such is the fate of any true witness dressed in sackcloth, in the image of the One who died on the cross.

Once a martyr, a prophet can rise not only from the dead, but also to power. Justice demands that bearers of the divine light be delegated powers of conquest and vindication. As in Revelation 7, the sealing of those destined to suffer great tribulations presupposes their survival and victory over their satanic foes. By turning their sufferings into sacrificial offerings, children of the Lord can conquer death and the world. Examples of conquest through martyrdom have already been set by Moses and Elijah, two Old Testament witnesses of the oppression of the chosen and followers of the Lord. Words of the sixth verse hark back to the plagues that Moses inflicted on Egypt, a nation now equated with the Great City ruled by the antigod. Other verses of Revelation 11 take their cue from the story of Elijah, his power to destroy by fire and to confine rainwater to the sky (1 Kings 17: 1; 2 Kings 1: 10ff.; Luke 4: 25).[16]

Martyrs rise from the dead, above mountains of idolatry evoking the horns and the Beast-led uprising directed against the saints (Isa. 5: 1; Dan. 7: 21). The resurrected can cause the earth to tremble with fear as the wrath of the Lord falls upon the lowest depths of humanity. **Seven thousand** persons are killed, and **a tenth** of the city is destroyed, with the implication that the whole of humanity adds up to 70,000 (L. Morris 1983: 152). Why the latter restriction? Perhaps because the last seven years are a pale reflection of what has yet to come. They represent only one-tenth of those calamities that will put an end to the whole era of seventy years. They act as a prelude to the Second Advent, which is when the Lord shall tread on all ten horns of the ruling Beast.

The story of two heavenly witnesses dying at the hand of the Beast goes back to the Epic of Creation. In the Babylonian epic, the dragon Tiamat humiliated the two freshwater gods named Anu and Ea. Only the sun-god Marduk, the god of vengeance riding on the wings of a mighty lion, could triumph over the creature from the Abyss. Having conquered the beast, Marduk brought Anu and Ea to heaven and put them in charge of the ecliptic and southern bands of stars. Marduk kept control over the northern way of Tammuz, the hot sun-god flying high in the sky and descending upon the earth from the north. Analyses presented in the next chapter point to a similar resolution of the grand battle between the Lord and the dragon as portrayed in Revelation: a hot-tempered Lord giving vent to his divine wrath through winds from the north (Bousset 1906: 321; Caird 1966: 137; Heidel 1951; Jacobsen 1976: 168–83; Langdon 1931: 84, 94ff., 278, 291f., 297).[17]

The third and final woe comes with the proper angelic announcement and the sounding of the seventh trumpet. What we are about to witness lies at the heart of John's prophecy. Visions to come offer a clear demonstration of astrocalendrical influences lurking behind the New Testament Apocalypse. They begin with heavenly voices proclaiming the eternal reign of the Lord. The twenty-four elders enthroned before God prostrate themselves and give thanks to their everlasting God named He-Is-and-He-Was. The time has come for the Lord to confront rebellious nations with his own wrath; to judge the dead; to destroy the destroyers of the earth; and to reward the prophets, the saints, and all the faithful. The sanctuary opens in heaven and the ark of God's testament is then seen inside the temple. The scene is accompanied by flashes of lightning, peals of thunder, a violent hail, and an earthquake.

The first two woes were associated with manifestations of the heavenly altar (Rev. 8: 3, 9: 13). The final woe is no exception. It too begins with the celestial appearance of the Ark of the Covenant inside the Holy of Holies, the innermost shrine of the temple. It also comes with signs and sounds of heaven announcing the millennial kingdom followed by the reign of God. In Jewish tradition, the ark used to be visited by the high priest on the Day of Atonement, around the time of the fall equinox. The altar, the seventh trumpet, and the enthronement symbology thus converge on the seventh month of the sacred year (Sweet 1990: 192f.; Farrer 1964: 137; Caird 1966: 144). Accordingly, the elders of Revelation 11: 16 take up Psalms 2, a messianic enthronement psalm that 'was probably used originally in Solomon's temple at the annual celebration of the king's accession, understood as his enthronement as God's "son" or vice-regent. This may have been accompanied by a ritual combat between God, represented by the king, and the powers of evil (often symbolized by a dragon), a triumphal procession and a "sacred marriage", in line with the Near Eastern "myth and ritual" investigated by S.H. Hooke' (Sweet 1979: 191n). The season in question is one of judgment carried out in the light of a heavenly altar known as Ara, a constellation near Scorpio. These connections confirm our autumn reading of earlier verses.

Plans Folding and Unfolding

The conflict between true and false gods is not merely a struggle over truth. More significantly, it is a struggle between forces vying for control over a material cosmos governed by the solar pact, a primordial covenant involving the sun, the moon, the planets, and all the spheres of heaven. We saw that the prologue and greeting to the seven churches of Asia (Rev. 1) gave little foretaste of this grand battle. Signs of Revelation's cosmic struggle were none the less prefigured in the claims and evocations a sevenfold Church, the day of a resurrected Lord portrayed as Alpha and Omega, an Almighty God with a solar face, eyes of fire, seven stars in his right hand, the keys of death and the underworld in his possession, and secrets of the future about to be told. Although written in a secular tone, the letters to the seven churches (Rev. 2–3) also deployed an array of astromythical imageries pointing to the cult of stars and emperors, acts of idolatry to be reprimanded by empyrean forces under God's command. The letters harnessed the cosmos to the higher rule of God, using the language of the Morning Star, the Book and crown of life, a new name engraved on stone, white robes, manna, and the blessings of wine and love. To these reassuring imageries were added signs of a great downfall echoing the southward descent of the summer sun and the yearly cycle approaching the End. Instruments of God's wrath issued from the heavens included the Lord's double-edged sword, his iron sceptre, and the sickbed of trials and tribulation inflicted upon Nicolaitans and followers of the Serpent, Balaam, and Jezebel.

The author of Revelation is concerned about rulers of the temporal world (emperors and stars) and the regulations of time trying to elevate themselves above God's eternal order. In an attempt to counter these threats against the Everlasting, the prophet takes it upon himself to reorient the language of Chronos and the heavens towards a loftier purpose going into two directions: announcing the *End of Time* while also glorifying the *above-timeness* of the Lord. Revelation 4–5 achieves the latter purpose by means of an ecstatic throne-room vision painted on a cosmic scale, with all the signs of triumphant solarism being put to the service of the enthroned Spirit. While appearing in colours of vernal resurrection, the Passover Lamb is pictured in such ways as to transcend all measurements of Time. The Root of David is surrounded by twenty-four elders and four living creatures stationed in the heavenly throne-room, representing the full heavens and circle of seasons attending the One who lives for ever and ever.

Paradoxically, the rule of God expresses itself through both an atemporal reality and a course of events that brings Time closer to the End. While Revelation 4–5 emphasizes the everlasting-enthronement imagery, Revelation 6 shifts back to the woes briefly suggested in the letters to the churches, thereby following up the warnings made in earlier chapters. The timeless spectacle of the Spirit gives way to signs of the times, those of the last day. As the Lamb breaks the seven seals, four catastrophes are followed by three. Four horsemen usher in the darker End-season of human history, playing havoc with all keepers of cyclical time: the sun is darkened, the moon turns red as blood, the stars fall like figs from a tree, and the sky disappears like a scroll rolling up in heaven.

Revelation 7 interrupts the beginning of the End and reverts to and elaborates on the equinoctial blessings of John's throne-room vision, in anticipation of the immortal life to be enjoyed by the martyrs redeemed in God's deathless heaven. The reversion is achieved through words of sevenfold praise combined with images of palms, white robes, and springs of living waters. To these signs of future rewards are added the Lord's exodus sky-tent spread over a fourfold and twelvefold universe and an angel rising to the east with the seal of the living God in his possession. As in a spiral movement, Revelation moves back and forth between the Timeless and the actual End, two complementary sides of the same Apocalypse.

Visions of the End are resumed in Revelation 8. The seventh seal opens on to an altar pouring fire over the earth, a scene followed by seven woeful trumpets sounding the 'day of blowing' usually heard at autumn, a season of repentance and judgment. Signs of the earth's final days include several woes modelled after the plagues of Egypt, all the stars of heaven partially darkened, a huge star falling on earth, an eagle flying in midheaven, and the sun presumably descending to the south. In Revelation 9, a cloud of scorpion-tailed, golden-crowned, female-haired locusts covering the sun and hurting humans for five months reinforces the wrathful autumn-Fall aspect of Revelation 6 and 8. Correlatively, calculations of threeness, fourness, and tenness deployed in these two chapters point to normal measurements of time and space being redirected towards an entirely new end: a dramatic reordering of the earth and the universe at the End of Time.

Revelation 10–11 follows up on previous visions of wrath, starting with seven thunderclaps and a scroll of bittersweet revelations of things that have yet to come. The scroll is held in the hand of a roaring-lion angel, an estival sun-faced giant pictured with the right foot in the sea and the left on the land. To this menacing material is added the godly use of a measuring-rod, fire burning the earth, waters locked up in the sky, and a period of trials lasting three and a half years. While in keeping with earlier forebodings, the latter symbolism allows the Lion of Judah and his followers to assert their supremacy *vis-à-vis* the whole visible cosmos, thereby countering the demons' claims (in Rev. 9) to powers of the sun and the stars. Having secured the powers of heaven and corresponding instruments of wrath for the Lord and his followers, Revelation can now stop shifting back and forth between words of satanic evil and scenes of divine glory, if only for a while, it is to be hoped, the last. The narrative can move on to an even clearer exposition of the grand battle of the New Testament Apocalypse. In Revelation 12, John finally unfolds a theme already 'contained' (conveyed/withheld) in all previous chapters: an eschatological (and primordial) struggle pitting good against evil – Christ against Antichrist, the Lord against contenders to his heavenly throne.

As we are about to see, a combat scene starring the dragon and the sun-robed woman of Revelation 12 brings out many implications of earlier visions. But an unfolding will capture our imagination only if it brings new secrets into its fold. We have seen that references to Old Testament sources of Revelation such as Ezekiel will not exempt the analyst from looking into the 'origins' of such sources – hence, 'pagan' texts and religions to which Ezekiel was speaking in veiled terms. The same can be said of texts that bring previous words or scenes to their conclusion, unravelling and resolving the complications of the story at hand: they too revel in their own secret conversations with the unspoken word. Revelation 12 brings clarity to the conflict of good and evil pervading the visions and prophecies of John, but it does so without undermining the central goal of our Christian Apocalypse. In the final analysis, Revelation's end is to impose silence on the cult of Nature – on all pagan cults that dare treat the heavenly bodies as full-fledged divinities governing the order of Time.

9

The Sun-Robed Woman

The Woman and the Dragon

Revelation 12 offers a cosmic tableau that sheds considerable light on the polemical underpinnings of Revelation. The vision merits quoting at length.

Now a great sign appeared in heaven: a woman, adorned with the sun, standing on the moon, and with the twelve stars on her head for a crown. She was pregnant, and in labor, crying aloud in the pangs of childbirth. Then a second sign appeared in the sky, a huge red dragon which had seven heads and ten horns, and each of the seven heads crowned with a coronet. Its tail dragged a third of the stars from the sky and dropped them to the earth, and the dragon stopped in front of the woman as she was having the child, so that he could eat it as soon as it was born from its mother. The woman brought a male child into the world, the son who was to rule all the nations with an iron scepter, and the child was taken straight up to God and to his throne, while the woman escaped into the desert, where God had made a place of safety ready, for her to be looked after in the twelve hundred and sixty days.

And now war broke out in heaven, when Michael with his angels attacked the dragon. The dragon fought back with his angels, but they were defeated and driven out of heaven. The great dragon, the primeval serpent, known as the devil or Satan, who had deceived all the world, was hurled down to the earth and his angels were hurled down with him. Then I heard a voice shout from heaven, 'Victory and power and empire for ever have been won by our God, and all authority for his Christ, now that the persecutor, who accused our brothers days and night before our God, has been brought down. They have triumphed over him by the blood of the Lamb and by the witness of their martyrdom, because even in the face of death they would not cling to life. Let the heavens rejoice and all who live there; but for

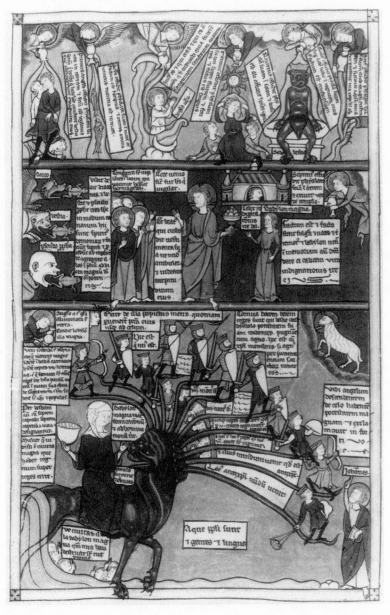

Apocalyptic scenes, Cod. lat. 8865, Liber floridus, f.41, LA73219. Bibliothèque Nationale, Paris, France; Foto Marburg/Art Resource, New York

The Woman Clothed in the Sun (Apoc. 12: 1–18). Commentary on the Apocalypse by Beatus de Liebana. Spain (Leon), *c.* 950 CE. M.644, f.152v–153. The Pierpont Morgan Library, New York; Art Resource, New York

you, earth and sea, trouble is coming – because the devil has gone down to you in a rage, knowing that his days are numbered.'

As soon as the devil found himself thrown down to the earth, he sprang in pursuit of the woman, the mother of the male child, but she was given a huge pair of eagle's wings to fly away from the serpent into the desert, to the place where she was to be looked after for a year and twice a year and half a year. So the serpent vomited water from his mouth, like a river, after the woman, to sweep her away in the current, but the earth came to her rescue; it opened its mouth and swallowed the river thrown up by the dragon's jaws. Then the dragon was enraged with the woman and went away to make war on the rest of her children, that is, all who obey God's commandments and bear witness for Jesus.

While Revelation 12 may not be derived from any particular myth or religion, the comparative findings of Dieterich (1891), Gunkel (1895), Bousset (1906), and later scholars have led most twentieth-century commentators of Revelation to agree on the international inspiration of this grand battle between the sun-clothed woman and the dragon. The scene betrays the influence of astrally inspired myths known throughout the Semitic lands and the world of John's day. Even Charles, who usually shies away from such interpretations, recognizes that the mythical scenario of this chapter can not been attributed to Christian or Jewish writers alone. In his words (1920, 1: 314), 'into this primitive international tradition [pitting light and order against darkness and disorder] Judaism had read its own religious history and its longings for a divine Redeemer.'

The parallels that can be drawn between John's cosmic vision and mythologies of the ancient world are many. To begin with, readers will recall an older version of the Lord's conflict with the dragon from the abyss: the Akkadian story of celestial deities and the sun-god Marduk fighting against the female sea-monster Tiamat. A summary of the great **Babylonian epic** has already been given. Suffice it to mention here that Tiamat was also a seven-headed creature associated with bitter waters of the deep, that she too caused the downfall of a third of all stars (cf. Dan. 8: 10), and that her mother (Damkina, 'the lady of the heavenly tiara') was described in terms reminiscent of verse 12: 1. In her train there was Mushussu, the horrific serpent coloured 'gleaming red' in the Temple of Marduk at Esagil.

Mention should be made of the **Persian** story of Azhi Dahak, a dragon sent by Ahriman, who competed with Ormuzd for the honours and powers of kingship. The god Ormuzd was the one who created the twelve constellations now reflected in the twelve-star crown worn by John's sunrobed woman. The dragon stood on a third part of the heaven and wore seven diadems that stood for the seven planets he had created (Charles 1920, 1: 311). Iranian myths also refer to the dragon casting a third of the stars to the earth (Beasley-Murray 1974: 193).

The **Greek** story of Apollo born from Zeus and Leto, however, offers a closer parallel to John's narrative. Hyginus's variant form of the myth features the great dragon Python and his pursuit of Leto, the mother-to-be of a child destined to conquer the dragon. Boreas carried off the mother to Poseidon, who placed her on an island, and then sank it beneath the sea, where it stayed until Python had gone away. Leto then gave birth to a fully grown Apollo, who went on to kill the dragon. A similar story tells of the dragon raising the waters against Leto so that she could not bear Apollo, and then the earth rescuing the mother by letting the island of Delos rise above the flood. As Collins (1976) and Charles (1920, 1: 312) argue, the parallels between these stories and John's narrative are striking.

The last source usually cited comes from **Egypt**. The myth concerns the sun-capped goddess Isis who gave her husband, Osiris, a son called Horus, the hawk-headed god of day. Draconic Typhon, also known as Set, was his enemy. The beast was coloured red and had the shape of a serpent or a crocodile. He killed Osiris, and then went after Isis, who was about to give birth. The pregnant woman made her miraculous escape on a papyrus boat to the island Chemnis, where Horus was born. Another variant describes Isis as bearing Horus in the solitude where she had fled. The dragon ends up being imprisoned and killed by fire at the hand of Horus (see Rev. 20: 1ff.). As Collins argues (1976: 84, 252–61), all indications are that John enriched the ancient combat imagery with this lunisolar story of the heavenly Isis, a goddess depicted nursing the divine infant and worshipped throughout Western Asia Minor at the time when Revelation was written.

John's red dragon with seven heads can be assigned various **Old Testament** designations: the sea-dragon (Job 7: 12), Behemoth (Job 40: 15ff.), Rahab (Ps. 89: 9f.), the serpent of the sea (Amos 9: 3), the crocodile (Ezek. 29: 3ff.), the oppressing nation, or the antichristian kingdom and tyrant dominating the world (Isa. 51: 9f.; Ezek. 32: 3ff.; Dan. 7: 1ff.). There is also Leviathan (Ps. 74: 12ff.), the seven-headed serpent of the sea who was conquered by Baal, the stormy son of El and the Canaan counterpart of Marduk; the monster's defeat caused the heavens to 'wilt and drop slack as the belt of his own robe' (quoted in Beasley-Murray 1974: 192). Biblical connections between the draconic figure and images of chaos, darkness, and the deep sea – the primeval ocean and the flood that befell the first creation – are not lacking (Charles 1920, 1: 317f.). The same can be said of the snake associated with the whores of Rome and Babylon (Rev. 17), or the satanic serpent and the sinful woman of Genesis 3. As for the model woman, she denotes the faithful nation of Israel, the labouring mother or daughter of Zion, or Jerusalem bringing forth the Messiah and children for the age of salvation (Isa. 26: 16–27, 66: 7; Jer. 4: 31, 13: 21). Her flight into the wilderness under the protection of the Lord and an eagle, towards the promised land of the New Jerusalem, echoes the chosen people's exodus in the days of the Old Covenant (Exod. 19: 4).

While many motifs of Revelation 12 can be understood against an Old Testament background, other important images such as the dragon chasing the woman and her child betray an effort on the part of John to combine traditional elements from a variety of Near Eastern cultures. As Collins (1976: 58, 209) suggests, these pagan influences converge on ancient combat myths of Sumerian-Babylonian, Hittite, Canaanite-Ugaritic, Greek, and

The Devil Chained in the Abyss (Apoc. 20: 1–3). Commentary on the Apocalypse by Beatus de Liebana. Spain (Leon), *c.* 950 CE. M.644, f.212v. The Pierpont Morgan Library, New York; Art Resource, New York

Egyptian origins, stories that circulated so widely in the early imperial period of the first century C.E. as to be cross-culturally intelligible (see also Sweet 1990: 196n). The myths in question show a pattern that closely resembles the imagery of Revelation 12:

Basic pattern (Fontenrose)	*Revelation 12 (Collins)*
A. The dragon pair (husband and wife and/or mother and son)	A. The dragon (vs. 3)
B. Chaos and disorder (represented by the opponent)	B. Chaos and disorder (vs. 4a)
C. The attack	C. The attack (vs. 4b)
D. The champion	D. The champion (vs. 5a)

E. The champion's death (confined
   to the underworld)
F. The dragon's reign: destructive,
   lecherous, god's wife/mother
   attacked
G. God's son, sister, wife or mother
   saves the champion
H. Battle renewed and victory
I. Order restored and confirmed

E. The champion's death (vs. 5b)

G. Recovery of the champion (vs. 7a)

H. Battle renewed and victory (vss. 7b–9)
I. Order restored and confirmed (vss.
    10–12a)
F. The dragon's reign (vss. 12b–17)

Source: Collins 1976: 59–61

Revelation 12 brings together ancient Isis imagery and Near Eastern combat mythology, both of which were based on solar symbolism: 'the dragon of darkness tries to kill the sun god, only to be killed by him when the new day dawns' (Caird 1966: 147). Heliolatry was common at the time when Revelation was written. There is ample epigraphical and numismatic evidence pointing to the solar cult of Isis in Western Asia Minor during the last century B.C.E. and the first century C.E. There is also a wealth of evidence suggesting Jewish exposure to the Leto-Python combat myth. The material includes ancient literary references to the cult of Apollo and Leto in Ephesus, and passages from the writings of Lucan, Tacitus, Strabo, Hyginus, and Lucian of Samosata evoking elements of this mythology. Many coins, paintings, statues, and monumental inscriptions representing Python's attack on Leto have been observed throughout the region (Collins 1976: 245–52). Some coins show the emperor's radiant head, suggesting that 'in the drama of man's existence, where light and darkness are at constant warfare, the role of Apollo was now being played by imperial Caesar' (Caird 1966: 149).

Against the latter interpretation, Prigent (1959: 144; 1981: 179–82, 186f.; see also 1959: 121f.) argues that there are enough Old Testament parallels to account for the central plot of Revelation 12 and that some of John's imagery is entirely original (see also L. Morris 1983: 156; Sweet 1990: 194f.). Add to this Jewish inspiration John's tendency to project human history onto celestial events and several Jewish texts that make use of lunisolar metaphors, and you have a much simpler interpretation of the symbology at hand, a safer reading that tallies with the prophet's intolerance vis-à-vis all stellar myths and related expressions of idolatry. As Mounce (1977: 235) puts it: 'John probably borrowed some of his imagery from the thought-world of his day, but it is very unlikely that he consciously took over a pagan myth to explain the spiritual significance of the persecution coming upon faithful Christians. Would a writer who elsewhere in the book displays such a definite antagonism toward paganism draw extensively at this point upon its mythology?' The implication here is that 'any lesson we can learn by thinking of a pagan sun-goddess is purely incidental. John is an artist in words with a divinely-given message. We must not degrade him to the level of a copyist of ill-digested pagan myths' (L. Morris 1983: 156). Prigent also remarks that the fact that John's vision and pagan myths are 'undeniably related' cannot be construed as evidence for literary dependence.

These conclusions are somewhat surprising, given that most of these exegetes will recognize the impact of non-Jewish mythology on the imageries of Revelation. For instance, Prigent states that John's vision of a pregnant woman chased by a dragon is a Christian adaptation of Greek mythology (1981: 178). In an earlier text, Prigent (1959: 128) concedes that Revelation 12, although not a replica of any particular myth, constitutes an early Judaeo-Christian adaptation of heavenly child-saviour stories well documented in the Near East. Also, his comment regarding John's Old Testament inspiration begs the question: can Old Testament imageries be read in isolation from pagan mythologies in the first place? Are we not told by Prigent (1981: 186) that pre-Christian attributes of Satan should be read against the background of the Near Eastern dragon of chaos mythology? Finally, could it be that Prigent misses the point of intertextual analysis? After all, the interest of Revelation 12 does not reside in the parallels that can be drawn between John's apocalyptic imagery and mythologies foreign to Judaeo-Christianity. That such immediate influences should have had an impact on John's visions is not surprising. What should strike us more is the Seer's systematic avoidance of any explicit mention of other religions contending over his own imagery – a constant refusal to acknowledge political and theological battles over key signs of Near Eastern world-thought.

In hindsight, John's avoidance pattern has a relatively simple *raison d'être*. The prophet's silence is telling: as with other visions of Revelation, chapter 12 busies itself transforming alien imageries into forces struggling in the train of the true God. Once divested of their divine attributes, stellar figures are made to wear the cloak of metaphor, acting as signs and agents subserving the higher rule of Logos. Stars lose their own government: leaders of the heavenly spheres – the dragon and the moon under the woman's feet – are expelled from heaven (Rev. 12: 9) so as to be 'subjugated, trodden down, held in bondage' (H. Morris 1983: 215). John borrows symbolic material from astromythology with a view to countering the powers of the dragon and showing that only Christ can resolve the problems posed by paganism. As Kiddle (1940) suggests, 'the true mother of the incarnate Son of God is the messianic people – not Leto, nor any other goddess of pagan veneration. And the true son of God is Christ, not Apollo; it is Christ whose witness and warfare will result in the dragon's ultimate defeat – He and His loyal servants are the true actors in the great struggle between light and darkness.'

Parallels in Heaven

A critical lesson that can be learned from Revelation 12 is that, while John substitutes the messianic scheme of Incarnation for the cult of physical bodies in heaven, he recuperates ancient cartoons of redemption through a lavish deployment of astral metaphors. The two themes of Incarnation and astralism represent significant concessions to pre-Christian traditions other than the Judaic of the Old Testament. These concessions serve an important function, which is to respond to aspirations of Christian proselytism by casting the language of Christianity as broadly as possible, to include other cults and religions supporting or struggling against the tyranny of Rome.

Astralism implies a cosmic perspective on the struggle between God and the Devil. The cosmic formulation of the conflict of good and evil was already present in the writings of Paul (Eph. 6: 12; cf. Charles 1920, 1: 298). We know that Paul had some knowledge of astral mythology, to the point of quoting from the celebrated fifth verse of the *Phaenomena* of Aratus (*c.* 270 B.C.E.), a Greek astronomical poet from Cilicia, Paul's own country: 'for we are also his offspring' (Acts 17: 28). That John may have been exposed to similar beliefs is more than probable. Many of those who received the teachings of the apostles were under the immediate influence of the astral religions of John's day. Even when reluctant to read astrology into Revelation, most exegetes will readily admit that 'John's contemporaries were certainly versed in zodiacal lore and assumed that earthly destinies were determined by, and reflected in, the stars' (Sweet 1990: 204).

Combat myths of the ancient Near East contained astral imageries that closely resemble the heavenly composition deployed in Revelation 12. In his attempt to usurp the throne of Zeus, Typhon is said to have attacked the stars, knocking a few constellations out of the sky and throwing zodiacal Pisces into the sea (Collins 1976: 78f.). Rebellion against the divine thus involves a disruption of the stellar order, an imagery attested in both Greek and Semitic tradition. As with the dragon motif, John's woman pictured as

Queen of Heaven is also loaded with evocations of primitive astronomy. As Collins (1976: 72–5) notes, a woman adorned with the sun, standing on the moon, and wearing a twelve-starred crown is reminiscent of such goddesses of the Hellenistic and early Roman periods as Isis and the Ephesian Artemis, both of whom were typically represented with lunar and zodiacal iconography. Apuleius, a philosopher of the second century c.e., used similar astral imagery to describe the goddess Isis (Mounce 1977: 236n5).

O Queen of Heaven – whether you are bountiful Ceres, the primal mother of crops, who in joy at the recovery of your daughter took away from men their primeval animal fodder of acorns and showed them gentler nourishment, and now dwell in the land of Eleusis; or heavenly Venus (= Phoenician goddess Astarte), who at the first foundation of the universe united the diversity of the sexes by creating Love and propagated the human race through ever-recurring progeny, and now are worshipped in the island sanctuary of Paphos; or Phoebus' sister, who brought forth populous multitudes by relieving the delivery of offspring with your soothing remedies, and now are venerated at the illustrious shrine of Ephesus (= Diana/Artemis, also Lucina/Eileithya); or dreaded Proserpina (= Hecate) of the nocturnal howls, who in triple form repress the attacks of ghosts and keep the gates to earth fast, roam through widely scattered groves and are propitiated by diverse rites – you who illumine every city with your womanly light, nourish the joyous seeds with your moist fires, and dispense beams of fluctuating radiance according to the convolutions of the sun ... (*Metamorphoses* 11: 2; quoted in Malina 1995: 156–7)

The text continues with evocations of the lady's long hair, her crown adorned with ears of wheat and snakes coiling on each side, a lunar disc glistening with white light placed above her forehead, and a black cloak covered with glittering stars scattered around a full moon. The queen of the universe is said to manifest the aspects of all gods and goddesses and to rule the starry heights of the sky. Apuleius equates Isis with other female divinities such as Cybele, Athene, Venus, Diana, Proserpina, Ceres, Juno, and Hecate.

The association between Virgo and the sun-robed woman of Revelation 12 was already emphasized in Charles Dupuis's *L'Origine de tous les cultes*, first published in 1798. In this book Dupuis argues that

the author of the Apocalypse turns his gaze to the heaven of the fixed stars, and specifically to the Zodiac, and on that part of the sky where at midnight the beginning of the year at the winter solstice was situated and which in springtime, at sunset, rose the first on the horizon of the Eastern Part. These constellations were vessels

called Ara, and the Celestial Virgin, accompanied by the Serpent, which rose following her, and which appeared to pursue her in the Sky, while in the west the river
of Orion seemed to be swallowed up by the earth and disappear with its setting.
This then is the tableau with which the astronomical sky presents us at the time
when the equinoctial year ends and when the sun of springtime shines, bringing the
famous Lamb, chief of the twelve signs. (quoted in Malina 1995: 158)

In his analysis of the astral underpinnings of Revelation, Boll (1914: 102)
also equates the sun-robed woman with Virgo, a zodiacal constellation
associated with Isis. The dragon stood in turn for Hydra, the many-headed
Water-Snake of the southern sky. While Dupuis and Boll make an important contribution to our understanding of the many close connections that
bind Revelation to astromythology, one must never lose sight of a basic
feature of John's script: the distance taken by the Seer *vis-à-vis* astralism,
and therefore the impossibility of arguing a perfect match between Revelation 12 and any particular astral myth. The same comment can be made
about the sun-robed woman and dragon imagery: neither of them can be
equated with any particular heavenly configuration, be it lunar or solar,
equinoctial or solstitial, northerly or southerly. More than any positive
association, the negative command – thou shall not confound the divine
with the astral – constitutes John's central message conveyed anagogically,
through allegorical suggestion. In between the lines, the prophet insists on
saying that 'the woman is certainly not Virgo, the sixth of the signs of the
zodiac ... She belongs ... to the realm of vision. The dragon is not Draco,
nor Serpens, nor the many-headed Hydra, but a combination of all three ...
the stars are angelic representatives of pagan powers. We must look beyond
astronomy for an answer. The woman and the dragon are *figures of the
imagination, projected on to the starry heavens*' (Caird 1966: 149; emphasis
added). Both the prophet and his exegetic readers have in common the self-
appointed task of demoting astral gods to mere figures of speech.

John's negative command applies to a host of well-known stories written
all over the skies of early Christianity. To begin with, signs of astralism can
be conveyed and contested through figures of sevenness. Revelation 12
brings out the opposition between false and true gods struggling over the
sacred seven. In a Judaeo-Christian perspective, demons are prone to usurp
attributes of the divine, including signs of heptadic heavenliness. The
dragon aspires to sovereignty over the world as he 'proudly uplifts' himself
in the sky and wears a crown of seven diadems, those of the solar king leading the sacred Seven across the vault of heaven. For the first time in Revelation, the septenary principle falls under the dominion of a beast surging

from the abyss and overshadowing the luminaries of heaven. 'The seven diadems will have been viewed by John as blasphemous claims to sovereignty, in imitation of the divine royalty of the Christ (cf. 19:12)' (Beasley-Murray 1974: 199; see also Caird 1966: 156). Correlatively, the word *sign* (*semeion*) that John uses to introduce the chapter is given a demonic twist: the beast usurps the sign-making powers of God and mobilizes the forces of heaven to announce his own triumph (Prigent 1959: 183f.). Given that a *semeion* commonly meant not only a wonder or miracle, but also a constellation interpreted as a portent (Caird 1966: 149), little would be needed to transform this close association between false gods and 'their signs in heaven' into a full equation. Visible bodies of heaven stand accused of acting as divinities and sign-manifestations of their own will, makers of signs and sign markers all at once.

But what are we to make of the tenfold calculations applied to the horns of God's arch-enemy? When picturing the Lord in heaven and his immediate surroundings, scenes preceding the introduction of the sun-robed woman never resorted to the decimal scheme alone. Up until now, John combined figures of tenness with cardinal or lunisolar divisions based on heptadic and duodecimal calculations (24 hours in a day, 7 days in a week, 4 weeks in a month, 12 months in a year, 4 directions in the sky, etc.).[1] Through his vision of a dragon with ten horns, John separates the decimal principle from the septenary code. In the biblical literature, the two systems of computation, heptadic and decimal, lend themselves to different usages. While figures of sevenness are harnessed to the lunar cycle and are diachronically motivated, figures of tenness operate synchronically, as with toes that stand for coexisting kingdoms (Dan. 2: 42, 7: 7f., 23f.). The first principle is mapped onto calendrical motions of the moon, the second onto the human body. Given these connections, seven heads can be equated with successive kingdoms or crowns. By contrast, the ten horns suggest the simultaneous sprouting of powers not yet crowned; multiples of tenness are essentially secular and down-to-earth, removed from calendrical preoccupations with planets and stars evolving in heaven. In Revelation 12, the two methods of computation are brought together in a single imagery: all ten horns are reunited in a beastly creature that grows into a mega-kingdom or era of its own, the eighth. This is when all horns are crowned and given the strength of iron, but also the perishable attributes of clay and flesh (Rev. 13: 1, 17: 7–17).

Revelation 12 owes its numerical symbolism to measurements of the body coupled with lunisolar measurements of time. It also owes some of its inspiration to ancient struggles between dragons and godly figures covering the vault of heaven, astromythical images now written off as mere signs, mediators, and metaphors. Elements of Sabian inspiration appearing in Revelation 12 include:

- a pregnant lady adorned with the sun, standing on the moon and crowned with twelve stars;
- a heavenly serpent-dragon dropping one-third of the stars to the earth and pursuing the woman through a river of water vomited from his mouth;
- the lady receiving a huge pair of eagle's wings and taking refuge in the desert for a period of three and a half years;
- Michael and his angels driving the red dragon out of heaven and triumphing through the sacrificial pouring of the blood of the Lamb, a Saviour called upon to rule the world.

There are various ways in which the confrontation of man, god, and serpent can be mapped onto ancient configurations of the sky. Consider first the story of **Hydra and the Raven**. Briefly, the Water-Snake governs the meridional way of Ea, one of the three ways of heaven in Babylonian astrology. Its head and tail point to the draconic nodes – the equinoctial dragon swallowing the sun or the moon. The constellation extends over about *one-third of the lower heaven*, immediately above the southern horizon; accordingly, the late Sumerian ideogram for ghosts of darkness begins with the sign for one-third (Langdon 1931: 161ff.). Hydra was identified with the winter, the season of rains, the bitter fountains of the deep, the seven-headed Tiamat and her 'gleaming-red' companion known as Mushussu. It also stood for the well-known Ereshkigal of Sumerian and Akkadian origin, queen of the underworld, a goddess married to the falling sun-god celebrated at autumn. John's seven-headed red dragon dropping a third of the stars from his tail, threatening to devour the child of a lunisolar mother in labour, and then pursuing the woman with a flood of water, is a kindred spirit of the ancient Hydra.

The male child's mother flees to the desert on the wings of a huge eagle. The bird can be likened to the Raven or Bird of the Desert flying on Hydra's back, a bird thriving on a land rid of the Flood (Gen. 8: 7) and rising in the company of a solar woman called Virgo. Although this astral scenario has much in common with John's vision, there is a problem with the ten-starred Corvus appearing near the ten-starred cup known as Crater: the raven does not enjoy a good mythical reputation. Could it be because it fails to look after the young? Or is it because it keeps close company with the Water-Snake? For the bird to become an enemy of the serpent and a protector of the young, Corvus would have to become an eagle (Exod. 19: 4; Deut. 32: 11). Viewed astrologically, the scene would have to shift from southern Hydra and Corvus to the equatorial battle of **Aquila and Ophiuchus against Serpens and Scorpio,** on the darker side of the Milky Way river. Malina (1995: 162) thus suggests that 'the scenario described by John would consist of a Pregnant Woman (Virgo), with the traditional Heads (later Claws, now Libra) of the Dragon (old Scorpio) right at her feet awaiting her offspring's birth.' As with Michael battling against the Dragon at the beginning of Creation, the light-bearing Orion rising to the east causes Scorpio's fall to the west (Aratus 634–41; see Malina 1995: 170). The shift is not entirely reassuring though. Readers should recall that both the Eagle and the Scorpion marked the beginning of the darker half of the year. Both symbols were ascribed to the tribe of Dan, a man compared to a serpent by his own father, Jacob.

The Babylonian lion-headed Eagle identified with Zu (in the train of Mushussu) was an enemy of the sun-god Enlil and an ally of the serpent. On the brighter side of the Eagle's story, however, there is the predator's morning culmination just before the arrival of spring, followed by its descent in the summer, a season dominated by Leo standing above the Water-Snake. Another positive aspect of the Eagle is that it keeps company with the anti-serpent figure of Ophiuchus, the Serpent-Holder standing with a foot on Scorpio. Also, the bird fought victoriously against the evil snake in the legend of Etana and contributed to the defeat of its own inverted image, Zu the rapacious eagle. Finally, mention should be made of the Sumero-Babylonian myth of Ninurta and Marduk, victorious war-gods associated with the *Sol Invictus.* The myth evokes the solar body rising or fully risen, that is, the beginning and the end of the spring season, a time of the year governed by Leo and Aquila (Kramer 1961: 126; Jacobsen 1970: 4; 1976: 132f.; Langdon 1931: 115–19, 166–74, 234f.).

But the autumn coordinates of the scene are more compelling than its vernal implications. The ascent of Aquila trailing Serpens and Ophiucus trampling Scorpio signals indeed the rise of demonic forces and the corresponding changes in climate: the scene ushers in the beginning of autumn rains and the darkness of winter. This is also time of the year when Satan alias the Devil (both 'accusers' in Hebrew and Greek) is deprived of his power to accuse humans before God. As noted by Charles (1920, 1: 328), 'Satan accuses men all the days of the year except the Day of Atonement,' which comes in the seventh month of Tishri, in the season of Judgment. Since Revelation 12 is concerned with the dragon's expulsion from heaven

– the downfall of the satanic 'accuser of our brethren' (Revelation 12: 10) –
we can infer that the scene takes place at the appropriate time: about the
autumn equinox.

While the story of the Water-Snake and the Raven covers the southern
sky, images of the Serpens and the Eagle are essentially equatorial. To
understand the cosmic struggle of man and serpent, readers may also look
at another portion of the sky, that is, the highest heaven, the circumpolar
north. In the vicinity of the polestar, there is the telling story of **Hercules
and Draco**, to which we now turn. According to Caesius, Draco and the
Great Dragon worshipped by the Babylonians are one and the same. Some
have identified this dragon of the high north with the sea-monster Tiamat,
'overcome by the kneeling sun-god Izhdubar or Gizdhubar, our Hercules,
whose foot is upon it' (Allen 1963: 204). The Old Testament portrays the
dragon as a crocodile (Job 41: 1; Ezek. 29: 3), a widespread connection confirmed on the planisphere of Denderah and the walls of the Ramesseum at
Thebes. About 2,000 to 3,000 years before our era, this imposing creature
occupying the crown of heaven marked both the ecliptic's north pole and
the equator's polestar. Since then, the constellation has shifted. It now coils
round the polestar like 'the crooked serpent' in the Book of Job (26: 13).
The Chaldean version of Draco was so enormous that it clasped the seven-
starred arctic bears in its fold, whence the combined title *Arctoe et Draco*.
Thuban, the star that used to mark the pole, was synonymous with the
entire constellation and was known as the Judge of Heaven in the days of
the first Sargon, King of Akkad. Both Thuban and Dubhe (α Ursae
Majoris) were objects of Egyptian temple worship (Allen 1963: 208f.).

Like the primeval serpent in Revelation 12, Draco never plunges beneath
the horizon and the earth. But it does suffer a yearly fall that starts with the
rise of Aries and the Pleiades at spring. The fall is caused by Hercules,
whose 'right foot is planted on the twisting Serpent's head,' to use the
words of Aratus. Hercules rises to glory as the Serpent descends to the
earth. The victory is not without cost. Like the nearby Eagle, Hercules was
destined to fly high, and then swoop low. While he rises above and gets the
upper hand of Draco, the hero is bound to decline as he kneels on the
demon's head. The scene is *remarkable for its association with events of the
vernal equinox*. In the words of Maunder, the 'meridian at midnight at the
time of the spring equinox is called a "colure," – the "autumnal colure,"
because the sun crosses it in autumn. Now the Serpent was so arranged as
to be shown writhing itself for some distance along the equator, and then
struggling upwards, along the autumnal colure, marking the zenith with its
head. The lower part of the autumnal colure was marked by the Scorpion,

and the foot of the Serpent-holder pressed down the creature's head, just where the colure, the equator, and the ecliptic intersected' (Maunder 1923: 159).[2] In this scene, the ascent of the Ram and the Passover Lamb at spring-time causes the downfall of three leading demons (Scorpio, Serpens, Draco) and the victory of vernal light over the forces of darkness.

Stories featuring the Water-Snake, the Serpent, and the Dragon suggest that the confrontation of good and evil increases in intensity as protago-nists rise in heaven, closer to the high north. The greater success the dra-conic creature has in mounting the sky, the more potential it has to rise against the Lord, and the more powerful the godly forces deployed against it. While southern Hydra is virtually on the loose, the equatorial Serpent is held firmly by Ophiuchus. As for northern Draco, it is trampled underfoot by Hercules and the Almighty enthroned above the vault of heaven. Given these levels of confrontation, it stands to reason that calamities befalling the entire creation should come from up north.

As in Genesis, feminine characters will also play an important role in conflicts between man, god, and serpent. This brings us to issues of gender and to connections between John's sun-clothed woman and the queens of heaven portrayed in antiquity. When one speaks of goddesses of the sky, the constellation that comes immediately to mind is **Virgo**, a divine lady that stands immediately above the tail-end of Hydra, is closely followed by the Serpent and the Scorpion, and ends up being rescued by the Eagle (Far-rer 1964: 148). The maiden was identified with the sun-capped goddess Hathor of the Nile, or Isis the Queen of the Stars, a lady that Egyptian Hellenistic sky maps pictured with the young Horus (the infant southern sun-god) in her arms or ears of wheat (the star Spica) in her left hand. An Egyptian text depicts her as a circumpolar constellation that keeps Typhon or the northern Bear in chains (Boll 1914: 110). Isis was the Egyptian coun-terpart of the Aphrodite of Greece, the Venus of Rome, the Astarte of Syria, the Ashtoreth of Canaan, and the Ishtar of Babylon, the goddess of the morning star. In the Epic of Creation, Virgo was Zarbanit, the mother, sister, and virgin wife of the sun-god Marduk. She was commonly known as Our Lady, a title applied to West Semitic goddesses and the Virgin Mary (Jacobsen 1976: 138f.; Langdon 1931: 317, 341; Malina 1995: 162). Her month was the sixth of the sacred year, which marked Gabriel's visit to Mary and the annunciation of Jesus' birth (Luke 1: 26).

The association of Isis with the summer sun heading south evoked the companionship of Leo and Virgo; the union of a maiden and a lion pro-duced the Sphinx of Egypt, a creature that consisted of a woman's head and a lion's body. Virgo's heliacal rise at the beginning of the sixth month marked the inundation of the Nile and the midsummer sun turning hot and falling towards the nether world, below the celestial equator. Like the sun heading south, the celestial Virgin was bound to suffer a great fall. To use Canaanitish symbolism, the lady was expected to accompany the sun-god Ninurta, a deity assimilated to the Sirius complex (the stars of Canis Major rising as the sun goes through Leo). After Ishtar descending with Tammuz, Virgo partook in the destiny of Ninurta who perished with the dying corn as he entered the second, darker half of the year (Jacobsen 1976: 55–63; Langdon 1931: 28, 135, 233). In Revelation 12, the queen of heaven suffers a similar fate. She turns into a sunlit woman fleeing into the desert, a place of permanent heat and drought. Her flight marks the beginning of the darker half of time (in a cycle of seven years) and a sojourn in the wilderness coinciding with the serpent's dominion over the world.

All indications are that the Lion of Judah is an infant born from the sun-clothed woman of the zodiac, menaced by two draconic figures or beasts (Scorpio, Serpens) attacking her from below and behind. The latter chase is taken up by the two beasts of Revelation 13 and modelled after God's primordial battle against Leviathan and Behemoth (Collins 1976: 164f.). The imagery evokes the Virgin's appearance high in the vernal sky at midnight – hence, autumn memories of the Scorpion, the Serpent, and the Serpent-Holder meeting at the intersection of the colure, the equator, and the ecliptic. The scene is preceded by Virgo shining to the east, rising on the eve of the paschal lamb's ascent to the sky. It ends with the woman's decline towards the west and the downfall of the draconic creatures chasing her (as in Rev. 12: 4). The final descent coincides with the culmination of the Eagle in the morning sky followed by the ascent of the sun entering the Ram, father of the Lamb. The fate of the maiden is thus tied to two opposite manifestations of the solar cycle: the birth of life at springtime and death striking at the end of summer.

For yet an even clearer expression of a beast pursuing a goddess in the sky, one should look farther north, closer to the crown of heaven, directly across from Virgo, in the vicinity of Aries. I am alluding to the daughter of King Cepheus and Queen Cassiopeia, or a chained woman called **Andromeda**, a figure known for her exposure to the southern sea-monster Cetus as punishment for her mother's vanity. 'Andromeda, though far away she flies, dreads the Sea-monster, low in southern skies,' used to say Aratus. In the words of Manilius: 'Cetus undulates its scaly body; it rises aloft upon a spiral of coils and splashes with such a belly as drove the sea beyond its proper shores when it appeared from the waves to destroy the daughter of Cepheus exposed upon the cliffs' (*Astronomica* 1: 431–7). The whale monster (Cetus) bathing in Eridanus had in common with Draco, Hydra, and Serpens that it served as a substitute for the Euphratean Tiamat. The heavenly creature was thought to cast a great river out of his mouth, Eridanus the heavenly Nile – the Ocean Stream flowing around the earth according to Homer (Maunder 1923: 208). In keeping with John's vision, this lowest River of the Sky flows to the south as if swallowed by the earth.

Perseus was the one who rescued Andromeda from the Whale. The hero held Satan's severed head in his hand and lived up the celestial river formed by the Milky Way. His conflict with the Sea-Monster echoed the battle of the sun-god Bel Marduk against Tiamat. Close to Andromeda, there is also Pegasus, a constellation whose wings evoked the flight of the eagle and the horse of the Jewish god Nimrod (Allen 1963: 322f.; Langdon 1931: 115–19).

In short, just as the southern Water-Snake/Lion opposition mirrors the higher antagonism between Hercules and Draco, so too the conflict between Water-Snake and Virgo rises in intensity when translated to the north, towards the scene of Cetus pursuing Andromeda.

All of these astral evocations throw light on what Revelation 12 insists on not saying. But which of these counter-texts should be privileged? Should it be the zodiac? Beasley-Murray (1974: 197) argues that John's sun-clothed woman cannot be attached to any particular asterism, not even Virgo. After all, if zodiacal effects had been intended, the lady's crown of twelve stars would convey the complete cycle of the zodiac as opposed to one constellation only. In spite of this difficulty, the zodiacal overtones of the sunlit woman scene are commonly acknowledged, even by Charles (1920, 1: 315f.) and Prigent (1959: 130), following the example of Gunkel (1895: 386), Zimmern (1903), and Bousset (1906). Charles cites Josephus, Philo, and Martianus Capella, whose views on the subject point to a correspondence between the zodiac, the tribes of Israel, the apostles heading the Christian Church, and the twelve stones on the crown of the Assyrian Juno and the breastplate of the high priest. To use Old Testament symbolism, the beauty of John's heavenly woman is that she embodies unity between the solar father, his lunar wife, and their twelve star-like sons (Gen. 37: 9). A similar vision occurs in the Testament of Naphtali (v. 1ff.), where Levi and Judah rise like sun and moon, with twelve rays sighted beneath their feet.

The projection of a twelvefold zodiac on to specific portions of heaven (such as Virgo) is none the less problematical. The maiden embodies the principle of cosmic unity; she appears as a composite image embracing many attributes, a creature marching to the four winds, around the crown of heaven. Fixed, as they are, to the vault of heaven, Andromeda and Virgo cannot fulfil this synthetic function. Given this interpretive problem, the scene could be made to prompt a different thought: the two constellations could be seen as reflections of Isis and other goddesses of her kind, all of whom were commonly assimilated to Venus and the moon. In the background of our twelve-starred woman adorned with the sun, standing on the moon, and giving birth to Christ *the Morning Star* (2 Peter 1: 19; Rev. 2: 24, 28, 22: 16), there is indeed a rich corpus of pan-Semitic mythologies centred on the relationship between the dying sun-god and Venus or the moon, two queenly 'planets' that travelled with the sun along the ecliptic path and covered the entire zodiac.

Jacobsen (1976: 138f.) and Langdon (1931: 14, 23–5, 34ff.) have shown how the Sumerian cult of the morning and evening star is at the origin of the Babylonian story of the virgin Earth-goddess Ishtar and its Syrian variant starring Astarte, heiresses of the divine creatress of humanity (Aruru or Mami) in the older Sumerian mythology. Like **Venus**, these goddesses accompanied the god of earthly vegetation, the sun-god that died every summer, only to be reborn yearly in midwinter or at the beginning of spring. The Queen of Heaven thus acted as precursor or follower of the rising or declining sun. In Sumerian mythology, Venus was the evening star (Ishtar of Erech) appearing as a heavenly maiden, but also the morning star viewed as a male god (Ishtar of Agade). The planet stood for love and harlotry when setting with the sun, and war when rising in the morning. Accordingly, the Babylonian Mother-Earth represented Fate, but also the goddess of battle, after the manner of Athena, Greek protectress of the state and defender of kings.

The cult of Venus was widely observed in Canaan and by the Hebrews as well (Jer. 7: 18). The lady's relationship to the sun-god incorporated images of divine sisterhood, motherhood, and wifehood. The brightness of Venus was such that she was titled the twin sister of the sun-god Shamash. The queenly star, however, was also portrayed as a mother with a child at her breasts, after the Babylonian Nintud or Aruru, queen of the gods. In the religious system of Sumer and Babylon, the Earth-goddess Astarte was the wife, mother, or sister of the sun-god. John's sun-clothed woman takes after these goddesses in that she personifies the labouring nation of Zion – hence, 'our mother Jerusalem' bringing forth a Saviour hailed as the newborn king (Isa. 26: 18, 66: 7; Jer. 4: 31, etc.). Faithful Israel mothered a Saviour who stood as her divine bridegroom and also her own brother, the son of her Father in heaven (Gal. 4: 26; Rev. 19: 7, 21: 9).

The lunar aspect of the Queen of Heaven should also be mentioned, for it is in conjunction with the **moon** that Venus and the sun governed the laws and covenants of the universe. With the sun, the moon was appointed 'for signs and for seasons, and for days and years,' an expression referring to the moon's role in the ordering of time and festivities instituted by the Hebrews. The lunar divinity was known to the Hebrews as Sin, a name of Sumero-Babylonian origin. Sin was masculine, yet in Egypt the moon was worshipped under the form of Isis. In Syria she became the Astarte surnamed Karnaim, from the horns of the crescent moon which typified her (cf. Gen. 14: 5). Rituals dedicated to the moon prevailed in Canaan and Judah before the reign of Josiah (cf. 2 Kings 23: 5; Jer. 7: 18). Readers of Job will also recall the prophet's words of remonstrance against lunisolarism: 'Has the sight of the sun in its glory, or the glow of the moon as it walked the sky, stolen my heart, so that my hand blew them a secret kiss? That too would be a criminal offense, to have denied the supreme God' (Job 31: 26–7).

Like Virgo heralding the second half of the year, lunar symbols can be used to evoke the second half and the End of Time. This can be done through a womb and a lunar footstool 'fully waxed,' positioned midway between the beginning and the end of the monthly cycle. When assimilated to a pregnant woman (as in Rev. 12), however, a full moon announces a new life, not the reign of death or the end of time. In the long run, the lunar woman can be counted on to fulfil the same mission as assigned to the virgin creatress and Earth-goddess called 'Mother Womb.' Like the Babylonian Mami (= Aruru = Ishtar), the sun-robed woman of Revelation 12 will give mankind a new life, through the birth of a redeemer (Jacobsen 1976: 196f.). Still, the new creation will emerge only after the first creation is brought to a close. Redemption must come after total destruction by drought, famine, and pestilence. It must come after a great sacrifice, as on the festal day of the fifteenth of each Babylonian month, or day of the full moon known as the *sabattu*. This is the day that ushers in the darkness of the moon in the second half of the month, a darkness which the Epic of Creation attributes to seven devils of the lower world (Jacobsen 1976: 121–3). The ritual sacrifice could also be held at the beginning of the civil year, on 15 Tishri, on the occasion of the Feast of Ingathering. In keeping with the imagery of Revelation 12, the date commemorates the flight of God's chosen bride (Israel) into the desert, a place of mourning and propitiatory atonement, away from the tyranny of her Egyptian persecutor (Jacobsen 1976: 53–5; Langdon 1931: 152, 356f.). Alternatively, the sacrifice could take place two weeks after the first new moon of the sacred year, on the eve of 14 Abib. This is when the paschal Lamb is sacrificed to mark the beginning of Passover and the deliverance of Israel from bondage and death. The scene is set against the background of Virgo shining to the east and a full moon pregnant with signs of vernal resurrection and the end of winter rains and the Flood (Gen. 8: 13).

To sum up, a woman falling in the company of a solarized god yields to forces of darkness. In the language of primitive astronomy, the appearance of Virgo on the eve of spring is overshadowed by the ascent of Hydra to the south and Draco to the north. To make things worse, the maiden's appearance is followed by Scorpio guarding the gates of the underworld along the ecliptic (Jacobsen 1976: 204). When these creatures climb into heaven, they chase away God's celestial allies (Aquila, Ophiuchus, Hercules) and rise against the sun-god, causing him to fall towards the deep and the darkness of winter. As the sun falls, he brings down with him the maiden of heaven – the moon or Venus setting with the sun declining in old age. Yet the lady's descent causes in turn the downfall of the draconic colure and the heliacal birth and rise of Christ, a morning star going to war at spring or at autumn, the season of Judgment. The triumph of the faithful woman and her son/spouse is announced by the culmination of King Cepheus to the north and also Aquila, protector of the young. To these signs of godly victory can be added the rise of Andromeda flying on the wings of an eagle-like horse named Pegasus. The daughter of Cepheus is rescued by Perseus, who saves her from the satanic sea-monster while holding the head of Medusa in his hand.

Revelation 12 brings profound modifications to older religions. For instance, it innovates by substituting the model woman, the angel Michael, and Christ the martyr and redeemer for the star-gods and – goddesses of ancient mythology. But the substitution is only partial. In its reactive mode, innovation presupposes a debt towards foreign traditions; the new vision is 'alienated' by its opposition to the alien. To say that 'John is never restricted by the sources of his imagery' (Mounce 1977: 246) is to leave unexplored the restrictions placed by John on his own sources. In the final analysis, what distinguishes John's script from Sabian mythologies is not an absolute distance between the two scripts, as if the biblical text could squarely 'transcend' its context or counter-text, as Prigent (1959: 137) would have it. The innovation of Revelation lies rather in its constant effort to leave the astral deities unnamed, reducing them to a shadowy existence, an obscure presence felt by metaphorical proxy. Christian prophets preoccupied with the spread of idolatry have little to gain from exposing pagan plots against the Lord; a more profitable strategy consists in recuperating the Sabian code for higher purposes. Stars receive as much attention as before, but only as reflections of the Lord and his Light. Astral gods are bridled so that they can be forced to die in harness, never in earnest.

Arresting the Order of Time

The suggestion made by Collins (1976: 1f., 117ff., 129, 187ff.), Caird (1966: 148), and Beasley-Murray (1974: 191ff.) that key motifs of Revelation 12 be explained as polemical adaptations of Graeco-Roman mythology and pro-paganda is central to our understanding of John's visions of the End of Time. Signs of lunisolarism, Isis imagery, the Leto-Python combat myth, Apollonianism, emperor-worship modelled on the deification of Augustus, the legend of Nero returning as Saviour-King to avenge the East on Rome (see Rev. 13 and 17), all these elements of non-Jewish culture were known throughout the world of John's day, and even more so to Jews of the diaspora. In Revelation 12, this material is rewritten so as to contradict its current political application and bring back memories of messianic strug-gles of the Old Testament. By casting this material in a Jewish-Christian mould, John turns paganism into a parody of the divine, an expression of self-adulation and satanic idolatry.

The killing of the dragon *is* being re-enacted, but not by the emperor, who turns out instead to be one of the dragon's minions. It is not the emperor who is son to the Queen of Heaven. We have seen that the goddess Roma was worshipped in the cit-ies of Asia and closely associated with the local cults of the Mother Goddess [Cybele]. On a coin of Pergamum there is the head of Augustus and a female figure with the legend, THEAN ROMEN (the goddess Roma). On another coin, from the reign of Tiberius, Augustus and Livia, the ideal embodiments of Roman imperial authority, are represented as sun and moon. The coinage was the one universal form of propaganda for the imperial ideology, which declared that Roma was the new queen of the gods and mother of the world's saviour. John is going to portray her as the new Jezebel, the seducer of the world, clad in all the finery of earth. She who claims to be the queen of earth (xviii.7) must be seen to be a travesty of the resplen-dent Queen of Heaven. (Caird 1966: 148)

Pagan elements are fused into an international text, co-opted in such ways as to underscore Jewish opposition to Rome expressed on a cosmic scale. By reinterpreting the Apollo myth and related symbology to depict the birth of the Messiah and his triumph against the dragon, 'the author of Revelation formulated a further element in the antithesis of Christ and Nero. The claims of the Apollonian Nero are rejected by the depiction of Christ as the true bringer of order and light' (Collins 1976: 190). Similar adaptations of Graeco-Roman, Egyptian, or Babylonian mythology to express Jewish messianic expectations can be found in the Sibylline books, in a hymn to wisdom composed by Jesus Ben Sirah, and in the second-century writings of Pseudo-Eupolemos and Artapanus (Collins 1976: 128f.; see Charlesworth 1983, 1: 356).

In spite of the overwhelming evidence pointing to the political and historical underpinnings of Revelation 12, Lohmeyer (1926: 103–6) contends that John's vision is strictly eschatological. The text speaks essentially of spiritual events, a transcendent reality or timeless order that escapes all accounts of real history. In this perspective, the exegete should avoid reading an historical allegory into John's visions of *the End of Time*. Although more inclined to accept historical explanations, other biblical scholars have made the same argument with respect to particular details of Revelation (see Prigent 1981). Gunkel (1895: 374–8), for instance, objects to equating the 666 motif of Revelation 13 with any particular emperor. Likewise, Charles (1920, 1: 345–7) argues against granting any precise historical meaning to the ten-horn motif and the rising-out-of-the-sea imagery. Other exegetes such as Allo (1933: 289), Bonsirven (1951: 230, 270f.), and Caird (1966: 161–5) invert the historical-allegorical interpretation by treating implicit references to the Roman Empire as symbolic of demonic power (see Collins 1976: 198n87). All in all, Revelation 'does not encourage the reader with clear hints, as does the Animal Apocalypse, for example, to look for a continuous series of historical events to which the story corresponds' (Collins 1976: 124).

While cautions expressed about historical explanations are understandable, Lohmeyer's argument is untenable. But Lohmeyer's thesis is faithful to the spirit of John's text. His thesis points to an important feature of Revelation: the systematic reluctance on the part of John to spell out the connections between his eschatological imagery and the order of time. The prophet indulges in visions of signs of heaven, yet he never treats these signs for what others saw in them: divine stars, planets, and spheres of heaven fighting and succeeding one another as they mark the repeated passage of days, weeks, months, and seasons. On the political level, his visions can hardly be isolated from Jewish opposition to Rome, yet no reference is ever made to real historical figures or events. Gematria is used to evoke Nero (Rev. 13: 8), Babylon is substituted for Rome, military and judicial actions against early Christians are allegorized via combat and heavenly court mythology, emperor worship is never clearly mentioned, and prophecies are never assigned precise dates (unlike astrological oracles). The Messiah has yet to come, which means that the life and deeds of Christ mothered by a woman named Mary seem to be wholly forgotten (Charles 1920, 1: 308f.). Surely, there must be a reason for these blatant omissions, other than the notion that John was simply concentrating on something else, or that there was no need to spell out what the Church already knew (L. Morris 1983: 159; Sweet 1990: 197).

If connections to the order of time (astrology, worldly history) are so compelling, why should John show so much discretion? The reasons are many. Through eschatological language, John gives maximum weight to contemporary political issues seen from a Jewish perspective. In lieu of chronicling a sequence of events situated in context and predicting those that have yet to come, the prophet expresses the universal and transcendent significance of the struggle of the chosen people against their unholy enemies. The plight of first-century Jews is elevated to the rank of a final confrontation embodying all battles against the forces of darkness, a holy war to end all wars. Cosmic dualism is thus substituted for the conflict between Rome and the Jews, with the implication that earthly and heavenly adversaries of God and his chosen people are fated to share Satan's defeat (Collins 1976: 117, 131, 144).

Until the world of Satan comes to an end, the fusion of many religious traditions into a full-scale cosmogony allows John to overcome the infidels and all false gods in a single vision. In the name of the Messiah, John appropriates key signs and symbolic fields claimed by competing divinities of Western Asia Minor and the ruling powers of his day. Through his Revelation, pagan hopes of redemption vested in divinities that govern the order of Time (kings, the sun, the moon, the stars) are revamped in the service of Christian messianism. The prophet strikes a fatal blow on evil forces by divesting them of all godly authority and control over the cosmos, reducing them to signs of tribulational chaos. Efforts on the part of kings and star-gods to harness the motions of Time (cycles of the sun and the planets, the passing of seasons, the unfolding of worldly history) are thus in vain. Even when bound to the passing of days and seasons, rulers and false gods rebelling against the Eternal can generate nothing but chaos. This is to say that the temporal must be governed by the eternal less it lapse into troubled times. In Revelation, the 'constant tension between creation and chaos' (Collins 1976: 164) – enlightenment and obscurantism (Sweet 1990: 204) – is surreptitiously substituted for the struggle between two competing orders: the eternal (logocentric) and the temporal (imperial, astromythical, calendrical).

The substitution entails a flight from the tensions and battles of real history. While John's use of eschatology magnifies a particular reality, it also has the opposite effect, which is to reduce the tensions of worldly history, hiding the strains of contemporary politics under a thick cloak of allegori-

cal apocalypse. In its own discreet way, Revelation is an advice against the
Zealot policy of fighting openly against the Roman rule in Palestine (Collins 1976: 234). John's vision precludes overt defamations of Rome and
direct appropriations of her imperial symbolism. The latter includes astral
and lunisolar titles and the corresponding measurements of time performed
through oracles of primitive astronomy – acts of divination performed with
rebellious intent, strictly forbidden in biblical texts, and severely punished
by Roman magistrates as well. On the surface level, Revelation is concerned with court actions instigated by Satan against followers of the Lord
represented by Michael, their heavenly advocate (Caird 1966: 155; L. Morris 1983: 161; Sweet 1990: 199f.). But the text also betrays the author's and
readers' fear of the well-known first-century *delator*, the informer paid to
bring charges against people using astrology and other means to challenge
the imperial and divine power vested in Rome.

The author of Revelation is constantly careful about what he says of
human history, or rather about what he should never say. As suggested
above, the Seer also keeps a watchful eye on all references to measurements
of time based on observations of the cyclical motions of sun, moon, and
stars. As a result, correspondences between John's visions and the calendrical aspects of life and death, be it on earth or in heaven, are never spelled
out. Given their objections to introducing lunisolar ideology into the apocalypse, some biblical scholars have taken John's reservations about calendrical time at their face-value. Prigent (1959: 122ff.; 1981: 185) is a case in
point. The exegete objects to Gunkel's stellar reading of the Apocalypse
and other related themes borrowed from ancient formulations of naturalism and realism. He also rejects Gunkel's notion that Revelation 12
deploys images of winter darkness and birth that give way to vernal light
and glory in Revelation 19. Finally, Prigent criticizes the idea that the parallels between Revelation 12 and non-Jewish mythologies may result from
common calendrical and ritual markers of scenes of resurrection and
enthronement held at springtime.

The last point can serve to illustrate the limitations of Prigent's anti-
astrological approach to Revelation. One way to explain the similarities
among various religious texts of the ancient Near East is to attribute common ritual patterns associated with agricultural calendars, royal cults, and
New Year enthronement festivals observed throughout biblical lands
(Hooke 1933, 1935, 1958). Despite his rejection of astral and calendrical
interpretations, Prigent (1981: 184, 189, 191) resorts to this 'myth and ritual' approach in his discussion of the impact of paschal symbolism on Revelation 12. The approach is particularly useful as it accounts for the cyclical

features of John's visions and the principle of recapitulation that governs the whole Book of Revelation. As pointed out by many scholars such as Bousset (1906: 57), Bornkamm (1937), and Collins (1976: 13–16, 215), to name just a few, John's Apocalypse repeats the same basic pattern through a series of combat scenes. Why repeat the same theme over and over again? In my view, the recapitulation phenomenon does not point to the reiterative features of mythic language or the universal opposition between order and chaos (see Collins 1976: 44, 232). It points rather to the calendrical underpinnings of Judaeo-Christian cosmogony and morality. As Collins (1976: 117; emphasis added) puts it: 'the victory of order over chaos, fertility over sterility was not something which happened once and for all *in illo tempore*, but must be *won repeatedly with the ebb and flow of the seasons and of dynasties.*' The grand battle in question is culturally specific in that it is played out against the background of pan-Semitic world-views centred on cyclical motions of heavenly bodies and divinities falling and rising from the sky *in due season*. These world-views involve context-specific measurements of cycles of light and darkness – hence, codifications of the repeated fall and rise, death and resurrection of the sun and the planets marching through the Near Eastern sky.

In retrospect, Prigent's refusal to translate John's imageries into principles of calendrical realism and astral naturalism has in common with Lohmeyer's thesis that it emphasizes elements of everlasting spirituality over astrology and worldly history – over 'signs of the times.' Actually, both scholars have in common with the author of Revelation a tendency to privilege signs of a timeless Logos over temporal implications of the Verb.

To conclude, Collins (1976: 207) warns us that the search for symbolic parallels (as between logocentric and naturalistic mythologies) can produce oversimplifications, a tendency to overlook significant differences, and a temptation to assume that similarities imply literary dependence. The claim made by the pan-Babylonian school that much of Judaeo-Christian symbolism goes back to the Babylonian world-view illustrates the latter fallacies. But the notion that one should not look beyond the Old Testament and Jewish religion to understand the raw material of Revelation is equally extreme. Actually, both approaches to Revelation err on the side of monological naïvety. A particular tradition monopolizes the entire conversation, either by detaching itself completely from all foreign influences or by repeating itself through countless cross-cultural variations on similar themes. For an alternative to monology, one should consider the polemical features of the Verb: that is, critical struggles occurring over current signs and powers of speech, struggles involving neither relations of full independence nor absolute dependence, neither radical differences nor perfect similarities. This is to say that comparative literary analysis (searching for similarities and/or differences) is but a first step towards a better understanding of the complex interaction between one text and another: in other words, the intertext and discursive contest.

Of Seasons and Sacrifice

The notion that victory comes after repeated, seasonally regulated gestures of sacrifice and mourning is a recurrent theme within pan-Semitic stories of stars and kings. 'This great cult of a dying god, which was intensively practised from prehistoric times by the Sumerians, adopted by the Babylonians, Assyrians, Aramaeans, Phoenicians, Canaanites, Hebrews, and Egyptians, is based upon the belief in a martyred saint, who died and rose again, and became a god' (Langdon 1931: 346, see also 52, 76, 341f.). The idea that an afterlife can be attained through self-sacrifice lies at the heart of the Syrian festival of the *dies natalis Solis invicti*, 'Natal day of the unconquerable Sun,' an event held at the end of the winter season. The Babylonian New Year festival dedicated to Marduk rising from his tomb also points to a sacrificial morality embedded in natural cycles of life and death, cycles that apply to all forms of life on earth and to gods dwelling in heaven (Jacobsen 1976: 47–63). Laws of the universe were such that deified kings had to follow the example set by the father of Tammuz and sacrifice some of their children to the gods, at least when great dangers beset the land. All humans must find inspiration in the Supreme Sacrifice of Tammuz. Readers will recall that the sun-god Tammuz had to suffer decline and death after the summer solstice before he could rise from the dead at spring. Prior to rejoicing in the rebirth of Tammuz, Ishtar-like women had to weep the death of the sun-god descending to the nether world at summertime. The renewal of solar life requires that the elderly sun-god be immolated on his own altar, burning in the heat of his estival flames.

The yearly descent of the sun and his bride suggests that the fall of gods is not without purpose. The sun had to immolate himself in his own fire and cause the death of the motherland and the lamb so that all of them could languish for the fresh water of life renewed at spring. The Earth-goddess and the sun-god of vegetation and corn will not be protected from death by means of an uncomplicated marriage between heaven and earth, without the trials of a great Fall. A deity that stays high in heaven without ever falling presents little interest (lofty Shamash was never a principal figure in Sumerian or Akkadian mythology).

The same moral applies to earthly and heavenly mortals alike: to conquer death, all of them must first become martyrs – victims of the seven gods of destruction and the beasts in their host. In Revelation 12, the trials of godly sacrifice are merely announced, which means that the blood of martyrdom has yet to be poured over the earth. For the time being the sun-clothed woman is spared a tragic fall as she takes refuge in the wilderness, the place where God fed the daughter of Israel with manna rain, saving her from death during her wanderings in the desert. Unlike Ishtar, the heroine flees from the demons of heaven and is not swallowed by the waters of Tiamat (Jacobsen 1976: 55–63, 190; Langdon 1931: 97, 219f.). Nor is the male child devoured by the beast. It is rather the Mother-Earth who swallows the river issued from the dragon's mouth. As a result, the male child ascends to the throne of heaven; he triumphs like the sun-god of vegetation resurrecting at spring, the male counterpart of the wheat-bearing Virgin.

Until the woman and her child are truly sacrificed, the woman can expect to lose her children to devils and strange gods, thus provoking God to jealousy (Deut. 32: 15ff.; Ps. 106: 37). Other demons have yet to rise from the abyss, including seven bulls known as the *sedim*, 'strong ones of the pit' in Canaanitish mythology. These beasts used to play a central role in astromythical formulations of the heavenly life cycle. They stood as the inverted image of Taurus led by the seven Pleiades, the sacred bull sacrificed on the fifth day of the Babylonian spring festival. As argued in previous chapters, the heptadic team also pointed to a seven-headed, bear-footed beast of the high north, a demonic creature now about to rise from the sea (Rev. 13).[3]

The persecution of the lamb child and his mother by dragons of heaven is part of the lesson of life obtained through cycles of rebirth and sacrificial death. In the words of the Seer, 'they have triumphed over him [the persecutor] by the blood of the Lamb and by the witness of their martyrdom, because even in the face of death they would not cling to life' (Rev. 12: 11). Great rewards are promised to martyrs who in the face of death refuse to cling to life. In his visions of the End of Time, however, John gives the sacrificial teachings exemplified by yearly motions of the sun a different twist. The powers accorded to those who follow the sacrificial ways of the Lord differ from those granted to astral divinities falling and resurrecting in due season. For one thing, the prophet dissociates his vision of the Saviour and his bride/mother from Semitic stories of the lunisolar pantheon, stories that portray astral bodies as divinities given to outbursts of lust and wrath. When John assigns star symbols to God, he treats them as signs of spiritual glory and divine retribution. Revelation makes no concession to the Gnostic principle of tolerance towards chaos or sexual licence sought by humans, let alone by the gods. By contrast, the ways of Tammuz and Ishtar involve greater violence and licence. In Babylonian mythology, the goddess Ishtar was unfaithful to her Lord and was responsible for sending her dying son/husband to hell. She wreaked havoc in heaven and was known as the goddess of discord. The sun-god Tammuz was forced to join her many victims, all of them seduced to their destruction. Her victims included the lion for whom she dug seven pits, the magnificent bird whose wing she broke, the herdsman she turned into a jackal, and the gardener she reduced to misery.

The cult of this goddess of war and lust, also pictured as Venus, was found throughout Western Asia under various titles, including Astarte, queen of the harlots. In many ways Astarte resembled Tiamat, the mortal foe of Tammuz; actually, she was the sister of this underworld serpent elsewhere known as Ereshkigal (= Hydra). Her close association with creatures of the abyss meant that she could take the shape of a serpent and have a scorpion between her legs. Like her, Tammuz could assume the identity of the dreaded serpent, the draconic lion, or the ram gone wild. Alternatively, the sun-god could take in marriage the serpent of the salt sea, as in legends of Nergal, the Sumerian counterpart of Tammuz.[4]

In the writings of John, associations of this sort are inconceivable. The sunlit woman is sharply contrasted with the harlot, and the serpent figure is clearly opposed to God. The snake is not a representation of godliness, but rather the leading contender to God's throne. The reptile aspires to godly status as it possesses what any true god must attain and also retain: the power over life and death. Snakes are envied by mortals as they can inflict great sufferings on their enemies. Also they can survive in the desert and save their own skin, even when shedding it. We know from the Babylonian epic of Gilgamish that the annual rejuvenation of the serpent resulted from the serpent's theft of the plant of metamorphosis (named 'the old man becomes a young man'), at the expense of man. 'From that time forth reptiles cast their aged slough, but evil old age envelops men; while the deadly beast received "Brayer's" complaint, and inflicts a scarce-seen wound' (Langdon 1931: 229; see Jacobsen 1976: 207, 217–19).

Revelation must keep its distance from pagan characterizations of God and his virgin mother or bride, which include expressions of astralism and also the serpent and harlot imagery. Empyrean signs of war and lust can none the less be recuperated by godly forces, if only indirectly and with great circumspection. Revelation 12 thus alludes to the vernal enthronement of a Passover Lamb turned into a fearsome Ram. Christ is portrayed as a newborn sun exercising power over his enemies, launching a decisive expedition, presumably at spring (which is when real wars used to take place). The exultation of a solarized Lord implies the downfall of forces of evil, or the final judgment that comes at the beginning of the winter season. This is when the sun-god descends to the world of the dead and the trials of darkness befall humanity. In keeping with these calendrical signs, Christ is given an iron sceptre to rule over the world, an instrument of power closely tied to Arcturus, shepherd of the heavenly flock, and to the combined equinoctial imagery of sword, stone, manna, and name (see chapter 5).

Just as God recuperates the powers of older star-gods, so too his bridal nation recovers the beauty the unfaithful whore possesses but never deserves. In order to regain her glory and beauty, however, the model woman must in some way resemble the lady who vainly usurped her role. While there are two expressions of lust, one obtained through sacrificial passion and the other through sinful conduct, both employ similar imageries. This paradox can be explored through the sun-robed woman's relationship to Eve, the mother of humanity. Despite the distance that lies between Genesis 3 and Revelation 12, the two women have much in common. Both are possessed with the blessings of God and are confronted with the same serpent, a satanic creature to be crushed by the Lord. They both suffer the pains of travail and are expelled from a heavenly habitat because of their demonic enemy. Finally, both stories speak of a woman whose seed is destined to trample the forces of darkness. On the astral plane, the imagery is reminiscent of wheat-bearing Virgo standing above Hydra and Scorpio, Ophiuchus stepping on Scorpio, and Hercules on Draco.

Eve and the woman of Revelation 12 differ in that one falls under the influence of the serpent while the other falls as she flees from the dragon. The first woman was tricked into eating the fruit of the tree of immortal life and divine knowledge. Together with Adam, she tried to elevate human beings to the rank of God, in vain. As a result, humans became mortal. Eve and her male companion never assimilated the secrets of the plant of metamorphosis originally stolen by the serpent.[5] Because of her sin, the mother of humanity was condemned to give birth in pain. By contrast, John's sunlit woman is freed from satanic persecution because of the pain she endured when giving birth to the Messiah and giving her son away on the cross. Eve's curse is turned into a show of virtue: the fall a harlot suffers at the hand of the Lord becomes a woman's sacrifice. To compensate for her pain, the Saviour's mother is granted the assistance of an Eagle rising in the season of Judgment, a bird that can show her where the 'plant of birth' is hidden, as in the legend of Etana. Like Ishtar, the woman's quest for a shepherd wearing a crown brings about a kingship descending from heaven, a new reign to counter the chaos caused by the gods' hatred for humans.

Eve and the sun-robed woman of Revelation 12 differ in many respects. Still, few modifications would be needed to transform the sun-clothed woman into a harlot or an infidel. The lady's fall can be viewed as a sacrifice, yet the language used to describe her misfortune could also be applied to expressions of immoral conduct. Events that caused the woman of Revelation 12 to suffer the pangs of birth have yet to be explored. Could it be that the lady fell prey to temptations of the flesh? Could it be that her relationship to the serpent lends itself to signs of evil rapture? Although adorned with the sun, our model woman may have let herself be raptured by the seediest part of creation surging from the pit. Parallels in heaven point that way. The serpent's position beneath or behind the Maiden of Heaven (Virgo) allows the beast (the Water-Snake, the Serpent held by Ophiuchus, Scorpio) to bruise the heel of the woman or her seed, the Morning Star. As she falls prey to the serpent's sting, the woman becomes like Eve. She succumbs to the serpent and is condemned to bring forth children in sorrow. When she took the serpent's advice and swallowed the apple, Eve caused her womb to shed blood with as much regularity as the moon going through her twelve *menses* (Latin for 'months'). John's sun-robed woman suffers the same fate in that she too must shed a lot of blood – the blood of her son and the twelve tribal/apostolic stars in her train.

Although performed in a spirit of purification and propitiation, gestures of sacrifice imply expressions of self-degradation. In order to undergo sacrifice, deities have to be deprived of their heavenly splendour and be brought down so low as to become virtually 'depraved.' Like the Janus-faced sun, martyred gods are inherently two-faced. The story of the vegetation goddess is a case in point. She was the one 'who brings verdure in abundance,' yet when she disappeared from heaven she became the 'woe for the leafing plant.' Her descent to the nether world to which her solar lover had gone caused her to lose her beautiful apparel. The last article (the seventh) to be removed from her body consisted of a shame garment; when the garment was removed, the goddess became like a whore. Her fall meant that she became like her sister, Ereshkigal, the demoness that governed the underworld and that led demons rising against the living.

To conclude, myths and rituals centring on the death and rebirth of the sun-god and his wife, sister, or mother were commonly found throughout Syria, Phoenicia, and Palestine. Heliolatry marked the religious history of Sumer, Akkad, and Babylonia and goes back more than 4,000 years. This astral mythology caught the imagination of all Semitic peoples for a simple reason: it tackled basic problems of human existence, such as the fate of vegetation at the hand of the scorching sun heading south in the midsummer season. People's concern for the death of Tammuz and Ishtar reflected a preoccupation with the withering of leaves and food-plants in the torrid heat of the summer, and the fear of droughts plaguing the Mesopotamian valley. Measures had to be taken to protect the cycle of life, ensuring that the solar shepherd would return at springtime with rains to feed his flock on earth and the plants to feed humans and animals. Paradoxically, the downfall of all life forms (godly, astral, human, animal, botanical) provided the imagery that was needed to explain the calamities suffered because of the Fall but also the means to counter them: gestures of sacrificial devotion performed by lowly men and women falling on their knees before God, hoping to rise again with the sun resurrecting and the greenery of the earth growing a new life again.

Conclusion:

Signs of Logomachy

The notion that astral lessons of cyclical time can be read into ancient mythologies dates back at least to late antiquity. In his *Saturnalia*, Macrobius claimed that Adonis stood for the sun. The Latin grammarian found confirmation of this in religious practices of the Assyrians and Phoenicians, including the sun-related cult of Venus. The goddess was said to mourn the sun that journeyed through the twelve zodiacal signs of the lower hemisphere, the realm of Proserpina. This was the time of the year when days got shorter, as if the sun had been carried off for a time by death. Venus mourned until Adonis rose back to life, an event occurring in springtime, when the sun had left the 'circle of the earth.'

On Mount Lebanon there is a statue of Venus. Her head is veiled, her expression sad, her cheek beneath her veil is resting on her left hand; and it is believed that as one looks upon the statue it sheds tears. This statue not only represents the mourning goddess of whom we have been speaking but is also a symbol of the earth in winter; for at the time the earth is veiled in clouds, deprived of the companionship of the sun, and benumbed, its springs of water (which are, as it were, its eyes) flowing more freely and the fields meanwhile stripped of their finery – a sorry sight. But when the sun has come up from the lower parts of the earth and has crossed the boundary of the spring equinox, giving length to the day, then Venus is glad and fair to see, the fields are green with growing crops, the meadows with grass and trees with leaves. This is why our ancestors dedicated the month of April to Venus. (Macrobius, quoted in Malina 1995: 143)

In the same interpretive vein, Macrobius claims that the story of the boar that killed Adonis *signifies* the winter season inflicting a wound on the sun, 'for the boar is an unkempt and rude creature delighting in damp, muddy and frost covered places and feeding on the acorn, which is especially a winter fruit.'

Many ancient philosophers and theologians objected to this naturalistic interpretation of religious beliefs, treating divine personages as stand-ins for the heavenly spheres. Hippolytus (c. 160–c. 235) was one of them. In his *Refutation of all Heresies*, the Church Father makes it clear that scriptural characters cannot be understood astrologically. He admonishes heretics who assert that Eve is Cassiopeia; that Logos is Perseus, 'the winged axle that pierces both poles through the center of the earth, and turns the world around'; and that Adam is Cepheus or Hercules (Engonasis) guarding the head of the Dragon, in compliance with God's command. No concession is to be made to those who 'endeavor to seduce the mind of those who give heed to their [tenets], drawing them only plausible words into the admission of whatever opinions they wish, [and] exhibiting a strange marvel, *as if the assertions made by them were fixed among the stars*' (quoted in Malina 1995: 75; emphasis added).

The polemic regarding the role of stars and planets in the Scriptures continued throughout the ages and found its way into exegetic commentaries of the twentieth century. In 1914 Franz Boll offered an astrological reading of Revelation, using modern genealogical methods to cast light on what he thought to be the true literary sources and origins of John's prophetic imagery. Given his naturalistic approach and lack of exegetic expertise, Boll's work was soon discounted, to be taken up by few students of Revelation (Gundel, Kroll, Festugière). Freundorfer's assessment of his work (published in 1929) raised some fundamental objections that sealed the fate of Boll's astrologism in the field of New Testament scholarship. Among other things, Freuendorfer rejected the notion that John had direct access to Near Eastern texts and documents containing astrological lore, translating these motifs into prophetic visions of his own.

More recently, Malina has attempted to resurrect the astrological hypothesis from a scholarly perspective. His contention is that John's work fits into a particular genre, an ancient literature that may be described as 'astral prophecy.' By this he means 'those ancient narratives reporting the interaction of prophets and seers with star-related, celestial personages and the outcomes of that interaction' (1995: 19, cf. 26, 30). This astronomic writing involves prophets reporting on their interaction with celestial entities and their impact upon regions of the earth. Astral visions commonly reported in the first century of our era were based on the widespread notion that sky beings controlled natural forces and human reality as well.

Groups and persons believed they had access to those cosmic personages who controlled the socially unknown. And they gained this access either through the initiative of the celestial beings themselves (e.g., the appearance of a deity) or through human initiative (e.g., a person prepares for ecstasy). Hence by means of such access, one might, on behalf of a group or its central persons (e.g., the king), contact those controlling beings and, thanks to their help, enter their space by means of visions, sky trips, and the like, with a view to learning directives and obeying. Such access was part of the social role of prophets, seers, magicians, astrologers, and astronomers. At times such access agents simply observed events as they unfolded, while at other times they attempted to coerce such controlling beings to do their own bidding. In either case the information sought was not about some distant future but about the present and forthcoming events that would impact their lives. In other words, there was nothing 'eschatological' about astral prophecy, at least not in any usual sense of the 'study of the last things.' (1995: 44f.)

The implication of this approach is that vertical relations between humans and sky beings are projected onto relations in time; for instance, heaven denotes not merely distant spaces, but also immediate future horizons. But if the short-term future is to be portrayed on a large scale, as the astral-prophecy genre requires, then the prophet must combine vertical spatial interaction with recollections of the distant past, using themes of the First Creation to enlarge the battle stakes of contemporary religious politics. The tendency to assign cosmic scope to developments of the near future thus accounts for the prophet's focus on scenes of Genesis and the struggles of primordial times. Forces of the remote past explain current troubles, giving issues of the day a magnitude matched by forthcoming events (1995: 199, 266).

According to Malina, celestial characters appearing in the New Testament Apocalypse are to be understood for what they were: sky beings encountered through visionary experiences. When John talks of Jesus the heavenly Lamb or the seven stars in the right hand of the Lord, he must be taken literally. Through his vision, the prophet did see the Lamb of God ruling the cosmos from beyond the vault of the sky, and he did see a seven-starred constellation in the Lord's hand. But if this is the case, why is it that later readers of Revelation have had so much difficulty understanding the literal meanings of John's narrative account? Malina's answer to this question is essentially twofold. First, our society no longer recognizes the validity of knowledge obtained through altered states of awareness, experiences considered quite normal in most cultures. Second, our Western world-view no longer acknowledges the many life forms and visible spirits that used to dwell in the ancient heavens. Since we are ignorant of older notions of astromythology, we can hardly recognize 'sky servants' in the literature that evokes them. If there are still many things that the Book of Revelation leaves unexplained, it is mostly because 'the seer presumes all readers know about these items. This sort of authoring is called high context writing ... The author supposes that his audience is quite well informed about everything to which he refers, such as the comets, the sky Altar or holy ones, and the like' (1995: 141, cf. 70, 75).

The evidence marshalled by Malina in support of an astrological rendering of Revelation is impressive; the overall argument cannot be ignored. The author's insights into the Apocalypse are all the more commendable as there is little scholarly work that shows the close connections between the history of astronomy and the science of mythology, two disciplines that have taken separate roads since the early eighteenth century. To suggest that John was an astral prophet, a visionary who was exiled to Patmos because he practised astral prophecy (1995: 259), is none the less untenable. Malina's thesis is problematic in several important ways. To begin with, Malina fails to reflect on the functions of John's metaphorical rhetoric. As argued in previous chapters, the prophet insists on treating heavenly imageries as tangible signs made 'in the likeness of the appearances' of immaterial spirits. This precludes a literal reading of astralism into Revelation. The creatures appearing in Revelation 4 were *like* a lion, a bull, a man, and an eagle, which is to say that that *they were not what they seemed to be*. Righteous souls that shine *like* stars in the firmament, as in Daniel 12: 3, are not necessarily thought to exist as stars, as Malina suggests (1995: 131). Unlike identity attributions, metaphors have two interrelated effects: they establish a relationship of similarity between one thing and another, but they also maintain the distance required to distinguish the two things compared, thereby eschewing a relationship of full identity. While it is easy to recognize the first effect, which tends to be more explicit, the implications of the second effect are less obvious.

In the case of Revelation, allegorical connections erected between spirits and stars are based on the principle of approximation, not of consubstantiation. While logocentrism can use astrological imageries to unfold its doctrine of history and spirituality, it cannot afford to be confused with astralism and the deification of visible rulers of heaven and the earth. The language of metaphor will permit a squaring of the circle – reconciling reverence for the stars with logocentrism – provided that the correspondences posited between spirits and stars be close enough to cause the desired impact, but never so close as to eliminate all 'flickers of doubts' regarding the identities involved. From an exegetic perspective, the implications of the language of approximation is that *a perfect match between one dominant mythology (logocentrism) and another subserving it (astralism) can never be firmly established.* John's text is constructed in such ways as to leave room for various astrological interpretations.

Effects of dialogical ambiguity and indeterminacy do not mean that literary comparative exercises should never be attempted. The point rather is that we should move the hermeneutic exercise beyond the simple quest for similarities and sources, to include questions about a text's sustained effort to distance itself from competing compositions and the precise formulations they deploy. Interpretive doubts caused by such distance are to be explained, never to be dispelled.

The Book of Revelation reflects an early Christian way of activating stellar motifs while losing track of contemporary sidereal cults. The erasure of astralism is all the more important as it allows the teachings of Logos to be elevated above the lessons of cyclical time. In other words, logocentrism requires that *battles of the times* (day versus night, spring versus autumn, Orion versus Scorpion, etc.) be turned into a *battle against time.* Star signs regulating calendrical motions are still useful inasmuch as they can make a contribution to a prophetic apprehension of God's timeless order and supportive events of the End of Time. The Verb demands that blurred reformulations of smaller-scale engagements of one zodiacal sign or season against another be put to the service of a much larger-scale combat: the struggle of an atemporal God against all temporal rulers, be they stars governing the heavens or their kingly allies ruling on earth.

Unless stars and kings keep the subordinate places appointed to them by their Creator, they will suffer the wrath of God and go to war among themselves. Stars will fight other stars, kings will defeat other kings, nations will destroy other nations. The end-result is *universal logomachy,* by which I mean a religious dispute coinciding with a cosmic battle between signs in heaven – hence, total chaos. This is what prevails before history but also at the End of Time. A vivid description of this apocalyptic 'star war' can be found in the Sibylline Oracles:

The stars travailed in battle; God bade them fight. For over against the sun long flames were in strife, and the two-horned rush of the moon was changed. Lucifer fought, mounted on the back of Leo. Capricorn smote the ankle of the young Taurus, and Taurus deprived Capricorn of his day of return. Orion removed Libra so that it remained no more. Virgo changed the destiny of Gemini in Aries. The Pleiad no longer appeared and Draco rejected its belt. Pisces submerged themselves in the girdle of Leo. Cancer did not stand its ground, for it feared Orion. Scorpio got under its tail because of terrible Leo, and the dog star perished by the flame of the sun. The strength of the mighty star burned up Aquarius. Heaven itself was roused until it shook the fighters. In anger it cast them headlong to earth. Accordingly, stricken into the baths of ocean, they quickly kindled the whole earth. But the sky remained starless. (5: 512–31)

Seneca uses similar imagery to portray the triumph of a 'formless chaos.' The first-century Roman philosopher describes a scene where stars no longer guide the procession of the seasons and the years. The thrones of gods and constellations of the zodiac are thrown into the abyss. The Ram plunges into the Ocean, the Bull and the Scales drag the Twins and the fierce Scorpion down with them, the Virgin falls back to the earth she once abandoned, and the Wagon 'which was never bathed by the sea, shall be plunged beneath the all engulfing waves; the slippery Serpent which gliding like a river, separates the Bears shall fall and Icy Cynosura, the Lesser Bear, together with the Dragon vast, congealed with cold; and that slow moving driver of his wagon, Arctophylax, no longer fixed in place, shall fall' (*Thyestes* 827–74).

According to Malina (1995: 166ff., 171), this sky-war theme known throughout ancient Mesopotamia and the Mediterranean world takes us back to the primordial times that preceded the beginnings of God's Creation. This is precisely the kind of astral material that inspired John's vision of a Second Creation, a new cosmos heralded by stars falling on earth and all hell let loose. The times foreseen by John are so chaotic as to be populated by monstrous creatures composed of limbs and parts taken from different animal species. This state of anatomical confusion is reminiscent of the mystical Scorpion-and-Dragon period described by Berossus of Babylon, third century B.C.E. (1995: 181).

In a Judaeo-Christian perspective, the star-war effects of logomachy preside over small-scale floods sent to punish sinful humans during normal world history or, what is more usual, the larger-scale floods of tribulations preceding or following the advent of Time. Readers will recall that the fallen angels – spirits who failed to keep time in heaven, had sexual commerce with the daughters of humans, taught them the secrets of the sky, and generated a race of monstrous giants – ended up playing havoc with the entire universe. But the chaos and diluvian sufferings they provoked were never meant to last. In Genesis, the Noahic Covenant put an end to the Flood. It offered a solid lunisolar pact that guaranteed the fixity of the eternal transients, or the everlasting recurrence of days and nights and seasons of the year. Likewise, the New Jerusalem offered by John is essentially reassuring. It too gives the impression that the order of time will be unproblematic. Come the Second Creation, the motions of time will cause no problem in that they will be simply discontinued. They will give way to a timeless cosmos where the Light of God will be forever substituted for the luminaries of heaven (Rev. 21).

A language that eliminates the embattlements of signs evolving in heaven is hard to imagine. Notwithstanding the reassurances of the solar pact and of the sunless and moonless Jerusalem, logocentrism has never been able to do away with logomachy. Visions of the Endtime can hardly be expressed without resorting to the powerful imageries of seasons and signs of the equinoxes struggling in heaven. As in 'pagan' mythology, cyclical tensions and altercations between signs of life and death written all over the sky provide a 'most natural' screen against which rivalries of the Great Beyond can be projected and visualized. But 'signs in dispute' derived from astrological lore provide more than useful calendrical metaphors to express visions of a world beyond history. Over and beyond their metaphorical implications, sign altercations – imageries that go into contradictory directions – can also serve to create *the confusion required by God to subjugate and harness the powers of astrology in history. Provided that they be distorted and reproduced through monstrous formulations at best,* astral bodies in movement constitute effective means to express the grandest battle of all: the historic war waged by Logos against cults devoted to nature and the heavenly rulers of time.

Postscript:

In the Nearness of Evil

Revelation 12 offers hopes of eschatological redemption vested in such powerful figures as the man-child and the woman adorned with the sun. Both figures stand as signs of the future 'containing' (conveying, withholding) hopes of an older astrological imagination. As is the case for other interpretations offered throughout this book, this argument rests on evidence obtained from a comparative reading of Revelation and ancient astromythology, evidence often recognized by biblical scholars themselves. My interpretation, however, is intended to cast this evidence in a new light, one that emphasizes the polemical implications of John's dream-like symbolism. To the extent that it stresses the tensions inherent in John's language, my reading of his visionary text reinforces some of the conclusions reached by Jung in his *Answer to Job*. Jung's book was originally written as a contribution to psychology, using an anagogical and teleological perspective that differs radically from the genealogical concerns of modern biblical scholarship (looking for the root principles, original meanings, and historical circumstances of the text). As shown below, Jung's reading of John is none the less a valuable contribution to our understanding of Revelation (with a particular emphasis on Revelation 12), the articulations of scriptural and pagan mythologies, and the general process of symbolling. I now turn to a discussion of the insights of the *Answer to Job*, followed by a assessment of how studies of logomachy depart from the findings and claims of Jungian phenomenology.

According to Jung, Revelation is symptomatic of Christianity striving for so much perfection, brightness, and goodness that it invites an equally excessive outburst of darker forces of the unconscious, negative feelings invading the conscious mind of the Seer. The prophet's effort 'to secure an absolute and final victory for good is bound to lead to a dangerous accu-

mulation of evil and hence to catastrophe' (Jung 1954: 80). From a psychological viewpoint, 'irritability, bad moods, and outbursts of affect are the
classical symptoms of chronic virtuousness' (143). When the conscious ego
insists on the light and moral nature of the total self, it is to be expected that
an 'unusual tension between conscious and unconscious' will result, and
that the self will counteract and appear as something 'dark and menacing'
(133, 135). Under these conditions, the apocalyptic Christ ends up behaving like a savage avenger and cruel judge, 'a bad-tempered, power-con-
scious "boss" who very much resembles the "shadow" of a love-preaching
bishop' (123). The sombre wrathful-lamb figure is so 'shadowy' that it no
longer bears any resemblance to the light-bearing Saviour proclaimed elsewhere in the New Testament (132). John's vision of wrath 'blatantly con-
tradicts all ideas of Christian humility, tolerance, and love of your
neighbour and your enemies, and makes nonsense of a loving father in
heaven and rescuer of mankind. A veritable orgy of hatred, vindictiveness,
and blind destructive fury that revels in fantastic images of terror breaks
out and with blood and fire overwhelms a world which Christ had just
endeavoured to restore to the original state of innocence and loving communion with God' (125).

When the Creator is pitted against his creation and 'man' (to use Jung's
gendered language) is burdened with 'a positively cosmic or demonic grandeur in evil,' an uncontrollable will to destruction is bound to turn against
humanity (Jung 1954: 154). Logically, the unleashing of sentiments of
wrath proceeds through imageries rejected from Christian consciousness –
symbols borrowed from pagan mythology of astrological inspiration (e.g.,
the Leto myth). Pagan contents thus 'lay just below the surface.' Jung
claims that 'the more Christian one's consciousness is, the more heathen-
ishly does the unconscious conduct itself, if in the rejected heathenism
there are values which are important for life' (129f.). The unconscious does
this without retaining positive symbols of the pagan world. Vital values
forsaken by Revelation include the spring-like beauty of a divine youth
embodied in the lovely and lovable Tammuz or Adonis. The vitality of love
and sexuality are irremediably jeopardized: witness all of life's joys and
pleasures that are destined to be destroyed together with Babylon come the
End of Time (131–3, 139, 142).

A lack of dialogue prevails between the John of the Epistles and the John
of Revelation. All is as if the gospel of absolute charity had led John to use
the gospel of fear to supplement the one-sided lessons of Christian love
(Jung 1954: 145, 150). But the antagonisms deployed in Revelation are not
without hints of potential mediation. Although suggesting a brutal colli-

sion of opposites verging on psychosis, John's imagery offers signs of a long-term solution to the tension pitting light against darkness, good against evil. These hopeful signs revolve around Christ, the sun-robed woman, and the man-child, crucial images of hierogamy ('sacred marriage') that Jung lumps with the Holy Ghost and the Virgin Mary.

In response to humanity's pursuit of wholeness, Christianity allowed God to become flesh, or a divinity and a creaturely man all at once, a mediator hanging (crucified) between two thieves, one destined to go to heaven and the other to hell (Jung 1954: 154). From a psychological perspective, Christ is to man what the total self is to the conscious ego. He is a powerful symbol appealing to man's pursuit of a harmonious self, striving, as he does, for the 'ascendancy of the "complete" – *teleios* – or total human being, consisting of the totality of the psyche, of conscious and unconscious, over the ego, which represents only consciousness and its contents.' Jung adds that, by following the teachings of the son of God, the faithful Christian strives to become 'the perfect man formed in the image of God, the second Adam' (131). The son of God teaches the nearness or immediate presence of God, 'and it is just this nearness which has to be empirically real if it is not to lose all significance' (178).

The sun-robed woman of Revelation 12 is another symbol of unity. Although an ordinary woman conceived on earth, she is portrayed as a heavenly figure wearing the sun, with the stars above her and the moon below. As such, 'she contains in her darkness the sun of "masculine" consciousness, which rises as a child out of the nocturnal sea of the unconscious, and like an old man sinks into it again. She adds the dark to the light, symbolizes the hierogamy of opposites, and reconciles nature with spirit' (June 1954: 127). Her marriage to her bridegroom in heaven signifies perfection and wholeness, a powerful synthesis announcing the reunification of God and the Old Testament Sophia or New Testament Church (140). The archetypal impact of this divine-woman imagery is none the less limited. Since Revelation is committed to an excess of light and the subjugation of 'the lust of this world,' the text ends up celebrating the marriage of the mother-bride in heaven, 'where "nothing unclean" enters, high above the devastated world. Light consorts with light' (Jung 1954: 158f.). Correlatively, the redemptive potential of the sun-robed woman is relegated to a distant future, not to be fully realized until the last days of the Christian aeon.

The divine man-child of Revelation is also a product of *hieros gamos* symbolism. He is portrayed as a Christ-like figure who has yet to come, a higher and complete man representing 'our totality, which transcends consciousness' (Jung 1954: 157). Born of the sun-robed woman, the man-child acts as 'a *complexio oppositorum*, a uniting symbol, a totality of life' (127). He stands as a morality of evil, a boy 'born from the maturity of the adult man, and not the unconscious child we would like to remain' (158). But John's man-child motif has yet to be further developed and is not to be confused with the birth of Christ: the man-child will rise to life in the eschatological future and is associated with feelings of hatred and vengeance embodied in the retributive Lamb. John could have developed the man-child imagery independently of the Lamb and vengeful Christ motifs but did not do so, thereby failing to tap the archetype's positive function. Had this messianic potential not escaped his notice, the prophet could have used the man-child to 'compensate the intolerable devastation wrought by the outburst of long-pent-up passions,' restoring the balance between principles of love and fear, charity and revenge. Instead of doing this, the child-figure is condemned to remain latent for an indefinite time. Like the Jewish Messiah, the Saviour is 'caught up' to God and is relegated to the distant End (128, 134).

As with Christ, the man-child points to God who 'wanted to become man, and still wants to' (Jung 1954: 153). This yearning for a reconciliation of opposites illustrates once more Jung's notion of the all-embracing individuation process. As a product of the symbolic mind pursuing the total self, the idea of God 'acts out of the unconscious of man and forces him to harmonize and unite the opposing influences to which his mind is exposed from the unconscious. The unconscious wants both: to divide and to unite.' That is, God has a paradoxical nature: he wants to become man, 'but not quite,' for an excess of light and human consciousness achieved through full incarnation threatens to destroy the vital forces of darkness dwelling in the unconscious. The conflict emerging from the unconscious 'is so great that the incarnation can only be bought by an expiatory self-sacrifice offered up to the wrath of God's dark side' (155). No sooner has the divine chosen to commune with the human that man chooses to kill the God made man.

Revelation betrays an even more wrathful response to God's wish to reproduce himself in a dark creature, which is but the other side of man's wish to dwell in the full light of his Creator. But the instinct of destruction deployed in the New Testament Apocalypse is never fully divorced from signs of hopeful redemption. Revelation 12 proposes the image of a messianic man-child harking back to the Incarnation in Christ, 'the prototype which is continually being transferred to the creature by the Holy Ghost' (Jung 1954: 156). Like the Holy Ghost dwelling in the human soul, the man-child mediator is a 'third thing' that arises from the unconscious, one of those irrational 'symbols of a reconciling and unitive nature' that show up in prophetic visions, dreams, and belief systems such as alchemy (151). Although Christ tends to stand as the one and only God-man, the indwelling of the man-child and the Holy Ghost in the creaturely man permits a 'Christification of many' – hence, an invitation to a full individuation of the self (180).

Jung adds that Christianity has yet to show us the way to a higher level of 'self'-realization. In his own prophetic way, John understood and suffered from the early Christian ambivalence between the teachings of absolute love and the warnings of apocalyptic wrath. Accordingly, he laid down a tentative symbolism (the sun-robed woman giving birth to the man-child and wedded to her heavenly bridegroom) for a future resolution of unresolved tensions. Actually, the prophet went so far as to outline a program for the whole zodiacal age of Pisces. The first half of the Pisces aeon corresponds to the millennium, the preordained thousand years allotted by astrology to the reign of Christ. The second half is marked by the 'enantiodromia' of the Christian aeon and 'the reign of the Antichrist, whose coming could be predicted on astrological grounds' (Jung 1954: 81, 139–40). This 2,000-year period will be brought to a dramatic conclusion in the twentieth century, justifying Jung's 'catechizing' reflection on the pressing problems of our age.

Notwithstanding modernity's claims to enlightenment, Jung finds in our age 'a considerable admixture of darkness' (1954: 157). The spiritual differentiation of Reformation has created great divisions and schisms in the modern world, and the growth of sciences has laid in our hands formidable powers of destruction: the atom bomb, chemical weapons, and so on. In his drive to become man, God has chosen 'the creaturely man filled with darkness – the natural man who is tainted with original sin and who learnt the divine arts and sciences from the fallen angels. The guilty man is eminently suitable and is therefore chosen to become the vessel for the continuing incarnation, not the guiltless one who holds aloof from the world and refuses to pay his tribute to life, for in him the dark God would find no room' (163). But while the worldliness of modern humanity mitigates the impact of evil forces and the triumph of a sheer will to destruction, it makes us more vulnerable to dangers of a 'dark end which we have still to experience, and before whose – without exaggeration – truly apocalyptic possibilities mankind shudders ... Could anyone in his right senses deny that John correctly foresaw at least some of the possible dangers which threaten our world in the final phase of the Christian aeon?' (146). Given this sombre outlook on our age, Jung argues that more light, love, and moral strength are needed to protect us against outbursts of obnoxious blackness. 'Otherwise we shall not be able to assimilate the dark God who also wants to become man, and at the same time endure him without perishing' (157).

Tensions between light and darkness are often expressed in the dreams of modern man (Jung 1954: 152). As in Revelation, oppositional symbols surfacing from the depths of the unconscious reflect these tensions and conflicts that consciousness and pure reason can hardly resolve. But unconscious archetypes can be counted on to offer hints of a solution to man's fragmentation and excess of darkness. Whether it be through dreams, theological doctrine, or mass-culture religion, instinct is always there to guide the individuation process, 'ensuring that everything which belongs to an individual's life shall enter into it, whether he consents or not' (161).

The modern lesson of the *Assumptio Mariae*, a Catholic dogma since 1950, is a case in point. The ascent of the Virgin Mary to heaven is but a step towards a new incarnation of a Christ-like saviour and the rise of a triumphant peacemaker. The incarnation of God began with Christ, it was prefigured in the apocalyptic marriage of the Lamb, and it is perpetuated through the Holy Ghost dwelling in Christian souls. It is now given a new life through hopes vested in the bodily reception of the Virgin in heaven. Notwithstanding the negative reaction of rational and male-minded Protestants, Jung views this dogma of the Mother Church (Catholic) as 'the most important religious event since the Reformation' (Jung 1954: 169). The papal declaration is clearly a sign of the times, expressing, as it does, greater equality between man and woman and also 'a renewed hope for the fulfilment of that yearning for peace which stirs deep down in the soul, and for a resolution of the threatening tension between the opposites' (171). Images of this archetypal sort are designed 'to compensate the truly apocalyptic world situation today,' placing upon everyone 'a new responsibility toward the worldly spirit of our age' (168, 174).

Symbolically formulated dogmas and hermeneutic imageries appeal to the masses because they play an active role in man's instinctive pursuit of his total self, the *teleios anthropos* sought by way of the unconscious individuation process. But why should we bother to explore and understand the functions of archetypal symbols, if not because of the benefits that conscious reflection can bring to the instinct of self-realization, individual and collective? Jung claims that logic and reason are unable to produce the union of deep-seated opposites, yet his own observations and explications regarding the effects of symbolling are intended to elevate the individuation process to a higher plane. The latter plane lies well above linear logic, the archaic language of theology, or the unconscious convolutions of religious dogmas and allegories – unconscious operations where 'the end [of the natural individuation process] remains as dark as the beginning.' Jungian consciousness takes it upon itself to confront the unconscious with a view to finding a balance between the opposites and amplifying the individuation process (Jung 1954: 153, 175f.).

Jungian phenomenology and psychotherapy is the individuation process in conscious action, a process where 'so more darkness comes to light that the personality is permeated with light, and consciousness necessarily gains in scope and insight. The encounter between conscious and unconscious has to ensure that the light which shines in the darkness is not only comprehended by the darkness, but comprehends it' (Jung 1954: 176). Reaching this higher plane of awareness and self-realization is all the more important as modern man must gain better knowledge of self, God's nature, and the relationship between symbolic language and the individuation process. Without this active probing of his greater self, man will remain a passive victim of the unconscious mind and mishandle the 'superhuman powers which the fallen angels have played [placed?] in his hands' (163).

Jung's reading of Revelation is rarely taken seriously by biblical scholars. And yet his *Answer to Job* is remarkable in many ways. Jung should be credited for having grasped the central role of codification in the process of symbolling, using Revelation to illustrate what later semioticians, mostly of structuralist affiliation, have theorized as the logic of unconscious oppositions and mediations governing the intellect. Unlike structuralists, however, Jung managed to go well beyond the Lévi-Straussian aesthetics of *l'esprit* and discover in Revelation a complex dialogue between consciousness and the unconscious, moral thinking and the human psyche. As with Freud, Jung emphasized the active tensions that are constantly played out between different levels of the mind and that evolve through time, a far cry from Lévi-Strauss's neo-Kantian conception of an unconscious mind gone excessively synchronic and logical.

Jung can also be credited for developing two interpretive strategies that play a negligible role in the Freudian literature. First, Jung's *Answer to Job* shows a sensitivity to the rivalry that may exist between sign systems: for instance, the doctrine of Christ versus the lessons of astromythology (deployed in Revelation though rejected into the Christian unconscious). Instead of reducing battles of the mind to operations of language hiding and signifying motions of the libido, Jungian phenomenology unravels conflicts that develop within the realm of language – hence, battles between signs and symbols rising from the unconscious. As with Lacan, Jung allows a substitutive signifier to be 'put in the place of *another signifier* to constitute the effect of metaphor. It refers the signifier that it has usurped elsewhere' (Lacan 1979: 248f.; emphasis added).

Second, Jung is careful to avoid all overly rational, moral, and theoretical flights from the unconscious. In lieu of revelling in a conceptual language that takes great distance from the symbols it is supposed to account for, Jung accepts to play what has now become the postmodern game *par excellence*: the scholar speaks of symbols through symbols, metaphor through metaphor, thereby encountering and confronting language on its own terrain – the concrete, the bodily, the emotional (Habermas 1987: 107). *Answer to Job* is a dialogical contribution to our understanding of the emotive and moral appeal of signs of the unconscious, effects of symbolling that are fundamental to all acts of language and an essential ingredient of moral thinking as well. In hindsight, Jung's collusion with the powers of symbolling – his rejection of strictly scientific explanations that collide with their object of study, the symbolic and the irrational – leads to a remarkable squaring of the circle: an empirically founded, clinically informed reading of Revelation that turns into a vibrant plea for peace, gender equality, and the powers of the imaginative mind.

Jung's *Answer to Job* is a far-reaching dialogue between scholar and text, a profound conversation between acts of signification and the interpretive process. As do Derrida (1982: 213) and feminist theorists such as Young (1987, 1990), Jung challenges all formulations of 'white mythology' founded on the exclusion of what is natural, sensible, female, dark, and metaphorical – vital forces denegated by Western metaphysics and bourgeois claims to ethnic and gender neutrality. As Lawrence (1974: 88) suggests in his commentary on the Apocalypse, 'men are far more fools today, for stripping themselves of their emotional and imaginative reactions, and feeling nothing. Our bald processes of thought no longer are life to us.'

The drawbacks of the Jungian answer to signs of Revelation are none the less many. Jung should not be reproached for having failed to do something he never planned: he never promised a scholarly, historically informed exegesis of the Book of Revelation, an exercise he recognizes to be useful in its own right. And yet readers of Jung are left to wonder if the author has not fallen prey to John's temptation: imposing too much darkness because of too great an anxiety to 'see the light' and bring the human mind closer to perfection. Had he shown a greater interest towards the 'worldly spirit' of Science and Reformation, Jung would have paid more attention to the spiritual *differentiation* of religious thought systems. He would have acknowledged the particular 'genealogy' of Revelation, its inner texture and historical complexity, and the precise modalities of the apocalyptic individuation process. When overly committed to anagogy and teleology, the archetypal quest for universal meanings and processes of growth can end up stripping all products of language of their inherent thickness and historicity, wishing the 'empirical humanity' out of its concrete existence in no time.

Jung's treatment of astrology in Revelation may serve to illustrate the latter difficulties. Although he correctly situates astromythology in the shadow of the Christian Logos, Jung fails to delve into the historical and ideological factors that make astralism either intolerable or attractive from a Yahwistic perspective, reverting instead to explanations that are essentially moralistic. On the one hand, he suggests that the positive (hedonistic, light-bearing, springtime) aspects of astrology are left out of John's sombre vision of wrathful sentiments. The distance between one language and another tends to be exaggerated, allowing Jung to condemn one archetypal configuration while condoning the other. On the other hand, Jung's reading of John is full of references to the radiant lunisolarism of key passages of Revelation. Actually Jung goes so far as to assign real powers of astrological foresight to John: through his use of astrology, the Seer was able to prophesy historical developments of our age, a period of history that marks the end of the Pisces aeon.

The problem with the latter interpretation is that no evidence is given as to what role the fish motif actually played in Revelation; in point of fact, the motif never appears in John's visions, unlike the Aries-like lamb imagery. Also Jung fails to ask whether early Christian prophets had any real knowledge of precession, the astronomical phenomenon that accounts for the 2,160 years that the vernal sun takes to move from one zodiacal sign to another; some historians suggest that these astronomical calculations were foreign to authors of the Scriptures (Feldman 1978: 77). Nor are the incompatibilities between astrological divination and Judaeo-Christian prophecy discussed. By not asking these questions, the distance between Yahwism and Sabaism is underestimated, a strategy that allows Jung to bring all forms of teleology (pagan and Christian) into the service of his vision of the collective individuation process governing Western history.

In short, signs of future resolutions of the dualisms deployed in Revelation are disembodied and disembattled: they convey eternal principles (the individuation process), they suffer no internal contradiction (astralism versus logocentrism), they unite past and present (through correct prefigurations), and they verify the interpreter's own vision of history. The Romantic pursuit of unity and harmony triumphs over the darker aspects of Romantic thought: the subjective, the emotional, the worldly, the unpredictable, the tragic.

In his interpretation of Revelation, Jung leaves us without a consistent and thorough account of how one *particular* symbolic regime (Yahwism) manages to silence and speak to another regime (Sabaism) – hence, how consciousness interacts with the unconscious *in history*. Theories of signification that neglect the contextual aspects of the unconscious run the risk of universalizing their own discursive battles, spreading such issues as the dogma of the Assumption around the world and across history. When transposed to the social plane, this interpretive strategy deprives us of the knowledge needed to evaluate what any mythology, movement, or event can do to resolve social issues of its time. The question as to whether the Ascension of the Virgin Mary or any other religious belief can help mend the modern divisions pitting man against woman, Protestants against Catholics, consciousness against the unconscious, reason against the imagination, can hardly be answered in isolation from broader issues: that is, the value system, social practices (e.g., gender relations), and political-economic conditions associated with religious dogmas. In the absence of thorough analyses of doctrinal systems and their social contexts, psychological assessments of the cultural impact of any religious event are suspect from the start.

As we approach the year 2000, we may ask ourselves what relevance the Book of Revelation has for our own age. Answers to this question are many, depending on one's own social background, value systems, and ideological commitments, factors that invite a sociological investigation of religious history. The interpretive analyses developed in previous chapters can hardly be read as a full-fledged exercise in the sociological history of astrology and the apocalyptic literature. My reading of Revelation and astrology and their respective histories none the less raises a question central to our late-twentieth-century society. While committed to a future-oriented vision of time, the New Testament Apocalypse was a critical step in our Western journey beyond humanity's worldly existence, closer to the eternal, the immaterial, the universal, the transcendental. Following the rise of the Church to power, anagogical theology was used to drive additional nails into earlier astrologically informed visions of time – into 'cycles of life' driven by visions of the future and hopes and fears of the End. With the Enlightenment and modernity, the 'high cultural' achievements of the genealogical *Weltanschauung* (looking into the root principles and origins of nature and history) have further weakened our ability to invest the passing of time with plans of our collective future. If anything, postmodernity has made things worse, for time no longer has a sense of its own End. Through a surface celebration of diversity and freedom, we now revel in the proliferation of individual 'ends,' particularistic movements and islands of histories that ignore the actual world-system we live in, the enormous tragedies we face, and the potential for utopian rewritings of global history. Although there is no point in going back to astrology or prophecy for an answer to this loss of far-sighted perspectives on time, it is still time to ask ourselves if it is in our power and truly our wish to arrest the formidable and wondrous wheels of Time.

The End.

Notes

Chapter 2 Music of the Spheres

1 'The primitive astrology thus produced was refined by the Greeks, with their astronomical and philosophical ideas – especially perhaps Pythagoreanism with its number symbolism, and Stoicism with the ideas of cosmic sympathy and the universal rule of Fate – to bring about the confusion of systems and parts of systems found in the early sources, with dodecatemoria and single degrees, *loci* and Lots, planetary aspects and characters, genders and spheres of influence, the four elements and stones and metals and plants' (Tester 1987: 56).

2 Orosius, a disciple of Augustine, said of the Priscillianist heretics in Spain that 'they believed in the soul's journey through the spheres, when it was influenced by the planets in turn, and in the allocation of the parts of the body to the signs of the zodiac – the *melothesia*' (Tester 1987: 112).

Chapter 3 A History of Revelations

1 Some scholars (e.g., McGinn 1992: 14) distinguish between theological approaches to Revelation and the cyclic, recapitulative readings of the same text. In my view, the recapitulation principle constitutes, not an overall perspective on Revelation, but rather a particular method that has been used predominantly – but not always – in the context of anagogical and genealogical readings of John's apocalypse. The rule of recapitulation does not constitute a distinct theory: its actual application depends entirely on whether Revelation is thought to express visions of chronological history (with the same sequence of events being expressed in various forms) or the playing-out of constant struggles in Church history. See Court 1979: 6.

2 According to Charles (1913: 13), Tyconius predicted that the second advent was

to take place about 380 C.E., but successors of Tyconius removed all historical references from his interpretive method.

3 Primasius understands the woman of Revelation 12 as typified by the Virgin Mary, an equation picked up by influential exegetes such as Quodvultdeus (*c.* 450), Cassiodorus (*c.* 575), and Ambrose Autpert. This issue was to become highly polemical in later discussions of Revelation.

4 Later echoes of Joachim's exegesis can be found in the sixteenth-century commentaries of Petrus Galatinus and Onus Ecclesiae.

5 Sixteenth-century proponents of the spiritual method include Gagnaeius (1545), Tacitus Nicolaus Zegerus (1553), Pet. Bulengerus (1589), Benedictus Arias Montanus (1588), Antoine Pignet (1543), H. Bullinger (1557), and J. Calvin (1565) (see Prigent 1959: 73f.)

6 In most reviews of studies of Revelation, exegetes who hold that the major prophecies of Revelation were fulfilled in the fall of Rome (476 C.E.) are classified as preterists (e.g., Mounce 1977: 41). In my view, the preterist strategy should be confined to first-century contextual analyses of Revelation. Studies that establish one-to-one connections between the New Testament Apocalypse and events occurring well *after its writing* have more in common with prophetic-historical approaches than with preterism.

7 Although generally in agreement with Alcásar, the Dutch Protestant scholar none the less found in John's Apocalypse prophecies of later events occurring under Constantine and some events of universal history as well. Grotius is also remembered for having refuted the polemical Beast–Pope equation.

Chapter 4 Alpha and Omega

1 Exod. 13: 6f., 34: 18; Lev. 14: 38, 23: 42; Num. 23; Deut. 16: 8, 13.

2 Prigent questions the polemical nature of the Lord's Day motif, yet he admits to the political origin of other expressions used by John (1981: 24, 90).

3 Langdon 1931: 58, 102, 158, 160, 318, 323–4.

4 Josephus (*The Antiquities of the Jews* 3: 6, 7; *The Jewish War* 5: 217). To quote Philo (1956–62, iv: 221–5), the 'holy candlestick and the seven candle-bearers on it are a copy of the march of choir of the seven planets. How so? perhaps we shall be asked. Because, we shall reply, each of the planets is a light-bringer, as the candle-bearers are. For they are supremely bright and transmit the great lustre of their rays to the earth, especially the central among the seven, the sun. I call it central, not merely because it holds the central position, which some give as the reason, but because apart from this it has the right to be served and attended by its squires on either side, in virtue of its dignity and magnitude and the benefits which it provides for all that are on the earth. Now the order of the

planets is a matter of which men have no sure apprehension – indeed is there any other celestial phenomenon which can be known with real certainty? – and therefore they fall back on probabilities. But the best conjecture, in my opinion, is that of those who assign the middle place to the sun and hold that there are three above him and the same number below him ... So the Master-craftsman, wishing that we should possess a copy of the archetypal celestial sphere with its seven lights, commanded this splendid work, the candlestick, to be wrought." The Targum version of Exodus 39: 37 and 40: 4 speaks of 'the lampstand and its lamps, the lamps of order which were arrayed to correspond to the seven stars (or "planets") in the firmament day and night,' or 'the seven lamps corresponding to the seven stars (or "planets") which resemble the just that shine unto eternity in their righteousness' (see McNamara 1966: 192–9).

5 Although conceiving the earth as a sphere floating in mid-air, first-century astronomers such as Manilius were still describing the land as being 'afloat, encircled by the crown of ocean which clasps the round world within it in an embrace of water. The land also receives the sea to its bosom ...' (Manilius 4: 585ff.).

6 Gen 1, 2: 10ff.; Job 22: 14, 40: 22; Ps. 19: 6, 48: 2f., 75: 6–7; Isa. 14: 12–14, 40: 22.

7 Actually Polaris is a variable star. The North Pole pointed at Draco's Thuban star in the year 3000 B.C.E. and at Kochab in Ursa Minor about five centuries before Christ. It now points at empty space two full moons away from our present-day Polaris. Pytheas, the Greek astronomer (320 B.C.E.), had already noted this distinction between the pole and a Polaris situated somewhere between the two Bears.

8 Gen. 45: 25; Hos. 8: 9; Acts 18: 22, 19: 1.

9 The bears were charged with so much evocative strength that Caesius, a Dutch astronomical writer of the seventeenth century well versed in Roman and Greek mythology, assimilated them to the bears David slew and Elisha sent to punish his juvenile offenders, and also to the chariots of Elijah and Joseph received from the Pharaoh. Interestingly, the god Thor has been described as sitting naked and high, with 'seven stars in his hand and Charles's Wain' (Allen 1963: 427–8).

10 Zeph. 2: 13; Jer. 1: 13ff., 4: 6, 6: 1, 25: 9, 46: 6; Eze. 26: 7, 38: 6–15, 39: 2.

11 On these attributes of heaven, see also Job 22: 12; Ps. 75: 3–6, 77: 17f.; Isa. 13: 10, 66: 1; Ezek. 40: 2; Eph. 1: 21, 4: 10; Rev. 21: 2, 10.

12 This observation was astronomically accurate thousands of years before and also centuries after Homer's day. Ursa Major was then circling nearer the North Pole than now, because of precession – 'the occurrence of the equinoxes earlier in each successive sidereal year, caused by the gradual westward movement of the equinoctial points along the ecliptic as the result of the change in direction of

the earth's axis as it turns around the axis of the ecliptic so as to describe a complete cone every 26,000 years' (*Webster's* 2d ed.). We can therefore assume that the constellation never did 'bathe in th' ocean wave.' The same can be said of the lesser Bear, alias the Dog's Tail, Cynosura, or the Little Dipper of modern days.

13 These remarks generally apply to our Christian era and also the Age of Aries which preceded it (approximately from 2100 B.C.E. to 100 C.E.). They are true of northern latitudes, and also of ancient biblical lands, where the Wain used to be sighted higher in the sky.

14 Mention should be made of the legend involving a nymph named *Kallisto*, who, because she was loved by Jupiter (Zeus), was turned into a stellar bear by jealous Juno (Hera). Her son Arkas was changed into Ursa Minor in Ovid's version of Kallisto's story. Helice of Arcadia happens to be Kallisto's birthplace and another Greek name for the larger Wheel; the same name was given to a Cretan nymph who nourished the infant Jupiter only to be transferred to the skies where, in the words of Dante, she keeps 'revolving with her son whom she delights in.'

15 The Arabic language had other names for Ursa Minor: that is, *Al Dubb al Ashgar,* or Lesser Bear; *Alrucaba,* as first mentioned in the Alfonsine Tables, probably for the Vehicle, after the Hebrew *Rekhubh;* and the Bier, a smaller Coffin followed by three other mournful daughters. For those living along the Nile, it was the *Jackal of Set,* as drawn in the zodiacal planisphere at Denderah. Romans spoke of *Ursa Minor* and *Septentrio.* Another title was *Phoenice,* or *Ursa Phoenicia,* apparently because of its use in navigation by Phoenician sailors as reported by Thales about 600 B.C.E. In Scandinavia, it became the *Smaller Chariot* or *Throne of Thor.* Dante called it *Cornu,* which became the Horn through Eden's translation, a motif that fits nicely the Spanish designation of *Bocina,* the *Bugle* (Allen 1963).

16 In the English language, a person who 'loses his tramontane' is reputed to have lost his bearings, 'perdre le nord' in French.

17 It is in a cave located inside this sacred mountain that the Seven Sleepers of Ephesus, elsewhere associated with the seven stars of Ursa Major, apparently spent many years (Allen 1963: 452).

Chapter 5 The Seven Churches of Asia

1 Job 9: 9, 38: 31f.; Acts 19: 13ff., 20: 29; Rev. 22: 15. See Allen 1963: 434 and Unger 1957: 813.

2 Job 9: 9, 38: 31; Amos 5: 8; see Langdon 1931: 28, 55.

3 John 6: 27; Eph. 1: 14, 4: 30; 2 Cor. 1: 22; Rev. 3: 12, 7: 4, 22: 4.

4 Exod. 28: 30; Num. 27: 21; see Chevalier 1990: 296 and Unger 1957: 1128f.

5 See Gen. 49: 9f.; Num. 24: 27; Ps. 23: 4; Isa. 11: 1.

6 Lev. 20: 2ff.; Deut. 32: 17; 1 Kings 11: 7; Ps. 106: 37; Jer. 32: 35, 48: 7ff.; see Langdon 1931: 13, 47.

7 On the question of morality, local belief systems prevailing in Asia Minor could always be cited for their exemplary inclusion of female divinities within their pantheons. By contrast, the Pauline conception of relations between women and God verges on misogyny. Modern commentators on Revelation should be careful not to reproduce this Pauline bias, as does H. Morris in his discussion of Jezebel: 'Paul had specifically forbidden women to speak in the church (1 Corinthians 14: 34, referring especially to the use of supposed supernatural gifts, such as tongues and prophecy) or to teach in such a way as to exercise authority over men (1 Timothy 2: 11, 12), *and ignoring such instructions had led to a tragic situation at Thyatira*' (1983: 60; emphasis added).

8 Hemer 1986: 138f., 259f., Thompson 1990: 141, Langdon 1931: 359f., Ford 1975: 410.

9 Deut. 6: 9; 1 Chron. 9: 27; Isa. 22: 22; Matt. 25: 10; John 10: 7ff.; Rev. 1: 18, 3: 7, 4: 1, 9: 1, 20: 1, 21: 12ff.; see Sweet 1990: 103.

10 Ps. 80: 8; Isa. 5: 1–7, 25: 6; Jer. 13: 12ff.; Joel 3: 12; Matt. 26: 27ff.; Rev. 19: 11.

11 Hemer 1986: 188, 247, Mounce 1977: 123, 125, 192.

Chapter 6 The Chariot of Fire

1 For a discussion of Ezekiel's influence on John, see Feuillet 1976: 472, 475 and Vanhoye 1962.

2 Two superscriptions apparently composed at different times are combined in the inaugural lines of Ezekiel's vision: the first verse, written in the first-person singular, and verses 2–3, which are in the third person, indicating a later insertion.

3 Jehoahaz acceded to the throne of his father Josiah immediately after his death. His reign lasted for three months only and was followed by that of Jehoiakim, lasting eleven years, and then that of Jehoiachin, a mere three-month period prior to his captivity (2 Kings 22: 3, 24: 6–17; Ezek. 1: 1–2).

4 On reproductive age, see Gen 11: 14, 18, 22; 2 Sam. 5: 4. On the association between the number thirty and children, see Jude 10: 4, 12: 9; 1 Chron. 27: 1–6. On soldiers, see 1 Sam. 4: 10, 11; 8. On golden bowls and pieces of silver, see Ezra 1: 9; Zech. 11: 12; Matt. 27: 3. On mourning, see Num. 20: 29; Deut. 34: 8.

5 Jude 2: 13; 1 Sam. 12: 10; 1 Kings 11: 5. See Unger 1957 and Langdon 1931. *Sin*, the Sumerian word for the lunar god, gave its name to the sacred Mount Sinai.

6 2 Sam. 6: 2; 1 Kings 7: 27–37, 22: 35; 2 Kings 9: 27, 10: 15, 19: 15, 23: 11; 1 Chron. 28: 18; Ps. 80: 1, 99: 1; Hab. 3: 8; Zech. 6: 1ff.

7 Cooke (1960: 97n) notes that the Jews have preserved the mournful character of the month of Tammuz 'by substituting national disasters for the heathen associations.'

8 See 1 Kings 14: 13; Isa. 17: 10; Jer. 22: 18; Dan. 11: 37; Zech. 12: 11.

9 The departure of a solarized Yahweh at summer and autumn, a season of vintage heralding the Day of Yahweh, finds another echo in the intriguing *zemorah* branch motif appearing at the end of Ezekiel 8. Elders engaging in idolatrous cults are said to put a 'branch to their nostrils' (v. 17). It is difficult to relate the gesture to a precise cultic rite performed with a vine branch (Greenberg 1983: 173). In any case, even when situated in its ritual context, the precise contribution of the branch-and-nose imagery would still call for an explanation. Other biblical passages involving the same imagery can provide us with some clues as to what the gesture might convey. When mentioned elsewhere in the Old Testament, the word *zemorah* is associated with grapes and wood used for burning or carving (Num. 13: 23; Ezek. 15: 2). It also stands for 'sprigs of foreign gods,' idolatrous shoots that flower on the same day that they are planted (Isa. 17: 10) and that are enemies of the Messiah known as 'Branch' (Zech. 3: 8ff., 6: 12; Isa. 4: 2). Readers are reminded that shoots are synonymous with royal rods and stars that rise in the morning and reign in heaven (Num. 24: 17; Jer. 23: 5, 15). As for noses, they are connected to the breath of life (Gen. 2: 7), the sense of smell, and the fragrance of fruit (Song 7: 8). Nostrils can also be used in expressions of anger (combined with smoke and fire; see 2 Sam. 22: 9; Ps. 18: 8; Isa. 65: 5), domination (Song 7: 4), bondage and humiliation (i.e., when hooked; see 2 Kings 19: 28).

Given these associations, the gesture of humans putting vine branches to their noses may allude to the gift of the breath and the fruit of life offered to carvings of wood and bodies in heaven. The branch imagery becomes all the more heathenish when equated with summertime Spica, the ear of wheat in the Virgo's hand, or springtime Betelgeuse, Orion's arm or hand (Fleming 1981: 21). Alternatively, the ritual action may coincide with Yahweh's departure from the temple, about the autumn equinox, which is when grain is sown and fruit harvested. Instead of mourning God's departure (Ezek. 10: 18) and submitting themselves to his rule, humans are enjoying the good life and worshipping false gods (as in Isa. 17: 10). As in the Septuagint Greek Version, these humans are guilty of 'turning up the nose' to the Lord or rebelling against the Almighty, thereby applying the twig to God's anger, 'adding fuel to the fire,' as it were (Ezek. 8: 11). The gesture is likely to rebound on humans who betray the Lord. Come the Day of Judgment, they shall lose the breath of life, their noses shall be cut off, their vines and their wood carvings (idols that have noses but never smell) shall be destroyed by fire and the sword (see Ps. 115: 6; Isa. 17: 9ff.; Ezek. 23: 25; Nah. 1: 14, 2: 2). Those who plant the seed of idolatry and worship the sun and the lights of heaven shall reap nothing but grief and the darkness of death (Isa. 17: 7).

10 For similar imageries, see Exod. 25: 18–22, 26: 31; 2 Sam. 6: 2; 2 Kings 19: 5; Ps. 80: 1.

11 While the Hebrew word *daron* means both the south and a bright sunny region, *teman* (also *yamin*) denotes the right-hand side or the south (Unger 1957).

12 Ezek. 3: 15f., 20: 1, 30: 20, 39: 9–14, 40: 22–6, 41: 3, 43: 25f., 44: 26, 45: 20–5.

13 Ps. 77: 18f.; Ezek. 10: 12f., 23: 24, 26: 10; see Cooke 1960: 112.

14 Assyrian myths spoke of the waters of the earth as feminine and the heavenly as masculine (1 Enoch 54: 8).

15 Gen. 22: 13; Exod. 12: 3–27; Isa. 53: 7ff.; Jer. 11: 19; Dan. 8: 3; John 1: 29, 19: 14, 21: 15, 31; 1 Cor. 5: 7; Rev. 1: 5f., 13: 11; 1 Enoch 89–90. See Beasley-Murray (1974: 125) and Mounce 1977: 144. Given the closeness of Aries and Taurus, bulls can be substituted for rams, as in representations of patriarchs from Adam to Isaac (1 Enoch 85–6; see Ford 1975: 88). The wrathful aspect of the paschal sun is echoed in the House of Mars anciently formed by the sign of Aries. Christ's death on the cross is a prelude to God's inevitable wrath – to the battering-ram (Heb. *kar*) and other military equipment deployed in the spring season, a time of the year that brought warfare to biblical lands (Maunder 1923: 312). For an argument in favour of the Passover-lamb interpretation but against an astrological reading of this paschal motif, see Prigent 1964: 73; 1981: 97f..

16 The harlot figure takes us back to the rule of Ninlil, a Babylonian earth-goddess equated with Margidda the Greater Bear (Langdon 1931: 109, 317)

17 Ps. 19; Isa. 6: 3; Ezek. 28: 13ff.; Dan. 7: 9; 1 Enoch 14: 11ff., 71: 7; 2 Enoch 11: 2–3, 21: 1. See Charles 1920, 1: 120–3; Ford 1975: 77, 79; Beasley-Murray 1974: 177f.

18 1 Enoch 47: 3, 81: 1f., 106: 19, 107: 1; Exod. 25: 9f., 26: 30, 32: 15; Ps. 139: 13; Ezek. 3: 3; Eph. 2: 10; and so on. See Mounce 1977: 142.

19 Gen. 49: 11f.; Isa. 1: 18; Lam. 4: 7. See Sweet 1990: 153 and Mounce 1977: 135.

20 Job 9: 13, 38: 8ff.; Ps. 74: 13f., 89: 10, 93: 3ff.; Prov. 8: 27ff.; Isa. 27: 1.

21 Gen. 6: 5ff.; Exod. 10: 21; Ps. 32: 6; Jer. 4: 23ff., 46: 7f.; Dan. 9: 26; Zech. 11: 10; Rev. 6: 12, 8: 12. See Caird 1966: 66f..

22 Isa. 43: 2; Ps. 124: 4f.; Matt. 7: 25ff.; Rev. 12: 15f., 15: 2f.

23 In his discussion of the four animals grouped around the throne, Prigent (1981: 86n) concedes that an astrological reading of Revelation 4 could be reconciled with his interpretation of John's throne-room vision.

Chapter 7 Seven Seals and Four Trumpets

1 While some commentators read Revelation 6: 8 as a characterization of all four riders, some view the 'authority over a fourth part of the earth' as an attribution

of the fourth rider only (Charles 1920, 1: 169; Mounce 1977: 156). But even if this authority were restricted to the last rider, the latter could still be said to fulfil a double function, 'both as a symbol for pestilence and as an epitome of all four plagues' (Caird 1966: 80f.). Thus the four horsemen are given power not over the entire world, only part of it.

2 Gen. 2: 8; Isa. 41: 2; Ezek. 43: 2; Matt. 2: 1f.; Luke 1: 78; Rev. 22: 16; see Beasley-Murray 1974: 142.

3 Gen. 49: 17; Deut. 33: 22; Num. 2: 25; Judg. 18: 30; 1 Kings 12: 28ff.; Jer. 8: 16. See Charles 1920, 1: 208, and Prigent 1981: 121.

4 Matt. 19: 28; Gal. 6: 16; Jas. 1: 1; 1 Pet. 1: 1, 2: 9f.; Rev. 21: 2, 12.

5 Lev. 24: 42f., 26; Exod. 13: 21f., 40: 34ff.; 2 Chron. 7: 1ff.; Isa. 4: 5f.; Ezek. 37: 27; Zech. 2: 10. See Charles 1920, 1: 215; L. Morris 1983: 118; Sweet 1990: 151; Mounce 1977: 175; Farrer 1964: 111; Prévost 1991: 129; Draper 1983; Ulfgard 1989. Unlike most commentators, Prigent (1981: 124, 127) finds the connection between Revelation 7 and the Feast of Tabernacles tenuous.

6 Isa. 49: 10; Zech. 14: 7f.; John 8: 12, 7: 37ff.; Rev. 7: 17, 21: 6, 22: 1, 17.

7 Wis. 18: 14ff.; Isa. 13: 10; Joel 2: 2; Amos 5: 18; Mark 13: 24; John 1: 14.

8 As there is only one altar in heaven, the altar of burnt-offering and the altar of incense are presumably one and the same (Charles 1920, 1: 227).

9 Isa. 14: 12–20; Jer. 51: 25, 42; Luke 10: 18; Rev. 18: 9–19; see Ford 1975: 133.

10 Judg. 5: 20; 1 Kings 22: 19; 2 Chron. 18: 18; Neh. 9: 6; Job 38: 7; Ps. 103: 21ff.; Isa. 13: 10, 29: 21; Ezek. 32: 7; Joel 2: 10, 3: 14f.; 1 Enoch 18: 13ff.; see Charles 1920, 1: 150; Ford 1975: 138f.; Mounce 1977: 192.

Chapter 8 The Last Three Trumpets

1 Ps. 33: 7; Isa. 27: 1; Amos 9: 3; Luke 8: 31; Rev. 11: 7, 17: 8, 20: 1ff.; 1 Enoch 18–21. See Ford 1975: 147.

2 The creatures could also be assimilated to long-haired, fiery-tailed stars falling from heaven, comets reputed to announce war, pestilence, and other plagues. They point to trials as bitter as the wormwood thrown into fresh waters of the earth (Rev. 8: 11).

3 Farrer (1964: 106f.) wrongly associates the Lion of Judah to the east. The title evokes rather the south, that is, the country of Judah located to the south of the Holy Land and the sun entering Leo to the southeast at summer.

4 Scriptural references to the north as the seat of gloom and the origin of winds of judgment have already been discussed. See Isa. 14: 31; Jer. 1: 14f., 6: 1, 22, 10: 22, 13: 20, 25: 9, 26, 46: 20, 24, 47: 2; Ezek. 26: 7, 38: 1–15, 39: 1f.

5 Joel 2: 20–5; 1 Enoch 76: 1ff. See Charles 1920, 1: 249 and Beasley-Murray 1974: 164.

6   1 Kings 14: 11, 21: 19; 2 Kings 8: 13, 9: 10; Ps. 22: 16; Isa. 66: 3; Jer. 15: 3; Matt.
    15: 26; Rev. 9: 20f., 22: 15.

7   In the Acts of the Apostles, Jesus is said to have appeared to the apostles for a
    period of forty days after his Passion and resurrection (Acts 1: 3).

8   Luke 3: 23, 4: 2; Heb. 3: 9; 2 Sam. 5: 4; 1 Kings 11: 42; 2 Kings 12: 1; Acts 13: 21.
    Likewise, Abdon had forty sons and thirty grandsons (Jud. 12: 14) and the
    Jerusalem Temple was forty cubits by thirty (Ezek. 46: 22).

9   Jer. 25: 11f., 29: 10; Ps. 90: 10; see also Dan. 9: 2, 24.

10 See Isa. 41: 15f.; Jer. 4: 11, 51: 2; Matt. 3: 12; also Maunder 1963: 263.

11 For detailed discussions of the Great City evoked by John, see Mounce 1977:
    226; Charles 1920, 1: 287; and Prigent 1981: 165, 168.

12 Between the holy interior and the evil periphery, there may be a wall impeding
    the Gentiles from entering the sanctuary on pain of death, as in the Herodian
    temple.

13 The seven-candlestick motif is readapted to the ancient tradition of using two
    emissaries on missions or witnesses for testimonials (Beasley-Murray 1974: 184).

14 See Luke's (4: 25) and James's (5: 17) mention of the drought of Elijah's days, a
    drought that lasted three and a half years. Cf. Beasley-Murray 1974: 186;
    Mounce 1977: 225, 227; Charles 1920, 1: 289n; Farrer 1964: 136; Sweet 1990:
    182; and Prigent 1981: 162.

15 In keeping with these signs of winter eve, the number 42 (the number of months
    in a period of three and a half years) is suggestive of the exodus story and the
    encampments of Israel in the wilderness (Num. 33: 5ff.; L. Morris 1983: 147).

16 A more detailed confirmation of this identification of the two lampstands with
    Moses and Elijah can be found in Charles 1920, 1: 281f. See also L. Morris 1983:
    147 and Farrer 1964: 133. Prigent (1981: 165) argues that John's two witnesses
    are symbolic figures and should not be confused with historical characters.

17 Charles (1920, 1: 283n) finds Gunkel's and Bousset's connection between Zoro-
    astrian Parsiism and the two witnesses of Revelation 11 purely hypothetical.

Chapter 9 The Sun-Robed Woman

1   John's evocation of angels ten thousand times ten thousand in number (Rev. 5:
    11) is the only exception to this rule. Unlike figures of tenness, fourness, and
    twelveness, the decimal scheme can be pushed beyond an uppermost limit,
    where calculations become meaningless and limitless, evoking a heavenly
    creation beyond measure.

2   The colures are two imaginary circles of the celestial sphere intersecting each
    other at right angles at the poles: one passes through the ecliptic at the solstice,
    the other at the equinox.

3 Langdon 1931: 75, 80–2, 90, 99, 109, 117, 130, 136ff., 155, 171, 194, 220, 314, 319, 361, 372; Jacobsen 1970: 27, 165; 1976: 79, 95, 201f., 229.

4 Jacobsen 1976: 56f., 139–41, 169, 187, 190, 229f.; Langdon 1931: 28ff., 78, 90, 110f., 128f., 134, 163, 178, 235, 330, 351, 367.

5 Interestingly, the widespread myth of Adapa inverts the story of snakes and mortals. It tells of Ea, god of the world below the ecliptic, who tricks predilu-vian Adapa into *not* eating the bread and water of life, thus bringing mortality on human beings. In retrospect, there is nothing that the first couple could have done to save mankind from the pangs of death (Langdon 1931: 181ff., 221).

Bibliography

Adorno, Theodor W. 1994. *The Stars Down to Earth and Other Essays on the Irrational in Culture*. Edited and with an introduction by Stephen Crook. London and New York: Routledge

Alexander, Ralph. 1976. *Ezekiel*. Chicago: Moody Press

Alexander, P.S. 1973–87. 'Incantations and Books of Magic.' In *The History of the Jewish People in the Age of Jesus Christ*, ed. Emil Schürer; rev. and ed. G. Vermes, F. Millar, and M. Goodman, 3 vols., III.1: 342–79. Edinburgh: Clark

Allen, Richard Hinckley. 1963 [1899]. *Star Names: Their Lore and Meaning*. New York: Dover

Allo, P.E. Bernard. 1933. *Saint-Jean – L'Apocalypse*. Paris: Firmin Didot

Altman, Alexander. 1971. 'Astrology.' In *Encyclopedia Judaica*, vol. 3, cols. 788–95. Jerusalem, NY: Macmillan

Arnold, Clinton E. 1989. *Ephesians, Power and Magic: The Concept of Power in Ephesians in Light of Its Historical Setting*. Cambridge: Cambridge University Press

Augustine, Saint. 1950. *The City of Gods*. Transl. by Marcus Dods. New York: Modern Library

Aune, D.E. 1990. 'The Form and Function of the Proclamations to the Seven Churches (Revelation 2–3).' *New Testament Studies* 36, 182–204

Avienus, Rufus Festus. 1843. *Description de la terre. Les régions maritimes. Phénomènes d'Aratus et pièces diverses*. Trans by E. Despois and Ed. Saviot. Paris: C.L.F. Panckoucke

Avi-Yonah, M. 1964. 'The Caesarea Inscription of the Twenty-Four Priestly Courses.' In *The Teacher's Yoke: Studies in Memory of Henry Trantham*, ed. E.J. Vardaman and James Leo Garrett, J.B. Adair, assoc. ed., 46–57. Waco, TX: Baylor University Press

Bakhtin, M.M. 1981. *The Dialogic Imagination*. ed. by M. Holquist; trans. by
C. Emerson and M. Holquist. Austin: University of Texas Press

Barbault, A. 1961. *De la psychanalyse à l'astrologie*. Paris: Seuil

Barthes, R. 1957. *Mythologies*. Paris: Seuil

Beasley-Murray, G.R. 1974. *The Book of Revelation*. The New Century Bible
Commentary. Grand Rapids, MI, and London: Eerdmans & Marshall, Morgan &
Scott

Beckwith, I.T. 1967. *The Apocalypse of John*. Grand Rapids, MI: Baker

Beer, Arthur. 1971. 'Astronomy.' In *Encyclopedia Judaica*, vol. 3, cols. 795–808.
Jerusalem, NY: Macmillan

Benjamin, Walter. 1976. 'Theses on the Philosophy of History.' In *Illuminations*,
ed. H. Arendt; trans. H. Zohn, 253–64. New York: Shocken

Boismard, M.-É. 1949. 'L'Apocalypse ou les Apocalypses de saint Jean.' *Revue
biblique* 56, 507–27

– 1968. 'The Apocalypse.' In *Introduction to the New Testament*, ed. A. Robert
and A. Feuillet; trans. P.W. Shekan et al., 691–722. New York: Desclée

Boll, Franz J. 1914. *Auf der Offenbarung Johannis: Hellenistiche Studien zum
Weltbild der Apokalypse*. Berlin: Teubner

Bonsirven, Joseph. 1951. *L'Apocalypse*. Verbum Salutis 16. Paris: Beauchesne

Bornkamm, Günther. 1937. 'Die Komposition der apokalyptischen Visionen in der
Offenbarung Johannis.' *Zeitschrift für die neutestamentliche Wissenchaft* 36,
132–49

Bouché-Leclercq, Auguste. 1879. *Histoire de la divination dans l'Antiquité*.
Brussels: Culture et Civilisation

– 1963 [1899]. *L'Astrologie grecque*. Brussels: Culture et Civilisation

Bousset, Wilhelm. 1906. *Die Offenbarung Johannis*. Göttingen: Vandenhoeck und
Ruprecht

Bowman, J.W. 1955. 'The Revelation to John: Its Dramatic Structure and Message.'
Interpretation 9, 436–53

Boyarin, Jonathan. 1995. 'At Last, All the Goyin: Notes on a Greek Word Applied
to Jews.' In *Postmodern Apocalypse: Theory and Cultural Practice at the End*, ed.
R. Dellamora, 41–60. Philadelphia: University of Pennsylvania Press

Burr, D. 1992. 'Mendicant Readings of the Apocalypse.' In *The Apocalypse in the
Middle Ages*, ed. R.K. Emmerson and B. McGinn, 72–88. New York: Cornell
University Press

Caird, George Bradford. 1966. *A Commentary on the Revelation of St. John the
Divine*. Black's New Testament Commentaries. New York: Black and Harper &
Row

Calloud, J., J. Delorme, and J.-P. Duplantier. 1977. 'L'Apocalypse de Jean. Propositions pour une analyse structurale.' *Apocalypses et théologie de l'espérance*,

351–81. Association catholique française pour l'étude de la Bible, Congrès de Toulouse, 1975. Paris: Cerf

Calvin, Jean. 1985 [1549]. *Advertissement contre l'astrologie judiciaire*. Edition critique par Olivier Millet. Geneva: Librairie Droz S.A.

Carpenter, Mary W. 1995. 'Representing Apocalypse: Sexual Politics and the Violence of Revelation.' In *Postmodern Apocalypse: Theory and Cultural Practice at the End*, ed. R. Dellamora, 107–35. Philadelphia: University of Pennsylvania Press

Cassirer, Ernst. 1963. *The Individual and the Cosmos in Renaissance Philosophy*. Oxford: Blackwell

Charles, Robert Henry. 1913. *Studies in the Apocalypse, Being Lectures Delivered before the University of London*. Edinburgh: Clark

– 1920. The *Revelation of St. John*. The International Critical Commentary, 2 vols. Edinburgh and New York: Clark and Scribner's

Charlesworth, James H., ed. 1983. *The Old Testament Pseudepigrapha*, 2 vols. Garden City, NY: Doubleday

Chevalier, Jacques M. 1990. *Semiotics, Romanticism and the Scriptures*. Approaches to Semiotics 88. Berlin and New York: Mouton de Gruyter

– 1995. 'The Great Sign in the Book of Revelation – Le Chant du Signe.' In *Beyond Textuality: Asceticism and Violence in Anthropological Interpretation*, ed. Gilles Bibeau and Ellen Corin, 111–44. Berlin and New York: Mouton de Gruyter

Chevalier, Jacques M., and Daniel Buckles. 1995. *A Land without Gods: Process Theory, Maldevelopment and the Gulf Nahuas*. London and Halifax: Zed and Fernwood

Choisnard, P. 1908. *Preuves et bases de l'astrologie scientifique*. Paris. Chacornac

Claudel, Paul. 1952. *Paul Claudel interroge l'apocalypse*. Paris: Gallimard

Collins, Adela Yarbro. 1976. *The Combat Myth in the Book of Revelation*. Missoula, MT: Scholars

– 1984. *Crisis and Catharsis: The Power of the Apocalypse*. Philadelphia: Westminster

Cooke, G.A. 1960. *A Critical and Exegetical Commentary on the Book of Ezekiel*. The International Critical Commentary. Edinburgh and New York: Clark and Scribner's

Court, John M. 1979. *Myth and History in the Book of Revelation*. Atlanta, GA: John Knox

Cramer, Frederick H. 1954. *Astrology in Roman Law and Politics*. Philadelphia: American Philosophical Society

– n.d. *Astrology in Roman Law and Politics*, vol. 2. Philadelphia: American Philosophical Society, Manuscript Collections

Cumont, Franz. 1960 [1912]. *Astrology and Religion among the Greeks and Romans*. New York: Dover

Daniel, E.R. 1992. 'Joachim of Fiore: Patterns of History in the Apocalypse.' In *The Apocalypse in the Middle Ages*, ed. R.K. Emmerson and B. McGinn, 72–88. New York: Cornell University Press

Dellamora, Richard. 1995. 'Introduction.' In *Postmodern Apocalypse: Theory and Cultural Practice at the End*, ed. R. Dellamora, 1–16. Philadelphia: University of Pennsylvania Press

Derrida, Jacques. 1984a. 'No Apocalypse, Not Now (Full Speed Ahead, Seven Missiles, Seven Missives.)' *Diacritics* 14/2, 20–31

– 1984b. 'Of an Apocalyptic Tone Recently Adopted in Philosophy.' *The Oxford Literary Review* 6/2, 3–37

– 1982. 'White Mythology: Metaphor in the Text of Philosophy.' In *Margins of Philosophy*, 207–72. Chicago: University of Chicago Press

– 1978. *Writing and Difference*. Trans. by Alan Bass. Chicago: University of Chicago Press

Dieterich, A. 1891. *Abraxas: Studien zur Religionsgeschichte des spätern Altertums*. Leipzig: Teubner

Dobin, Joel C. 1983 [1977]. *The Astrological Secrets of the Hebrew Sages*. New York: Inner Traditions International

Draper, J.A. 1983. 'The Feast of Tabernacles: Revelation 7.1–17.' *Journal for the Study of the New Testament* 19, 133–47

du Plessis, J. 1936. *Les Derniers Temps d'après l'histoire et la prophétie*, 2 vols. Paris: Desclée de Brouwer

Eliade, Mircea. 1976. *Occultism, Witchcraft and Cultural Fashions*. Chicago and London: University of Chicago Press

Ellul, Jacques. 1975. *L'Apocalypse, architecture en mouvement*. Paris: Desclée (L'athéisme s'interroge)

– 1977. *Apocalypse: The Book of Revelation*. New York: Seabury

Exel, Jerry. 1986. *Bible et astrologie*. Paris: Atlantic

Farrer, Austin Marsden, 1949. *A Rebirth of Images: The Making of St. John's Apocalypse*. Boston: Beacon

– 1964. *The Revelation of St. John the Divine*. Oxford: Clarendon Press

Fekkes, Jan. 1994. *Isaiah and Prophetic Traditions in the Book of Revelation: Visionary Antecedents and Their Development*. Sheffield: JSOT

Feldman, Wilhelm Moses. 1978 [1931]. *Rabbinical Mathematics and Astronomy*. New York: Hermon

Feuillet, A. 1961. *L'Apocalypse; État de la question*. Paris: Desclée de Brouwer

– 1975. 'Jalons pour une meilleure intelligence de l'Apocalypse. Les Lettres aux Eglises (Ch. 2 et 3).' *Esprit et Vie* 85, 209–23

– 1976. 'Quelques Énigmes des chapitres 4 à 7 de l'Apocalypse. Suggestions pour l'interprétation du langage imagé de la Révélation johannique.' *Esprit et Vie* 86, 455–9, 471–9

Fiorenza, Elizabeth Schuessler. 1985. *The Book of Revelation: Justice and Judgment.* Philadelphia: Fortress

- 1991. *Revelation: Vision of a Just World.* Proclamation Commentaries. Minneapolis: Fortress

Fleming, Kenneth Charles. 1981. *God's Voice in the Stars: Zodiac Signs and Bible Truth.* New York: Neptune

Flint, Valerie I.J. 1991. *The Rise of Magic in Early Medieval Europe.* Princeton, NJ: Princeton University Press

Fontenrose, J. 1959. *Python: A Study of Delphic Myth and Its Origins.* Berkeley: University of California Press

Ford, J.M. 1975. *Revelation.* The Anchor Bible. Garden City, NY: Doubleday

Foucault, Michel. 1984. *Histoire de la sexualité 2: L'Usage des plaisirs.* Paris: Gallimard

Fredriksen, P. 1992. 'Tyconius and Augustine on the Apocalypse.' In *The Apocalypse in the Middle Ages,* ed. R.K. Emmerson and B. McGinn, 27–37. New York: Cornell University Press

Freud, Sigmund. 1973. *New Introductory Lectures on Psychoanalysis.* London: Pelican

- 1976. *The Interpretation of Dreams.* London: Penguin

Frye, Northrop. 1957. *Anatomy of Criticism: Four Essays.* Princeton, NJ: Princeton University Press.

- 1962. *Fearful Symmetry: A Study of William Blake.* Boston: Beacon

- 1981. *The Great Code: The Bible and Literature.* New York: Harvest/HJB

Gager, J.G. 1975. *Kingdom and Community.* Englewood Cliffs, NJ: Prentice-Hall

Gandz, Soloman. 1970. *Studies in Hebrew Astronomy and Mathematics.* New York: Ktau

Gauquelin, Michel. 1985. *La Vérité sur l'astrologie.* Paris: Rocher

Giet, S. 1957. *L'Apocalypse et l'histoire: Étude historique sur l'Apocalypse johannique.* Paris: Presses Universitaires de France

Gleadow, Rupert. 1968. *The Origin of the Zodiac.* London: J. Cape

Goodenough, Erwin Ramsdell. 1958. *Jewish Symbols in the Greco-Roman Period,* vol. 8. New York: Pantheon

Goold, G.P., ed. 1977. *Manilius, Astronomica.* English trans. by G.P. Goold. Cambridge, MA, and London: Harvard University Press and Heinemann

Gordon, Cyrus H. 1961. 'Canaanite Mythology.' In *Mythologies of the Ancient World,* ed. S.N. Kramer, 181–218. Garden City, NY: Anchor

Grabar, André. 1982. 'L'Iconographie du ciel dans l'art de l'Antiquité et du haut Moyen Age.' *Cahiers archéologiques,* 30, 5–24

Greenberg, Moshe. 1983. *Ezekiel 1–20.* The Anchor Bible. Garden City, NY: Doubleday

Gunkel, Hermann. 1895. *Schöpfung und Chaos in Urzeit und Endzeit: Eine religionsgeschitliche Untersuchung über gen 1 und Ap Joh 12.* Göttingen: Vandenhoeck und Ruprecht

Habermas, Jürgen. 1987. *The Philosophical Discourse of Modernity.* Cambridge, MA: MIT Press

Hachlili, R. 1988. *Ancient Jewish Art and Archaeology in the Land of Israel.* Leiden, NY: E.J. Brill

Halsell, Grace. 1986. *Prophecy and Politics: Militant Evangelists on the Road to Nuclear War.* Westport, CT: Hill

Hastings, James, ed. 1921. 'Sun, Moon, and Stars.' In *Encyclopaedia of Religion and Ethics,* vol. 12, 48–103. Edinburgh: Clark

Heidel, Alexander. 1951. *The Babylonian Genesis: The Story of Creation,* 2d ed. Chicago and London: University of Chicago Press

Hellholm, D., ed. 1983. *Apocalypticism in the Mediterranean World and the Near East.* Tübingen: Mohr

Hemer, Colin J. 1986. *The Letters to the Seven Churches of Asia in Their Local Setting.* Sheffield: Journal for the Study of the Old Testament

Hollis, F.J. 1933. 'The Sun Cult and the Temple at Jerusalem.' In *Myth and Ritual,* ed. S.H. Hooke, 87–110. London: Oxford University Press

Hooke, S.H., ed. 1933. *Myth and Ritual.* London: Oxford University Press

– 1935. *The Labyrinth.* London: SPCK

– 1958. *Myth, Ritual, and Kingship.* Oxford: Clarendon

Howe, Ellic. 1967. *Astrology: A Recent History Including the Untold Story of Its Role in World War II.* New York: Walker

Jacobsen, Thorkild. 1970. *Toward the Image of Tammuz and Other Essays on Mesopotamian History and Culture.* Ed. by W.L. Moran. Cambridge, MA: Harvard University Press

– 1976. *The Treasures of Darkness: A History of Mesopotamian Religion.* New Haven and London: Yale University Press

Josephus, Flavius. 1926–65. *Works, Comprising the Antiquities of the Jews; A History of the Jewish Wars; and Life of Flavius Josephus.* Philadelphia: McKay

Jung, C.G. 1954. *Answer to Job.* London: Routledge and Kegan Paul

Jurist, Michele D. 1982. 'Astrology: Its History, Philosophy, and Relation to Religion, with Special Emphasis on the Early Hebrews and the Bible.' *Journal of Religious Studies* 10, 58–76

Kiddle, Martin. 1940. *The Revelation of St John.* Moffat New Testament Commentary. London: Hodder and Stoughton

Kirschbaum, Engelbert. 1959. *The Tomb of St. Peter and St. Paul.* London: Secker and Warburg

Kraabel, A.T. 1978. 'Paganism and Judaism: The Sardis Evidence.' In *Paganisme, Judaïsme, Christianisme,* 13–23. Paris: Editions E. de Boccard

Kraft, H. 1974. *Die Offenbarung des Johannes*. Handbuch zum Neuen Testament 16a. Tübingen: Mohr

Kramer, Samuel Noah. 1961. 'Mythology of Sumer and Akkad.' In *Mythologies of the Ancient World*. ed. S.N. Kramer, 93–138. Garden City, NY: Anchor

– 1969. *The Sacred Marriage Rite*. Bloomington: Indiana University Press

Lacan, J. 1979. *The Four Fundamental Concepts of Psycho-analysis*. Trans. by A. Sheridan. London: Penguin

Lambrecht, J. 1980. 'A Structuration of Revelation 4, 1–22, 5.' In *L'Apocalypse johannique dans le Nouveau Testament*, ed. J. Lambrecht, 77–104. Gembloux and Leuven: Duculot and Leuven University Press

Langdon, Stephen. 1931. *Semitic Mythology*. New York: Cooper Square

Lawrence, D.H. 1974. *Apocalypse*. Intr. by R. Aldington. London: Secker

– 1980. *Apocalypse and the Writings of Revelation*. Cambridge: Cambridge University Press

Lerner, R.E. 1992. 'The Medieval Return to the Thousand-Year Sabbath.' In *The Apocalypse in the Middle Ages*, ed. R.K. Emmerson and B. McGinn, 51–71. New York: Cornell University Press

Lévi-Strauss, Claude. 1958. *Anthropologie structurale*. Paris: Plon

– 1962. *La Pensée sauvage*. Paris: Plon

– 1975. *The Raw and the Cooked*. New York: Harper

Lohmeyer, Ernst. 1926. *Die Offenbarung des Johannes, Handbuch zum Neuen Testament*, 16. Tübingen: Mohr

Lyotard, Jean-François. 1988. *The Differend: Phrases in Dispute*. Trans. by Georges Van Den Abbeele. Minneapolis: University of Minnesota Press

McGinn, B. 1992. 'Introduction: John's Apocalypse and the Apocalyptic Mentality.' In *The Apocalypse in the Middle Ages*, ed. R.K. Emmerson and B. McGinn, 3–19. New York: Cornell University Press

McNamara, Martin. 1966. *The New Testament and the Palestinian Targum to the Pentateuch*. Rome: Pontifical Biblical Institute

Mailly Nesle, Solange de. 1981. *L'Astrologie: L'Histoire, les symboles, les signes*. Paris: Fernand Nathan

Malina, Bruce J. 1995. *On the Genre and Message of Revelation: Star Visions and Sky Journeys*. Peabody, MA: Hendrickson

Matter, E.A. 1992. 'The Apocalypse in Early Medieval Exegesis.' In *The Apocalypse in the Middle Ages*, ed. R.K. Emmerson and B. McGinn, 38–50. New York: Cornell University Press

Maunder, E.W. 1923. *The Astronomy of the Bible*. Chatham: Clements Brothers

Minear, P.S. 1968. *I Saw a New Earth*. Washington, DC: Corpus

Moffat, J. 1951. 'The Revelation of St. John the Divine.' In *The Expositor's Greek Testament* 5, 279–492. Grand Rapids, MI: Eerdmans

Moore, Joan André. 1981. *Astronomy in the Bible*. Nashville: Abingdon

Morin, Edgar, dir. 1981. *La Croyance astrologique moderne (diagnostic sociologique)*. Lausanne: L'Age d'homme

Morris, Henry. 1983. *The Revelation Record*. Wheaton, IL, and San Diego: Tyndale and Creation-Life

Morris, Leon. 1973. *Apocalyptic*. Leicester: Inter-Varsity

– 1983. *The Revelation of St. John*. Tyndale New Testament Commentaries. Leicester and Grand Rapids: Inter-Varsity and Eerdmans

Mounce, Robert H. 1977. *The Book of Revelation*. Grand Rapids: Eerdmans

Ness, L.J. 1990. 'Astrology and Judaism in Late Antiquity.' PhD dissertation, Department of History, University of Miami

Neugebauer, Otto. 1957. *The Exact Sciences in Antiquity*. Providence, RI: Brown University Press

Palmer, F. 1903. *The Drama of the Apocalypse*. New York: Macmillan

Paley, Morton D. 1986. *The Apocalyptic Sublime*. New Haven, CT, and London: Yale University Press

Pecker, Jean-Claude. 1995. 'L'Effet Mars.' *Sciences et avenir* 101, 20–7

Philo of Alexandria. 1956–62. *Quis rerum Divinarum Heres*. In *Works*, 221–5. London and Cambridge: Heinemann and Harvard University Press

Pilch, John L. 1992. 'Lying and Deceit in the Letters to the Seven Churches: Perspectives from Cultural Anthropology.' *Biblical Theology Bulletin* 22, 126–35

Pingree, David. 1968. 'Astrology.' In *Dictionary of the History of Ideas*, ed. Philip P. Weiner, 118–26. New York: Scribner

– 1990. 'Astrology.' In *Religion, Learning and Science in the Abbasid Period*, ed. M.J.L. Young, J.D. Latham, and R.B. Serjeant, 290–300. Cambridge: Cambridge University Press

– 1993. 'Occultism.' In *The New Encyclopaedia Britannica*, 15th ed., vol. 25, 75–98

Prévost, Jean-Pierre. 1991. *Pour lire l'Apocalypse*. Ottawa and Paris: Novalis and Editions du Cerf

Prigent, P. 1959. *Apocalypse 12, Histoire de l'Exegèse*. Tübingen: Mohr

– 1964. *Apocalypse et liturgie*. Cahiers Théologiques 52. Lausanne: Delachaux et Niestle

– 1980. 'L'Apocalypse. Exegèse historique et analyse structurale.' *New Testament Studies* 26, 127–37

– 1981. *Apocalypse de Saint Jean*. Lausanne: Delachaux et Niestle

– 1990. *Le Judaïsme et l'image*. Tübingen: Mohr

Rahner, Hugo. 1963. *Greek Myths and Christian Mystery*. London: Burns & Oates

Ricoeur, Paul. 1984. *Time and Narrative*, vol. 1. Trans. by K. McLaughlin and D. Pellauer. Chicago and London: University of Chicago Press

Rissi, M. 1966. *Time and History: A Study on the Revelation*. Trans. by G.C. Winsor. Richmond, VI: John Knox

Robson, David. 1995. 'Frye, Derrida, Pynchon, and the Apocalyptic Space of Postmodern Fiction.' In *Postmodern Apocalypse: Theory and Cultural Practice at the End*, ed. R. Dellamora, 61–78. Philadelphia: University of Pennsylvania Press

Rozanov, Vasily. 1977. *The Apocalypse of Our Time*. Ed. with an introduction by R. Payne; trans. by R. Payne and N. Romanoff. New York: Praeger

Schiaparelli, G.V. 1905. *Astronomy in the Old Testament*. Oxford: Clarendon Press

Scott, Alan. 1991. *Origen and the Life of the Stars: A History of an Idea*. Oxford: Clarendon Press

Seznec, Jean. 1953. *The Survival of the Pagan Gods*. New York: Pantheon

Shakespeare, William. 1974. *Complete Works*. Ed. by W.J. Craig. London: Oxford University Press

Shepherd, M.H. 1960. *The Paschal Liturgy and the Apocalypse*. Ecumenical Studies in Worship. Cambridge: Lutterworth

Sickenberger, Joseph. 1942. *Erklärung der Johannesapokalypse*. Bonn: Hanstein

Stauffer, E. 1965. *Christ and the Caesars*. London: SCM

Suetonius. 1967. *The Twelve Caesars*. Rev. with an introduction by Michael Grant; trans. by Philemon Holland. New York: Ams

Sweet, John. 1990 [1979]. *Revelation*. London and Philadelphia: SCM and Trinity

Swete, Henry B. 1951 [1906]. *The Apocalypse of St John*. Grand Rapids, MI: Eerdmans

Tester, S.J. 1987. *A History of Western Astrology*. Suffolk and Wolfeboro: Boydell

Theissen, G. 1982. *The Social Setting of Pauline Christianity*. Philadelphia: Fortress

Thomas, Keith. 1971. *Religion and the Decline of Magic*. New York: Scribner's

Thompson, Leonard L. 1990. *The Book of Revelation, Apocalypse and Empire*. New York and Oxford: Oxford University Press

Toynbee, Jocelyn, and John Ward Perkins. 1956. *The Shrine of St. Peter and the Vatican Excavations*. London: Longmans

Touilleux, P. 1935. *L'Apocalypse et les cultes de Domitien et de Cybèle*. Paris: P. Geuthner

Ulansey, David. 1989. *The Origins of the Mithraic Mysteries; Cosmology and Salvation in the Ancient World*. Oxford: Oxford University Press

Ulfgard, H. 1989. *Feast and Future. Revelation 7: 9–17 and the Feast of Tabernacles*. Coniectnaea Biblica, New Testament Series, 22. Lund: Almqvist & Wiksell International

Unger, Merrill F. 1957. *Unger's Bible Dictionary*. Chicago: Moody

Urbach, E.E. 1953. 'The Rabbinical Laws of Idolatry in the Second and Third Centuries in the Light of Archaeological and Historical Facts.' *Israel Exploration Journal* 9/3, 150–1

Vanhoye, A. 1962. 'Ezéchiel dans l'Apocalypse.' *Biblica* 43, 436–72

Wevers, John W. 1969. *Ezekiel.* The New Century Bible Commentary. Grand Rapids, MI, and London: Eerdmans & Marshall and Morgan & Scott

Young, Iris Marion. 1987. 'Impartiality and the Civic Public.' In *Feminism as Critique,* ed. S. Benhabib and D. Cornell, 57–76. Minneapolis: University of Minnesota Press

– 1990. 'The Ideal of Community and the Politics of Difference.' In *Feminism/ Postmodernism,* ed. L. Nicholson, 300–23. New York: Routledge

Zahn, T. 1924. *Die Offenbarung des Johannes (Kommentar zum Neuen Testament, Ausgelegt v. T. Zahn).* Leipzig: Werner Scholl

Zimmerli, Walther. 1979. *Ezekiel: A Commentary on the Book of the Prophet Ezekiel.* Trans. by Ronald E. Clements. Philadelphia: Fortress

Zimmern, H., ed. 1903. *Keilinschriften und das Alte Testament.* Berlin: Reuther & Reichard

Index